THE NEAR ABROAD

Socialist Eastern Europe and Soviet Patriotism in Ukraine, 1956–1985

The Near Abroad

Socialist Eastern Europe and Soviet Patriotism in Ukraine, 1956–1985

ZBIGNIEW WOJNOWSKI

UNIVERSITY OF TORONTO PRESS
Toronto Buffalo London

Toronto Buffalo London
www.utppublishing.com

ISBN 978-1-4426-3107-6

Printed on acid-free, 100% post-consumer recycled paper with vegetable-based inks.

Library and Archives Canada Cataloguing in Publication

Wojnowski, Zbigniew, 1983–, author
The near abroad : socialist Eastern Europe and Soviet patriotism in Ukraine, 1956-1985 / Zbigniew Wojnowski.

Includes bibliographical references and index.
ISBN 978-1-4426-3107-6 (cloth)

1. Patriotism – Ukraine – History – 20th century. 2. Patriotism – Soviet Union – History – 20th century. 3. Ukrainians – Ethnic identity – History – 20th century. 4. Socialism – Europe, Eastern – History – 20th century. 5. Ukraine – History – 1944–1991. 6. Soviet Union – History – 1953–1985. 7. Europe, Eastern – History – 1945–1989. I. Title.

DK508.84.W64 2017 947.708'5 C2016-907329-7

University of Toronto Press acknowledges the financial assistance to its publishing program of the Canada Council for the Arts and the Ontario Arts Council, an agency of the Government of Ontario.

Canada Council for the Arts
Conseil des Arts du Canada

Funded by the Government of Canada
Financé par le gouvernement du Canada
Canada

In loving memory of my grandad, Władysław Wojnowski (1922–2015). For me, the twentieth century ended with his death.

Contents

Illustrations

Maps

Figures

Acknowledgments

The work that led to this book, *The Near Abroad*, began at the School of Slavonic and East European Studies, University College London. Susan Morrissey, who influenced the writing of this work more than anyone else, was as demanding as she was supportive. Susan had a way of pushing me to my limits without crushing my spirit; she challenged my ideas but never imposed her own agenda. I am immensely grateful that she has continued to provide much-needed advice since I graduated in 2011. During my years at SSEES, I learnt a lot from Andrew Wilson, Polly Jones, Geoffrey Hosking, Svetlana McMillin, and the entire faculty. Sarah Davies and Kevin McDermott gave me faith in the project and pushed it in new, exciting directions. I was also fortunate to share my miseries, doubts, and joys with a wonderful cohort of PhD students at SSEES. Maks Fras, Sarah McArthur, Dragana Obradovic, and Claire Shaw have remained very close friends (and this is despite all the trials and tribulations of travelling together in Central Asia and the Caucasus). Unfortunately I have lost touch with others, but I would like them to know that they made an imprint on my twenties in ways that cannot be erased.

The year I spent as a postdoctoral fellow at the University of Toronto was one of the best in my life. Generous funding from the Petro Jacyk Foundation helped me take a step back from my thesis and broaden my academic horizons. Tracy McDonald, Alison Smith, Peter Solomon, and Lynne Viola were very generous with their time. Anka Hajkova and Lilia Topouzova organized a reading group that provided a source of intellectual stimulation and comradeship. I am very grateful to have met Auri and Olia Berg, Svitlana Frunchak, and Misha Kogan. Last but not least, I have to thank Seth Bernstein for saving my skin and ruining his rucksack after one fateful night in Hamilton, Ontario.

I completed much of the research and writing for this book as an Assistant Professor at Nazarbayev University in Astana, Kazakhstan. My colleagues at the Department of History, Philosophy, and Religious Studies have been a constant source of critique, enthusiasm, and support. Sam Hirst, Don Leggett, Alexander Morrison, Beatrice Penati, Danielle Ross, Scott Savran, and Stephen Wheatcroft in particular have helped me look at history from a whole new angle. Brendan Pietsch has repeatedly burst my enormous ego. Aighanym Ayazbayeva, Mwita Chacha, Zach Cofran, Tiffany Hong, Malavika Jaganathaan, Saniya Karpykova, Jon Powell, and Almira Zholamanova kept me (reasonably) happy in the depths of the Kazakhstani winter. I want to thank Gabriel McGuire for not leaving me out in the steppe the first time I tried cross-country skiing; Alima Bissenova for getting those policemen and their AK-47s off our backs; Jenni Lehtinen and Zarina Rakhmanova for my body image problems; and James Nikopoulos for his wonderful head of hair.

The inspiration for this project came from many other sources. The editors and anonymous reviewers at *Kritika: Explorations in Russian and Eurasian History*, *Slavic Review*, and *Nationalities Papers*, as well as discussants and fellow panelists at various conferences and workshops, have greatly shaped my thinking about this project. I would like to thank Rachel Applebaum, Claire Kaiser, Uku Lember, and Anna Wylegała in particular. My understanding of Ukrainian, East European, and Soviet history has also been enriched by knowledgeable and generous librarians at SSEES, the British Library, and Robarts Library, as well as archival staff in Kyiv, Lviv, Odesa, Moscow, Warsaw, and Budapest. Special thanks go to Liudmila Ivanovna Stepanich at RGANI. Last but not least, I have only fully come to understand why and how this project matters through teaching Soviet and East European history. My students at University College London, Anglia Ruskin, the University of Durham, the University of St Andrews, the University of Toronto, and Nazarbayev University have been a real source of inspiration.

I have been very lucky to work with Richard Ratzlaff at the University of Toronto Press. He has been kind, inspiring, and supportive throughout the publication process. The book's anonymous reviewers wrote wonderfully constructive and selfless reports. They challenged me, but also engaged with what I wanted to say. I would like to thank the organisers and participants of the conference "Recovering Forgotten History: The Image of East Central Europe in English-Language Academic Textbooks," where a full draft of this manuscript was discussed in June 2015. I am especially grateful to Juraj Marusiak and Iryna Sklokina for their rich feedback. Many thanks go to Anne Fullerton for a very thorough reading of the manuscript.

My friends outside work and graduate school have kept me sane. Ukraine became a home away from home thanks to Khrystyna Chushak, James and Sveta Marson, Anna Prymakova, and Lusiena and Serhyi Shum. Verity Allison, Paweł and Basia Brzezińscy, Romy Danflous, Agnes Frimston, Neil Jenkins, Lika Kvitsiani-Fras, Digby Levitt, Alicja Mans, Sara Modzmanashvili-Kemecsei, Alex Nice, Magda and Witek Płotka, Roshan Saleh, Kinga Vorbrich, and Marta Wojnowska have been impressively tolerant of my many quirks. Working on this project was never a lonely experience.

The research for this project would not have been possible without generous funding from the Arts and Humanities Research Council, the School of Slavonic and East European Studies, the Petro Jacyk Foundation, and Nazarbayev University.

Most importantly, I would like to thank my parents, Basia and Jurek, and my sister, Ola, for their unwavering support.

Abbreviations

AAN	Achiwum Akt Nowych (Archive of Contemporary Files)
CDSP	*Current Digest of the Soviet Press*
CPSU	Communist Party of the Soviet Union
CPU	Communist Party of Ukraine
CPWU	Communist Party of Western Ukraine
DAKO	*Derzhavnyi arkhiv Kyivs'koi oblasti* (State Archive of Kyiv Oblast)
DALO	*Derzhavnyi arkhiv L'vivs'koi oblasti* (State Archive of L'viv Oblast)
DAOO	*Derzhavnyi arkhiv Odes'koi oblasti* (State Archive of Odesa Oblast)
DSUP	*Digest of the Soviet Ukrainian Press*
GARF	*Gosudarstvennyi arkhiv Rossiiskoi Federatsii* (State Archive of the Russian Federation)
KhTS	*Khronika tekushchikh sobytii* (Chronicle of Current Events)
MS	*Materialy samizdata* (Samizdat Materials)
OSA	Open Society Archive
PUWP	Polish United Workers' Party
RGANI	*Rossiiskii gosudarstvennyi arkhiv noveishei istorii* (Russian State Archive of Contemporary History)
SDS	*Sobranie dokumentov samizdata* (Collection of Samizdat Documents)
SMOT	*Svobodnoe mezhprofessional'noe ob"edinenie trudiashchikhsia* (Free Interprofessional Union of Workers)
SWPW	*Stowarzyszenie współpracy Polska-Wschód* (Union for Cooperation between Poland and the East)
TsDAHO	*Tsentral'nyi derzhavnyi arkhiv hromads'kykh ob"ednan' Ukrainy* (Central State Archive of Social Organizations of Ukraine)

Note on Spelling and Transliteration

I use the Library of Congress transliteration system for Russian and Ukrainian. For the sake of consistency, all place names in Ukraine are given in the Ukrainian version. They therefore differ from some well-established forms which the English reader may be accustomed to: I have, for example, chosen to write Kyiv, Lviv and Odesa rather than Kiev, Lvov and Odessa. I have omitted transliterating soft and hard signs in common place names.

Wherever the sources allow me to ascertain that a particular individual lived in Soviet Ukraine, I cite names, patronymics, and surnames in the Ukrainian form. I thus refer to Volodymyr Shcherbyts'kyi rather than Vladimir Shcherbitskii. In ambiguous cases, such as the member of the CPU Central Committee in Kyiv Mykola Pidhornyi who then became better known as Nikolai Podgornyi after moving to the CPSU Central Committee in Moscow, I provide both versions.

Map 1. East Central Europe, 1945.

Source: https://faculty.unlv.edu/pwerth/Europe-East-Central-1945.jpg (retrieved 17 January 2016).

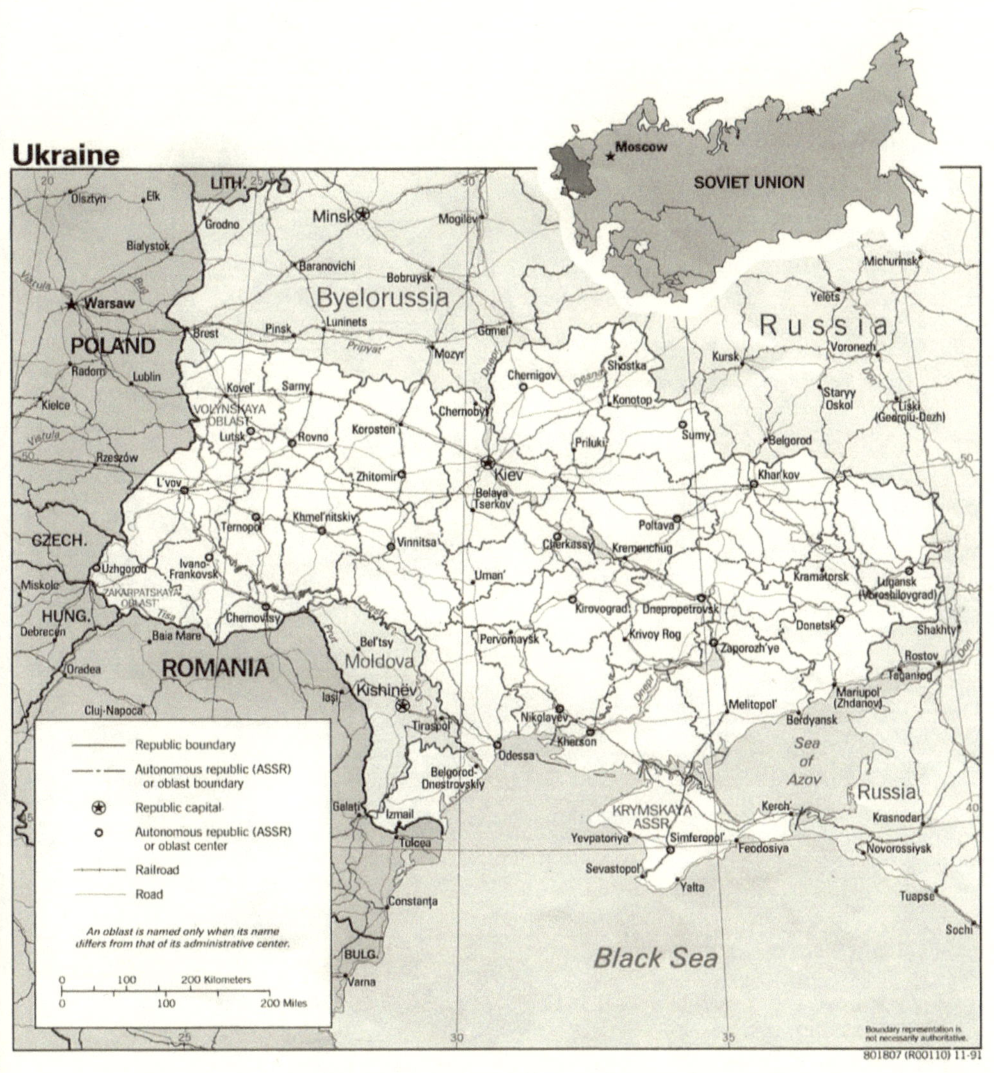

Map 2. Ukraine.

Source: University of Texas Libraries, Perry-Castañeda Library Map Collection, https://www.lib.utexas.edu/maps/europe/ukraine_pol_1991.pdf

THE NEAR ABROAD

Socialist Eastern Europe and Soviet Patriotism in Ukraine, 1956–1985

Introduction

On 9 March 2014, a rally in the east Ukrainian city of Donetsk attracted some ten thousand participants. They came out to support Russian military intervention in the Crimea, as well as to protest against Ukraine's closer ties with the European Union. "The USSR is our homeland! The West will turn us all into slaves!" chanted the protesters. Violent clashes between these self-identified Soviet patriots and the new pro-Western government in Kyiv would rock Ukraine for months. By summer, the hostility escalated into a hybrid war involving regular armies and volunteers from both sides of the Russian-Ukrainian border.

As protesters in Donetsk climbed onto a makeshift stage and fought over the microphone, divisions quickly came to the surface. Some called the Donbas a part of Russia, while others stressed that the region should enjoy greater autonomy within Ukraine. Rumours spread that many participants in the rally had been shipped in from Russia during the night, but Ukraine's fragile borders, both physical and cultural, made it difficult to discern locals from their eastern neighbours. One thing united the protesters on this cold March morning in Donetsk: almost everybody evoked memories of a shared Soviet past. Waving hammer and sickle flags, many speakers recalled the USSR's exploits during the Great Patriotic War and condemned pro-Western politicians in Kyiv who challenged Soviet-made geographies. Russian and Ukrainian identities were not useful markers of political preferences in Donetsk, for both were interpreted through the Soviet lens of Russo-Ukrainian friendship. "My two sons serve in the Ukrainian army," yelled a middle-aged woman from the stage. "The older one is stationed in the Crimea and he knows that the Russians are our friends," she continued, evoking Soviet-made notions of Ukraine to support closer ties with Russia. But her younger son had clearly developed a different understanding of Ukrainianness that he defined in opposition to the USSR and Russia: "He married a girl from Lviv and he thinks that the Russians have occupied Crimea. I argue with him on the phone every day, I don't know how we can be a family from now on."

The Soviet-era mental geographies that still shape international relations and domestic politics in the former USSR are the subject of *The Near Abroad*. The book explores the history of Soviet patriotism and its discontents in post-Stalinist Ukraine. To gauge what it meant to be a Soviet patriot in Ukraine, I examine the USSR's relations with Eastern Europe from the Hungarian uprising of 1956, through the Czechoslovak Prague Spring of 1968, to the rise and fall of Solidarity in Poland during the 1980s. This transnational approach is key for understanding identity dynamics in Ukraine. Just as protesters in 2014 Donetsk argued about Ukraine's position between Russia and the European Union, identities in Soviet Ukraine were formed not only in relation to Moscow, but also to European countries further west.

The Near Abroad and Soviet Politics of Empire

In December 1967, an eighteen-year-old Ukrainian student from Lviv was excluded from the Komsomol. Born and bred in the Ukrainian-speaking west, Viacheslav Mykhailovych Eres'ko had tried to organise a paramilitary group to defend Soviet power in Ukraine from supposed foreign and domestic enemies. Having heard his older brother's horrifying stories about service in the Soviet army during the Hungarian uprising of 1956, Eres'ko was afraid that "nationalist elements" in Lviv would follow the East European example and rebel. Along with several like-minded young people from Lviv, convinced that the party authorities had not done enough to eliminate the nationalist threat, he printed leaflets calling for the USSR to invade China to avoid a surprise attack from abroad as witnessed in 1941, and set out to rob shops to obtain money for weapons. Detained by the KGB, other members of his group soon renounced their views, but Eres'ko refused to capitulate.[1]

Viacheslav Eres'ko was not a typical west Ukrainian. Clandestine military groups in the USSR's western borderlands were crushed long before 1967, and those that operated in the region during the late 1940s and the early 1950s opposed Soviet power. Though his group was weak and short-lived, Eres'ko was certainly an extremist by the standards of his time. Soviet leaders did not face much organised resistance in western Ukraine in the late 1960s. Neither was Eres'ko terribly consistent in his views. By the early 1970s, he was active in Lviv's hippie movement, donned fascist insignia, and expressed a clear sense of alienation from the Soviet state.[2]

Still, his story reveals the dilemmas of Soviet identity politics in Ukraine. In 1967, Eres'ko was both a self-identified Ukrainian and a Soviet patriot prepared to defend the USSR against Ukrainian nationalism. He was a loyal citizen and an outlaw. Concerned that inhabitants of Lviv mobilised Ukrainian identities to oppose the USSR, Eres'ko also defined what it meant to be Soviet in national and geographical terms. In his view, Chinese imperialists and Hungarian nationalists outside the USSR's borders threatened Russians and Ukrainians at home. That a pro-Soviet clandestine organization appeared in Ukraine's western borderlands is particularly surprising. Post-Stalinist western Ukraine was home to anti-Soviet nationalism and dissent,[3] but it also witnessed some of the starkest expressions of Soviet patriotism defined in opposition to the world outside the USSR's borders.

Eres'ko's obsession with outside threats to Soviet stability was far from uncommon in post-Stalinist Ukraine. In the second half of the twentieth century, many Soviet citizens found it difficult to imagine that the Soviet system could ever end.[4] At the same time, the first postwar generation grew up listening to the dramatic stories of their fathers and older brothers who came of age during a more unstable time. Memories of Second World War violence pushed inhabitants of Ukraine to discuss what life might have been like without the USSR. Major breakdowns in state-society dynamics in socialist Eastern Europe, as well as Cold War rivalries in the Middle East, Asia, Africa, and Latin America, raised further questions about not only the USSR's foreign policy, but also the viability of Soviet-style systems.[5]

Events and developments in the Soviet satellite states of Eastern Europe acquired particular significance for Soviet citizens concerned about the future of the USSR. Even the war in Afghanistan – the only conflict in the second half of the twentieth century that stirred Soviet popular opinion more than the military interventions in Eastern Europe – was less ideologically charged than Moscow's policies in Czechoslovakia, Hungary, Poland, and other countries of the Warsaw Pact.[6] Although Soviet visions of socialism were adopted and remade in different parts of the world, it was primarily Eastern Europe that Soviet leaders looked upon as a potential source of controversial ideas and instability in the USSR itself.[7] This was largely because Soviet relations with Eastern Europe were more protracted and multifaceted than with Afghanistan and other Third World countries. They encompassed long periods of economic cooperation, large-scale cultural exchanges, and mass tourism, as well as armed interventions and political crises.[8]

From the Soviet perspective, East European socialist countries formed the Soviet near abroad – more familiar and accessible than the capitalist West, yet also unambiguously foreign.[9] Eastern Europe was part of what Stephen Kotkin calls the "post-Mongol space." Close links between Soviet and East European communist parties, special organisations devoted to promoting cross-border travel within the socialist camp, and trade across the Soviet western border (both legal and illicit) lent a great degree of uniformity to the Soviet bloc.[10] At the same time, as East European institutions enjoyed increasing autonomy from Moscow after the death of Stalin, their politics, culture, and everyday life diverged from the Soviet model. For example, Russian language was not nearly as widely spoken in the people's democracies as in the USSR itself, and in contrast to domestic travel between Soviet republics, inhabitants of the USSR needed to obtain a foreign passport to visit the satellite states. Most strikingly, Soviet-backed regimes in Eastern Europe faced mass opposition of the kind unseen in the USSR.

The "not-quite-foreign" status of Eastern Europe had broad implications for state-society dynamics in the USSR itself. In the words of Roman Szporluk, the people's democracies provided an example of socio-political innovation, which "subverted the position of the Soviet Union as the one prototype of the socialist future of mankind."[11] The near abroad was a testing ground for Soviet policies and ideas which compelled many Soviet citizens to look at and ultimately take a stance on issues of foreign policy, political reform under state socialism, and the role of nations in the Soviet camp.

Interactions between Soviet citizens and inhabitants of Eastern Europe ultimately shaped the USSR's politics of empire. Patryk Babiracki suggests that the Soviet bloc can be viewed as a "composite interface" – a web of multiple, overlapping spaces united by common visions, challenges, and disappointments. The socialist camp (or the "interface") was an empire "that both mediated and was destabilised by ... institutions of communication and transport." Far from carrying any moral implications, the term "empire" here designates a political space distinct from a nation state whose discrete parts functioned together and shaped one another in an unequal relationship. In Babiracki's model, Eastern Europe was an imperial periphery: a politically and militarily subordinate part of an interconnected socialist world, and subject to Moscow-led Sovetisation, but also a source of ideas that challenged dominant power relations and thus reshaped political, cultural, and economic practices in the Soviet bloc as a whole.[12]

After the establishment of Soviet hegemony in Eastern Europe, the socialist camp can in fact be seen as an empire twice over. From the outset, the USSR itself was an "empire of nations" in which "Soviet leaders, administrators, and experts combined colonial forms of economic and administrative organization" with multiple state-sponsored nation-building projects.[13] These prewar approaches to nation building informed the USSR's policies in Eastern Europe after 1945, as Moscow granted the people's democracies a comparatively greater degree of national autonomy than Soviet federal units. At the same time, the outer empire in Eastern Europe changed the status of non-Russian republics in the USSR. Though still subject to Soviet attempts at what Hirsch described as a "nonimperialistic" model of colonisation,[14] Ukraine and other non-Russian republics emerged as part of the Soviet metropole in comparison to and in dialogue with the people's democracies. Their governments and communist parties exerted a much more direct influence over the Soviet centre than East European institutions. As well, it was the non-Russian republic-level institutions in western USSR that were often tasked with maintaining control over the near abroad.

Because of family ties, geographical proximity, and memories of common history, inhabitants of Soviet Ukraine were very exposed to events and developments in the satellite states. Yet it would be a mistake to assume that the proximity of Eastern Europe and its examples of resistance to Moscow's domination pulled Ukraine away from Russia.[15] After the death of Stalin, Soviet citizens in Ukraine articulated more diverse political identities in confronting the near abroad. In official and underground publications, as well as during public meetings and in such relatively uncontrolled contexts as queues outside shops, residents of Ukraine identified with a transnational socialist community or described Ukraine itself as part of Russia's near abroad. Most often, however, these residents expressed loyalty to a Soviet community defined in opposition to socialist Eastern Europe. These discussions shaped Soviet notions of internationalism, ethnicity, and citizenship.

The Limits of Soviet Internationalism

The post-Stalin era was a time of renewed commitment to internationalism, both among the Soviet leadership and on a broader level.

Internationalism meant state-sponsored attempts to prove the validity of the Soviet experiment for Eastern Europe and countries emerging from colonial rule, as well as campaigns to promote a positive image of the Soviet system in the capitalist West.[16] Internationalism expressed itself through public and cultural diplomacy: international travel, for example, was supposed to spread Soviet practices in the near abroad and to establish direct contacts between Soviet citizens and factory workers on both sides of the Iron Curtain.[17] The authorities further sponsored heavily controlled contacts between cultural (and even religious) elites in the USSR and the Third World, as well as popularised Soviet film and literature abroad.[18]

The post-Stalin era was also a time of globalization. Partly because of the new internationalist spirit, but also due to developments beyond Soviet leaders' control, inhabitants of the Soviet bloc often participated in the same cultural trends and aspired to the same consumer goods as the rest of the world. For Soviet leaders, this was a very ambiguous development. While raising hopes for spreading Soviet influences across the world, transnational contacts and globalisation also encouraged party apparatchiks to question whether Soviet culture could really hold its own in a cosmopolitan environment.[19] From the Soviet perspective, the transnational and the global were not necessarily internationalist. Welcoming some global cultural trends as signs of "internationalism," Soviet leaders rejected others as examples of "cosmopolitanism."

To be sure, Soviet internationalism had its limits. While a worldwide culture of sorts grew stronger during the 1960s, transnational political and organisational links across the Iron Curtain remained relatively weak.[20] New technologies, while global, paradoxically helped create cultures that were perhaps more inward looking than ever before. Stephen Lovell argues that the rise of television in the 1970s marked the end of Soviet internationalism and helped create a set of cultural references that mostly only made sense to Russian-speaking Soviet audiences.[21]

In fact, Soviet internationalism had long been overshadowed by the importance of ethnically and geographically defined identities in Soviet public culture.[22] During the 1920s and the early 1930s, when social class formed the most politically salient identity category in the USSR,[23] the Bolsheviks awaited a worldwide proletarian revolution.[24] Meanwhile, Soviet leaders also pushed citizens to adopt ethnically and geographically defined identities. Initially, the promotion of ethnic cultures and the creation of ethnically designated administrative territories were not seen as an alternative to worldwide revolution, but rather as the first step to the establishment of global communism. Party apparatchiks perceived ethnic identities as key to state building and overcoming bureaucratic resistance to the revolution after the collapse of Tsarism.[25] However, the looming threat of a Nazi invasion, the violence of the Second World War, and early Cold War rivalries overshadowed the hope that Soviet socialism would spread across the world after the mid-1930s. This effectively undermined internationalism in Soviet public culture. As Stalin promoted the notion that socialism could be built in one country, he also defined friends and enemies in ethnic terms. Sovietness was increasingly framed with reference to territory and national identity, rather than as a set of universal ideas.[26]

But just as Stalin dropped the *Internationale* as the USSR's anthem in 1944, Soviet socialism spread to the nominally independent states of Eastern Europe. This radically altered the parameters of Soviet public debates about the global and the local. It gave a new lease of life to the belief that Soviet-style socialism could conquer the world. At the same time, events and developments in Eastern Europe periodically challenged Soviet citizens' faith in the universal applicability of their system.

During the 1950s and 1960s, the Soviet mass media and party apparatchiks did not cast the USSR's relations with the near abroad as just a matter of great power politics. Despite growing concerns about the potential spillover of dissent from the near abroad into the USSR, post-Stalinist leaders of the socialist camp also facilitated the transfer of ideas across borders. They presented for the public the image of an internationalist community where borders and national identities faded in light of successful socialist cooperation.[27] International friendship was not just a term uttered at party meetings and in the press, for it also had real life consequences for many residents of Soviet Ukraine. In comparison to the 1920s and 1930s, many more Soviet citizens participated in public diplomacy after the mid-1950s, showcasing Soviet culture to foreign socialist countries.[28] The cautious opening of the Soviet border was part of a larger attempt to find fresh sources of popular enthusiasm for the communist project. Before 1968 in particular, official policies and narratives of international friendship praised Soviet citizens who crossed the Soviet border for supposedly overcoming age-old hatreds to build a brighter future in Eastern Europe.[29]

Largely because they lived close to the border, residents of Soviet Ukraine played a prominent part in post-Stalinist public and cultural diplomacy in the near abroad. In the 1950s, the idea that Soviet Ukrainians would build friendly ties with East European citizens across the border was new and controversial. In prewar Stalinist Ukraine, Poland in particular was cast as a mortal threat to the very existence of Ukraine and Ukrainians, though Soviet (and Soviet Ukrainian) intelligentsia did seek to re-imagine the USSR's relationship with Eastern Europe in the immediate postwar years.[30] Memories of Polish-Ukrainian tensions were even more prominent in parts of western Ukraine that were annexed by the USSR during the Second World War, and that had recently witnessed widespread ethnic cleansing campaigns. Hitler and Stalin had effectively destroyed the multifaceted identities and complex networks of the borderlands, with the Holocaust and the brutal postwar "population exchanges" transforming the region into an unambiguously Ukrainian nation space.[31] On the Polish side of the new postwar border, the communist regime likewise employed violent means to remove Ukrainian people and culture from the borderlands.[32] In stark contrast to the late Stalinist era, during the 1950s and the 1960s party leaders and members of social organisations such as international friendship societies promoted new sites of contact between Soviet Ukrainian and East European citizens. This was enacted with the apparent belief that socialism would obliterate the importance of national divisions.

Despite these efforts, conviction that Soviet socialism held universal appeal failed to take deep roots in Ukraine. On a popular level, the first events that seriously undermined Soviet citizens' faith in transnational socialist friendship with Eastern Europe came as early as 1956. Following Khrushchev's denunciation of Stalin at the Twentieth Party Congress, the far-reaching reforms in Poland and the violent suppression of the Hungarian uprising inspired citizens to articulate various understandings of what distinguished them from their supposedly "socialist brothers" across the western border.

Internationalism was further discredited among residents of Ukraine in the late 1960s. The Warsaw Pact invasion of Czechoslovakia in 1968 made apparent that many East Europeans resented Soviet-style socialism, and that the USSR's control of the near abroad was still largely based on the threat of force. From the late 1960s, Soviet apparatchiks and mass media cast Eastern Europe not so much as a socialist commonwealth united by left-wing values and ideas, but rather as a confederation of closely related ethnic groups that looked to Moscow for protection against Western European and American aggression. Perceptions of Eastern Europe thus imbued the concept of Sovietness with undertones of power and international prestige, but also helped emphasise in public culture the permanence of borders and national identities under socialism. This came shortly before party leaders in Moscow intensified their efforts to support Soviet-style regimes in the Third World.[33] There was a growing discrepancy between top leaders' internationalist foreign policy goals founded on the assumption that Soviet socialism held universal appeal, and both official and popular understandings of what it meant to be Soviet that developed in dialogue with Eastern Europe.

East European departures from the Soviet model convinced many residents of the USSR that Soviet-style socialism simply did not spread across borders. This gradually turned public attention towards features that differentiated the USSR from the outside world. At the same time, after the establishment of socialist regimes in Eastern Europe, the old Stalinist slogans about building "socialism in one country" no longer made sense. Because transnational interactions in the socialist camp exposed significant differences between the USSR and its socialist satellites, socialism was no longer a sufficient indicator of Sovietness.

Soviet Ukrainian Identities

Both for Soviet leaders and on a broader level, ethnicity was a particularly useful marker that helped to distinguish Russians, Ukrainians, and other Soviet ethnic groups that had their own republics in the USSR from foreigners in the near abroad.[34] Although some citizens mobilised Ukrainian ethnicity to oppose the Soviet state, Ukrainian national activism cannot be reduced to anti-Soviet views and behaviours. Ukrainian ethnic identities, albeit only when refracted through the prism of Russo-Ukrainian friendship, were a key source of legitimacy for the post-Stalinist Soviet state.

National identities in Ukraine were hotly contested after the Second World War. Most strikingly, Ukrainian integral nationalism framed some radical anti-Soviet and anti-Russian attitudes. Its roots lay in the first half of the twentieth century and in the regions of Galicia and Volhynia that had been under Polish rule before 1939. Despite a significant Ukrainian movement for independence, which centred in formerly Hasburg-governed Galicia, the 1919 Paris Peace Treaties did not grant Ukrainians the right to national self-determination. During the interwar period, apart from Soviet Ukraine, there were consequently large Ukrainian communities in Poland, Czechoslovakia, and Romania. Ukrainians in Galicia and Volhynia adopted a variety of responses to Polish rule. Their far-left and centre parties suffered crushing defeats in the 1930s.[35] In contrast, the far-right Organisation of Ukrainian Nationalists (OUN) which called for the violent removal of all non-Ukrainian people from what they deemed to be Ukrainian lands (including Soviet Ukraine) grew stronger prior to 1939.[36] The OUN became still more important as Stalinist terror, radical social and cultural policies, and deportations of local Polish elites polarised west Ukrainian society along overlapping ethnic and social lines during the first period of Soviet rule in Galicia and Volhynia between 1939 and 1941.[37]

Ultimately, the Nazi occupation of Galicia, Volhynia, and Soviet Ukraine sparked off an explosion of Ukrainian nationalism that combined anti-Soviet rhetoric with extreme anti-Semitism and xenophobia. Although the OUN's hopes to establish an independent Ukraine under German protection were quickly disappointed in 1941, and despite Nazi repressions of Ukrainian nationalist activists and the population at large, Hitler's racial policies boosted the appeal of OUN's far-right ideas. Some self-identified Ukrainians rallied behind the OUN between 1941 and 1943 because they came to perceive ethnicity as the primary locus of identity, and indeed a matter of life and death.[38] In formerly Polish-ruled territories, as well as further east, the German occupation regime implicated OUN supporters and other local Slavs in the Holocaust. Apart from outright coercion and greed, Ukrainian and Polish participation in the Final Solution was underpinned by the popular stereotype that Jews supported the USSR and thus harmed Poles and Ukrainians.[39] Taking advantage of Nazi-supplied weapons and training, though also largely in defiance of the German authorities, the OUN further stepped up campaigns to turn Ukraine into an ethnically pure nation in 1943. Its military wing, the Ukrainian Insurgent Army (UPA), conducted brutal ethnic cleansing of Poles in Volhynia, and to a lesser extent, in Galicia. The UPA and so-called Polish "self-defence" units, as well as Soviet partisans and the German police force that included locals of different ethnicities, were likewise complicit in the mass murder of Ukrainians.[40]

The OUN's far-right ideology continued to polarise society in western Ukraine after Soviet rule returned to the region in 1944. The most radical UPA activists rose up against the Soviet regime.[41] In response, the Stalinist authorities launched brutal retaliation campaigns and attacked local Ukrainian institutions. In particular, in 1946 they banned the Greek Catholic Church, which had played a crucial part in Ukrainian nation building in Habsburg and subsequently Polish-ruled Galicia.[42] At the same time, Soviet propaganda mobilised Ukrainian identities against the OUN and UPA, portraying them as "traitors to the

Ukrainian people and as henchmen to the Nazis."[43] While the Soviet state destroyed organised nationalist resistance before the death of Stalin, the idea that Soviet rule was alien to Ukraine and that "foreigners" should be removed from the country continued to shape attitudes among a small section of the population through the 1950s and 1960s. Following the Hungarian Uprising and the Prague Spring, for example, some residents of western Ukraine claimed in public that they should follow the East European example, end "Russian" political dominance, and redistribute "Russian" property among local "Ukrainians." Still, anti-Soviet nationalism was a minority faith after the death of Stalin.

Meanwhile, the relaxation of terror and censorship after the mid-1950s fuelled very different types of Ukrainian national activism. During the Thaw, many Ukrainian intellectuals and political activists pushed the limits of permissible national expression without rejecting the Soviet system as such. In parts of western Ukraine annexed by the USSR during the Second World War, local inhabitants retained strong memories of a non-Soviet past and pushed for the Ukrainianisation of Lviv's public spaces. They also took advantage of Soviet opportunities for social mobility, and more broadly, "developed a general set of strategies from a society in which they lived."[44] Attempts to promote Ukrainianness through Soviet institutions were also strong in parts of Ukraine that had belonged to the USSR before 1939. In early 1960s Kyiv, for example, young poets and artists promoted Ukrainian language and culture through the Komsomol and the Writers' Union. Yet even these forms of Ukrainian activism led to conflict with the authorities, as a series of government crackdowns in the mid-1960s dramatically shrank the limits of the "controlled freedom" that intellectuals had enjoyed under Khrushchev.[45] Many members of the creative intelligentsia found the confines of official Soviet Ukrainian culture too stifling. They consequently turned to underground books and pamphlets (known as *samvydav* in Ukrainian or *samizdat* in Russian) to promote Ukrainian identities in defiance of the state.[46]

That Soviet institutions both promoted and suppressed Ukrainian culture is not a new discovery. In the 1960s, examining the range of Ukrainian resistance to Sovietisation, Yaroslav Bilinsky also pointed to the importance of Soviet schools in promoting Ukrainian language.[47] More recently, Serhy Yekelchyk has argued that compromises between Moscow, Kyiv, and the Ukrainian intelligentsia led to the emergence of Soviet organisations devoted to the promotion of Ukrainian culture even before the death of Stalin.[48]

For most scholars, the promotion of Ukrainian identities through Soviet institutions was a source of tension that ultimately undermined the USSR's cultural and political integrity.[49] Borys Lewytzkyj casts Ukrainian national activism as "resistance to [the state's] attempts to curtail the rights of the republics and to all forms of Russification and discrimination."[50] Within at least some contexts, intellectuals, students, and even Communist Party officials in Kyiv pit the "Ukrainian" against the "Soviet." As Natalia Shlikhta argues, for example, the officially recognized Ukrainian Exarchate, a semi-autonomous part of the Russian Orthodox Church supported by republic-level party authorities in Kyiv, provided a focus for former Greek Catholic priests seeking to preserve a separate religious identity for Ukraine. Keen to use the Exarchate to channel Greek Catholic influences and to appease the population of western Ukraine, Soviet leaders sponsored an institution which cultivated anti-secularist, anti-assimilationist, and ultimately anti-Soviet attitudes.[51]

But national contestation did not always mean antagonism between the Ukrainian and the Soviet. Equally important, citizens mobilized Ukrainian identities to highlight their belonging in the wider Soviet community. As Tarik Cyril Amar demonstrates for Lviv, Sovietization sometimes meant Ukrainianization.[52] Although the authorities initially deemed local Ukrainians backward and non-yet-Soviet, by 1950 some members of Lviv's prewar intelligentsia echoed late Stalinist 'anti-cosmopolitan' rhetoric to defend themselves against accusations of disloyalty. They emphasised that local Ukrainians who understood borderland realities were useful Soviet citizens. Especially after the death of Stalin, propaganda drew on a repertoire of western Ukrainian historical events and contemporary local heroes to define what it meant to be Soviet in Lviv.[53] In other words, Sovietness in Lviv was framed in both local (western) and ethnic (Ukrainian) terms, making the city a very distinct part of Ukraine.

At the same time, western Ukraine was not different from other parts of the republic in the sense that Sovietness elsewhere was also defined in geographical and ethnic terms. Throughout Ukraine, identities that were at once Soviet and Ukrainian developed in dialogue between top political leaders in Moscow, republican authorities in Kyiv, Ukraine's regional institutions, and citizens who voiced their views in such public forums as agitation gatherings. To be sure, this was not a dialogue of equals, but local communities in Ukraine played an important role in what Peter Sahlins calls "the formation and consolidation of nationhood." In his study of the early modern Pyrenees, Sahlins argues that national identity cannot be seen as a state-sponsored ideology emanating from the centre to the periphery. On the contrary, "national identity – as Frenchmen or Spaniards – appeared on the periphery before it was built there by the centre." Borderland communities appropriated national rhetoric to resolve local conflicts and to pursue local interests. For example, community leaders in the Pyrenees represented themselves as French or Spanish to seek more powerful allies in battles over scarce regional resources.[54] At times, state-led attempts to draw clear boundaries between "Frenchmen" and "Spaniards" challenged borderland inhabitants' values and practices.[55] Yet other case studies suggest that tensions between central governments and regional communities did not necessarily fuel regionalism or separatism; rather, these tensions were in themselves constitutive of national identities. In Switzerland, for instance, where nation builders faced the challenge of uniting distinct linguistic and religious groups, "contestation [was] instrumental in popularising the modern nation itself." It was because regions, localities, and other cultural and political groupings struggled for status within the modern nation-state "that men and women were drawn into a modern public sphere and became engaged with national institutions."[56]

Although the USSR was not a nation state like France or Spain, many residents of Ukraine came to resemble Sahlin's Frenchmen and Spaniards from the borderlands in their approaches to Soviet identity-building projects. They saw Sovietness not as a foreign identity imposed by Moscow or an alternative to Ukrainian nation-building projects, but rather as a vehicle for promoting personal, regional, and Ukrainian interests cast in opposition to neighbours across the western border. These tendencies were most pronounced in Galicia. Recalling local resistance to Polonisation, for example, political and cultural activists from Lviv claimed the right to promote Ukrainian language in Soviet public culture, and demanded Soviet pensions for veterans of the Communist Party of Western Ukraine who had struggled against Polish authorities before 1939. Residents of other parts of Ukraine also defined Sovietness in opposition to the near abroad. Underlining that Russians and Ukrainians were more committed to building communism than their western neighbours, they frequently used Eastern Europe as a scapegoat for the major economic problems that plagued the USSR, condemned Soviet subsidies to the satellite states, and stressed that the USSR should instead improve supplies in Soviet Ukraine's shops.

Soviet Ukraine's identity politics was thus a mirror and a consequence of nineteenth-century nation-building projects in the Russian Empire and Habsburg Galicia. As Faith Hillis demonstrates, the idea that Orthodox East Slavs formed a distinct political group whose interests diverged from Poles and Jews originated in the Dnieper region of modern-day Ukraine. Precisely because of their location in multiconfessional borderlands, Orthodox notables, Cossacks, regional governors, and intellectuals found it important to distinguish and privilege local Orthodox residents as Little Russians.[57] The Little Russian movement was the foundation of both Ukrainian and Russian nation-building projects. Some political and cultural activists began to refer to the cultural peculiarities of right-bank Ukraine to describe local inhabitants as "Ukrainians," supporting both populist and liberal movements that challenged Tsarist rule. Meanwhile, many members of the local Orthodox elite described Little Russian language and culture as the most authentic expressions of what it meant to be "Russian," casting opposition to the Tsar as unpatriotic.[58] Both the Russian and Ukrainian national identities, albeit conflicting, were thus articulated to distinguish East Slavs from Poles and Jews, often through the means of what we would today identify as Ukrainian culture.[59]

The Polish and Jewish "others" were equally important in fuelling Russian and Ukrainian nation building in Habsburg-ruled Galicia. East Slavic narratives offered an attractive alternative to the "Ruthenian" project that defined the local Greek Catholic population as a nation in its own right, largely because they provided a more powerful platform to oppose the Polish elites.[60] That Ukrainian identities eventually gained the upper hand among the Greek Catholics in Galicia owed much to the influence of right-bank intellectuals with roots in the Little Russian project.[61]

Framing social problems in national terms, Ukrainian and Russian activists competed with early Bolshevik calls for internationalist solidarity.[62] Yet East Slavic nationalisms soon became a key part of Soviet public culture. Nationalism was of course a heavily loaded term in the USSR. Propaganda celebrated the flowering of Soviet "nations" but reserved the label of "nationalism" for anti-Soviet views and organisations.[63] But if we follow John Breuilly and understand nationalism as a political movement that claims to represent the imagined nation's needs and values, the USSR itself emerges as a nationalist state.[64] To mobilise the population against foreign threats and to legitimise Soviet rule at home, Stalinist propaganda revived prerevolutionary notions of Little Russian patriotism. It accomplished this by emphasising that East Slavic "masses" had always striven for social liberation together, and crucially, under the auspices of strong authoritarian states that had helped them defeat foreign class oppressors.[65] Especially in newly annexed parts of west Ukraine, the establishment of Soviet rule was linked with the promotion of Ukrainian identities. This helped to legitimize the Soviet project among local Ukrainians, to obliterate what Soviet leaders considered subversive memories of Romanian, Hungarian, Polish, Jewish, and German past in the region, and to create a legible system of Ukrainian cultural references and institutions to replace the complex mosaic of languages and cultures.[66]

Interactions with the nominally socialist countries of Eastern Europe further solidified the importance of Eastern Slavic identities as the most important markers of what it meant to be Soviet in Ukraine. Contrasting the core ethnic groups of the USSR with foreigners in the near abroad, citizens defined Sovietness as a composite East Slavic identity. Memories of the Great Patriotic War were especially important in fuelling notions of Soviet patriotism understood in East Slavic terms. War veterans celebrated the Soviet "liberation" of Eastern Europe as a Russian (and to a lesser extent Ukrainian) achievement.[67] While notions of what it meant to be Russian and Ukrainian were closely entangled in Soviet public culture, Soviet patriotism became less Russocentric than under Stalin.[68] In official publications, during agitation gatherings, and even in relatively informal settings, residents of Ukraine emphasized that ethnic Ukrainians had always protected Tsarist Russia, the USSR, and their East Slavic inhabitants from East European nationalism, and now formed a crucial bulwark against the forces of instability in the near abroad. Citizens continued to outline a special role for Ukraine and Ukrainians in the socialist camp, even after the pace of Russification in the USSR picked up in the early 1970s.[69] Residents used various public forums to suggest not only that Ukrainian identities were an important part of what it meant to be Soviet, but also that culture and history from the western borderlands around Lviv (traditionally seen as the "least Soviet" part of Ukraine) were an important part of what it was to be Soviet Ukrainian. Therefore, popular reactions to events and development in the near abroad do not fit the stereotypical divide into "pro-Soviet" east and "anti-Soviet" west, for Ukrainianness throughout the republic was often defined against Eastern Europe and not against Russia or the USSR.

Post-Stalinist Soviet patriotism was deeply xenophobic. The centrality of East Slavic identities in Soviet public culture left very little room for non-titular nations.[70] There were about 800,000 Jews in Soviet Ukraine after the Second World War.[71] Although most Poles had been exiled from the newly annexed regions of western Ukraine in the 1940s, some 9,000 Soviet citizens of Polish ethnicity still lived in the city of Lviv in 1956.[72] There was also a Polish community further east, especially around Zhytomyr, because the regions which had been part of the USSR prior to 1939 were not affected by the Polish-Ukrainian program of population exchange in the 1940s.[73] There were nearly 50,000 Hungarians in Transcarpathia,[74] as well as smaller communities of Czechs and Slovaks. Finally, while Crimean Tatars had been deported to Central Asia and were not allowed to return to their homes after the death of Stalin, some tried to move closer to home and settle in southern Ukraine.[75] Representatives of all these minorities were Soviet citizens with "Jewish," "Polish," or "Hungarian" ethnicity written into their internal passports. The KGB and Soviet Party officials deemed these communities inherently less loyal to the Soviet Homeland than Russians and Ukrainians. Members of non-titular nations consequently found it difficult to register their grievances as citizens, though they did at times publicly challenge conceptions of rights defined in ethnic terms.[76]

Albeit "socialist," Czechs, Slovaks, Poles, and Hungarians were construed as outsiders who provided an important source of in-group definition for Soviet Ukrainian people. Whereas domestic policies exposed tensions between Soviet and Ukrainian identities, Ukrainian language, history, and literature turned into positive markers of Sovietness in the context of transnational interactions with Eastern Europe. To be Soviet meant to be Ukrainian and to be Ukrainian meant to be Soviet.

The New Big Deal in Soviet Ukraine

It was not just ethnic identities that determined the limits of belonging in the imagined Soviet Ukrainian community. Soviet Ukraine was also divided along overlapping professional and educational lines. Some categories of citizens, such as doctors, engineers, and war veterans were deemed more reliable supporters of the USSR's policies in Eastern Europe than others. These individuals formed an "aspirational middle class" which enjoyed the most opportunities to define what it meant to be Soviet and Ukrainian.

During the late Stalin period, the authorities struck what Vera Dunham calls a "big deal" with the educated strata of Soviet society.

The regime effectively created a "middle class" by bestowing material incentives on certain groups of specialists in return for their political conformism, "unequivocal nationalism, ... and professionalism."[77] This was not a middle class in the Marxist sense, for it had little to do with the means of production. Rather, it was a literary construct that helped to distinguish individuals with key technical expertise from the top party leadership on the one hand, and the mass of Soviet workers on the other.[78]

The Soviet middle class grew after the death of Stalin. The expansion of bureaucracy, rising party membership, urbanisation, and the increasing number of Soviet citizens with secondary and higher education put pressure on Soviet leaders to bridge the gap between citizens' growing aspirations and the still relatively poor quality of life.[79] The regime therefore marked and rewarded ambitious citizens deemed most important for economic success and political stability, helping to shape a middle class in a society where party membership was no longer a sufficient indicator of status.[80] As in other socialist countries, social status in the USSR was marked by conspicuous consumption.[81] Educated professionals – especially engineers – thus enjoyed easier access to single-family apartments and received higher wages than other members of Soviet society.[82] For Soviet leaders, granting access to high-quality consumer goods to the "most important" citizens was a way to address the perennial problem of work discipline that plagued the USSR.[83]

From the 1970s, however, consumption was no longer a useful marker of distinction for the Soviet aspirational middle class. Leonid Brezhnev struck a "little deal" with a large proportion of the USSR's urban population. In contrast to the postwar "big deal," this new social contract meant that access to much-coveted consumer goods was not the exclusive privilege of a handful of technocrats and specialists. Under Brezhnev, many more Soviet citizens accessed consumer goods by taking advantage of lax state controls, the second economy, and nepotistic connections.[84]

Yet the aspirational middle class remained a distinct group in Soviet society throughout the post-Stalinist era. This is because the middle class was not just a class of consumers – it was also defined in national and patriotic terms. The establishment of Soviet hegemony in the near abroad shaped the mechanics governing the big deal after the death of Stalin. There was now a large and growing group of citizens who publicly claimed that they made a special contribution to strengthening Soviet influences in the near abroad. The Soviet empire in Eastern Europe thus provided a new means to distinguish low-level party activists, engineers, writers, artists, war veterans, workers with some managerial responsibilities, as well as citizens who received various official titles and state awards (such as "shock workers"). There was a strong performative dimension to the Soviet aspirational middle class: citizens had to seek public recognition that their talents, hard work, or war record helped to advance Soviet interests in the near abroad.

My notion of middle class refers to an activist norm of socio-political identity, as citizens aspiring to middle class status claimed the right to guide the rest of Soviet population and the near abroad on the path of progress. The term which comes closest to encapsulating the aspirational and elitist attributes of the middle class is *obshchestvennost'*, which the 1958 Academy of Sciences dictionary defined as "the advanced portion of society." In the 1930s, the Soviet *obshchestvennost'* "did not in any sense approximate 'a new class' or an actual social grouping," but was rather "a fanciful construction that served ... to express a wishful image of the body politic."[85] The postwar aspirational middle class was likewise an idealised propaganda image of the active public. Mass media and official reports described certain groups of citizens as key actors who strengthened Soviet influences in the socialist bloc, aiming to provide a model of how all citizens should speak and behave. However, the protagonists of these propaganda campaigns came to resemble a class because they boldly evoked their supposedly high level of advancement to claim special perks and privileges for themselves.

The term "middle class" would not have meant much in the USSR;[86] nevertheless, it is useful precisely because it describes a reality that Soviet citizens and their leaders never acknowledged. A geographically and ethnically defined Soviet patriotism, articulated in confrontation with the near abroad, created spaces for citizens to cultivate social capital. The Soviet aspirational middle class was not a social group autonomous from the state. On the contrary, Soviet citizens belonged to the aspirational middle class because they were deemed important for the success of Soviet domestic and foreign policy. Members of the aspirational middle class were therefore the staunchest patriots who recognised that their fate was linked intimately with the vicissitudes of the USSR.[87]

Soviet Citizenship

All in all, Soviet citizens' perceptions and interactions with Eastern Europe encouraged expressions of Soviet patriotism. The resulting sense of belonging in the Soviet Ukrainian community – be it as East

Slavs or the aspirational middle class – had surprising implications for state-society dynamics after the death of Stalin. Popular and official views of what it meant to be Soviet and Soviet Ukrainian were not always the same. In contrasting themselves with residents of the near abroad, many inhabitants of Ukraine claimed the right and the duty to criticise official policy as engaged citizens.

Citizenship was a problematic concept in the USSR. Immediately after the October Revolution in 1917, the Bolsheviks did not accept familiar dichotomies of state and society. The state aimed not only to eliminate dissent, but also to transform citizens so they would identify with and further the revolutionary cause.[88] State-society dynamics in the USSR were underpinned by what Yanni Kotsonis identifies as a paradox of citizenship, in that "the self-reliant person was made so by the activist state." In the Soviet context, this translated into extensive use of state repression and indoctrination to shape the ideal citizen who would support and embody revolutionary goals. It also fuelled the rapid rise of the welfare state that was supposed to provide the basis for social inclusion and participation in power.[89]

These notions of participatory citizenship were turned on their head after the Second World War, and especially after the death of Stalin. During the late 1940s and the early 1950s, residents of Soviet Ukraine evoked notions of citizenship as they entered into subtle negotiations with volunteer agitators who addressed them during mass political events. These agitators, drawn from local communities, "played a complex and ambiguous role of speaking on behalf of the state before the people and on behalf of the people before the state." They were ready to respond to some questions and concerns among their audiences to avoid any appearance of trouble, which created spaces for ordinary citizens to "use [political rituals] to express criticisms of the state."[90]

Immediately after Khrushchev's Secret Speech in 1956, being a Soviet citizen further meant to participate in the deliberation and implementation of state policy. Inspired by Khrushchev's promises to build communism and fix mistakes of the past, some Soviet citizens, and young people in particular, expressed loyalty to the Soviet state. The post-Stalinist Thaw therefore witnessed new types of political and social activity, as well as heated debates about the Stalinist past and the post-Stalinist future. People asserted "their right to challenge the status quo as engaged members of society."[91]

Conventional wisdom holds that Soviet citizenship subsequently declined in the late 1960s.[92] Alexei Yurchak suggests that members of the "last Soviet generation" did not engage in meaningful public debate. Because the language of politics had become opaque, repetitive, and self-referential, Brezhnev-era citizens did not have the tools to discuss what their country was or what it should become. Dependent on official Soviet institutions, most citizens pledged loyalty to the USSR and 'socialist values.' At the same time, they developed very diverse lifestyles and conflicting ideas about what it meant to be Soviet.[93]

The idea that most Soviet citizens no longer engaged with Soviet politics in the last decades of the twentieth century owes much to the influence of Stephen Kotkin's study of Stalinist Magnitogorsk. This newly built Soviet city "encapsulated the novelty of socialist industrialisation" during the 1930s, Kotkin famously argues. He continues that local officials and ordinary inhabitants functioned as if the USSR was a "socialist civilization" in which all thoughts and actions had to be measured "against the goals and pronouncements of the party leadership."[94] For all the similarities between the USSR and other modernising regimes, Kotkin suggests, a uniquely Soviet vision of progress "acquired institutional forms which had some important resemblances to, and many important differences from, both liberal projects ... and other forms of anti-liberal modernity" in the interwar period.[95] State-society dynamics in Magnitogorsk were therefore animated through "a process of searching for socialism."[96] Officials shaped production norms and laws governing everyday life with reference to Bolshevik ideology, and citizens likewise commented on and even criticised state policies (and each other's behaviour) by employing Bolshevik rhetoric.[97] In Kotkin's paradigm, Soviet society cannot be divided into conformists and dissidents, as all ideas were refracted through the Bolshevik master narrative. Although people drew on a range of nationalist, anti-Semitic, and populist discourses to describe their relationship with the state,[98] Kotkin claims that these forms of speech did not necessarily rival Bolshevik ideas. In any case, periodic transgressions never undermined the widespread belief that Soviet socialism was superior to capitalism.[99]

While the binary categories of consent and dissent are indeed unhelpful, obscuring the fact that what Soviet citizens said and did was inescapably a product of their cultural environment, Kotkin's identification of Sovietness with Bolshevism is equally problematic. Knowledge and understanding of what Soviet policies should be were often shaped by non-party specialists in the regions of the USSR, rather than just the top party leadership in Moscow.[100] In some contexts at least, Soviet leaders formulated policy goals with little or no reference to Bolshevik ideas on class, revolution, or communalism, as well as encouraged citizens to draw on prerevolutionary notions of right and wrong to comment on social phenomena.[101] For example, the construction of the mining town of Karaganda in northern Kazakhstan reflected ethnic prejudices and considerations of economic expediency that made it difficult to distinguish the Soviet from American approaches to resource extraction and urban design.[102] Moreover, 1930s propaganda often framed "Soviet" goals and values in primordialist and great power terms, which was a far cry from early Bolshevik ideas about class and nation and rather resembled nationalist regimes elsewhere.[103] In Anna Krylova's words, Kotkin never makes the Bolshevik ideology "the subject of critical examination in and of itself."[104] It is therefore unclear what was "Bolshevik" about Soviet policies and culture.

Yet the assumption that Bolshevik ideology was the only vocabulary through which the Soviet state and citizens made sense of each other's relationship has often been transplanted to the postwar period. It has led historians inspired by Kotkin's work to suggest that late Soviet society "stagnated." For instance, a transplantation of Kotkin's ideas about the 1930s to the post-Stalinist period has shaped Amir Weiner's studies of the USSR's western borderlands.[105] In Weiner's view, Soviet citizens' speech and behaviour in the 1950s were judged against the party leadership's utopian, Leninist ideas about communalism and class.[106] People who supported the USSR's foreign and domestic policies were complicit in "post-Stalinist totalitarianism," embodying Khrushchev's "spirit and policies."[107] In contrast, anyone who described reality in a language that differed from the top Communist Party leadership was simply anti-Soviet.[108] Weiner suggests that once East European resistance to socialist regimes undermined Soviet citizens' faith in the Leninist utopian project,[109] the "revolutionary" regime and its citizens lost all meaningful ways to interact with each other. From the 1960s, youth in particular were "beset primarily by material concerns [... and] the regime responded in kind, offering commitment for material improvements in exchange for unchallenged political and ideological hegemony."[110] Weiner thus equates late Soviet social stability with political stagnation. Because people no longer "spoke Bolshevik," he implies, they lost interest in what the aging "Bolshevik" regime was doing.[111]

It is imprudent to study postwar USSR as a revolutionary regime in which state-society dynamics were only interpreted through the prism of old Bolshevik slogans. By the 1950s the Soviet project had gone through so many permutations that almost nobody took seriously the notion that a single "Bolshevik" discourse existed. What Krylova calls the "post-Bolshevik socialist culture" in the USSR was much less self-consciously unique than the prewar revolutionary regime.[112] Especially after the establishment of satellite regimes in Eastern Europe, the USSR was not the only socialist civilisation, but rather one socialist state among many. The Soviet Communist Party was therefore not the only source of ideas on what it meant to be socialist. More importantly, as citizens grew to see the USSR as an embodiment of geographically specific, East Slavic interests that differed from other socialist countries, they also perceived and judged Soviet practices and ideas against the background of foreign states that likewise claimed to represent national communities.[113] To be sure, citizens' perceptions of the Soviet Union and the outside world were filtered by party censors and propagandists. Nevertheless, while national identities had previously been seen as mere instruments in the Bolshevik project of constructing socialism,[114] they later turned into the central locus of identity. Post-Stalinist party apparatchiks and citizens rarely judged policies, beliefs, and behaviours against imagined 'socialist' standards, but rather sought to understand and fulfil the needs of a Soviet community defined in geographical and ethnic terms.

After the Second World War, and especially after the death of Stalin, citizens of the USSR did not "speak Bolshevik"; they spoke Soviet instead. The central point of speaking Soviet was to manifest one's loyalty to the Soviet homeland and its titular ethnic groups, rather than the Communist Party of the Soviet Union (CPSU). For many citizens in the 1940s, for example, to be Soviet was to be a Soviet soldier and not necessarily to be "Bolshevik."[115] In later decades, party leaders and ordinary citizens frequently spoke about the need to strengthen the Soviet military and to protect the Soviet border without making any explicit references to the Communist Party and its ideology. Citizens understood what formed "Soviet" and "Ukrainian" interests through national histories and literatures, memories of the Second World War and fears of foreign invasion, examples of reform in other socialist countries, conversations with foreign tourists travelling in the USSR, as well as the party's pronouncements.[116] Ultimately, Sovietness was not an ideology that the party vanguard bestowed upon society, but a set of values and goals that citizens formulated in dialogue with – or indeed in opposition to – other nations around the globe.

"Speaking Soviet" fuelled new types of citizenship in the USSR. It allowed many residents of the USSR to debate and criticise official policy outside the confines of "Bolshevik," without appearing anti-Soviet. While the party and the KGB labelled some such criticisms as "mistakes" or "misunderstandings," they welcomed others as expressions of genuine concern about Soviet politics, culture, and society. This was especially because the widespread identification of Soviet citizens with East Slavs extended imagined citizenship to former "class enemies," "bourgeois nationalists," and most party members and non-members alike. Whereas Jochen Hellbeck claims that bottom-up attempts to "redefine the objective revolutionary narrative" were ultimately unsuccessful under Stalin,[117] the war, de-Stalinization, and – crucially – the establishment of Soviet hegemony in Eastern Europe allowed citizens to invest official ideas with new meanings.

My study of Soviet patriotism challenges dominant chronologies of late Soviet history. Patriotism framed heated debates about the future of the Soviet project during the Thaw, but also in the supposedly stagnant 1970s and 1980s. People cared about politics not because they believed in Bolshevism, but because geographically and ethnically defined patriotism was a very effective means of political mobilisation.

Conservative and Reformist Patriotisms

Political attitudes filtered through patriotic rhetoric ranged between what I refer to as "conservative patriotism," which was most common, and "reformist patriotism." Far from denoting coherent sets of attitudes, these terms prove useful in classifying a very diverse set of opinions expressed in different settings. They do not refer to any clear social divisions in Soviet Ukraine, as it is conceivable that individuals voiced multiple and even contradictory views.

Central to both reformist and conservative patriotisms were a sense of loyalty to the Soviet community, and various understandings of the USSR's role as the centre of the socialist camp. Reformist patriotism generally held that excessive interference in the domestic affairs of other countries prevented Soviet leaders from implementing far-reaching reform at home. It thus reflected a sense of Soviet responsibility. Proponents of reform first highlighted that the USSR should guide the satellite states towards de-Stalinization, and then increasingly maintained that the Kremlin must prove more responsive to progressive ideas emanating from the satellite states. In contrast, expressing ideas of conservative patriotism, citizens generally pit the peaceful and cultured Soviet people against more "unreliable" foreigners in other socialist states. They articulated a sense of Soviet pride by insisting that Moscow should at all costs preserve its hegemony in Eastern Europe.

Reformist patriotism was at its peak in 1956, when some university students and members of the creative intelligentsia stressed that Khrushchev's "liberalisation" should be taken further, both in the USSR and in the near abroad. In subsequent years, as the space for the articulation of critical views grew narrower, reformist opinions were fewer, but also more coherent and concentrated in underground publications. The geography of reformist patriotism in Ukraine did not conform to the stereotypical division into unstable borderlands and a compliant east and south.[118] Bar a few scattered calls for Ukrainian independence, dissenting voices did not normally echo ideas of anti-Soviet nationalism or a sense of cultural and historical distinctiveness associated with western Ukraine. Rather, they were mostly grounded in a sense of Soviet patriotism that was more geographically widespread.

However, positive perceptions of reform were overshadowed by conservative concerns. A growing number of Ukraine's inhabitants voiced support for the Kremlin's repressive measures in the outer empire. Conservative patriotism also helped ostracise the regime's reformist critics at home. Resembling anti-dissident campaigns in late 1970s Czechoslovakia, Soviet agitators fanned popular fear of social instability and mobilised xenophobic sentiment, encouraging citizens to publicly condemn the regime's critics as tools of Zionist centres, "dregs of society, [and] people who had failed to become productive members of socialist society and so were willing to sell themselves to foreign bourgeois schemes."[119]

The public articulation of conservative patriotic ideas acquired a crucial social dimension, as it provided forums for the performance of middle-class identities. Whereas the Czechoslovak authorities relied on television celebrities to lend credence to anti-dissident campaigns,[120] the Soviet leadership turned to local community leaders to organise the public naming and shaming of enemies. Conservative patriotism consequently shaped the nature of claims asserted by the aspirational middle class. By manifesting their commitment to spreading Soviet influences abroad, its members sought improved access to perks associated with international travel. Professing to foster the correct opinions and attitudes towards Eastern Europe among the wider Soviet public, members of the aspirational middle class further criticised Soviet mass media. They not only demanded better access to news and information for themselves, but also pointed to gaps and inconsistencies in official coverage of international affairs, arguing that this could lead to the rise of malicious rumours and misunderstandings among residents of Soviet Ukraine.

Nonetheless, conservative patriotism was not an exclusive trait of the aspirational middle class. To borrow E.P. Thompson's expression, conservative patriotism was also a "moral economy of the poor." In parallel with eighteenth-century English peasants, Soviet citizens retained a strong attachment to the strong "paternalist state," perceived free market economies as a threat to their very existence, and complained in public about subsidised exports at times of dearth. In contrast to Thompson's peasants, however, advocates of conservative patriotism rarely took matters into their own hands to correct perceived abuses through the use of force.[121] They rather limited their criticism to statements voiced during official meetings and in such relatively uncontrolled contexts as market places. In these forums, proponents of conservative patriotism claimed that lax censorship and the opening of Soviet borders fuelled unrest at home and abroad. Demanding that the authorities take better care of their own citizens, residents of Ukraine did not normally demand access to luxury consumer goods, but rather pursued much more modest goals such as better supplies of soap and potatoes. The nature of these demands revealed just how impoverished the population of Ukraine remained well into the Brezhnev era.[122]

Patriotic criticism of Soviet domestic and foreign policies rarely took the form of organised and sustained dissent. But neither did it correspond to what Vladimir Kozlov defines as "*kramola*" or "sedition." Kozlov argues that *kramola* reflected "the traditional opposition in Russia between the state and the people," and as such, did not represent any coherent ideology.[123] In contrast, this book suggests that apart from clearly eclectic engagements between the state and its citizens (such as drunken outbursts directed against militia men), the post-Stalinist period witnessed the rise of new types of active citizenship underpinned by strong attachment to the Soviet state. The most important source of criticism and political engagement in post-Stalinist USSR was nationalism and geographically defined patriotism.

Popular Opinion and Sources

To be sure, it is extremely difficult to ascertain how inhabitants of Ukraine spoke about Soviet patriotism, national identities, and state borders in the twentieth century. In order to analyse the evolution of

Soviet and Soviet Ukrainian identities, I first examine official narratives about the near abroad as they evolved in official statements and publications.[124] To gauge popular responses to these narratives, I have had to rely mostly on reported opinion. With the exception of a few samizdat documents, which reflected first-person views of Soviet dissidents, and at times their assessment of what the broader public thought,[125] I draw on official party and KGB sources. The most important documents are informational reports compiled for internal use by communist apparatchiks at different levels of the party hierarchy in Ukraine. The stated aim of such reports was to assess popular reactions to major events and developments in the Soviet bloc in the regions of Ukraine.

For the most part, party-produced reports convey what inhabitants of Ukraine said in official and heavily controlled settings, such as agitation meetings held at factories and collective farms. Other important sources for my analysis are compilations of readers' letters that newspaper editors sent to top officials of the CPSU, in which they summarised the content of both signed and anonymous letters received from readers. To be sure, these sources do not reveal what people said in such relatively uncontrolled contexts as the home, but they do expose diverse patterns in which citizens related to the state and its officials in public.

In order to gauge what people said in less official settings, I have examined dozens of KGB surveillance reports, most of which were produced by senior officers for the use of obkom (regional party committee) secretaries and apparatchiks at the CPSU and CPU (Communist Party of Ukraine) Central Committees. Here I draw heavily on work conducted by the Ukrainian historians Volodymyr Dmytruk and Oleh Bazhan who collected and analysed fascinating KGB surveillance reports that reflect a wide range of popular reactions to major crises in Eastern Europe, particularly the Prague Spring of 1968.[126] These sources may well distort what people said about Eastern Europe, reflecting Soviet apparatchiks' own prejudices and vested institutional interests (although the reports sometimes claimed to relay *verbatim* the views expressed in private conversations and illegal pamphlets found in various parts of Ukraine). The KGB often focused on monitoring those people who had already been considered suspicious. Consequently, their reports may well construct certain groups and individuals as "hostile." This problem is partly alleviated by the fact that the KGB also made attempts to assess the spread of "hostile" and "incorrect" opinions, and consequently outlined a whole range of attitudes expressed by seemingly random individuals in various public sites such as queues outside shops or public transport. Furthermore, after the relaxation of Stalinist terror, KGB reports likely offered a more diverse picture of popular opinion than Stalinist-era NKVD (The People's Commissariat for Internal Affairs) documents. This is not only because citizens were more likely to voice controversial views in various public (if unofficial) forums, but also because the KGB itself was not only a coercive organ, but also a source of information that party leaders used to shape policy once coercion became a relatively less prominent instrument of power. Still, it is conceivable that secret police reports devoted disproportionate attention to opinions that the regime considered problematic, as KGB officers needed to justify their *raison d'être*.[127] Moreover, KGB officers may have assigned official categories to an otherwise broader range of views, creating a false impression of uniformity. Although they do not allow us to accurately assess the spread of different views in Ukrainian society, KGB surveillance reports reveal that opinions articulated in various unofficial forums ranged from expressions of support for the Soviet regime and its policies, through mild criticism, to outright rejection of the Soviet system.

Soviet popular opinion after the end of the 1960s is especially difficult to gauge. Surveillance reports from the era are often inaccessible, while increasingly formulaic reports from public agitation gatherings held after the end of Khrushchev's Thaw offer the historian an insight into citizens' public self-representation strategies, though they do not allow us to gauge conflicts and contradictions in Soviet society. Even internal party correspondence had become extremely formulaic by the 1970s, which makes it difficult to trace Soviet apparatchiks' responses to popular opinion. I therefore supplement Soviet-produced sources with Polish reports about public and cultural diplomacy and travel between Poland and the USSR. Especially during the early 1980s, when the rise of the Solidarity Trade Union shook up the Polish system, these reports discuss problems in Polish-Soviet and Polish-Ukrainian cooperation very openly, and even offer insights into Soviet apparatchiks' opinions that are kept out of internal Soviet reports. For the late Soviet period, I further explore interviews that Radio Liberty researchers conducted with Soviet tourists travelling in the West, as well as with recent émigrés from the USSR. To be sure, opinions contained therein cannot be taken at face value, not least because émigrés seeking to justify their right to remain abroad and the privileged Soviet citizens permitted to travel in the West might have exaggerated the extent to which official propaganda shaped popular opinion in the USSR. Nevertheless, the interviewees expressed a broad range of opinions, exposing important contradictions in Soviet society.

All these sources allow me to trace the development of popular opinion in twentieth-century Ukraine. In this book, I use the term "popular opinion" to refer to a process of communication involving Soviet citizens and the government that does not easily fit into the three categories of "public," "authorised," and "non-public" opinion outlined by Jürgen Habermas.[128] Neither does it correspond to the Soviet notion of *obshchestvennoe mnenie* (public opinion), which referred to those views that the regime recognised as "correct."[129] Although no official Soviet category corresponds to my notion of popular opinion, the term encompasses what official surveillance reports normally described as "moods," "reactions," "views," and "voiced opinions." On one level, popular opinion thus refers to the attitudes of citizens who expressed their alienation from the Soviet system and its ideology. However, popular opinion often consisted of the same terms and slogans as official propaganda, all the while encompassing differing ideas about life in the USSR. For example, individuals who participated in reproducing official slogans expected perks and privileges in return for their conformity. Furthermore, Soviet citizens invested official slogans with a range of meanings, seeking thereby to obtain power: in Michel Foucault's words, they sought "access to knowledge and language, which confer the ability to classify ideas, behaviours, and experiences and impose that classification, as norms, on others."[130] My concept of popular opinion therefore includes the claims that people made on the basis that they embraced the Soviet patriotic point of view.

Outline of the Book

The Near Abroad combines chronological and thematic structures across its five chapters. Chapters 1, 3 and 5 form its backbone, examining the evolution of Soviet identities in Ukraine by analysing the range of popular reactions to the dramatic events in the Soviet camp which unfolded in 1956, 1968, and the early 1980s. In order to understand the claims that Soviet citizens made through speaking about Eastern Europe, chapters 2 and 4 trace how interactions with Eastern Europe shaped Soviet society and culture between 1956 and 1968, and between 1968 and 1980.

Chapter 1 argues that Władysław Gomułka's reforms in Poland and the Hungarian uprising inspired heated debates about the costs of de-Stalinization among the population of Ukraine in 1956. Despite the violence in Eastern Europe, Soviet leaders were committed to salvaging the claims of Soviet internationalism. Yet citizens who commented on events across the border downplayed the importance of socialism as a force that brought the Soviet bloc together, and commented instead on the importance of national identities and borders in the region. Both conservative and reformist patriotism encouraged the expression of new notions of citizenship in 1956.

Chapter 2 examines ways in which Soviet and East European apparatchiks used public and cultural diplomacy to heal the wounds of 1956. It argues that the twelve years between the Hungarian uprising and the Prague Spring witnessed important attempts to revive Soviet internationalism, but it also shows that a transnational, socialist identity did not take root in Eastern Europe.

Chapter 3 argues that popular reactions to Czechoslovak events in 1968 revealed the rising importance of geographically defined patriotism and ethnicity in Soviet public culture. As Sovietness was increasingly defined in territorial and ethnic terms, many Soviet citizens developed new social identities and engaged with the state in dynamic ways.

Chapter 4 explores the further ethnicisation of Soviet public culture in the 1970s. Uneasy about the rise of new subcultures and the growing importance of television, Soviet officials sought new ways to promote patriotism among the population. Irked by conflicts with their East European colleagues, Soviet Party apparatchiks and artists turned towards epic historical narratives, not only to draw a clear boundary between loyal Soviet citizens and the "conniving" foreigners in Eastern Europe, but also to capture popular imagination.

Chapter 5 examines how these nationalist and xenophobic narratives conditioned Ukrainian responses to the Solidarity crisis during the early 1980s. While rejecting both the Polish trajectory and earlier reformist calls for the relaxation of state control over society in the USSR itself, Soviet citizens who commented on Solidarity nevertheless began to call for limited economic and social reforms in the USSR. The desire to transform the Soviet polity that began to manifest itself by the mid-1980s represented ideas of conservative patriotism shared by the Soviet regime, its socially mobile educated citizens, and many Ukrainians who identified with the USSR as an empire of East Slavs.

Finally, the epilogue highlights the importance of Soviet identity politics for understanding the social and political dynamics of Gorbachev's perestroika and nation building in Ukraine after 1991.

Soviet notions of near abroad developed during interactions with socialist Eastern Europe are today evoked to justify Moscow's interventionist policies in Ukraine. At the same time, world views shaped in dialogue and in confrontation with the Soviet satellite states underpin divergent attitudes towards Russia and the West among the population of Ukraine. In this sense, identity dynamics in the former USSR are an echo of Soviet relations with socialist Eastern Europe.

1 De-Stalinization and Soviet Patriotism: Ukrainian Reactions to East European Unrest in 1956

The Polish and Hungarian unrest of 1956 could not have caught Moscow at a more fragile time. Khrushchev's not-so-Secret Speech at the Twentieth Party Congress in February had raised troubling questions about the "cult of personality" and the excesses of Stalinism. With the country unsettled by waves of returning Gulag prisoners and the dramatic shifts in state policy in the years following Stalin's death, the future seemed uncertain.

The dramatic events in the Soviet satellite states did not help inspire confidence in Khrushchev's reforms among the population of Ukraine. In Poland, many citizens rejected Khrushchev's rhetoric about the "cult of personality" and condemned the entire CPSU and Stalinist-era Polish communist leaders.[1] Top Warsaw apparatchiks searched for new sources of legitimacy, especially after the bloody workers' riots in Poznań in June 1956. Elected to serve as the first secretary of the Polish United Workers' Party on 19 October 1956, Władysław Gomułka announced a new Polish "way to socialism," halting collectivization of agriculture and allowing (at least temporarily) a greater degree of freedom of expression. The Soviet army came close to invading, and the Soviet press raised alarm about the rise of "anti-Soviet" moods in Poland, but Khrushchev eventually accepted the new leadership in Warsaw.[2] The Secret Speech also triggered heated debates about the need to reform the regime in Hungary. In contrast to the relatively peaceful resolution to the crisis in Poland, fighting broke out on the streets of Budapest on 23 October, and after a brief Soviet military intervention, Imre Nagy took over the reins of the Hungarian Party. As he made chaotic attempts to end the violence and restore the authority of the Hungarian Party, Moscow grew concerned that his reforms went too far, especially as Hungary announced it was going to withdraw from the Warsaw Pact. On 4 November, Soviet armies moved in to Budapest again to crush the popular uprising, resulting in bloodshed on both sides. Hungarian resistance was crushed by 10 November, and the new Soviet puppet government destroyed all forms of public opposition within the next two months.[3]

Many scholars who explore Soviet citizens' attitudes towards reform and de-Stalinization in 1956 focus on reactions to the Secret Speech and changes within the USSR itself. However, as Mark Kramer and Amir Weiner have shown, this story of 1956 is incomplete.[4] This is because, in the Soviet Union itself, East European crises were seen as a direct consequence of Khrushchev's policies. Inhabitants of the USSR judged Khrushchev as an international leader, widely discussing his policies vis-à-vis the socialist satellites. More importantly, Poland and Hungary were treated as a testing ground for de-Stalinization. The brutal events in the near abroad inspired Soviet citizens to argue about the extent to which it was possible to reform Soviet-style regimes without inducing violence and instability.

To be sure, top CPSU leaders in Kyiv and Moscow were well aware that foreign crises reverberated in the USSR, particularly in the borderlands. After the cataclysm of the Secret Speech when public debates slipped out of control,[5] these leaders were determined to constrain discussion surrounding the Polish and Hungarian events more effectively. In order to communicate the party line and keep people under control, they sought to outline clear rules about how to conduct special agitation meetings for rank-and-file party members, as well as non-party workers and collective farmers.

In this chapter, I examine dozens of reports about these public "explanatory gatherings" to gauge attitudes towards Eastern Europe in 1956. Most of these documents date to October and November 1956, with some carrying on well into 1957.[6] An additional source for my analysis is the information that party officials obtained about private conversations, anonymous letters, and illegal pamphlets that cropped up in different regions of Ukraine in late 1956.

The most radical reactions to East European unrest were filtered through anti-Soviet nationalism, especially (though not exclusively) among Gulag returnees in the borderlands. Inspired by the Hungarian example in particular, some residents of western Ukraine spoke about the need to rise up against Soviet power. But Soviet patriotism was a more potent idea which inspired inhabitants of Ukraine not only to criticise Khrushchev, but also to voice demands of the state and articulate various understandings of what it meant to be a good citizen.

Getting the Story Straight

Debates about the crises in Eastern Europe acquired a particularly large scope between October 1956 and January 1957. During this period, senior officials and activists on the ground struggled to communicate the party line and control public discussion, which reflected Moscow's own ambiguous attitudes towards reform.

The Soviet press published the first news of unrest in Poland on 30 June. Coverage of the Poznań riots in the *Pravda* and *Izvestiia* newspapers set the tone for debates surrounding the Polish and Hungarian crises in the autumn. The media echoed party leaders' concerns about the unity of the socialist camp and their renewed commitment to improving living standards in the USSR and the near abroad. Newspapers thus blamed "international reactionary forces" for the outbreak of violence, but also pointed to "bureaucratic distortions" which aggravated economic shortages in Poland.[7] This language was certainly vague and open to interpretation, but it is striking that the press played on readers' fears of foreign anti-Soviet alliances, all the while emphasising that it was possible and necessary to raise the standard of living for "ordinary" workers in Soviet-style regimes. This was an attempt to preserve the unity of the socialist camp without abandoning the reform agenda: although de-Stalinization had led to instability, these narratives suggested, it could still succeed. Problems were not inherent in the socialist system, but were rather a product of foreign interference.

Despite obvious dissatisfaction with Soviet-style socialism in the near abroad, party apparatchiks tried to salvage the image of Soviet socialism as an ideology that spread across state and national borders. This goes some way towards explaining why Moscow did not articulate a clear Soviet point of view about the changes taking place in Poland in September and October 1956. As the Polish debates about reform gained momentum during the autumn, the CPSU Central Committee Presidium received reports about the publication of anti-Soviet materials in the Polish press,[8] but there seemed to be no consensus about how the Soviet media should react to this.[9] *Pravda* printed the news of Gomułka's takeover on 20 October 1956, raising alarm about the rise of "anti-socialist" forces in Warsaw,[10] but Khrushchev remained reluctant to define his attitude. On 21 October, he informed the Presidium that no statement about the Polish situation should yet be sent out to party organisations.[11]

It was not until 23 October that the CPSU Central Committee began to draft a letter about the situation in Poland, which was supposed to be read alongside Gomułka's speech outlining his new policies during regional party cell meetings throughout the USSR. The speech once again outlined the limits of de-Stalinization as Gomułka promised to protect Polish sovereignty, address bureaucratic abuses, and improve living standards, but it also reaffirmed Poland's loyalty to the Warsaw Pact and Soviet-style communism.[12] Even then, the authorities sought to limit the flow of information from Poland, instructing officials at the regional level (*obkomy*) to read the letter to their subordinates in sub-regional party structures (*raikomy*) but not to leave any copies with them.[13] Meanwhile, *Pravda* continued to produce ambiguous images of Gomułka's Poland over the next two weeks or so, informing its readers about the influence of anti-Soviet political forces in the country, but also expressing faith that Moscow and Warsaw would find a way to resolve their differences.[14] With Gomułka attacked by the Soviet press and yet ultimately accepted as the new leader of Poland, Moscow's attitudes towards the "Polish way to socialism" remained unclear.

News reports from Hungary were much less ambiguous. On 25 October 1956, *Pravda* and *Izvestiia* wrote about a "counterrevolutionary rebellion" in Budapest, organised by "reactionary underground organizations."[15] The language was harsh and uncompromising: the Hungarian protesters were unmistakably defined as enemies, and the threat to the Soviet bloc was framed in both ethnic and ideological terms. *Pravda* pointed to the supposed links between the "fascist" rebellion in Hungary and German revanchism.[16] On 3 November, the CPSU Central Committee informed leaders in each republic and region that Nagy's government had prepared the way for "reactionary forces," which sought to re-establish the capitalist system in Hungary. At the same time, despite Molotov's opposition,[17] Central Committee officials criticised Hungarian leaders for their reluctance to introduce reform after 1953.[18] In line with this, on 5 November the editorial in *Pravda* stated that "the Hungarian Revolutionary and Peasants Government … requested the Soviet troops to help the people smash the dire forces of reaction and counterrevolution." It continued that the new Hungarian government established under Soviet protection would pursue a program of reform, "ensuring the country's national independence," "raising the standard of living of the working people," and "establishing indestructible fraternal ties with the socialist states."[19] Popular acquiescence would be achieved through granting economic concessions to the Hungarian workers, and preserving a degree of Hungarian autonomy within the socialist camp.

The issue of national autonomy and cultural freedom under the Soviet aegis had a particularly strong resonance in Ukraine. The press mobilized both Soviet and Soviet Ukrainian identities to frame discussions about the near abroad. *Pravda Ukrainy* celebrated openness in Ukrainian-Polish cultural relations as a key aspect of Ukrainian national development, as well as an important step towards de-Stalinization of the Soviet information sphere.[20] Likewise, when the 1957 Moscow Youth Festival offered a fresh opportunity to reflect upon the Hungarian events and the role of nations in the Soviet bloc, *Literaturna hazeta* wrote about the distinct role of "Ukrainian" as well as "all Soviet" youth in strengthening fraternal unity with Hungary.[21]

Through thus shaping their portrayals of Eastern Europe, the official media suggested that Soviet-style regimes had first to strengthen top-down control, and second to concentrate on reform to gain mass legitimacy. The Soviet authorities made a concerted effort to transmit this message to residents of Ukraine through agitation meetings. In the last week of October, party officials organised special explanatory gatherings about the situation in Poland and Hungary, where press articles were read out and discussed. The meetings were tailored for the broader public, rather than just party members.[22] Throughout the first half of November, each regional party leader in Ukraine produced a few reports about the repercussions of the Polish and Hungarian events, informing the CPU Central Committee about the conduct of agitation meetings held at large industrial enterprises and collective farms, and passing on information obtained from the local KGB branches.[23] Such careful monitoring of popular opinion was underpinned by party leaders' belief that crises in the near abroad inspired Soviet citizens to question the viability of Soviet-style socialism.

Before the CPSU Central Committee issued the telegram about Hungary on 3 November, it seems that agitators relied exclusively on the official Soviet media in preparation for meetings.[24] During this time, regional Communist Party leaders blamed their superiors in Kyiv and Moscow for providing insufficient information, as well as requested clearer top-down instructions about how to deal with news and agitation on the local level.[25] For their part, top officials in Kyiv reprimanded local party organisations throughout Ukraine for their lack of "flexibility" and reluctance to answer citizens' questions.[26] It is not surprising that regional officials looked for clear top-down instructions before explaining current events at public meetings. Stalinist purges of those who expressed the "wrong" views were still within very recent memory, and it was far from clear whether Khrushchev's reforms would hold. For the same reason, bureaucrats at the regional level were not satisfied with the work of their subordinates in charge of organising agitation work on the ground. The harshest criticism of all resounded in Lviv, reflecting concerns about the limits of Sovietization in the western borderlands annexed to the USSR during the Second World War.[27] Party apparatchiks at the regional and city level in various parts of Ukraine were also very alarmed that debates among students escaped the confines of the official agitation meetings, which they blamed on the incompetence of low-level officials.[28] This indicated that party leaders in the regions of Ukraine took seriously the need to speak to rank-and-file members, and to enthuse them about the Soviet project at such an unstable time. But communication between regional leaders and communists on the ground still left a lot to be desired: there was not a clear party (or "Bolshevik") interpretation of the East European crises in autumn 1956.

By issuing their special telegram on 3 November, Khrushchev and other members of the CPSU Presidium in Moscow hoped to improve the quality of agitation work. They explicitly instructed local officials that the "state and party *aktiv*" – low-level officials entrusted with mobilising and controlling other citizens – should be informed about the situation in Eastern Europe first; only then should they organise "explanatory work" at factories, collective farms, and other institutions.[29] In this way, Khrushchev and other Presidium members in Moscow recognised and maintained strong hierarchies in Soviet society. Unsure of how most citizens would react to the tumultuous events of 1956, and despite party leaders' commitment to promoting public discussion after the death of Stalin, the Presidium maintained strict censorship in the mass media. They simply took it for granted that information available in Soviet newspapers was less complete than news obtained through internal party channels. To learn about events in Eastern Europe, most people had to rely on either the activists who filtered and explained the news to them, or the heavily controlled mass media. Only the "middle class" of community leaders, including agitators who addressed workers and collective farmers on the ground, enjoyed direct access to relatively reliable information.

It is not entirely clear whether all community leaders charged with explaining current affairs in public were in fact familiar with the telegram, and in any case, it appears that they failed to control popular opinion to the satisfaction of officials in Moscow. On 21 November, the Presidium of the Central Committee in Moscow began to compose "an extremely harsh and impatient letter" to all party organizations down to the level of primary cells. In it, they chastised low-level party officials for failing to root out "negative reactions" to Khrushchev's de-Stalinization and the East European crises among the creative intelligentsia, academics, Gulag returnees, "bourgeois nationalists," and others.[30]

The letter had gone through several drafts before being sent out on 19 December, as the Party Presidium in Moscow discussed how to infuse Soviet citizens with the "correct" understanding of the East European crises, rather than just punishing those individuals who expressed undesirable views. It stressed that the party should find new sources of legitimacy to maintain calm and stability in the USSR. For instance, CPSU Presidium members called for combatting "bureaucratism" throughout the USSR; in this way, they put pressure on factory managers, local party bosses, and trade union officials to become more responsive to popular demands (including calls to improve safety standards at work).[31] In line with this, the letter also instructed party secretaries on the local level to hold meetings with workers and engineers in the spirit of "healthy criticism and self-criticism." Low-rank officials were supposed to take a big chunk of the blame for social and economic problems in the USSR, publicly admit to the mistakes they had made, and promise improvements.[32]

The letter was above all an attempt to define the limits of permissible public expression at a time when many citizens still argued about the implications of Khrushchev's Secret Speech and the East European crises. While making sure that writers accepted state control over the arts and ascribed to "Leninist principles," for example, the letter also stated that party officials were to avoid the vulgarity of Stalinist interventions in literature.[33] In other words, it was acceptable to say or write that mistakes had been made, but not to question whether the USSR and its allies had made the right choice by rejecting capitalism. Khrushchev's Presidium hoped thereby to win over some citizens who had grown critical of the USSR. While some of them were clearly beyond redemption, the top brass reasoned, others could still be convinced that the system was fixable. Party officials in the regions were therefore explicitly told not to punish or ostracize ideologically immature and "lost" (*zabluzhdaiushchiesia*) citizens, who were not be confused with "hostile elements."[34]

Exactly one month after sending the letter, the CPSU Central Committee evaluated how its resolutions were implemented in the regions. They still complained about the quality of public lectures in the USSR, claiming that the agitators who explained party and state policy were often immature, unprepared, and sometimes untrustworthy. However, feedback from the regions suggested that the Central Committee's letter had created an "atmosphere of intolerance" towards "anti-Soviet" opinions, at least within party organisations. Local community leaders had brought discussion under control and exorcised views that the top brass deemed especially threatening. Sometimes this happened retrospectively. Comrade Kapusta, the director of a Transcarpathian lumberjack collective and a party member, had previously attacked the Soviet army for killing children in Hungary and claimed that the USSR crushed a popular revolt against tyrannical governments. Whereas the lumberjacks' party organisation had ignored this at the time, they remembered Kapusta after reading the Presidium's letter in December. Only then did they pass a resolution condemning his statements.[35] Exclusion from the party was an important means of keeping discipline after 19 December. At the genetics institute in Odesa, for example, the party cell condemned the "anti-party" behaviour and expelled a third year postgraduate student, A.I. Chaiko, who had criticised Soviet policies in Hungary.[36]

Thus, public discussion about the East European crises was most lively between late October and mid-December 1956, and it became more constrained by early 1957. The gradual taming of public meetings has important implications for understanding the significance of participants' questions and comments. On one level, in clamping down on public debate, the authorities outlined a set of "correct" views that citizens should evoke to show loyalty to the regime. In doing so, inhabitants of Ukraine claimed perks and privileges in return for their loyalty, and asserted that their social and regional groups made a special contribution to Soviet society. Through revealing which categories of citizens were most successful at manifesting their patriotic credentials, therefore, official reports expose complex social and regional dynamics in Ukraine.

At the same time, the confusion and excitement that characterised at least some of the agitation gatherings provided for the expression of diverse opinions. In this sense, agitation meetings devoted to Eastern

Europe resembled the primary party gatherings held earlier in the year.[37] Between October 1956 and January 1957, citizens used the opportunity to speak in public to express diverse opinions about Soviet foreign and domestic policy. By the very act of organising informational gatherings, the authorities encouraged citizens to talk about foreign affairs and reform within the Soviet bloc, as well as to demand more information from party leaders. The lack of a clear party narrative encouraged diverse public expressions of Sovietness. Whereas official narratives concentrated on the power of Soviet-style socialism to bridge the gap between the USSR and its allies in Eastern Europe, citizens' public statements focused more on what distinguished Soviet people from their supposedly "socialist brothers" across the border.

Conservative Patriotism and the Aspirational Middle Class

In speaking about Eastern Europe, some citizens underlined their special status in Soviet society. In various public forums, they articulated notions of conservative patriotism in such a way as to claim they made an outstanding contribution to maintaining Soviet power abroad. Debates about crises in the near abroad presented inhabitants of Ukraine with the opportunity to perform middle-class identities. Citizens keen to emphasise their loyalty to the USSR dominated public meetings, repeating propaganda slogans in long and jingoistic speeches. On the one hand, this stifled public debates about the Stalinist past and the post-Stalinist future. Citizens who addressed public meetings claimed that true Soviet people must always speak in one voice, and thus exorcised dissent as foreign and unpatriotic. On the other hand, evoking their supposedly high level of advancement, these self-styled community leaders criticised official policy and expressed strong anti-reformist views that undermined Khrushchev's authority.

Middle-class articulations of conservative patriotism drew on memories of the Second World War. During late 1956, war veterans in particular evoked Soviet sacrifices in Eastern Europe and called on Khrushchev to protect the fruits of victory. In the Crimea, local residents gathered together to listen to Soviet radio. During the meeting, veterans were quoted as saying the country must remain within the socialist camp since Soviet soldiers "spilt blood" for Hungary.[38] In a similar vein, during a public gathering a primary party organisation secretary from Kyiv claimed that "the Polish workers and villagers remembered that it was the Soviet army that liberated their country from German fascism."[39]

Statements like these helped frame the Soviet bloc in great power terms that bore little explicit relation to official ideas about socialism: the USSR had the right to shape policies in the near abroad not necessarily because it represented progressive socialist ideas, but rather because its army had won the war. Sovietness was thus defined with reference to the state and its institutions, rather than the party and its ideology.

In 1956, surveillance reports presented war veterans as a group that unanimously supported Moscow's repressive policies in Hungary. This may suggest that debates about foreign affairs provided one forum where veterans – otherwise divided along generational lines and facing various degrees of discrimination and outright repression in the USSR – began to speak in one voice. Recently united in the Soviet Committee of War Veterans, they were an important part of Cold War propaganda, as Soviet leaders mobilised memories of the USSR's victory over Nazi Germany to justify their foreign policy.[40] At the same time, even though the veterans did not yet articulate demands for privileges as clearly as they would after avenues for formal organisation were closed again in the 1970s,[41] they used public meetings about Poland and Hungary to assert that they were a distinguished group in Soviet society.

Citizens' public statements implied that what made them Soviet was the professional expertise that helped strengthen the Soviet homeland and their local communities. A doctor of orthopaedics from Kyiv publicly condemned the "deplorable degenerates" (*zhalki vyrodki*) and "pitiful animals" (*zhaluhidni tvaryny*) in Hungary "as a surgeon and a participant in the Great Patriotic War."[42] Citizens presented themselves as important local leaders by speaking on behalf of entire communities. Although the participants who actually spoke at agitation meetings were a minority, they commonly used such rhetorical devices as "together with the entire Soviet people" to preface public calls to "punish fascists" in Hungary.[43] While these speeches did not necessarily reflect people's "real" attitudes, they gave rise to a public culture in which Soviet society was defined as indivisible, united against enemies framed in both geographical and ideological terms. Conservative patriotism thus fused the rhetoric of imperial pride with a sense of elitism at home.

The paternalistic claims of conservative patriotism as expressed in public forums posed a major challenge to the Soviet state in 1956. Following the opening of the Gulag, many Soviet citizens were concerned that Khrushchev "left the country at the mercy of its enemies."[44] Rising concerns about the spread of anti-Soviet attitudes in Ukraine and the bloody events in Hungary, coupled with the confusion and incompetence of local officials, offered a stimulus and a fresh opportunity for some citizens to criticise the Kremlin's reforms and to advance a more positive image of Stalin. Members of the aspirational middle class gave little credence to Khrushchev's promises to breathe a new life into the communist experiment at home and abroad, calling instead for the restoration of Stalinist great power politics.

Stalin nostalgia was common among army officers who criticised Khrushchev's foreign policy.[45] The KGB informed the CPU Central Committee that officers complained about shortages in the military budget and Khrushchev's leniency, though the circumstances in which they voiced such opinions were often unclear. On 3 November, a party member and lieutenant from the Kyiv aviation school stated that the Hungarian crisis "would never have happened under Stalin," whose authority was strong enough to hold Eastern Europe together. "Our talk of peace," he lamented, had led to the "weakening of alertness." Soviet leaders spent copious amounts of money on receiving foreign delegations, which gave them a false sense of security. The lieutenant continued that this money would be better spent on defence.[46] His opinions were echoed by an engineer and army captain who claimed that "we have been talking too much about the cult of personality, becoming too democratic and losing any semblance of discipline."[47] In no uncertain terms, these individuals asserted their right to comment on policy and criticised Khrushchev's reforms that expanded the limits of permissible expression. The implication was that Khrushchev should abandon the utopian project of trying to fix socialism, and focus instead on strengthening the USSR's army and borders.

Party leaders found it difficult to suppress or ignore these forms of anti-reformist criticism, expressed as they were by prominent members of Soviet society. Army officers who had seen service in Hungary were particularly alarmed about Khrushchev's reconciliation with Yugoslavian statesman Josip Broz Tito. Two officers who visited officials at the Khmelnytskyi obkom on 16 November claimed that Yugoslavia actively supported the Hungarian rebels, which outraged Soviet army personnel. Nikolai Khramtsov, an officer in charge of propaganda work among soldiers, and especially his colleague Leonid Zholudev, a decorated lieutenant of the Soviet airforce, clearly enjoyed some clout among senior Communist Party apparatchiks. They were greeted by not only the first secretary of the Khmelnytskyi region, Vasilii Begma, but also the deputy head of the Ukrainian Council of Ministers, G.P. Onishchenko.

The party bosses tried to explain that the USSR should strive to maintain good relations with a fellow socialist country, Tito's Yugoslavia (according to Wanda Michalewska, the Polish consul in Kyiv, Begma in particular was keen on establishing strong transnational ties with socialist Eastern Europe). As they put it, however, the officers' "facial expression" showed that they did not agree with them.[48]

Paradoxically, in condemning Khrushchev's liberalisation and referring to their yearning for Stalin's iron fist, members of the aspirational middle class asserted their right to hold the authorities accountable to themselves. Most surprisingly, perhaps, they criticised Soviet mass media and claimed the right to know the facts, portraying themselves as responsible citizens concerned about the failure of Khrushchev's leadership to outline a clear point of view about the foreign crises. In this vein, an inhabitant of Uzhgorod expressed support for the military invervention in Hungary but also charged that Soviet newspapers provided very little information, thus encouraging the growth of all sorts of incredible rumours and creating the impression that the Soviet authorities did not trust or care about their own citizens.[49] This man evoked notions of Soviet citizenship and looked to the state for an internally consistent narrative about the crisis. Indeed, demands for more information from the Soviet media were quite widespread in late 1956 because self-identified leaders of local communities claimed they needed reliable news to guide popular opinion. As the head of a primary party organisation from Lviv put it in early November, "the workers would really like someone to come and explain what is going on in Hungary, because newspapers give very little information about it."[50]

Commenting on major events that unfolded across their western border, some inhabitants of Ukraine (war veterans prominent among them) claimed they were the most important patriots who maintained stability at home and looked after Soviet interests abroad. They thus performed what I call middle class identities in public, which allowed them to voice limited criticism of Soviet foreign and media policy, but also to stifle meaningful public debate about reform.

Economic Complaints

At the same time, party-sponsored notions of what it meant to be Soviet and socialist were challenged by citizens who voiced economic complaints in 1956. Ignoring or implicitly rejecting the party's internationalist rhetoric, citizens argued that the authorities should take care of their own citizens before sending aid to other (socialist) nations across the border. In voicing economic demands, citizens drew on Khrushchev's promises that "socialism" would bring improvements to ordinary workers,[51] but more prominently evoked notions of Sovietness defined in geographical and ethnic terms: they suggested that Soviet leaders should improve supplies because citizens of the USSR deserved to live at least as well as foreigners across the border. It was their interactions with and observations of Eastern Europe, and not simply party pronouncements, which shaped citizens' expectations and behaviours in 1956.

Food and fuel shortages created problems for Soviet authorities in Ukraine during late 1956 and early 1957, raising doubts about the USSR's ability to deal with the escalating crisis. After the news of unrest in Poland and Hungary reached Ukraine, some citizens began to panic. They took money out of their savings accounts and bought basic necessities in preparation for war, which normally included "soap, salt, and matches."[52] Panic buying was particularly prevalent in the western regions, and it was impossible to buy sugar and flour in some parts of the Lviv oblast.[53] At the height of the East European crises, the key task of regional party organisations was to prevent panic by improving supplies of the products citizens purchased in mass quantities.[54] Some party officials found this to be a difficult task, with the Bila Tserkva town party organisation still experiencing significant problems on 19 November 1956.[55] Nevertheless, authorities in Ukraine felt confident that they brought supply and demand largely under control by the second week of November. Most reports emphasized that local party bosses had reacted to panic buying promptly and efficiently: trading organisations made sure that the products in question were restocked, and party activists conducted agitation work among the population to encourage them to collectively denounce any signs of panic-mongering.[56]

While Soviet citizens did buy up basic food and fuel products, regional-level communist leaders such as Petro Shelest in Kyiv were equally concerned about the way in which they described economic problems. Most daringly, perhaps, some inhabitants of Ukraine underlined that Soviet citizens should follow the example of Hungarian workers and strike to protect their rights. In a private conversation with two other factory workers, Nikolai Egorovich Kudriashov, a thirty-one-year-old non-party man from Kyiv, alleged that strikes were already breaking out in Zaporizhzhia and the Donbas.[57] Apart from strikes, individual inhabitants of Ukraine threatened the authorities with violence. Kozlov writes that "in the criminal and half-criminal milieu, it was common to hear the promise to construct a 'second Hungary.'"[58] Such statements were often underpinned by economic discontent. For instance, a non-party member from Bila Tserkva boasted in front of others, "had I been in Hungary during the uprising, I would have also killed a few communists, because they bring hunger to the people."[59] In a similar vein, in the village of Boiarka in the Kyiv oblast, some locals voiced ad hoc threats to do "what the Hungarians did" unless supplies of fuel improved.[60]

At the height of the Hungarian crisis, party officials in Ukraine classified many radical economic complaints and attacks on the local bureaucrats as acts of "hooliganism." However, while ascribing "hooligan" behaviour to the influence of the Polish and Hungarian events, official reports cited some examples that bore no explicit relation to the foreign developments; rather, they indicated that local party authorities were very alert to signs of disturbance in late 1956, particularly among groups they already considered unstable.[61] Hence, it seems that the label of hooliganism was employed to describe individuals who disobeyed the law, and thus departed from the official vision of a harmonious Soviet community underpinned by notions of socialist legality. Convictions for hooliganism exploded in 1956 as the authorities sought to eliminate all forms of "deviancy," including both serious crime and petty offences.[62] In this way, through criminalising the more aggressive forms of economic complaints as instances of hooliganism, the authorities not only implied that they would not give in to threats of violence, but also promoted the image of a Soviet community united against crime and deviancy.

While it is difficult to assess the extent to which citizens believed in this vision of Sovietness, it seems that they learnt to articulate economic demands by evoking the ideas of harmony and patriotism, rejecting both radical demands for economic reform discussed below, and violent "hooligan" rhetoric. Discussions about the East European crises provided a forum where Soviet citizens voiced some very concrete demands. During agitation meetings at higher education institutions in Lviv, for example, students and lecturers alike talked about increasing scholarships and raising living standards in the city.[63] Meanwhile, blue-collar workers and other residents of Ukraine talked about the need to improve supplies of building materials and children's shoes.[64] Economic complaints represented attempts by ordinary citizens to exact benefits from the state as part of the Soviet "social contract." This brings to mind those individuals whom Christine Varga-Harris describes in her study of housing petitions during the Thaw, when citizens were much more assertive in demanding that Soviet officials help them with their "individualistic aims," often claiming "a right to decent housing simply by reason of having been born 'Soviet.'"[65]

How citizens understood what Soviet standards of living should be was formulated in comparison to and in contrast with the outside world. For example, during a special meeting for party activists in Lviv, participants asked a senior lecturer to compare the standard of living in Czechoslovakia and the USSR, and even dared to enquire when the economic situation of the workers "of our country would be raised to the standard of the leading capitalist states."[66] They thus pushed the limits of the party's promises and yet presented themselves as loyal citizens. It was not uncommon to hear complaints to the effect that the USSR helped the satellite states while Soviet citizens themselves lived in poverty.[67] For instance, while explaining the Hungarian crisis to his colleagues at a factory in Lviv, party member Liubyms'kyi claimed that the crisis erupted because East Europeans faced very similar economic problems to Soviet citizens. Ignoring his colleagues' statements that life in the USSR improved from year to year, this east Ukraine-born communist complained that the USSR should send fewer products abroad and improve material conditions for its own people instead.[68] In comparing and contrasting the USSR to other countries in the Soviet camp, he evoked notions of conservative patriotism to press for the satisfaction of Soviet citizens' material demands.

Yet unlike in the early 1980s when the rise and fall of the Solidarity movement in Poland pushed Soviet leaders to reflect more deeply on the roots of discontent among the population of Ukraine,[69] apparatchiks showed relatively little interest in citizens' economic complaints in 1956. Despite the fact that the Central Committee Presidium criticised local party leaders for ignoring the population's material needs, the authorities discouraged industrial workers and collective farmers from voicing complaints. Already before the Hungarian uprising, central authorities had grown suspicious of the kind of criticism that Vladimir Dudintsev had levelled against managers in his controversial novel *Not By Bread Alone*, which "pitted upright champions of social benefit against corrupt self-seeking bureaucrats." After late November, the press abandoned the initial "qualified praise" of the novel in favour of "reserved censure" and even "outright rejection."[70] In line with this, party officials were reluctant to engage in meaningful discussion about working and living conditions in the USSR. Although Moscow failed to reform the system of work relations to raise labour efficiency in the post-Stalinist period,[71] it appears that party officials were successful in maintaining the outward manifestations of labour discipline and productivity in the aftermath of the Polish and Hungarian unrest. During public gatherings called to discuss foreign affairs, most of the recorded workers' and collective farmers' comments were about Soviet economic progress, and making official pledges to over-fulfil their production targets. This is not to suggest that they actually worked efficiently, but rather that despite the many economic grievances voiced in late 1956, most of them did not publicly question the nature of the Soviet economic system.[72] This was particularly significant in western Ukraine, where the authorities remained concerned that Gulag returnees would turn the local population against collective farms and other Soviet institutions, but were also confident that most collective farmers would work as long as they were protected against the minority of what they called "saboteurs."[73]

Conservative Patriotism in Western Ukraine

As conservative patriotism was underpinned by fears of instability, it took on a special significance in parts of Ukraine annexed by the USSR during the Second World War. Regional party activists and some members of the local intelligentsia emphasised that they made a special contribution to spreading socialism across borders. Official slogans about socialist internationalism therefore reverberated in west Ukraine more often than in other parts of the republic. At the same time, it was here that the geographical aspect of Soviet patriotism acquired the greatest significance. Because the Polish and Hungarian crises unfolded so close, local residents stressed that they relied on the Soviet border to protect them from war and instability.

Divisions between 'local' Ukrainians and recent arrivals from further east ran strong in the borderlands.[74] But locals and easterners often spoke in one voice in 1956, underlining their loyalty to the Soviet homeland in the aftermath of the East European crises. Outward manifestations of support for Soviet policies among indigeneous inhabitants of western Ukraine attracted the wrath of anti-Soviet nationalists in the early post-war years.[75] Soviet patriotism nevertheless became widespread by 1956 due to brutal repression of dissent, as well as the rapid incorporation of locals in Soviet power structures, culture, and industry.[76]

By 1956, western Ukraine had produced its own aspirational Soviet middle class. While many prominent members of local society had migrated to the region from eastern Ukraine and other parts of the USSR, others grew up in the borderlands.[77] Many local leaders had recently participated in constructing Soviet socialism in the region, and so had a stake and perhaps even an emotional attachment to maintaining the status quo. They therefore actively criticised East European deviations from the Soviet model. For example, composer Mykola Kolessa spoke in public about the need to establish cross-border contacts with the Polish "progressive intelligentsia," and raised alarm about "deviations from socialism" in the Polish press.[78] Kolessa echoed party narratives about internationalist friendship and thus manifested his loyalty to the Soviet Union, which was no doubt necessary if he ever wanted to cross the border. Similarly, a west Ukrainian-born pensioner and former deputy of the Ukrainian Supreme Council named Buia was clearly disturbed by Warsaw's new agricultural policy when he described a recent trip to Poland to a group of local workers in late 1956:

> All of us old Lvivians have known Gomułka for a long time and we think he will sort things out in Poland … I saw my sister, who lives in a Polish village … I told her that … we [also] had slackers and bandits destroying collective farms, but we dealt with them decisively and our collective farms are now strong.

With their superior experience, he suggested, Soviet people should travel to Poland to guide their Polish brothers along the road to socialism.[79] This former Polish citizen turned his west Ukrainian origin into a positive marker of Sovietness. He implied that indigenous inhabitants of Galicia, the "old Lvivians," were uniquely suited to assess Gomułka's credentials as the new communist leader in Warsaw. For both men, internationalism was a key aspect of the Soviet identity. As people like them were sent on foreign trips and tasked with spreading the USSR's influences abroad, they embraced the notion that to be Soviet in the borderlands meant to build new transnational ties.

Other inhabitants of the region, equally keen to maintain their status as local community leaders, were less emphatic in articulating internationalist ideas. Before the second Soviet invasion of Budapest, a west Ukrainian-born party member and manager at a local factory named Zaverbnyi was very cautious when a group of workers asked him to explain the causes of the Hungarian unrest over lunch:

> I don't know what is going on in Hungary. They say that the American imperialists want to restore capitalism, but workers don't want that to

> happen. And they don't want to work … The government they had before committed many excesses; in particular, many people were put in prison. Apparently, these people are now coming out and causing unrest.[80]

This statement was likely a desperate attempt to avoid voicing "incorrect" opinions at a time when official narratives were still in flux: Zaverbnyi seemed uncertain as to whether the crises in Eastern Europe could or should be described with reference to socialism and anti-imperialism.

Articulations of Soviet patriotism in western Ukraine were underpinned by fear of violence. A lecturer from Uzhgorod State University echoed many other public statements as he argued that just as the Budapest revolt was supported by reactionary classes in Hungary, some residents of Transcarpathia could also provoke unrest at home. There is a reason why the Uzhgorod furniture factory is dubbed the "bourgeois" factory, he claimed, pointing out that many people who worked there had enjoyed a privileged status under the Hungarians but were now "forced to work."[81] These fears were articulated in the party's language of class, and yet pushed residents of the borderlands to criticize Moscow for failing to maintain stability, both at home and in the outer empire. In this vein, talking to a group of workers over lunch, a resident of Lviv who had migrated from the eastern oblasts, a former NKVD officer by the name of Savelev, claimed that "nationalists" and "speculators" in western Ukraine could follow the Hungarian example. The KGB was doing "a bad job of combatting hostile elements," he added.[82] His was a version of conservative patriotism specific to the borderlands (and likely most widespread among recent migrants from the east): he suggested that the East European crises awoke demons that were almost unique to the region.

In fact, conservative patriotism underpinned by a lack of confidence in Khrushchev's ability to maintain peace spread beyond west Ukraine's elite as more people spoke about an imminent war in public places.[83] An unidentified man thus approached a crowd outside a shop and told them that stocking up would help nobody when they drop an atomic bomb on Lviv.[84] Such open fatalism was rare, but even more restrained citizens took to criticising Khrushchev's foreign policy. Talking to his colleagues at work, for example, a senior worker from Lviv supported Soviet policies in Hungary, but also suggested that the Soviet army should have prevented the crisis in the first place.[85] Another man openly and publicly stated that the Hungarian uprising was "our fault," because the USSR had not been alert when the "fascists" in Budapest prepared their revolt.[86]

It is then not surprising that the authorities took popular fear of war very seriously, seeing it as a potentially destabilising influence in parts of western Ukraine annexed to the USSR during the Second World War, and other regions of the republic that lay close to the USSR's border. The first secretary of the local Communist Party in the region of Khmelnytskyi, the same Vasilii Begma who struggled to convince army officers about the rightfulness of Khrushchev's Yugoslav policy, was equally concerned about fears and discontent on a more popular level. He personally witnessed panic among women at a collective farm who misinterpreted radio broadcasts about the bombing of the Suez Canal and thought that western powers had attacked the "Soviet canal." Begma talked to them about the Suez crisis, and they laughed at their mistake, but he reprimanded them for their lightheartedness. That the regional first secretary travelled to villages to speak to collective farmers testifies to how seriously he took agitation work during this period.[87]

Notably, concerns about the future of the Soviet homeland were not only expressed in public meetings, but also permeated informal discussions in western Ukraine. As rumours spread and doubts about the Soviet future multiplied, west Ukrainian responses to the Polish and Hungarian crises were varied and contradictory. Inhabitants of the region took a strong interest in foreign affairs because they unfolded just across the border. "Unhealthy rumours" appeared in the town of Khmelnytskyi, noted Begma, as some locals claimed that the town hospital was full of the wounded from Hungary, "which was not in fact true."[88] When a non-party Ukrainian laboratory worker from Lviv told her colleagues that she and her husband condemned Soviet interference in the internal affairs of Hungary, she was opposed by another employee who argued that events in the Soviet satellite states concerned them directly due to their geographical proximity: the "American imperialist border" could move right down to our doorstep, she argued. Nevertheless, other employees including a non-party Russian woman supported the controversial opinion, and the laboratory worker boldly resisted her colleague's criticism by accusing her of being afraid to voice her true beliefs.[89] A strong sense of instability thus encouraged residents of Ukraine to argue about the current crises and to criticise Soviet policies in Eastern Europe. This was felt especially keenly in regions that lay close to the border. Articulations of Soviet patriotism exposed conflicts in west Ukrainian society, which did not neatly correspond to any ideological, ethnic, or regional fault lines.

Conservative patriotism was highly paradoxical. In calling for greater top-down control in the USSR and the Soviet empire as a whole, its adherents emerged as active citizens who criticised the leaders in Moscow. Even though the conservative vision of Soviet society put a strong emphasis on hierarchy and thereby appealed to privileged members of Soviet society such as war veterans, army officers, and members of local party cells entrusted with some managerial responsibilities, it was also embraced by other residents of Ukraine. This was because conservative patriotism was underpinned by a belief that the state had the power and the responsibility to assure stability at a time when many citizens feared the outbreak of war.

Reformist Patriotism

Frustration with the Soviet state found more politicised forms of expression in 1956 and 1957. Small numbers of people, including students and members of the creative intelligentsia, voiced support for Gomułka's policies and hoped that they would be emulated in the USSR itself. This was especially evident in Lviv, where even some blue-collar workers blamed the foreign crises on the fact that mistakes of the Stalinist era were being removed too slowly, which allowed "hostile forces" to turn people against Soviet-style regimes.[90] More broadly, proponents of reformist patriotism wanted to limit the power of the state and encourage citizens to comment on Moscow's domestic and foreign policy. They rallied behind a vision of participatory citizenship that held all citizens should enjoy free access to information.

Proponents of reformist patriotism underlined that they were committed to fixing socialism, but also went beyond what the party authorities defined as de-Stalinization. Their views occurred along a relatively wide spectrum, ranging from mild reformist comments that the state was prepared to tolerate, to more challenging calls for better access to information that formed the backbone of future dissent. These views were underpinned by national (Soviet Ukrainian) and supranational (Soviet) identities.

The East European crises inspired residents of Ukraine to reflect upon the importance of national identities in Soviet-style regimes. Those who expressed support for the Polish reforms explained Gomułka's rise to power as an expression of Polish nationalism. During an informal conversation, for example, a senior lecturer from the Institute of Trade and Economics in Lviv emphasised that the recent events across the border were natural and entirely predictable:

> The Poles had always been distinguished by a strong drive for autonomy and independence. They grew accustomed to a different way of life during the thirty years of their country's independence. Even many blue-collar workers were then better off than now.[91]

Other commentators expected the USSR would now crack down on national dissent in Eastern Europe. The chief accountant of the oblast branch of the Gosbank in Zhytomyr publicly claimed that Poland would be incorporated in the USSR.[92]

The example of "national roads to socialism" in Eastern Europe inspired some members of the creative intelligentsia to call for expanding Ukrainian cultural autonomy in the USSR. Citing the example of independent satellite states, they suggested that Ukraine could also enjoy more autonomy without betraying socialist ideals, arguing in particular that the authorities should improve Ukraine's cultural contacts with the satellite states.[93] To use Kenneth Farmer's expression, they posed a "reformist challenge" to Soviet leaders.[94] These ideas fit into the wider framework of reformist patriotism, for their proponents sought change in the Soviet Union and indeed within the confines of what they understood Soviet socialism to be, calling for the restoration of the principles of "Leninist nationalities policy." While this became more prominent in the 1960s,[95] the East European crises of 1956 provided an important boost to the Ukrainian national cause, for members of the creative intelligentsia justified the reformist agenda by the need to strengthen Soviet power in Eastern Europe. According to the first secretary of the CPU Central Committee and Khrushchev's right hand man Aleksei Illarionovych Kyrychenko, members of the Ukrainian Writers' Union complained about the suppression of Ukrainian culture in the USSR when they discussed the situation in Hungary with their colleagues. The writers apparently described encounters with visitors from Eastern Europe who failed to understand why there were so few Ukrainian language schools and cultural institutions in the republic. These members of the Ukrainian cultural elite suggested that Russification of Ukraine's public life discredited the Soviet nationalities policy in the eyes of the Hungarian comrades, which was particularly pressing at a time when the USSR should guide Hungary away from "counterrevolution."[96] Advocates of reform "searched for socialism," to borrow Kotkin's expression, with reference to not only the party's pronouncements, but also the views and opinions expressed by foreigners. Kyrychenko did not explicitly state when or where these conversations took place, but the writers' remarks were loud enough for the top party apparatchiks to hear.

Demands for increasing Ukrainian cultural autonomy in the USSR were voiced openly, and arguably, found some resonance among party leaders in the republic. The recently Ukrainianised local cadres in the western oblasts recognised that Ukrainian ethnic identities could be mobilised to strengthen pro-Soviet loyalties in the region. In order to demonstrate that local society was unified during such an unstable time, regional party leaders organised a special meeting in the Zankovets'ka theatre in Lviv. Not only did that gathering celebrate the 39th anniversary of the October revolution, but it also commemorated the 700th anniversary of the founding of Lviv. Furthermore, veterans of the "revolutionary struggle" from west Ukraine spoke during the meeting.[97] These forms of commemoration pointed towards a Ukrainian (and Galician) contribution to building socialism, distinct from the history of the Bolshevik Party and the rest of the USSR. The authorities in Kyiv also made nods in the direction of a Ukrainian nation, and proved responsive to demands voiced by members of the creative intelligentsia in the aftermath of the Hungarian crisis. On 12 November, Kyrychenko (the first ethnic Ukrainian to serve as Ukraine's party boss) insisted that regional administrators should work in the language of the local majority. In practice, this would amount to switching some offices from Russian into Ukrainian, particularly in the west.[98] The state would balance between the Russian and Ukrainian population of the republic, recognising their rights as separate entities: they would open Russian and Ukrainian schools "according to demand."[99] Party leaders in Ukraine echoed demands of the creative intelligentsia, articulating a vision of reformist patriotism that put a strong emphasis on increasing Ukrainian cultural autonomy in the USSR.

Still, in contrast to the Prague Spring of 1968,[100] the scope of debates surrounding the Ukrainian national question in the USSR was limited in 1956. Meanwhile, reformist patriotism posed a considerably more serious challenge to the CPSU when its proponents mobilised Soviet identities defined in terms of citizenship rather than ethnicity or language. In this way, some citizens who spoke in public tackled issues surrounding access to information. Demands for more openness in the mass media and during informational gatherings echoed some "conservative" concerns about inconsistencies in the official coverage of Eastern Europe, but they were underpinned by an anti-paternalist belief that a large number of people should engage in debates about the future of the socialist camp. Throughout 1956, as Cynthia Hooper demonstrates, Soviet citizens revealed a "keen awareness" of the extent to which they were denied access to information.[101] Participants in informational gatherings devoted to the Polish and Hungarian events demanded "more detailed information" in the Soviet press and enquired why the USSR blocked western radio broadcasts.[102]

University students were the most articulate advocates of openness.[103] Admittedly, many students did not question official portrayals of the Hungarian uprising, particularly outside large metropolitan centres. As the dissident Leonid Pliushch recalled in his memoirs, "clandestine and semi-clandestine organisations were founded in Moscow, Leningrad, and Kyiv. But we at Odesa University judged the events in Hungary on the basis of what we read in the newspapers."[104] Still, at least in Kyiv, party officials found it difficult to control public discussions among university students. Local apparatchiks who conducted a gathering at Kyiv State University infuriated M. Synytsia, the head of the Kyiv city party organisation, for having failed to give a decisive reproach to a student's provocative question. During the meeting, a student named Rudenko demanded to know why the Soviet state and press had not considered it necessary to inform the population about the content of Khrushchev's talks with Gomułka, which (according to the Soviet mass media) took place "in the spirit of friendliness and party openness." The student also attacked *Pravda*'s special correspondent who had claimed that all Soviet people were outraged by "anti-Soviet statements in the Polish press." Rudenko pointed out that the Soviet people could not possibly condemn any articles published in Poland, because they were not familiar with them.[105] The incident represented wider concerns about the limits of openness and information control. Taking advantage of the local officials' confusion and incompetence, Rudenko used the public meeting at his university to criticise central newspapers in the name of "Soviet people." Rejecting the idea that *Pravda*'s pronouncements could be read as an expression of popular opinion, he effectively asserted that citizens did not need party guidance to formulate their own views.

Reformist demands for information encouraged numerous students to bypass official channels, thus inspiring open criticism of Soviet policy and laying the grounds for future dissent. Disillusioned with the domestic mass media and public agitation meetings, students in Lviv turned to western broadcasters to obtain news about Eastern Europe.[106] Likewise, students in Kyiv "resorted to" listening to western radio stations, which inspired them to analyse Gomułka's reforms in more detail than the local apparatchiks desired. During an agitation meeting at Kyiv's Shevchenko University, for example, fourth-year history student Kornienko openly admitted that he listened to the BBC, claiming that this was now officially allowed: apparently, the Soviet minister of culture had recently signed a special agreement to that effect during his visit to the United Kingdom. A local agitator conducting the gathering asked Kornienko what he heard on the foreign radio, and the student reported that Khrushchev had called Gomułka a "traitor" and refused to shake his hand during an impromptu visit to Warsaw. Kornienko also asked whether the BBC could be considered to convey "fifty per cent of the truth."[107] It is notable that the student quoted western radio broadcasts during an official meeting and suggested that listening to the BBC was not a subversive act. As an active citizen, he thus sought to extend public debate through reporting what he had heard on foreign radio stations, compensating for the poor performance of Soviet journalists and agitators. Such demands for openness, voiced by self-identified Soviet citizens, lay at the heart of reformist patriotism in 1956.

In fact, the same logic can be applied to the more radical and isolated young people who used illegal means to raise public awareness about Gomułka's policies and to advance the cause of reform in the USSR. In Kyiv, for example, a small group held meetings to discuss Gomułka's speech, which they planned to translate and distribute in the USSR. They claimed that the USSR must follow the example of Poland in building socialism and democracy afresh.[108] In this way, they sought to redefine what it meant to be Soviet, encouraging citizens to participate in debates about reform and seeking unofficial sources of information to learn about Eastern Europe. Ultimately, however, they still wanted to improve the functioning of Soviet media and other Soviet institutions.

On the Fringes of Reformist Patriotism

As critical observers of the unfolding events, a small number residents expressed very controversial views, which should not however be classified as "anti-Soviet." They were likely aware that the KGB would deem their views to be "hostile," and grew to conceive of themselves as outsiders. At the same time, however, these citizens claimed they wanted to improve the Soviet system. In this sense, they operated on the fringes of reformist patriotism. These advocates of reform evoked a peculiar mixture of civic Soviet, ethnic, and class identities to justify their political agenda.

Some of the fringe demands were specific to 1956, such as people protesting against Soviet interference in the domestic affairs of Hungary.[109] Admittedly, criticism of Soviet policy in the socialist camp was often confined to private conversations, but with its implications of treason, it was inherently political and treated as a criminal act. For example, a student from Kharkiv and a teacher from the Donetsk oblast were both tried in court for condemning the invasion in private conversations. Meanwhile, dissatisfaction with Moscow's policy in Hungary found more public forms of expression during the autumn of 1956. In Odesa, the KGB discovered leaflets calling for the withdrawal of the Soviet army from Hungary.[110] More prominently, protests broke out at higher educational institutions in the USSR both before and after 4 November. Special anti-riot troops disbanded protests in Yaroslavl' and other cities, as students "organised rallies and carried banners demanding the withdrawal of Soviet troops from Hungary."[111] Citizens who expressed alarm at the invasion of Hungary did not agree with the accusations of disloyalty levelled against them; rather, they portrayed the invasion as a violation of Soviet values, evoking a Soviet identity to condemn the state's foreign policy and question the party's rhetoric. During explanatory gatherings, individual members of the public asked why the Soviet state led its army into Hungary despite promoting the principle of non-interference during the Suez crisis.[112]

Sovietness was not always identified with socialism. Like the anonymous authors of leaflets found near the shipbuilding institute in Mykolaiv, critics of the invasion identified themselves as "Soviet" even though they sometimes criticised "communism":

> Soviet citizens! Turn your attention to the Soviet government's aggressive policy in Hungary. Think about … the blood of the brotherly Hungarian people who are trying to free themselves from communist oppression. Protest against the violent and bloody actions of our armies in Hungary.[113]

Appealing to all "citizens," the authors understood Sovietness primarily in terms of territorial and legal belonging, rather than in ideological or ethnic terms. Their stark opposition to Soviet interference in Hungarian domestic affairs revealed a strong belief in the importance of state borders.

Similarly, at the end of November, the chief constructor of the Kyiv Krasnyi Ekskavator plant received an anonymous letter complaining about his statements on the radio and during a public meeting devoted to international events. The author professed faith in the principle of national self-determination:

> Listening to you on the radio … I was inspired to write this letter. Most people who speak during official meetings and gatherings simply read something that had been written for them from a piece of paper, but that was clearly not the case with you. Undoubtedly, you presented your own views. And that is what I found interesting; or was this a lie, were you not saying what you really thought … You were right as far as the Anglo-Franco-Israeli aggression against Egypt is concerned, but, at the end of the day, what has that got to do with us? We should concern ourselves … with what is going on in Hungary. As we know, the Hungarian people have risen up in a just war of liberation against Soviet oppression. For the last twelve years … they have suffered poverty and humiliation … The USSR has sent its armies … to deal a bloody blow to the Hungarian people: the elderly, women, and children. Why is nobody organising protest meetings against Soviet military interference in the internal affairs of Hungary, how can we justify this gross and inhuman violation of international democratic rights …?[114]

This statement was in many ways anti-Soviet, attacking Moscow's foreign policy in no uncertain terms. The author made no reference to the party's internationalist rhetoric used to justify the military intervention in Hungary, and instead suggested that Soviet policies should be judged by the same criteria as other great powers. By expressing these opinions in an anonymous letter, he or she clearly conceptualised them as an act of dissent. However, the author also took seriously the notion of Soviet citizenship. Even whilst attacking the USSR's repressive foreign policy, he or she wrote on behalf of the Soviet community. Most interestingly, perhaps, the author was encouraged to write the letter in the apparent belief that the addressee would take his or her arguments seriously and change the tone of public debate, thereby breathing a new life into Soviet public culture.

It is striking that complaints about the invasion of Hungary resounded across Ukraine in places such as Donetsk, Kharkiv, Mykolaiv, and Odesa.

Perhaps more surprisingly, some residents of the borderlands who had moved to the region from the eastern oblasts also attacked Moscow's foreign policy. A few days before the second invasion of Hungary, for instance, P.D. Malyi, a junior researcher at the Institute of Social Sciences in Lviv, was very bold in criticising the authorities during informal conversations with other employees, all the while clearly identifying with an imagined Soviet community:

> We should not have taken up arms in Hungary. We are following in the footsteps of the Tsarist government, which had also spilt the blood of peoples [*prolyvav krov narodiv*]. I heard that Imre Nagy called our representative in Budapest to ask why the Soviet armies were marching into Hungary instead of leaving ... Our government was right to criticise Stalin's cult of personality, but they have not yet sorted out such problems as the need for democratisation. Other countries have overtaken us as far as democratisation is concerned.[115]

It thus appears that, in the aftermath of Khrushchev's Secret Speech, it was a sense of belonging in the Soviet community – rather than just a sense of alienation from it – that fuelled notions of citizenship in the borderlands.

A potentially more sustained challenge came from representatives of the Jewish minority. After the anti-Semitic campaigns of late Stalinism, Soviet Jews enjoyed a somewhat more relaxed atmosphere under Khrushchev. A few books in Yiddish were published in the late 1950s, though not by contemporary authors; the yeshiva in Moscow's Great Synagogue was established, but it had few students, none of whom became rabbis; and in August 1961 the Yiddish periodical *Sovietish heimland* (*Soviet Homeland*) was started.[116]

Nonetheless, the dramatic events in Eastern Europe brought out the problem of anti-Semitism in Ukraine. Many party officials highlighted the opinions of Jewish citizens in their reports on public mood, and in doing so almost exclusively wrote about "misconceived" or "hostile" views, thereby implying that Jews did not fit in well with the bulk of the Soviet community. In part, this was because the Suez crisis inspired the rise of new forms of anti-Jewish rhetoric in the Soviet Union. The state of Israel was demonised in official propaganda, as the USSR chose to support Arab nationalism to weaken British and American positions in the Middle East.[117] The Jews continued to encounter official prejudice, as well as experience day-to-day tensions, especially since certain party circles in Ukraine encouraged anti-Semitism to "regain influence among the Ukrainian population."[118] Thus, reports about Jewish reactions to East European crises may have reflected the officials' own anti-Semitic prejudice, but it also appears that the events of 1956 increased Soviet Jews' sense of distinctiveness.

The dramatic turn of events on the international arena in late 1956 made many Jews in Soviet Ukraine particularly sensitive to manifestations of anti-Semitism at home. During a primary party cell meeting at an Odesa shoe factory, a man of Jewish origin complained that Soviet authorities persecuted the Jews in the aftermath of the Suez crisis.[119] The pervading sense of instability in the socialist camp likewise encouraged the spread of rumours about the rise of anti-Jewish violence. In what was likely an informal remark voiced outside official meetings, a Jewish engineer and party member from Kyiv alleged (mistakenly) that the "Hungarian fascists" had killed up to ten thousand Jews during the recent uprising.[120] During private conversations registered by the KGB, some Jewish citizens tried to defend Israel and "the Jews" from accusations voiced against them in official Soviet rhetoric, as well as anti-Semitic outbursts they personally encountered. Interestingly, they often expressed support for the Hungarian uprising in this context. For example, Franzin Mark Isaakovich, a fifty-nine-year-old Jewish man from Kyiv who "received Zionist literature from the Israeli embassy," stated that while the Soviet army shot at a peaceful population in Hungary, the Israelis defended their own lives from a fascist dictator in the war against Egypt.[121] Some citizens used illegal forums to draw links between Soviet repressive policies in Eastern Europe and discrimination at home. In February 1957, residents of a building in central Odesa discovered eighteen leaflets, which apart from expressing support for the Hungarian revolutionaries and calling for improved living conditions at home, also protested against "national" and "racial" oppression in the USSR. Hand-written on pages torn out of exercise books,[122] the pamphlets probably used these terms to refer to anti-Semitism.

Complaining about anti-Semitism, some Jews developed a paradoxical attitude towards the idea of Sovietness. Whilst they argued that socialist regimes must combat prejudice and economic problems, in this sense claiming their rights as Soviet citizens and drawing on the party's promises, they also stated that they should be allowed to emigrate from the USSR and even seemed to explicitly reject a Soviet identity. An office worker employed in the barbershop at Khreshchatyk 4 (in the very centre of Kyiv) denounced a Jewish hairdresser who had recently spent a holiday in Warsaw. Upon returning, he claimed, the hairdresser stated:

> There is no such anti-Semitism there as here. A Jewish newspaper is published daily and there is a Jewish theatre, which I often attended. Going back to Kyiv, I was literally coming to a foreign land. During my stay in Warsaw I had a chance to talk on the telephone to my sister in Tel-Aviv. She encouraged me to stay in Poland and to then emigrate freely to Israel ... Even our basic needs are not met here ... The hell with socialism ... We have had enough of the struggle for some sort of future communism.[123]

The hairdresser implicitly identified with the Soviet community that suffered economic hardship and seemed to despair that Kyiv was now "foreign" to him. However, while the man who denounced him may have distorted the hairdresser's opinions, the report demonstrates that his colleagues treated the hairdresser as an outsider because of his ethnic background, and suggests that anti-Semitic prejudice encouraged him to underline his alienation from the Soviet community and Soviet-style socialism. Clearly, the Jewish minority did not fit officially sponsored visions of a Ukraine united by its common ethnic roots. Whether such conflicts contributed towards the authorities' decision to allow former Polish citizens of Jewish origin to leave the USSR in 1957 is not clear, but approximately 300,000 Jews did emigrate at this time, most of whom used Poland as a transit point on the way to Israel or the West.[124]

Finally, some citizens articulated far-reaching demands for political and economic reform at home, amounting to demands for systemic change, but still grounded their grievances in Marxist-Leninist ideology. One extreme example of social disobedience rooted in the economic situation was an illegal workers' organisation formed in Donetsk; according to historian Anatolyi Rusnachenko, its leader was partly inspired by the example of the Poznań riots, which he saw as an attempt to defend workers' rights in Soviet-style regimes.[125] Calls for purifying the revolutionary cause and defending the proletariat against the party's interpretation of socialism were also apparent in the 1,300 leaflets that the KGB found across the Lviv oblast between 8 and 19 February 1957. Signed in the name of the Popular Trade Union of Russian Solidarists (*Narodno-Trudovoi Soiuz Rossiiskikh Solidaristov*), the brochures described the Polish and Hungarian events and called for workers' councils to rule factories.[126]

Apart from these organized forms of protest, some citizens indicated that they did not believe Soviet-style regimes were committed to improving the economic well-being of their citizens. Talking to his colleagues about the events in Poland, for example, a non-party Jewish engineer from Lviv expressed support for changes taking place in the aftermath of the Twentieth Party Congress, but also seemed to harbour little hope for long-term improvements: "The promises the government makes now are just a tactic, and they will return to their old ways once things settle down."[127] Similarly, a fifty-six-year-old teacher from Kyiv expressed support for the Hungarian uprising, stating the "Magyars" were right to reject the Soviet system, for it had "nothing to do with socialism." "The students in Budapest ... will force us to reflect upon the direction of our policy," he continued.[128]

Meanwhile, other residents who questioned the very foundations of the Soviet order focused on the issue of collective farming, voicing ad hoc comments during informal conversations with friends and colleagues. A local farmer from the Lviv oblast stated that collective farms in the USSR should be dissolved like they had been in Poland,[129] and an oblast inspector from Zhytomyr "tried to prove the impracticability of the collective farm system in the USSR."[130] A shop manager from Kyiv even suggested that reforming the countryside would help "Soviet people" establish friendly relations with foreigners in Eastern Europe.[131] Perplexed by Gomułka's drastic departures from the Soviet model, and emboldened perhaps by Moscow's acceptance of the Polish reforms, these individuals implied that radical economic restructuring was compatible with preserving a Soviet socialist system. Still, they explicitly rejected Khrushchev's notions of reform and the very idea that the Soviet Communist Party had the right understanding of socialism. In criticising the system, they echoed some anti-Soviet, nationalist outbursts, but also referred to examples of "socialist" reform in Eastern Europe to justify their complaints. The boundary between Soviet patriotism and what the authorities classified as "anti-Soviet nationalism" was therefore fluid.

Exorcising Nationalism

The Hungarian uprising, and to a lesser extent the Polish reforms, encouraged some inhabitants of Ukraine to question the very legitimacy of the Soviet system by calling for Ukrainian independence. The authorities were particularly concerned about the rise of what they called "bourgeois nationalism" among former members of nationalist organisations, "bandits" (a term which was often used as shorthand for the UPA), members of the illegal churches such as Greek Catholics, as well as the Hungarian and Polish minorities.[132] There is no doubt these fears and categories reflected party leaders' prejudices, but it does appear that nationalism framed some explicitly anti-Soviet views during this eventful period, especially among former Gulag prisoners. At the same time, however, such radical voices were very isolated, even in the borderlands.

Gulag returnees kept party apparatchiks awake at night. By 10 October 1956, the Ukrainian Ministry of Internal Affairs (MVD) registered over 45,000 "former nationalists and affiliates who [had] returned to the western provinces."[133] They included former members of Ukrainian nationalist organisations that had waged a war against Soviet power in the region a mere few years earlier.[134] Party officials in Ukraine's western borderlands were concerned that the return of the "banished other" would undermine the still fragile Soviet order in the region, raising the spectre of anti-Soviet nationalism. True, reports about "nationalists" questioning the legitimacy of the Soviet state were not exclusively confined to the western oblasts, likely because some Gulag returnees were resettled in other parts of Ukraine.[135] However, it was in the borderlands that most "aggressive anti-Russian statements" were recorded.[136] As rumours about an impending war spread in the region,[137] some Gulag returnees talked about an independent Ukraine. In Volhynia, a woman from the village of Boholiuby who had recently returned from imprisonment discussed the Hungarian developments with a group of collective farmers: "The same could happen here in the near future. We will live to see a time when we have our own, Ukrainian leaders, and we are the masters in our own home."[138]

For Soviet leaders, the Greek Catholic Church was another potential source of trouble in the west. Former Greek Catholic priests resisted attempts to eliminate the Ukrainian language from church services and provided a focus for the development of anti-Soviet Ukrainian nationalism.[139] In response, senior state and party apparatchiks shaped representations of the borderlands in such a way as to depict the faithful of the illegal Greek Catholic church as traitors and collaborators. Already in the 1940s, immediately after the incorporation of the western oblasts into Soviet Ukraine, Soviet publications depicted the Greek Catholic Church as a Polish and subsequently Austrian-German tool designed "to break up the unity and friendship of the

Russian and Ukrainian peoples."[140] As contacts with the outside world became more common after the death of Stalin, attacks on Greek Catholics in western Ukraine were especially aggressive because the authorities were determined to deny claims made in Ukrainian émigré publications.[141] Concerned that the "Catholics" who published in the Western press distorted the history of western Ukraine, the CPU Central Committee instructed *Pravoslavnyi visnyk* (*The Orthodox Herald*) to write that Ukrainian people, oppressed by the Greek Catholic clergy, had always striven to return to the Russian Orthodox faith of their ancestors.[142]

Still, it appears that the East European crises had little discernible influence over the reach and claims of anti-Soviet Ukrainian nationalism. While embedded in reports of popular reactions to the Eastern Europe events, many nationalist outbursts bore little explicit relation to Poland and Hungary. Surveillance reports attributed anti-Soviet statements to the usual suspects, pointing to the urgent need to resolve an old problem rather than constructing new enemies.[143] No doubt, this partly reflected the officials' predisposition to monitor the views of Gulag returnees more than other citizens, but also indicated their alienation from the rest of Ukrainian society. In fact, authorities in Lviv underlined that it was only a minority of Gulag returnees who caused problems.[144] Though it is conceivable that more locals articulated "anti-Soviet" sentiments in private, it appears that few residents of the borderlands went so far as to express support for the nationalist cause in any public forums. In a private conversation recorded by the KGB, a Volhynian-born member of the Komsomol, who had served in the Soviet army since 1953, stated:

> Everyone here wants an independent Ukraine, but people are afraid to state this openly and there is nobody to lead the people so that, instead of voicing individual views here and there, the majority of the population would write to the authorities, declaring that Ukraine is leaving the USSR. Ukraine has to be a sovereign state and not depend on anyone. Poland also wants to be a sovereign state.[145]

Resigned to accepting Soviet power, the speaker seems to have combined pro-independence sympathies with all the outward manifestations of conformity, joining the Komsomol and serving in the Soviet army. His statement suggests that nationalist views took the form of ad hoc comments and did not amount to any sustained resistance.

Furthermore, many party officials believed that members of the Polish and Hungarian minorities developed "hostile" opinions about the events in Eastern Europe. This reflected deep-seated suspicion of non-Russians and non-Ukrainians that was prevalent among state and party leaders in Soviet Ukraine. A "small number" of Polish residents of Lviv, as the officials would have it, expressed their joy at the recent developments in Poland and Hungary, using this opportunity to attack the Soviet system itself. Talking to other workers at the machine factory in Lviv, a Soviet citizen of Polish origin boasted that Soviet flags had been destroyed in Kraków, a sure sign that Poland would soon follow in the path of Yugoslavia.[146] Soviet officials were also concerned about the Hungarians in Transcarpathia,[147] especially because their proximity to the border exposed them to non-Soviet sources of information about the crisis. Party apparatchiks and the KGB were consequently very sensitive to any sign suggesting that "hostile" attitudes were on the rise among this group, and they did indeed register a few unsettling incidents. Some Soviet Hungarians, former Gulag prisoners in particular, spread illegal pamphlets and criticised the Soviet invasion of Hungary.[148]

In some ways, it was their ethnic identity as such that made Poles and Hungarians suspicious in the eyes of the authorities. The top brass was so concerned about the Poles in western Ukraine that when CPSU Central Committee member Pozdniakov visited Lviv to monitor the behaviour of "unstable elements," his report concentrated almost exclusively on the Polish minority.[149] Local Poles and Hungarians did not have to say anything to attract suspicion – staying quiet could also raise questions. For example, the man in charge of Lviv's party organisation F. Koval' complained that many Polish and Magyar lecturers who worked at the city's universities took no part in their local community's social life, remaining "passive" after hearing the news from Poland, Hungary, and Egypt. He named and shamed particular individuals including Kota, a party member and Hungarian lecturer from the Lviv Institute of Physical Culture. Koval' also relayed information obtained from primary party cell bosses at Lviv's universities and factories who portrayed members of non-titular minorities (along with indigenous inhabitants of western Ukraine) as particularly unstable. A certain Dogmarov, also from the Institute of Physical Culture, reported that a "local" (*mistsevyi urodzhenets*) colluded with a Czech student to translate a "counterrevolutionary" pamphlet.[150]

Meanwhile, some ethnic Poles in Ukraine added fuel to the flame by associating very strongly with their ethnic community, thereby furthering ethnic stereotypes. For one, they were particularly eager to listen to radio broadcasts from Poland.[151] They also talked about developments in Eastern Europe with other Soviet citizens of Polish nationality.[152] As one report argued, the Poles did not socialise with other inhabitants of the oblast.[153] This makes it difficult to establish how outspoken and "rebellious" the Soviet Poles and Hungarians really were, or to assess the extent to which they harboured isolationist ideas. Official reports suggest that party apparatchiks treated them as aliens within the Soviet community, and expected them to dispel accusations of disloyalty by explicitly denouncing East European distortions from the Soviet model.

More importantly, however, ethnic prejudices that underpinned many official reports reflected a broader social ostracism of Poles and Hungarians in Ukraine. The top brass was accordingly confident that the minorities exerted minimal influence over other inhabitants of the region. To the extent that the Poles featured prominently in nationalists' view as Ukrainian enemies,[154] the question of their national rights was bound to inspire heated debates among locals in western Ukraine. Rumours to the effect that Lviv would soon be given over to the Polish People's Republic did not help bridge the gap between the local Poles and Ukrainians.[155] It also appears that apart from condemning the Soviet intervention in Budapest, some Hungarians in Transcarpathia intimidated other Soviet citizens. For example, a Hungarian driver from Mukachevo told some non-Hungarians that a time would come when they would "crawl at his feet."[156] According to official reports, Hungarian nationalism was also closely associated with anti-Semitic prejudice. On 28 October 1956, an unidentified culprit distributed 152 anti-Soviet leaflets in the Russian and Hungarian languages in the town of Berehove; similar pamphlets, bulk-produced with the help of rubber stamps, appeared in Uzhgorod two days later. They praised the Hungarian revolution while attacking the Jews and communists.[157] In this sense, the "anti-Soviet" outbursts among the Hungarian minority were directed as much against the local Ukrainians, Jews, and Russians as they were against the Soviet state.

Ethnicity was a key marker of loyalty in Soviet Ukraine at the height of the 1956 crises. This was especially prominent in parts of Ukraine with large non-titular minorities, such as the western borderlands and Odesa. While Ukrainian identities were mobilised to oppose Khrushchev's reforms, to support further "liberalisation," and to undermine the legitimacy of the Soviet state as such, party leaders were ever suspicious of non-titular groups such as Hungarians, Jews, or Poles. Partly because they had no place in a Soviet Ukrainian community defined in such ethnically exclusive terms, it seems that members of non-titular minorities were more likely to voice anti-Soviet views than other citizens of the USSR.

Conclusion

The rise of popular interest in Eastern Europe and the growth of Soviet patriotisms transformed Soviet society, though not in the way that Khrushchev intended. Although Polish and Hungarian events provoked a predominantly conservative reaction, they also encouraged citizens to criticise the authorities, furthering the idea that Soviet patriots had the right and the duty to publicly comment on policy. The outbreak of violence in Hungary and Gomułka's reforms in Poland compelled citizens to discuss different ways the USSR and other Soviet-style regimes could develop. Confusion and incompetence of low-level officials created contexts where such discussions took place, allowing citizens to escape the confines of party rhetoric in defining what it meant to be Soviet.

Some reform-minded citizens criticised the shortage of information about Poland and Hungary, insisting on their right to obtain reliable news from the Soviet media and to participate in debates surrounding changes in the socialist camp. The Thaw also encouraged some members of ethnic minorities and the Ukrainian cultural intelligentsia to claim that their support for increasing national autonomies in no way undermined their loyalty to the Soviet state. These forms of reformist patriotism survived well into the 1960s. Sergei Zhuk demonstrates that many students in the eastern Ukrainian city of Dnipropetrovsk retained a patriotic commitment to improving the Soviet system, believing that their "activities in support of national cultures would lead to a restoration of the 'real, internationalist, and human, Leninist model of socialism.'" At the same time, however, reformist patriotism formed the backbone of future dissent. The "fringes" of Soviet patriotism expanded in late 1956, as citizens publicised their views through such illegal means as pamphlets, articulating demands for far-reaching political and economic reforms. Gradually, and especially after 1968, the KGB and Communist Party ideologists forced all proponents of openness underground, effectively limiting the appeal of reformist ideas.[158]

In fact, the appeal of reformist patriotism was already limited in 1956. As Vladislav Zubok argues, press reports about the lynching of communists in Budapest "cooled sympathies" towards the Hungarian rebels, even among the otherwise volatile university students, many considering the Soviet tanks in Hungary "our tanks."[159] Conservative patriotism represented support for Moscow's repressive policies in Hungary and the belief in a strong state. It was an anti-reformist platform that deprived Khrushchev of popular support for his de-Stalinization agenda founded in internationalist ideals. Whether advocates of conservative patriotism believed what they said is ultimately irrelevant. What matters is that they voiced public doubts about Khrushchev's ability to breathe a new life into Soviet-style socialism, and therefore called for the restoration of stricter controls at home and more traditional power relations with Eastern Europe. Citzens who rallied behind conservative patriotism in 1956 reinforced and in part created a political culture that contributed to Khrushchev's ouster in 1964.

Paradoxically, by criticising Khrushchev's policy, advocates of conservative patriotism undermined the very authoritarian state that they sought to preserve. Conservative patriotism underpinned economic complaints as citizens claimed that Soviets should live at least as well as their neighbours in Eastern Europe. It further facilitated the emergence of the Soviet aspirational middle class, whose members claimed the right to define what Soviet policies should be (with little reference to party ideology as defined by the top leadership in Moscow). Ultimately, Soviet conservative patriotism was an important limit on Khrushchev's de-Stalinization. It was a counter-reformist, xenophobic, and anti-pluralist ideology.

Soviet patriotism had a very dark side, as it implicitly excluded significant members of Ukraine's population from the Soviet community. As the numerous reports about conversations between friends and colleagues suggests, many loyal citizens denounced their acquaintances to the authorities. The officials thus constructed certain groups as inherently unreliable and "non-Soviet." Gulag returnees, former OUN members, and ethnic minorities whose members did not have their own ethnically designated republics in the USSR were always suspect. In that sense, party leaders defined "hostile" individuals with reference to who they were rather than what they did.

At the same time, the spread of Soviet patriotism helped integrate western Ukraine into the broader Soviet political community. It was in the west that Soviet patriotism acquired a particularly important role in fostering new types of citizenship. Because the spectre of war and instability seemed so real in the western borderlands, many inhabitants of the region found it important to publicly describe themselves as reliable Soviet patriots, and as such, to criticise Khrushchev for letting the situation get out of hand. Equally, however, calls for reforming the Soviet system resounded in the region, though they were by no means confined to the borderlands. In other words, notions of Soviet patriotism underpinned new types of citizenship in the western regions, and the borderlands witnessed the most heated debates about the USSR's role as the centre of the socialist camp.

2 Friendship in the Soviet Empire: Salvaging International Socialism in Eastern Europe after 1956

When representatives of the Polish youth movement visited Moscow in June 1957, they realised that establishing friendly relations with the USSR would be no easy task after the upheavals of 1956:

> The meeting with the Soviet comrades ... was rather cold and unpleasant. The first thing they said was that they did not know who they were dealing with ... Our comrades found that extremely embarrassing ... Judging from their questions, [Komsomol leaders] can only see anti-socialist tendencies [in the Polish youth movement] ... They wanted to know why the Twentieth Congress of the CPSU, which renewed people's faith in the power of socialism, provoked such a major breakdown in Poland ... They did not want to understand ... On 12 June, *Komsomol'skaia pravda* published a note about [our visit], which underlined that "discussions took place in the spirit of cordial friendship and full mutual understanding."[1]

This account indicated that the crisis of 1956 shook faith in internationalism on both sides of the Soviet-Polish border. Komsomol officials in Moscow knew that socialism diverged from the Soviet model in Poland, and therefore treated their Polish comrades as suspect revisionists. For their part, members of the Polish delegation described the USSR as a foreign and inhospitable land. Yet although it may have seemed that Soviet socialism had not spread across borders, activists from the USSR and Poland did not give up on the idea of building transnational ties. Komsomol officials took it for granted that the Thaw should breathe a new life into Soviet-style socialism and maintained an image of cordial Soviet-Polish relations in public. Although clearly made to feel uncomfortable and different, the Poles did not question the concept of transnational friendship either – in fact, they were frustrated that the Soviet Komsomol did not recognise them as legitimate partners.

The twelve years that separated the Hungarian uprising from the Prague Spring witnessed the last attempts to invigorate internationalism in the USSR and Eastern Europe. Soviet and East European leaders promoted the notion that Soviet-style socialism could and should spread across state borders. Just like the *Komsomol'skaia pravda* article cited above, newspapers and other publications created the framework of transnational friendship. Especially after 1958, Soviet officials suggested that national divisions and borders should become increasingly insignificant under state socialism. Ideas about internationalism and the role of the USSR in Eastern Europe were also forged during more problematic personal encounters in the socialist camp. Meetings between party and Komsomol activists, journalists, academics, tourists, and educated professionals from the USSR and Eastern Europe were supposed to heal the wounds of 1956. Nevertheless, participants often found that national tensions and organizational problems frustrated their efforts.

Soviet publications, correspondence between top Soviet and East European apparatchiks, as well as reports about the collaboration between Soviet and East European journalists allow me to trace how the concept of transnational friendship evolved in the late 1950s and late 1960s. I also examine plans for cultural and tourist exchanges compiled by state and party leaders in Moscow, Kyiv, Warsaw, and the Ukrainian provinces, which further demonstrate how Soviet and East European officials wanted to shape transnational interactions. Without revealing popular responses to the official narratives of friendship, these sources expose fractions and contradictions within them. Reports from foreign trips suggest that ideas about the USSR as an empire were also forged through the experiences of Soviet travellers. Compiled by tour group leaders who were also activists entrusted with mobilising and controlling the behaviour of other citizens, the reports offer a skewed picture of Soviet travellers' experiences. After all, "all trip leaders must have known that any possibilities for future trips, as well perhaps as possibilities for advancement at home, depended on their own behaviour and that of their charges while abroad."[2] Nevertheless, especially in conjunction with Polish reports which highlight the many practical problems inherent in organising and controlling international travel, they do reveal that citizens of the USSR witnessed many differences between the USSR and its East European satellites. This compelled travellers to comment on "non-Soviet" or even "anti-Soviet" attitudes and behaviours in public, thus redefining official ideas about state and national borders in the socialist camp. To be sure, the ways in which Soviet citizens commented on international friendship did not necessarily reflect people's genuine beliefs, but only how they defined their relationship to the Soviet state and its foreign policy in public.

Soviet notions of transnational friendship in the socialist camp had far-reaching implications for domestic identity politics. The act of crossing the border, both mentally and physically, encouraged citizens to reflect upon the relationship between Soviet patriotism, social class, and national identities. On one level, transnational interactions compelled citizens of the USSR to articulate ideas of Soviet patriotism between the late 1950s and late 1960s. In various public forums, residents of Ukraine described the satellite states as junior partners in the process of international cooperation, and claimed that they personally contributed to strengthening Soviet influences in Eastern Europe. The model citizen thus emerged as both a Soviet patriot and a conscious internationalist. While Soviet and East European party apparatchiks hoped that crossing borders would help foster new transnational identities in the socialist bloc, official policies and narratives of travel – and the actual experiences of Soviet travellers – ultimately helped construct the very idea of Sovietness by highlighting the importance of borders and national divisions in Eastern Europe and in the USSR itself.

Because Soviet citizens were expected to take part in public and cultural diplomacy in Eastern Europe, transnational interactions also contributed to the making of new social identities in the USSR. Strict vetting procedures served to determine the personal and social characteristics needed for an individual to represent the USSR abroad.[3] This turned travel into a privilege awarded to those who excelled, yet also conformed. Although trips to Eastern Europe were considerably less elitist than travel to the capitalist West,[4] transnational interactions in the socialist camp still served as both a marker and creator of social differentiation in Soviet Ukraine. Official narratives of travel highlighted the special contribution made to strengthening the USSR's ties with its satellites by Soviet professionals (especially engineers), party members deemed most active and important for their local communities, war veterans, artists, and "leading workers" (which normally referred to blue-collar workers with some managerial responsibilities, such as brigade leaders). International travellers were the Soviet aspirational middle class: one step removed from the top party leadership, yet also important community leaders distinct from "ordinary" citizens.

Narratives of transnational friendship acquired a particular importance in Ukraine. In comparison with the Soviet heartlands, travel to Eastern Europe was more easily accessible in Ukraine and its western borderlands. This made mishaps and conflicts between Soviet citizens and their East European counterparts all but unavoidable. Published accounts and face-to-face contact between Soviet Ukrainians and their western neighbours were also shaped by memories of bloody interethnic relations in the past. Both contemporary tensions that surfaced during travel and memories of historical conflicts highlighted differences between Ukrainians and East Europeans. In this way, discussions about transnational friendship fed into complex debates about the role of borders and ethnic identities in the USSR itself. Scholars, party activists, and international travellers claimed to represent both "Soviet" and "Ukrainian" culture during interactions with the near abroad. Ukrainian identities thus helped citizens write themselves and their republic into the imagined Soviet community, and to distance themselves from neighbouring Eastern Europe.

This chapter begins by analysing how Soviet and East European party officials shaped narratives of friendship after 1956. It then explores a range of reactions to these narratives in Ukraine, particularly among citizens with a professional interest in history. Finally, the chapter examines cross-border travel as a forum where narratives of internationalist friendship were tested and transformed between 1956 and 1968.

Reconciliation

Senior Communist Party apparatchiks in Moscow and East European capital cities created the ideological framework of transnational friendship. After 1958 in particular, the apparatchiks suggested that Soviet citizens should demonstrate an interest in the life of the near abroad. In this way, the post-Stalinist Thaw presented new opportunities for transnational friendship and cooperation in the socialist camp.

Mutual relations in the socialist camp were fraught with tension in the late 1950s. In June 1957, Polish diplomats in Moscow suggested that the Soviet press had still not come to terms with the new order that had arisen in Poland since October 1956, failing to publish a single article that offered a balanced and sophisticated view of Gomułka's government. With some newspapers staying clear of controversial topics altogether and Polish affairs remaining marginal in *Sovetskaia Ukraina*, other publications including *Pravda*, *Kommunist*, and *Komsomol'skaia pravda* focused exclusively on what they deemed to be negative phenomena in Polish society: the reversal of collectivisation, youth policy, and "anti-Soviet" articles in the Polish press.[5] Unlike in previous years, Soviet radio and television did not even broadcast the Polish ambassador's speech on the Polish national holiday of 22 July 1957 – to add insult to injury, they did transmit a speech by a Belgian embassy official the day before.[6] Problems persisted in 1958, as Polish diplomats in Moscow found state and party institutions reluctant to engage in cultural cooperation. Their reports mentioned the "bad atmosphere of mutual distrust" between Soviet and Polish unions of creative artists, and emphasised that cultural cooperation remained difficult, as Soviet officials considered such films as Andrzej Wajda's *Kanał* or Andrzej Munk's *Eroica* to be ideologically questionable.[7] Both films touched on the very controversial issue of the Warsaw Uprising staged by the non-communist Polish resistance in 1944, reminding viewers about the lack of Soviet assistance and postwar suppression of Polish anti-Nazi partisans. Soviet-Polish relations were particularly problematic because Gomułka's policies continued to raise troubling questions about the scope and nature of desired reform. According to Polish diplomats in Moscow, the Soviet press avoided writing about Polish farming, the church, and culture, all of which served as powerful examples of how Polish socialism diverged from the Soviet model.[8]

From the Soviet leaders' point of view, this state of affairs was far from ideal. For senior party apparatchiks such as Ekaterina Furtseva (head of the Moscow city party organization, soon to become a member of the CPSU Central Committee Presidium), tensions in Eastern Europe were a painful reminder that Soviet citizens and their western neighbours had yet to grasp the principles of class struggle and internationalism. In early 1957, she addressed an audience of primary party cell secretaries from Moscow's universities to claim that Soviet students failed to appropriately understand and react to the Hungarian uprising because universities had made little effort to recruit among the working class. Furtseva's solution to the breakdown of international relations in the socialist camp was not to shut the USSR off from Eastern Europe, but to reinstate class as an operational category in Soviet university admissions after it had disappeared from Soviet political culture in the second half of the 1930s.[9] She proposed that Soviet relations with Eastern Europe were a key indicator of how successful the Communist Party was in building socialism at home and abroad.[10]

1 A meeting with Soviet composer Aleksandra Pakhmutova at the Polish-Soviet Institute in Warsaw, 1964. Intensified cultural exchanges between the USSR and Poland were part of an attempt to breathe a new life into internationalism after the death of Stalin. National Digital Archives, Warsaw. Nac.gov.pl

Nikita Khrushchev likewise emphasised that Soviet leaders had a lot at stake in building friendly relations with Eastern Europe. "For now the international victory of Soviet power is in the region of 20 to 30 per cent," he estimated in a 1959 letter to Politburo members, "but should internal Polish forces ensure the victory of Soviet power in Poland, the international victory of the communist revolution would be around 40 to 50 per cent, maybe even 51 per cent."[11] How Khrushchev quantified the success of international revolution is far from clear, but he suggested that tensions with the near abroad discredited the idea that Soviet-style socialism could spread across borders. This explains perhaps why Khrushchev was personally involved in rebuilding transnational ties in the socialist bloc after 1956. During a meeting with Polish journalists held in the months after the Soviet invasion of Hungary, he claimed that his critical attitude towards Soviet policies had earned him the label of a "Polish" deviationist among some Communist Party officials in the USSR. At the same time, he also defended the USSR's policies at home and abroad. In particular, he acknowledged Polish resistance to collectivization, but emphasised that collective farming had a bright future in the USSR and in Poland (as he put it: "Why did our cows support us? Because we supported our cows"). He also keenly defended Soviet leaders' proletarian credentials. Khrushchev stated that Polish journalists were outraged that Soviet soldiers shot at blue-collar workers in Budapest in 1956, but this only betrayed their inexperience in class struggle. During the civil war in the USSR, as some factories in Siberia supported Kolchak, Lenin did not hesitate to shoot at blue-collar workers there. "There is the working class and then there are separate individuals. We serve the interests of the working class," Khrushchev claimed.[12] Khrushchev did not avoid controversial issues in his interactions with Polish journalists. His remarkable directness betrayed Soviet leaders' continuing commitment to overcoming mutual distrust and inspiring new faith in Soviet-style socialism in the late 1950s.

Pressure to establish friendly relations in the socialist camp also came from Eastern Europe, whose leaders sought to promote their cultural achievements and political reforms in the USSR. For example, despite continuing problems, the Polish embassy regularly produced informational bulletins for Soviet journalists,[13] as well as organised meetings between representatives of the Polish and Soviet writers' unions.[14] Diplomatic pressures to increase press coverage of East European affairs were sometimes effective, as Soviet apparatchiks condemned mistakes or omissions in the Soviet press as potentially offensive. In February 1958, the Soviet Minister of Culture Nikolai Mikhailov bemoaned the fact that *Pravda* and *Izvestiia*, while writing extensively about international sports, contained very little information about foreign artists visiting the USSR or Soviet artists performing abroad. This surprised "our friends" in socialist countries, he argued, especially because their newspapers reported on such events on a regular basis.[15]

Reflecting these developments, starting in 1958, top Soviet officials made a concerted effort to encourage journalists and editors to write more about socialist friendship in Eastern Europe. In a special resolution from 6 June 1958, the CPSU Central Committee instructed the Soviet press organs to systematically describe events and developments in the near abroad. Journalists were instructed to emphasise that cross-border cooperation between communist leaders increased standards of living in the Soviet bloc, but also to stress that these achievements of East Europeans were constantly threatened by the USA and its capitalist NATO allies.[16] The Communist Party Presidium outlined an important role for the press in deepening and improving transnational cooperation in the socialist camp. The news agency TASS was to refrain from publishing lengthy lists of foreign delegation participants who visited the USSR, and to promote more "analytical" materials instead.[17]

This pressure worked, for Soviet journalists and editors were keen to write more about Eastern Europe. Emphasising that foreign media should learn from the Soviet experience, they lobbied the Central Committee to increase the number of journalists' delegations travelling between the USSR and Eastern Europe.[18] As early as 1956, the chief editor of the satirical journal *Krokodil*, Sergei Shvetsov, boasted that his publication was popular throughout Eastern Europe, helping to deepen international cooperation and spread Soviet practices across the region. *Krokodil* and humorous periodicals from socialist countries, such as the Polish *Szpilki* and the Hungarian *Ludas matyi*, reprinted each other's cartoons and, he stressed, foreign editors carefully listened to Soviet advice. At the same time, although personal contacts with foreign journalists would allow *Krokodil*'s artists to find out more about life abroad and prepare appropriate materials, Shvetsov complained that his employees could hardly afford to visit East European countries and were even deprived of the opportunity to make international telephone calls. This undermined their position in the socialist camp: able to telephone the USSR on a regular basis, their foreign colleagues joked about Soviet formality when Moscow contacted them by post.[19] Naturally, Shvetsov sought to present the situation in such a way as to obtain more funding for his journal. Although his plight met with a rather cold reaction at the propaganda and agitation department of the CPSU Central Committee,[20] other editors had more success in lobbying party apparatchiks to increase the number of foreign correspondents in Eastern Europe.[21] Their justification reveals how they envisaged the role of the Soviet press. Editors and journalists depicted their work as an example of internationalist cooperation in the socialist camp, claiming both to familiarise readers at home with the life of the people's democracies, and to teach foreigners about the building of socialism.[22]

The number of Soviet articles about the European satellite states rose, with *Pravda* and *Izvestiia* publishing 1,500 items about Poland, Czechoslovakia, Bulgaria, Hungary, and Romania in 1961 alone. The strong presence of Eastern Europe in Soviet publications carried an important message to readers: Soviet citizens were expected to cultivate a level of erudition about the near abroad. The press department of the Communist Party Central Committee in Moscow went so far as to specify that the paper *Novoe vremia* should present a "more or less free view" of Soviet society, and not the "official position" on international affairs,[23] thus underlining the need for citizens to develop articulate views about the Soviet bloc. The CPSU Central Committee used the media to encourage industrial and agricultural specialists to learn from the experiences of East Europeans. In April 1966 the Soviet Ministry of Foreign Affairs resolved to facilitate direct contacts between newspapers targeting similar audiences in the USSR and Hungary. Because Hungary had recently "gained interesting experiences in the field of building socialism," Soviet journalists were instructed to analyse these developments in an "accessible and interesting way," albeit focusing on the "national particularities" (*natsional'nye osobennosti*) of Hungarian development and common Soviet-Hungarian industrial projects.[24] Motivated by the need to shape popular opinion in Eastern Europe and counteract accusations of Soviet economic exploitation, officials at the Communist Party Central Committee in Moscow instructed newspapers to discuss the performance of individual factories. Foreign journalists would visit Soviet enterprises that exported their products to Poland and Czechoslovakia, while Soviet journalists would write about Czechoslovak and Polish factories who geared production towards the USSR.[25]

In this way, managers and engineers were to study the process of international cooperation, and especially to learn about their colleagues and factories across the border. Some even needed to prove that they actively participated in common projects with East Europeans by speaking to foreign journalists. Publicly demonstrating a commitment to internationalism was therefore an important part of belonging to the Soviet aspirational middle class under Khrushchev. Soviet Ukraine would play a special role in this process of mutual education. As early as 1957, Khrushchev included senior Ukrainian apparatchiks such as Petro Shelest in a delegation to Hungary. As Shelest later recalled in his memoirs, the trip was tense and at times unpleasant, but it offered a key opportunity for Soviet Ukrainian leaders to learn about new agricultural technologies that had not yet reached the USSR.[26]

In line with the emphasis on learning from each other, Soviet publications helped to forge an idealised image of Eastern Europe as a mirror of the USSR. After 1956, Soviet guidebooks to Eastern Europe highlighted common achievements of the socialist countries. Visiting Warsaw in the late 1950s, the Soviet geographer A.K. Timashev thus emphasised the socialist nature of the city:

> Two wide thoroughfares – the rebuilt Aleje Jerozolimskie and ulica Świętokrzyska, which has replaced a tiny, narrow street – reflect the characteristics of the new, postwar city. The imposing building of the Party … is a masterly combination of glass and stone. Another, even more wonderful building, constructed in the middle of a huge square at the crossing of two thoroughfares, is the Palace of Culture and Science, which represents the great achievements of Soviet and Polish architecture.[27]

Timashev suggested that Soviet citizens should admire the socialist realist architecture of Warsaw. As Rachel Applebaum argues in her analysis of travel between the USSR and Czechoslovakia, travel was designed to emphasise the familiar.[28]

At the same time, official narratives suggested that friendship between the USSR and its satellite states was not a relationship of equals. While promoting the notion that the Soviet system spread across state and national borders, Soviet opinion leaders emphasised key differences between the USSR and the near abroad, turning public attention towards the continuing importance of states and nations under state socialism. In the case of Czechoslovakia, "vestiges of Soviet domination … remained."[29] This was even more prominent in Soviet relations with Poland and Hungary after 1956. In official narratives, these satellite states had much more to learn from the USSR than the other way round. Soviet travel writing about these countries was underpinned by a sense of pride or even superiority, as memories of troubling episodes in post-war history lingered. For example, an Inturist travel agency guide claimed that "with the support of the Soviet Union and other socialist countries, the Hungarian people … have quickly dealt with the consequences of the counterrevolutionary coup [of 1956] and continue to build a socialist society."[30] Similarly, publishing in 1959, one author reported on what he had supposedly heard when travelling in Hungary in the aftermath of the 1956 uprising:

> The country was gripped by fear. Who is going to save us, who is going to give brotherly help to the Hungarian people who have already suffered so much? And help arrived! At the request of the new Hungarian revolutionary government, the Soviet Army came to the rescue of the

> Hungarian people. It is in times of trouble that you get to know who your true friends are![31]

Unsurprisingly, official publications stressed that ideal East Europeans had always supported the USSR's hegemony in the region, but also implied that the near abroad needed Soviet guidance and military presence to build socialism.

Soviet publications suggested that personal contacts between Polish and Soviet citizens were especially tricky. Like Ekaterina Furtseva, who reportedly complained about a "role reversal" whereby "Polish students who came to study how to build socialism in the USSR had turned into teachers instead,"[32] Soviet opinion leaders tried to reassert the USSR's position as the centre of international socialism in light of Gomułka's substantial departures from the Soviet model. At times, travel accounts avoided mentioning controversial issues explicitly, but still instructed Soviet citizens how to understand Polish deviations. For instance, while Soviet authors did not normally deal with the problem of private agriculture, they stressed the central role of the socialist state in improving the Polish countryside.[33] Meanwhile, official publications were much more explicit in condemning Polish cultural policies. Expressions of outrage at discovering abstract art in hotels and other public spaces in Poland was a prominent theme in travel literature. The authors also concentrated on the public role of the Catholic Church and broader socio-cultural problems.[34]

Prominent Soviet intellectuals, including some outspoken critics of Soviet authorities, helped exoticise Eastern Europe in the 1960s. Lev Isaevich Slavin, the Odesa-born Soviet writer who signed a petition in defence of the dissidents Sinavskii and Daniel at the height of a state-sponsored campaign against them in 1966,[35] published a particularly humorous travel account from Poland. His 1965 publication noted that the Polish youth did not always resemble their Soviet contemporaries. Slavin was particularly puzzled to see "dandies" dressed with "carefully studied carelessness" – black turtlenecks, battered trousers, and demonstratively dirty shoes. The youth appeared bored, perhaps even cynical to him: "Dear God, I did not see such fops in the winter of 1945," he asserted, testifying to the importance of the Second World War and the USSR's defeat of Nazi Germany as central themes in Soviet portrayals of Poland. Slavin was more outraged by the popularity of abstract art in Poland, and "very surprised" to read positive reviews of Jean-Paul Sartre's drama in the Catholic press. He thus described the view from the Wawel castle in Kraków:

> I particularly liked a severe-looking building nearby, with Gothic, ogive windows. I asked the man next to me to explain what it was:
>
> – Oh, this is an old one! A seventeenth-century Bernadine monastery.
> – And what's there now?
> – A Bernadine monastery.[36]

The continuing centrality of the Catholic Church that the Poles took for granted was jarring, perhaps even amusing to the Soviet observer, Slavin suggested. He exoticised the outer empire, suggesting that Soviet-Polish friendship built on common socialist values had its limits. His account thus exemplified the limits of Soviet faith in internationalism during the Thaw.

International Friendship and Ethnicity

Narratives of East European friendship fed into Ukrainian debates about the role of ethnic identities in the USSR. The post-Stalinist Thaw created new opportunities for Soviet citizens to study and promote non-Russian languages, histories, and cultures. Ukraine and Ukrainians were consequently much more visible in Soviet public life in the 1960s than at any point since the mid-1930s. The prominence of Ukrainian ethnic identities in Thaw-era public life had an ambiguous impact on Soviet notions of internationalism. On the one hand, cultural leaders emphasised that Ukrainians and East Europeans overcame age-old hatreds under state socialism, and thereby evoked ethnic identities to suggest that the Soviet ideology united people across state and national boundaries. On the other hand, Soviet leaders' commitment to protecting Ukrainian national interests undermined narratives of socialist friendship. Particularly among Ukrainian academics, teachers, and members of the creative intelligentsia, powerful memories of Ukrainian-Polish conflicts overshadowed the Party's emphasis on internationalist friendship.

History was a particularly important arena in which Soviet Ukrainian and East European intellectuals worked out the meanings and limits of internationalism. While the general intellectual climate for historians remained oppressive under Khrushchev, as the purging of the editorial board of *Voprosy istorii* in 1957 demonstrated,[37] the Thaw witnessed the rise of a prominent group of historians who resisted excessive party interference in the Academy of Sciences.[38] Soviet historians hardly abandoned all the canons outlined in the Stalinist *History of the All-Union Communist Party (Bolsheviks) – Short Course*,[39] but Khrushchev's Secret Speech did attack the text. It was eventually replaced in 1959 by a considerably less dogmatic and crude book, *The History of the Communist Party of the Soviet Union*.[40] These factors encouraged some scholars to promote new ways of representing the past. It was in this spirit that they began to highlight the role of "masses as the creators of history," departing from the view that there was any inevitability in the "'lawfulness' of the historical process."[41] Focusing on the peculiarities of particular events and developments, they suggested, scholars should highlight the role of non-state actors in driving social change, and depart from sweeping Stalinist narratives that presented entire "nations" as homogenous historical actors striving towards progress.[42] The Thaw also presented new possibilities to write Ukrainian history outside strict Stalinist constraints – historian Vitalii Yaremchuk writes of a "Ukrainian historiographical micro-renaissance" between the late 1950s and the early 1970s.[43]

International histories of Eastern Europe, which celebrated class solidarity across national divides, helped promote such a de-Stalinised approach to the past. Soviet scholars wrote about various conflicts between Polish landlords and Ukrainian peasants, all the while emphasising that the Poles had their own class-conscious forces which not only fought against the rule of the landlords, but also helped to ease national conflicts in Ukraine. For example, they argued that the Polish "masses" supported the Cossacks during the seventeenth century, partly because Khmel'nyts'kyi's uprising helped alleviate Polish peasants' suffering at the hands of their class oppressors.[44] In Kyiv, historian Hryhoriy Marakhov was especially engaged in writing such international history. In the early 1960s, his work culminated in the publication of an edited volume on the history of the 1863 Polish uprising in Ukrainian territories.[45] These historical narratives were closely linked to de-Stalinization, as they helped bring back class as a key operational category in Soviet public culture. They were also an outcome of continuing state interference in the writing of history. When Marian Naszkowski's book about workers' movements in west Ukraine was translated from Polish to Ukrainian in 1960, for example, the CPU Central Committee removed references to Polish-Ukrainian conflicts and encouraged the translator to add phrases that would indicate that both Poles and Ukrainians supported communist movements in the region.[46] Censors therefore helped to de-emphasise the importance of national divisions in explaining East European history, highlighting instead interethnic class solidarity.

Cultural landmarks played a crucial part in the propagation of a transnational history of Eastern Europe in Ukraine. As the first secretary of the Ukrainian Communist Party during the 1940s, Khrushchev himself insisted that the statue of poet Adam Mickiewicz, unlike other Polish monuments, should not be removed from the streets of Lviv, stating that he was "a writer popular among the Ukrainian people and loved by them."[47] Echoing Khrushchev's appraisal of Mickiewicz, some Soviet scholars in 1950s Ukraine pointed to the importance of writers in leading the "masses" against their "exploiters." In June 1959 the Presidium of the Ukrainian Academy of Sciences resolved to celebrate the 150th anniversary of the Polish "revolutionary poet" Juliusz Słowacki, who had been born in the town of Kremenets' in modern-day Ukraine. Senior Ukrainian academics turned to the CPU Central Committee for permission to organise exhibitions and name the public library in Kremenets' after the poet. They presented Słowacki as an important social leader, claiming that his poetry "described the Ukrainian people and their struggle for independence."[48] The celebration of writers that Soviet academics deemed progressive was a common means of commemorating Eastern Europe's international history in which class loyalties and faith in progress mattered more than national belonging.[49] Literature was particularly attractive as a prism through which to understand transnational friendship because Ukraine was home to such poets, scholars, and translators of Polish literature as Maksym Ryl's'kyi. This group had a real interest in maintaining close literary ties with Poland. The republic was also a frequent travel destination for prominent Polish intellectuals, including writer Jarosław Iwaszkiewicz who had grown up in Ukraine and now cultivated friendships with local writers.[50]

Yet the writing and commemoration of transnational histories of Eastern Europe was undermined by bureaucratic resistance. Polish diplomats in Moscow complained that Polish historians found it extremely difficult to access unpublished Soviet archival materials, as reading room passes for foreigners were only issued at the highest levels of the Soviet academic establishment.[51] It is not altogether surprising that Soviet and Soviet Ukrainian officials looked upon Polish academics with suspicion. In practice, transnational cooperation in the sphere of culture and scholarship often translated to depleting west Ukrainian galleries and archives. In early 1968, for example, the Polish embassy in Moscow requested that some works of art and publications held in western Ukraine be transferred to Poland. They bypassed Ukrainian institutions and appealed to the all-Soviet Ministry of Culture instead – conceivably, they did not perceive Ukrainian colleagues as potential allies in this kind of cross-border cooperation. The Poles also lobbied the Soviet Minister of Culture Ekaterina Furtseva to build a monument in Lviv commemorating the city's Polish academics murdered by the Nazis. Although the issue had been raised before 1968, it had not reached senior Party apparatchiks in Moscow before the Poles directly approached the CPSU Central Committee, suggesting perhaps a degree of resistance to the commemoration of a common Ukrainian-Polish past in western Ukraine.[52]

Along with transnational histories of socialism, historians and party apparatchiks in Ukraine also promoted a much more ethno-centric version of the past. In these narratives, national differences overshadowed internationalist cooperation. Some Ukrainian historians promoted the notion that progress could only occur within national groups, and not through interactions between class-conscious representatives of different nations. In some publications, ethnic identities trumped class altogether. In 1959, for instance, the Shevchenko University in Kyiv published a history of the "age-old struggle of the Ukrainian people against the Vatican." The book claimed that the Roman Catholic Church had managed to wrestle Poland out from the Orthodox world in 966 (Poland had supposedly adopted Orthodox Christianity in 877) to turn it into an agent of Catholicism in the region.[53] In this vision, Poles were agents of the "West" not because of their class affiliation, but rather because of their national and religious identity – Polish Catholic workers and peasants were as much of a threat as the landlords and the bourgeoisie.

National history helped promote a neat, sanitised vision of Ukraine as a Ukrainian nation-space. Slowly but surely, the national paradigm overshadowed the international in Soviet Ukraine's politics of memory. This was partly because the CPSU Central Committee and the Soviet Council of Ministers grew determined to contain professional debates among historians.[54] As conservative establishment figures such as S.P. Trapeznikov and E.M. Zhukov set great store by official anniversaries and the publication of collective works,[55] scholars could no longer introduce new themes and topics.[56] With academic freedom under attack, simplistic national narratives won the day – there was simply too little room for subtle, original studies emphasising the complexity of national and class loyalties in the past. This process went hand-in-hand with the popularisation of history. At the beginning of the 1960s, the CPU Central Committee and its Institute of Party History made a concerted effort to encourage many residents of Ukraine to commemorate the history of Eastern Europe, compelling teachers, scholars, and low-ranking party members entrusted with mobilizing the rank-and-file to speak and write about it. For instance, they resolved to make the *Ukrains'kyi istorychnyi zhurnal* (*Ukrainian Historical Journal*) more accessible to a wider audience of agitators and university lecturers, rather than just senior academics at research institutions who had been reading the journal up until then.[57]

As an increasing number of Ukraine's residents discussed the past, they contributed towards the establishment of a fixed canon of East European history in which international cooperation played a less important role than ethnic conflicts. This was evident during the early 1960s, when the Ministry of Education in Kyiv commissioned the first Soviet school textbook specifically for teaching Ukrainian history.[58] School teachers, university lecturers, and party activists throughout Ukraine commented on two drafts of the manual during special meetings organised by local CPSU officials in March 1960 and July 1961. On the one hand, participants in these debates did not want to compromise on accuracy. In Mykolaiv, they charged that the textbook was imprecise as far as the history of southern Ukraine was concerned.[59] On the other hand, however, residents of Ukraine who commented on new textbook drafts were keen to convey historical knowledge in a manner understandable for as many people as possible. For instance, teachers from Dnipropetrovsk claimed that the authors did not use enough illustrative examples that would allow school children to imagine how the Ukrainian population lived under the Habsburgs, or to understand why they rebelled against foreign rule. The textbook only contained a very general statement that the life of the Ukrainian people had become even harder at the end of the eighteenth century, as it was now oppressed not only by Polish and Ukrainian feudal lords, but also the Austrian ruling classes.[60]

The teachers' call for more captivating portrayals of national communities was in line with broader trends, as those debating the new textbook typically promoted a simplistic vision of history in which nations acted as homogenous historical actors. Although Soviet scholars hardly abandoned Stalinist understanding of nations (*natsii*) as communities that emerged along with bourgeois societies (dating the emergence of

Ukrainians to the second half of the eighteenth century in particular),[61] the teachers and activists debating the textbook projected ethnic identities (*narodnosti*) into the Middle Ages. The "common people" in Ukraine's past were therefore not just workers and peasants, but also East Slavs: some teachers praised the textbook draft that demonstrated how this ethnic group achieved a high level of socio-economic, political, and cultural development, and played "an important role in Europe from ancient times."[62] They also devoted much attention to the Cossack uprisings and in this context promoted what amounted to a crude distinction between the "good" Ukrainians and Russians, and the "evil" Poles who exploited East Slavic lands.[63] Indeed, some teachers were worried that students would be left confused by any complicated analysis of the seventeenth century. For example, they pointed out that the authors discussed Khmel'nyts'kyi's uprising from the point of view of successes and failures, which made it difficult for students to understand the true "meaning of the national liberation struggle."[64] They insisted that Khmel'nyts'kyi should be seen as a great Ukrainian leader striving for reunification with Russia, and that was that.

All in all, inhabitants of Ukraine with a professional interest in history suggested that school textbooks should emphasise the close relationship between Ukraine and Russia, whilst distancing those nations from Western Slav Poland and other East European countries. Lecturers from the Chernihiv State Pedagogical University complained that the first draft failed to explain how the position of Ukrainians improved from Polish to Russian rule.[65] The need to maintain a close relationship with Russia would be made clear by reminding students that the Austrians occupied Northern Bukovyna as soon as the Russian army withdrew in the aftermath of the Russo-Turkish wars.[66] In trying to create a more approachable history textbook, therefore, inhabitants of Ukraine drew on well-established historiographical traditions, trying to "strike a balance between the grand narrative of the nation and class analysis," in which negative depictions of Polish landlords helped bring out the progressive role of Ukrainian national heroes.[67]

It is very difficult to establish the extent to which the reported opinions reflected broader attitudes of Ukraine's teachers and university lecturers. They took active part in shaping the textbook's contents, openly criticising the authors and suggesting very specific improvements and additions, but it also seems that they operated within the limits of what they considered to be permissible. This was partly because they knew that prominent historians and party apparatchiks expected them to discuss the role of the masses in socialist progress, and to focus on the Cossack period and the "reunification" of Ukraine with Russia. After all, they were commenting on a complete draft of the textbook that outlined a teleological vision of history during public meetings organised by party apparatchiks. However, it is striking that school teachers and university lecturers in the early 1960s actually tried to establish a coherent and "correct" vision of the past for students at schools. They argued that the past should be portrayed in a simple manner in order to ensure that as many residents of Ukraine as possible maintained a consistent vision of historical developments. It was partly because of this that they turned towards the simplistic national paradigm.

Awarding primacy to national development over class struggle, these narratives had far-reaching implications for nationalities policy in Soviet Ukraine. For one, they excluded ethnic minorities from the imagined Soviet Ukrainian community. In December 1960, discussing a new book about cross-border cooperation between Transcarpathia and socialist Hungary, the deputy head of the propaganda and agitation department at the Communist Party of Ukraine Central Committee rejected the proposed title *Friendship Has No Borders* (*Druzhba ne mae kordoniv*), and stressed that the authors should be careful not to overemphasise the importance of ethnic minorities on each side of the border.[68] In other words, Transcarpathia was to be portrayed as a Ukrainian nation space (despite the presence of a large Hungarian population in the province).

Furthermore, how to deal with the presence of Poles in Ukraine or Ukrainians in Poland was not just a historical question, but also a matter of some contemporary political controversy. During the late 1950s, the Polish-Soviet Friendship Society and the Polish consulate in Kyiv tried to reach out to the Polish minority in Ukraine, much to the chagrin of Soviet and Soviet Ukrainian officials in charge of cultivating transnational friendship in Eastern Europe.[69] For their part, Soviet Ukrainian writers and artists monitored the position of the Ukrainian minority in socialist Poland. In early 1968, poet Borys Oliinyk's article in *Literaturna Ukraina* bemoaned the fact that the Soviet authorities did not do enough to help them preserve their culture, resulting in Ukrainians in Poland having "no opportunity to hear their native language and song."[70]

It should be noted that while Ukraine was increasingly portrayed as a Ukrainian nation space in Soviet public culture, some forms of cultural activities that emphasized the multi-ethnic character of the republic survived into the 1980s. The Polish-language amateur theatre in Lviv, Ludowy Teatr Dramatyczny, enjoyed financial and institutional support (both in Poland and in the USSR) throughout the postwar period. The actors were local Soviet citizens identified as ethnic Poles by the Soviet administration, hailing mostly from the technical intelligentsia. Between 1947 and 1986, they prepared forty-one shows for audiences in Lviv and other parts of the USSR. Interestingly, the theatre's director in the 1980s was Valerii Bortiakov, an ethnic Russian who learnt Polish for the purposes of the job.[71] In the 1980s, the theatre was a shining example of the kind of transnational cooperation that had been more characteristic of the Thaw and later became overshadowed by interethnic tensions in the socialist camp. It focused public attention on west Ukraine's multi-cultural character and the potential advantages of interethnic cooperation, rather than emphasizing the political salience of ethnic divisions.

Ultimately, however, although the Thaw breathed a new life into Soviet internationalism, interethnic dynamics at home undermined the USSR's commitment to transnational socialism. Public potrayals of Ukraine and its role in Eastern Europe were an outcome of subtle negotiations between Soviet Party ideologues, East European officials, the Ukrainian creative intelligentsia, and educated professionals in the regions of Ukraine. During these negotiations, Ukrainian nationalism proved strong enough to undermine the idea that class and socialism eradicated the importance of nations and borders. Even on the level of official narratives, the socialist camp was often conceived not as a socialist brotherhood, but rather as a confederation of discrete national communities with separate histories and distinctive interests.

Friendship, Travel, and Social Differentiation

The meanings and limits of cross-border friendship were further shaped during international travel. Although Soviet leaders saw East European countries as troublesome and potentially subversive allies in the aftermath of the Polish and Hungarian unrest, crossing the USSR's western border became easier during the late 1950s and the 1960s. Soviet and East European officials were committed to promoting new sites of contact between prominent artists, academics, and journalists, as well as local community leaders such as factory managers, collective farm chairmen, doctors, and teachers from the USSR and Eastern Europe. Their ambiguous attitudes to international travel reflected key dilemmas of de-Stalinization. Fearful lest transnational contacts with Eastern Europe encourage Soviet citizens to question the limits of acceptable reform, Communist Party bosses also perceived travel in Eastern Europe as key to spreading Soviet influences abroad and rewarding certain categories of citizens at home.

State and party institutions in post-Stalinist USSR promoted three main types of international travel.[72] First, they coordinated the so-called "borderland exchanges" (*prigranichnye obmeny*) between towns and regions on either side of the Soviet frontier, which normally included local professionals, amateur artists, and activists recognised as the most active members of the local party organisations. Second, small delegations of CPSU officials and various cultural, scientific, industrial, and agricultural specialists from across Ukraine met their colleagues from the satellite states. Third, Soviet foreign tourism resumed in the mid-1950s, becoming better organised and more widespread, both geographically and numerically, from the early 1960s onwards.[73] Apart from relaxing and sunbathing at "international camps of rest" (*mezhdunarodnye lageria otdykha*), most tourists who travelled to Eastern Europe formed part of organised groups that often visited factories, farms, and other institutions abroad.[74]

Travelling between the USSR and Eastern Europe was not easy in the late 1950s, particularly outside carefully orchestrated tours. The visa application process was a discouraging hurdle in its own right. According to Soviet proposals, Polish citizens wishing to visit family in the USSR would need to receive a letter of invitation from their relatives, stamped by the local Soviet authorities, and submit their documents for approval to their regional (*voyvodship*) organs of the Ministry of Internal Affairs and Polish Foreign Office. Ministry officials in Warsaw would then apply to the Soviet consulate on citizens' behalf. Even as the Polish Foreign Ministry raised doubts about these measures, claiming that it was simply not their responsibility to deal with approving Polish citizens' visa applications, Moscow still insisted that some form of central control over travel would have to be implemented on the Polish side. In no uncertain terms, they informed the Polish side that they introduced these highly bothersome measures to limit the spread of "anti-Soviet" ideas into the USSR.[75]

Yet Soviet and East European officials were keen to expand travel as a means of promoting new types of cultural activity, forging economic links between the USSR and its satellite states, and proving that Soviet-type socialism spread across borders. Regional Party apparatchiks in

Kyiv and Kraków (including the future first secretary of the Communist Party of Ukraine, Petro Shelest) were thus involved in promoting face-to-face contacts between inhabitants of their regions in the late 1950s and the early 1960s. In 1958, artists from Kyiv and Kraków were supposed to enrich the cities' theatre repertoire. Young people from both cities would meet each other to give a personal dimension to socialist friendship. Meanwhile, specialists from the Kyiv region were to demonstrate to the Poles the advantages of collective farming, and engineers from Kyiv's Karl Marx and Kraków's Wawel chocolate factories would learn about each other's production technologies.[76]

The idea behind international travel during the Thaw was to establish permanent exchanges of artists, professionals, and political activists between Soviet and East European cities with a similar socio-economic profile.[77] The mining city of Katowice was thus twinned with Donetsk, while the port city of Szczecin was supposed to establish relations with Odesa. Kyiv was an especially fertile ground for the promotion of new transnational contacts with Poland. Key political players in the city had long-established personal relations with Polish communists, especially those active in Soviet Ukraine and Galicia before and during the Second World War. For example, as the regional party boss in the late 1950s and the CPU Central Committee secretary in charge of propaganda after 1960, Petro Timofiiovych Tron'ko was closely involved in establishing and running the Ukrainian branch of the Soviet-Polish Friendship Society. The Polish consul in Kyiv, Wanda Michalewska, later claimed that Tron'ko's interest in Poland had been fuelled by friendship with Marian Naszkowski, a prewar Polish communist activist in Galicia and the postwar Polish ambassador to Moscow (Tron'ko had himself been active in the Galician communist movement before 1939). Kyiv was also home to the Polish communist and writer Wanda Wasilewska (who was also the wife of the Soviet Ukrainian playwright Oleksandr Korniychuk). Long active on the Soviet political and literary scene, Wasilewska in a sense embodied official Soviet-Polish friendship.[78]

State and party apparatchiks in Moscow and Kyiv cast travel to Eastern Europe as a Soviet civilizing mission. Upon encountering foreigners from the near abroad, Soviet citizens were expected to speak about the USSR's great achievements in the war against Nazism, to perform Soviet popular music and Russian and Ukrainian folk dances, as well as to combat "petit-bourgeois" views among the creative intelligentsia in Eastern Europe.[79] In this way, East European satellites were cast as the "younger brothers" who owed a debt of gratitude to the USSR.

In the late 1950s, Soviet leaders were confident that this mission to Eastern Europe would be successful. In 1958, the man in charge of Soviet relations with Europe at the Union of Soviet Friendship Societies, I. Pronin, claimed that the Soviet-Polish Friendship Society and the transnational exchanges it organised gave a new lease of life to pro-Soviet movements in Gomułka's Poland.[80] In official reports, commanders of Soviet army units stationed in western Poland likewise underlined that music and theatre productions they organised for the local population helped combat malicious rumours about the USSR, and also set a "Soviet example" that "promoted high moral and aesthetic values" among the Polish population.[81]

At the same time, Soviet specialists who crossed the border sometimes emphasised that they also learned from East European experiences. In December 1967, for example, regional television in Kraków hosted the director of the Kyiv television studio, V. Iu. Vlasov. Reporting to the obkom, Vlasov described the Poles' short, dynamic news reports in very positive terms, and suggested that Ukrainian journalists could copy the Polish polemical programs where two speakers represented different views on a given topic and answered questions sent in by the viewers.[82]

Because travel was both exclusive and ideologically charged, it was an important marker of middle class status in Soviet Ukraine. Party apparatchiks took advantage of various new forms of travel, including "friendship trains" and "buses of friendship" to send Soviet specialists across the border. Every train contained approximately 330 tourists, including blue-collar workers and collective farmers, but also scientific, artistic, and cultural activists, state and party officials, journalists, and amateur artists.[83] While emphasising the wide-ranging social composition of each train, Soviet and East European reports paid particular attention to the types of travellers who, either through talent, political standing, or education, were seen to contribute the most towards establishing close transnational links. In addition, many so-called "workers" who visited the people's democracies as part of the trains were actually prominent members of their local communities: in October 1968, passengers of a train from Kyiv to Kraków contained blue-collar workers awarded official titles such as "Heroes of the Soviet Union and Socialist Labour."[84] Soviet partners were expected to manifest their knowledge through professional encounters during travel.[85]

Soviet travellers reproduced these ritualised narratives to emphasise that foreign travel made them special. Those who described their journeys on friendship trains in official reports presented them as a nobilitating experience, emphasising that, as Soviet people, they met with a fitting reception abroad. One report celebrated the fact that 3,000 people turned out to greet a Soviet group at the Kraków train station despite adverse weather conditions, and the tourists met "important people" and stayed in "the nicest hotels" in Warsaw.[86] This may well have reflected a truly friendly atmosphere that characterised some international trips. East European officials were keen to combat the pomp and formalism that often accompanied international travel.[87]

Describing their personal experiences of travel, Soviet citizens further emphasised that they guided popular opinion at home. The European department of the USSR's Foreign Ministry instructed the Soviet press to depict some categories of travellers as "authoritative observers" (*avtoritetnye obozrevateli*) who had a responsibility to inform the rest of the Soviet population about the people's democracies.[88] Prominent activists of friendship societies consequently printed newspaper articles, appeared on the local radio, and published books in which they highlighted their contribution to establishing friendly relations with twinned towns and regions across the border.[89]

Tour group leaders in particular emphasised their special status in Soviet society. In order to portray themselves as more sophisticated travellers than other Soviet citizens who came into contact with foreigners, they condemned untoward behaviour of other, "ordinary" tourists in official reports compiled upon returning from Eastern Europe. Soon after international tourism resumed under Khrushchev, tour group leaders criticised tourists for behaving in an "uncultured" manner. One report claimed that members of a Soviet group travelling around Czechoslovakia created a very bad impression on the local waiters because they had no table manners. Moreover, one writer allegedly discredited himself as a reliable international tourist by getting obscenely drunk and trying in vain to seduce a Slovak woman.[90] The report writer condemned what he depicted as undignified and politically immature behaviour of other travellers, thus proving his own patriotic credentials and suggesting that reliable Soviet citizens were polite, sober, and politically alert.

International Travel and Regional Identities in Ukraine

It was not just social status that set many travellers apart from Soviet society at large; where they lived was equally important. From 1958, the newly created Soviet friendship societies were instrumental in organising borderland exchanges between western USSR and eastern parts of Poland, Czechoslovakia, and Hungary.[91] From the perspective of Soviet officials in charge of international travel, borderland exchanges presented new opportunities for shaping ideas of what it meant to be a good citizen in the borderlands, especially in the regions of Lviv and Volhynia that bordered on socialist Poland.

In line with broader trends, strict selection criteria during borderland exchanges helped distinguish educated and talented inhabitants of western Ukraine from their "ordinary" compatriots. While the number of participants in borderland exchanges remained low, with approximately 1,000 people travelling between western Ukraine and eastern Poland in 1959,[92] SSOD (The Union of Soviet Friendship Societies) leaders demanded that the exchanges become increasingly "concrete and specialised."[93] Although borderland exchanges did include a small number of blue-collar workers and groups of Pioneers,[94] most citizens who participated in the program during the late 1950s and early 1960s were professionals (agricultural specialists, engineers, teachers, librarians, doctors, lawyers), party and Komsomol members who stood out in their local communities, sportsmen, and amateur artists.[95] Travellers from the borderlands were to act as representatives of their local communities, showcasing Soviet achievements and bringing new expertise from their foreign trips.[96] Both Soviet and Polish friendship society officials agreed that "social activists" should address large audiences during their trips to maximise the impact of the exchange program.[97] This helped promote in public and in internal party correspondence the image of western Ukraine as a region with its own Soviet middle class.

Cross-border travel had a strong cultural dimension. As Anne White argues in her analysis of houses of culture during the Thaw, Soviet and East European authorities sought to mobilise "the whole population by giving it the opportunity to truly participate in creative cultural activity."[98] In line with the broader policy, borderland exchanges provided a setting for cultural and intellectual pursuits. According to plans, librarians, museum employees, and theatre directors from various parts of the Lviv oblast would visit eastern Poland in 1959. In addition, ten employees from west Ukrainian houses of culture would travel across the border to Rzeszów to establish relations with their Polish counterparts.[99] Both Soviet and Polish officials saw these activities as a means of fostering amateur artistic activity and spreading theatre, dance, and music to the provinces. Discussing plans for improving borderland exchanges in

July 1959, for example, SSOD activists agreed to focus on exchanging smaller groups of artists – this would not only be cheaper, they reasoned, but would also allow them to perform in small villages.[100]

In west Ukraine, such cultural activism was seen as a means of challenging national stereotypes and overcoming mutual distrust between Soviet Ukrainians and their western neighbours. Official reports celebrated new friendships between Polish and Soviet children forged during international summer camps held in the borderlands.[101] The SSOD presented friendship between Polish and Ukrainian children as a major socialist achievement less than twenty years after brutal ethnic cleansing campaigns in the region. At the same time, official reports portrayed Ukrainian culture as an important means of strengthening Soviet-Polish relations. As Soviet friendship society leaders underlined, for example, exchanges of artists and professionals employed in various cultural institutions resulted in staging Soviet Ukrainian plays in Rzeszów and Polish plays in Lviv. Travellers from the borderlands also delivered speeches in the Ukrainian language, which reportedly "created a good impression on the Poles."[102] In this sense, narratives of borderland travel helped present Ukrainian language and culture from the borderlands as crucial parts of Soviet identities abroad.

The successes of borderland exchanges were especially impressive given that ambitious plans for establishing regular exchanges between twinned towns and cities often failed to take off the ground in other parts of Ukraine. Wanda Michalewska, the Polish consul in Kyiv, found herself dealing with numerous complaints from Polish bureaucrats keen to establish cross-border links. In 1960, Polish officials in Szczecin informed her that the Soviet apparatchiks in Odesa completely ignored their requests to establish friendly relations.[103] The consul, educated in Soviet Belarus and committed to spreading Soviet-style socialism across the Polish border during the interwar period, and later a prominent activist of the Polish-Soviet Friendship Society, likely offered a sympathetic ear.[104] Nonetheless, problems persisted through the 1960s and 1970s. With the exception of the borderlands and the cities Kyiv and Kraków, relations between most Ukrainian and Polish regions were rather sporadic.[105] This was at least partly because of excessive central planning of transnational travel, which made it difficult for friendship society activists to engage popular interests on the ground. Although the central Ukrainian town of Cherkasy was linked with the Polish Bydgoszcz, the relationship between both cities was limited to exchanging a few official letters. Meanwhile, local inhabitants in Cherkasy reportedly showed lively interest in obtaining news from the west Polish city of Szczecin because, during the Second World War, Cherkasy hosted Polish refugees resettled in Szczecin after 1945.[106]

In contrast, the western borderlands stood out as a region that had established the most systematic forms of cooperation with the Soviet satellite states. In 1968, for example, the man who would replace Petro Shelest as the first secretary of the Communist Party of Ukraine four years later, Volodymyr Shcherbyts'kyi, singled out the borderlands as a site where transnational contacts developed dynamically.[107] Eleven years later, the Polish Ministry of Administration likewise wrote about "borderland exchanges in particular" as a means of fostering political and ideological unity in the socialist bloc.[108] That the borderlands saw active transnational contact between Soviet Ukraine and Poland during the Thaw was not entirely surprising. Even more than Kyiv, Lviv was home to communist activists with long-established links to Poland. Maria Kikh, the deputy-head of the Lviv city council, had been active in the Communist Party of Western Ukraine under Polish rule in the 1930s and now headed the local branch of the Soviet-Polish Friendship Society. In addition, Lviv academics with an interest in Poland (such as literary scholar Teoksyst Pachovs'kyi and historian Ivan Belakevych) cooperated closely with the Polish consulate in Kyiv.[109]

Ultimately, borderland exchanges helped demonstrate that western Ukraine formed an integral part of the imagined Soviet community. Members of friendship societies directly involved in coordinating transnational travel underlined that inhabitants of the Soviet west resisted anti-Soviet attitudes in Eastern Europe. As they put it, many Soviet participants in borderland exchanges "tactfully showed" the Poles how to work hard.[110] In internal correspondence and meetings among Soviet officials, accounts of borderland exchanges helped to ground the image of west Ukraine as a home to activists who represented the Soviet community abroad, but also abided by crucial precepts of "communist morality" such as hard work, seriousness, and egalitarianism.[111] SSOD leaders in Moscow praised participants for helping to reinforce Soviet influences in troublesome Poland as early as 1959: "It is important to note that borderland exchanges have had a certain positive impact on the situation in many regions of Poland."[112] Friendship society officials further singled out particular groups and delegations. Agricultural specialists from Lviv had thus supposedly taught Polish farmers how to grow corn, while engineers from the local bus factory were said to have impressed the Poles, instructing them how to modernise production technologies.[113]

International Travel as Confrontation

But travel did not always work as planned. Personal conflicts, national tensions, and organisational blunders plagued face-to-face encounters in the socialist bloc. Commenting on blatant differences between the USSR and Eastern Europe, travellers from Soviet Ukraine defined what it meant to be Soviet and Soviet Ukrainian in opposition to their western neighbours.

Forging transnational friendships during travel was not easy. It appears that "international evenings of friendship" during which Soviet citizens met East European tourists travelling in the USSR were meticulously planned, with song and dance performances interspersed with long speeches. This likely made unstructured conversation difficult.[114] In addition, the language barrier remained an important obstacle through the 1960s, even between Soviet citizens and Slavic-speakers from the near abroad.[115]

More importantly, however, travel forced Soviet citizens to confront foreign ideas about what socialism and socialist friendship should mean in practice. In response to obvious Polish departures from Soviet norms, numerous members of Soviet delegations repeated conservative views on ideology and art (or at least they claimed to have done so in trip reports). For example, during a 1962 visit to Kraków, a group of regional party bosses from Kyiv asked their hosts why Polish agriculture had not been collectivised, and voiced outrage at the ever-present "Catholic propaganda" in Poland. They noticed small shrines decorated with fresh flowers all along the road from the Soviet border to Kraków, and were shocked to see two new churches being built en route to Lenin's former residence in Poronino. As responsible Soviet patriots, they alerted their superiors at the CPU Central Committee that the Catholic Church made extensive preparations to celebrate the millennium of Christianity in Poland.[116] Numerous academics, writers, and party apparatchiks also explicitly condemned Polish art that differed from Soviet standards. When a group of university lecturers from Kyiv visited Kraków in February 1960, they reportedly forced their reluctant Polish hosts to explain why abstractionism was so popular among students at the Academy of Fine Arts. The group was not satisfied with the dean's explanation that the students' interest in modern art stemmed from a Western style of teaching, where the role of university professors was limited to assisting young people in their individual creative explorations. The Kyiv academics retorted that abstractionism was promoted by the lecturers themselves and charged that primary party organisations exerted a weak influence over Polish universities.[117]

It is of course conceivable that delegation members played up the extent to which they resisted Polish ideological "deviations" as they compiled their reports upon returning to the USSR. What is significant, at least in these written reports, is that they performed Soviet identities and presented themselves as loyal citizens. They claimed that the party – and not the Kraków academics who escaped party control – had the right idea about the role of art in society. In this sense, they "spoke Bolshevik," citing party leaders' pronouncements to determine how society should function. Yet delegation reports also acknowledged that competing approaches to politics, culture, and society existed under state socialism: their conversations with Polish colleagues in no way resembled "speaking Bolshevik" in the sense that competing, non-party ideas were voiced and contested in the open (as well as in written reports compiled upon return to the USSR). The aspirational middle class blamed problems in Kraków on Polish national peculiarities such as Roman Catholicism, memories of medieval history, and particularly the adoption of Christianity in 966, suggesting that these were closely linked to their ideological deviations. Delegation members thus effectively claimed authority on the basis of their allegiance not only to the party, but also to the USSR and its nations defined in opposition to the near abroad.

Stressing just how different the USSR was from its satellite states was especially significant as national tensions rose along with increased cross-border travel in the late 1950s. In July 1959, for example, SSOD officials in Moscow complained about Polish tourists as smugglers and heritage-seekers:

> People working with Polish delegations from the borderland regions that come to visit the USSR have at times displayed unnecessary levels of trust (*proiavlialas' ne vsegda nuzhnaia doverchivost'*), forgetting elementary rules of alertness. Due to lax control, we have noted cases where our guests disappeared into the unknown for one or two days, claiming to visit places where they grew up or their "relatives." However, as it turned out later, these guests spent much time at market places and took care of their commercial dealings or, even worse, spread all sorts of hostile propaganda among the local Polish population.[118]

The report writers were clearly uneasy about the opening of borders and the relaxation of state controls over society after the death of Stalin, though they shied away from claiming that the Soviet authorities should not trust the Poles at all. After all, it was their job as SSOD activists to overcome transnational distrust. Aware of the troubled history of Ukrainian-Polish borderlands, however, even friendship society officials treated Polish ethnicity as a potential source of trouble both among foreign visitors and citizens of the USSR. They thus echoed broader suspicion of non-titular ethnic groups in Soviet Ukraine.

While travel was designed to strengthen Soviet cultural and political influences in Eastern Europe, Soviet citizens found that East Europeans refused to see them as the elder and more experienced brothers. Polish reports claimed that members of the Soviet creative intelligentsia were particularly offended by Poles' condescending attitudes towards Soviet society and culture, especially when Poles claimed to be more "European" than them.[119] By the second half of the 1960s, the KGB was also alarmed that foreigners travelling in the USSR directly confronted citizens about shortcomings of the Soviet political system, raising such sensitive subjects as Moscow's treatment of non-Russian nationalities in the USSR, economic shortages and the underdevelopment of the consumer industry, the rise of the "red bourgeoisie," and censorship.[120] Intensified contacts between intellectuals in Poland and Soviet Ukraine in particular exposed the latter to narratives of Ukrainian history that deviated from the Soviet script. For example, though V.F. Lobko's 1962 speech about the linguistic Russification of Ukraine was never published in the Soviet press, it reached residents of Ukraine by means of the Warsaw Ukrainian-language publication *Nasha kultura*.[121]

In public and in official reports, Soviet citizens who met East Europeans depicted themselves as defending the Soviet, Soviet Russian, and Soviet Ukrainian people from what they perceived as anti-Soviet attitudes in the near abroad. This was already evident in May 1956, when a group of Soviet journalists visited Czechoslovakia. The group leader was struck by the level of hostility they encountered on the streets of Prague, and offended to see that the people of Czechoslovakia were "proud and convinced of their superiority over other Slavic nations." He suggested that the USSR should make more effort to demonstrate the richness and splendour of "Russian and Soviet" culture, appealing to the CPSU Central Committee to send the best Soviet symphonic orchestras and opera singers to tour Czechoslovakia, and to invite a few hundred members of the Czechoslovak intelligentsia to the USSR to show them "our cultural and economic achievements."[122] To be Soviet, he suggested, was to take pride in Russian culture.

2 A Polish photographer captures a market in Lviv's Cathedral Square, Sepember 1969. Soviet officials complained that Polish tourists engaged in illegal trade and showed undue interest in Lviv's pre-Soviet sites. National Digital Archives (NAC), Warsaw.

Similarly, a few years later, writer Iosif Leonidovich Prut clearly stated that the USSR had "few friends" among the Polish intelligentsia, stressing that Poles harboured a range of anti-Russian and anti-Ukrainian stereotypes. He claimed in his report for the CPSU Central Committee that unlike the "simple people," Polish writers forced him to answer for all the evils of Tsarist Russia and the brutality of Khmel'nyts'kyi's uprising, and "crossed all boundaries of elementary politeness" by blaming the USSR for Katyn' and the scale of destruction during the Warsaw Uprising. Prut found that Soviet, Russian, and Ukrainian identities created important barriers between intellectuals in the USSR and abroad (the Poles attacked "Russian" Tsars, "Ukrainian" hetmans, as well as "Soviet" policies under Stalin). Interestingly, this led Prut to the conclusion that more Soviet writers should visit Poland to propagate "socialist" values in the arts and friendship towards the USSR. He specified that they should spend less time advertising their own personal achievements and focus more on exposing Soviet literature in general.[123]

Prut's account showed that international travel encouraged Soviet citizens to express a peculiar mixture of transnational "socialist," supranational Soviet, and ethnic identities. He took seriously the notion of transnational friendship, and looked for ways to overcome mutual distrust between Polish and Soviet intellectuals. At the same time, he posited himself as a defender of Soviet, Russian, and Ukrainian interests abroad. Like other travellers, he spoke and wrote about the continuing importance of the Soviet border and ethnic divisions that had not been obliterated by the establishment of socialist regimes in Eastern Europe.

Travel as Public Diplomacy: 1968

The patriotic and middle class nature of international travel was especially pronounced during the Prague Spring. Attempts to reform the socialist system in Czechoslovakia marked a major breakdown in Soviet relations with the near abroad in 1968, leading to a Soviet-led Warsaw Pact invasion in August 1968. Despite Soviet leaders' fears that Czechoslovak ideas for deep political, cultural, and social reform would spill across the border, tourist exchanges between Soviet Ukraine and Czechoslovakia intensified in 1968. As Grey Hodnett and Peter Potichnyj claim, this allowed Ukrainian party authorities to gather intelligence about the unfolding situation, and more broadly, formed part of the Ukrainian "quasi-diplomacy."[124] Because travel served as a means to secure Soviet influences in Czechoslovakia, the Ukrainian authorities instituted strict vetting procedures to determine who came into face-to-face contact with Czechoslovak citizens. They specified that members of amateur artistic groups, sportsmen, and war veterans should be encouraged to travel, while informal contacts between friends and relatives should be limited.[125] Consequently, even more than the various forms of travel that developed during the late 1950s and the 1960s, trips to Czechoslovakia in 1968 were clearly a perk awarded to the aspirational middle class.

Although a number of idealised accounts about face-to-face contacts celebrated how Ukraine's farmers welcomed Czechoslovak delegations "with bread and salt," while the latter, "moved to tears," laid flowers at monuments to Lenin,[126] this buoyant style clashed with the more factual tone of other reports. Questions of international cooperation became more complicated in 1968. Journalists and newspaper editors felt this strongly, which encouraged them to condemn the foreigners' "ignorance" in official reports. When Kyiv television showed the opening ceremony of the Ukrainian Culture Days in Bratislava, editors found their colleagues in Czechoslovakia incompetent and uncooperative. As a result, they could only show the picture with no sound during the live transmission in May.[127] Because of heightened tensions, Soviet visitors to Czechoslovakia interpreted similar problems as symptoms of hostility and political sabotage. For example, the deputy head of the Ukrainian radio and television committee Ia. complained that Czechoslovak journalists were simply unwilling to work with their Soviet Ukrainian colleagues. Soviet journalists were shocked that the Czechoslovak media failed to report on the Ukrainian Culture Days in Prague: it made their work difficult, because they had hoped to travel around the city and produce reports in cooperation with them.[128]

Furthermore, travellers who compiled reports upon returning from abroad complained about the rather chilly reception Soviet citizens encountered in Czechoslovakia. While it is not possible to determine whether tourists and members of Soviet delegations were indeed as appalled at their cold treatment as the reports claimed, it seems likely that they experienced Czechoslovak citizens' aloofness at this tense time. Both before and after the invasion of Czechoslovakia, leaders of tour groups complained about the rude attitude of waiters and tour guides, and emphasised that Soviet citizens were deprived of the usual opportunities to meet Czechoslovak citizens.[129] As one report put it, Soviet travellers did not feel in 1968 the "enthusiasm" and "love" so characteristic of visits to Czechoslovakia in previous years.[130] Indeed, personal conflicts with foreigners acquired new political significance due to their anti-Soviet or even xenophobic undertones. When a group of sixty-one Czechoslovak miners and engineers from Ostrava came to Lviv to visit the Soviet soldiers whom they had supposedly befriended back home during the autumn of 1968, the trip took a nasty turn. One guest from across the border approached a Czech woman who was dancing with a Soviet soldier, slapped her in the face, and called her a "Russian swine."[131] As the authorities encouraged their citizens to act as "bearers of peace" when they met residents of Czechoslovakia, they also exposed them to attitudes and opinions that challenged narratives of socialist friendship in Eastern Europe.

In particular, during their trips to Czechoslovakia, Soviet citizens often encountered opinions that questioned the USSR's leading position in the socialist camp. Many Czechoslovak citizens claimed the USSR did not always provide a good example for other socialist states in Eastern Europe. In this vein, a group of Czechoslovak workers laughed at the advice they were given by two Soviet industrial specialists who lectured them on leather production, underlining that Czechoslovakia was a highly developed industrial country that had adopted modern production technologies long before the USSR.[132] Some Czechoslovak statements levelled against the USSR were more pointed. During their stay in Bratislava, a group of Soviet students were confronted by a local man who claimed that "Soviet rule here was now over."[133] Unsurprisingly, similar attacks became more frequent after the August 1968 invasion.[134]

In response, the Soviet authorities demanded increasingly conformist forms of behaviour in return for the right to travel. Leaders of Soviet friendship societies who coordinated international travel, members of the Communist Party of Ukraine Central Committee, as well as communist leaders in the regions of Ukraine used tourism as a means of influencing the domestic situation in Czechoslovakia. The SSOD made a special effort to intensify cooperation with the Czechoslovak-Soviet Friendship Society,[135] thus strengthening "pro-Soviet" institutions in Prague. More broadly, citizens travelling to Czechoslovakia had to fulfil the mission of explaining the Soviet point of view on current affairs, counteract the influence of the Czechoslovak media, and popularise Soviet and Ukrainian culture. For instance, Kyiv fashion designers presented their work in Prague and Karlovy Vary in April 1968, and the SSOD assisted in preparing the Ukrainian Culture Days.[136] When the

Ukrainian republican dance ensemble toured Czechoslovakia between 7 and 29 May, the group leader emphasised that they had an impact on the local population: 40,000 spectators attended the performances, and claimed that the artists "socialized with the population of the Czech and Slovak parts" of the country.[137]

In 1968, travel to Czechoslovakia functioned as a reward for loyalty and conformity, but it also conferred certain responsibilities on Soviet citizens who took part in ritualistic affirmations of Sovietness. In order to manifest their patriotic credentials, during the trips and in their official reports, citizens needed to distance themselves from foreign criticisms leveled against their country, and confront conflicting interpretations of what it was to be socialist that Czechoslovak "reform communists" promoted. Articulations of Soviet and Soviet Ukrainian patriotism helped travellers emphasize that they made a special contribution to the USSR.

Conclusion

The process of reconciliation between the USSR and its satellite states was slow and uneven after the major upheavals of 1956. Still, by shaping mass media portrayals of the socialist bloc, top CPSU officials suggested that educated professionals, party activists, prominent members of friendship societies, and artists had a crucial role to play in spreading socialism across borders. Official narratives of travel outlined the idealised image of a transnational, East European "middle class" committed to transnational friendship. At the same time, they encouraged Soviet citizens to distance themselves from their neighbours in the near abroad, especially as the satellite states diverged from the Soviet model.

Because they emphasised the importance of nationhood under socialism, narratives of transnational friendship encouraged some residents to reflect upon the role of Ukrainian identities in the Soviet Union. Although the notion of transnational socialist friendship remained powerful before 1968, Ukrainian nationalism and memories of historical conflicts with Poland in particular ensured the continuing importance of borders and ethnic identities in Soviet public culture. Between 1956 and 1968, opinion leaders in the USSR conceived of the Soviet camp as a shaky alliance of different national groups, each with their distinct histories and characteristics, as well as a socialist commonwealth with a shared past and a shared future. This encouraged the expression of Ukrainian identities in the USSR itself, but also strengthened Soviet territorial integrity: Ukrainian identities were mostly defined against Eastern Europe and not against Russia.

Speaking and writing about Soviet friendship with the near abroad became a crucible where new notions of the USSR as an empire were forged. On the one hand, by speaking in public and compiling official reports, many citizens underlined their commitment to building transnational unity within the Soviet bloc. These narratives acquired particular significance in the borderlands, allowing many local inhabitants to challenge the nature of Ukraine's regional divisions by underlining their special contribution to strengthening East European friendship. On the other hand, the ritualised portrayals of travel were often a far cry from the actual experiences of Soviet citizens who encountered residents of Eastern Europe. Highlighting differences within the socialist bloc, international travel turned public attention towards themes that set the USSR apart from its satellite states.

Official narratives and increasingly ritualised practices of travel consequently helped establish a clear definition of what constituted Soviet identities in public rhetoric. Professional expertise, geographically defined patriotism, and ethnicity were key features of the Soviet person: they were at least as important as allegiance to the Communist Party. In 1968, as the following chapter shows, these notions of Sovietness posed a real challenge to top party apparatchiks in the USSR, and deepened divisions between titular and non-titular ethnic groups in Soviet society.

3 The Limits of De-Stalinization: The Prague Spring and the End of the Thaw in 1968

In October 1968, to mark the fiftieth anniversary of Czechoslovak independence, a Soviet citizen named Nekrasov from Putivl' in northeast Ukraine posted a letter to his friend in Czechoslovakia. It never reached the addressee, Stanislav, whom he had met eight years earlier convalescing in a Kyiv hospital. Writing to the Moscow newspaper *Literaturnaia gazeta* in early 1969, Nekrasov complained that the letter was stopped by Soviet censors. Return mail proved just as problematic, and Nekrasov expressed shock that a package from Stanislav with medicines unavailable in the USSR had recently been confiscated by the Soviet customs officials. Nekrasov believed these experiences not only testified to a major breakdown in Soviet-Czechoslovak relations after the Prague Spring of 1968, but also proved that the Soviet state was only concerned with its citizens' welfare on paper – he understood why the Czechs wanted freedom from Soviet tutelage. Expressing solidarity with the "highly cultured Czechoslovak people," Nekrasov was "ashamed to be Russian."[1]

Although Nekrasov was more openly critical of the authorities than most Soviet citizens, his comments reflect a broader crisis of faith that overcame the USSR in the late 1960s. The Warsaw Pact invasion of Czechoslovakia in August 1968 was a traumatic event for Soviet citizens. In contrast to the Polish and Hungarian events of 1956, which raised troubling questions about the scope and nature of Khrushchev's reforms after the death of Stalin, Moscow's reaction to the Czechoslovak crisis marked the end of debates about de-Stalinization in the Soviet bloc. As communist-led attempts to build "socialism with a human face" were stifled by Soviet soldiers, it was painfully clear that the Kremlin was now deeply suspicious of new ideas for liberalisation. This fuelled a sense of pessimism about the prospects of reforming Soviet-style regimes among the population of the USSR, both among proponents of conservative patriotism who considered reform dangerous, and among advocates of reformist patriotism who thought it impossible. At the same time, because the invasion of Czechoslovakia dealt a decisive blow to the idea of socialist friendship in Eastern Europe, it generated a heated public discussion about the importance of borders under state socialism. These debates revealed a shift in social and cultural identities, as ethnicity finally supplanted transnational socialist identities in Eastern Europe. The Prague Spring led to dramatic re-negotiations of Soviet identities, as many recognized it as a sign of failure in the attempt to create a transnational socialist identity for the Soviet bloc.

An important prelude to the Czechoslovak crisis occurred in Poland. In January 1968, the Polish authorities banned a Warsaw theatre production of Adam Mickiewicz's *Dziady*. Party officials claimed that the nineteenth-century play evoked excessive enthusiasm among audiences, who applauded the anti-Tsarist and, arguably, anti-Russian dialogue. The ban led to student demonstrations in Warsaw and other Polish university towns in early March. The authorities responded by launching a large-scale anti-Semitic campaign. In his infamous speech to communist activists in Warsaw, the first secretary of the Polish United Workers' Party, Władysław Gomułka, blamed the events on "the Zionists" and "fifth columnists." Polish Jews were expelled from the party, fired from their jobs, and effectively forced to emigrate.[2] The Polish crisis thereby extended debates about ethno-national identities, freedom of expression, and popular protest in Soviet-style regimes, all of which were to play a crucial role in the Prague Spring. The March events demonstrated that, despite decades of internationalist rhetoric, ethno-national identities still proved more effective at mobilising popular protest. Concerned about public displays of anti-Russian sentiment, the authorities attempted to redirect popular ire towards Jews.

The Czechoslovak crisis that began to unfold around the same time was the last serious attempt at social, cultural, and political transformation in Eastern Europe before Mikhail Gorbachev's *perestroika*. After Alexander Dubček replaced Antonin Novotny as the first secretary of the Czechoslovak Communist Party in January, the new leaders in Prague announced their action program in April 1968. Without questioning Czechoslovakia's role in the Warsaw Pact or the socialist system itself, they called for a more circumscribed place for the Communist Party in society, freedom of speech, and personal choice in profession and lifestyle. Brezhnev's response to the reform movement was at first cautiously encouraging. Though wary of allowing reformist impulses from Czechoslovakia to fuel resistance to Soviet authority, the Kremlin wanted to avoid jeopardising the "modernising and reforming claims of 'developed socialism.'"[3] Condemning the excesses of Dubček's reformism, including the relaxation of censorship and intra-party democracy, Brezhnev still wanted citizens to believe that gradual economic reform and limited intellectual and cultural openings could reinvigorate decaying socialist institutions without undermining strong state control over society.[4]

Yet by mid-1968 the developments had gone further than the Kremlin was prepared to tolerate. Many Czechoslovak students and intellectuals began to challenge the leading role of the Communist Party. Their views were embodied in Ludvik Vaculik's *Two Thousand Words*, published on 27 June 1968, in which he wrote about "foreign domination" of Czechoslovakia, the rule of "power-hungry individuals," and social inequality.[5] The Soviet leadership did not accept Dubček's calls for patience, growing increasingly convinced that the Czechoslovak party had lost control of the situation. On the night of 20 August 1968, armies of the Warsaw Pact marched into Czechoslovakia "to smother the Prague Spring with direct force and restore power to a reliable set of conservative leaders."[6] Protests against the Soviet domination of Czechoslovakia continued until April 1969, when Dubček was replaced by a more conservative and repressive leader, Gustáv Husák.[7]

Particularly in Ukraine and its borderlands regions, Soviet leaders were afraid of a potential spillover of the Czechoslovak crisis into the USSR itself. Unable to control the flow of information between the USSR and its satellite states, they turned to simplistic slogans that aimed to foster a sense of Soviet patriotism and distrust of foreigners among the population. In this vein, Soviet mass media repeatedly emphasized that foreigners in the socialist camp were prone to anti-Soviet views that threatened the peace and economic stability of the entire socialist bloc. Propaganda further suggested that national minorities such as Jews were inherently different from the Slavic majority in Soviet Ukraine. This arsenal of imperialist and anti-Semitic stereotypes was not new in 1968, but during the Prague Spring it shaped public rhetoric more than at any point since the death of Stalin. Xenophobia turned into a weapon that party leaders used to limit the spread of ideas from across the border in the late Soviet period.

Drawing on foreign sources of information and the domestic mass media, Soviet citizens commented on the unfolding developments in a variety of contexts.[8] As Soviet authorities cracked down on liberalizing impulses and dissenting speech, citizens from Ukraine developed a complex range of new social and cultural identities, blending elements of nationalism, anti-Semitism, middle-class aspiration, social criticism, and media sensibility into their constructions of what it meant to be a patriotic Soviet citizen.

This chapter begins by examining the failure of Soviet leaders to manage the information sphere during the Czechoslovak crisis. Whereas many historians point to the decline of the public sphere after the ouster of Khrushchev in 1964, I discuss the continuing importance of public agitation meetings as a space where inhabitants of Ukraine articulated what it meant to be Soviet and Ukrainian. The chapter then analyses the claims of conservative patriotism, pointing to the links between xenophobia and conservative notions of participatory citizenship in the USSR. The following sections examine the evolution of reformist patriotism (whose proponents developed a very different notion of citizenship), as well as the range and meanings of anti-Soviet opinions in 1968.

Mass Media Event

The Prague Spring was a mass media event in Soviet Ukraine. With the growth of radio and television in the post-war period, authorities could not stop the flow of news and ideas across the Soviet border.[9] Soviet leaders seemed at a loss about how to present an alternative vision of the Czechoslovak crisis in the domestic mass media, showing a great degree of unease about television in particular. Their sloppy attempts to counter the influence of foreign sources of information illustrated the symbolic significance of national boundaries in the socialist bloc, turning the act of listening, reading, and watching Soviet news into an expression of patriotism.

To learn about the Prague Spring, residents of Ukraine turned to Western radio stations, as well as Czechoslovak, Polish, Hungarian, and Romanian mass media. Party apparatchiks were especially concerned about the impact of foreign broadcasts in Ukraine's western regions,[10] but the crisis extended well beyond the borderlands. Even as far east as Sumy, local officials raised alarm about the popularity of "foreign, hostile" programming.[11] While Czechoslovak television was only available in the western oblasts of Ukraine, Czechoslovak radio – including Ukrainian-language programs produced by the Ukrainian minority in Prešov in eastern Slovakia – could be picked up throughout Ukraine.[12] For the authorities, this was especially concerning in the immediate aftermath of the August 1968 invasion. For example, the army command in Kyiv reported that an army captain and other officers collectively listened to Czechoslovak radio broadcasts during their free time.[13]

Particularly before August 1968, the Soviet authorities were reluctant to stop the flow of news from another socialist country. An obvious break from Czechoslovakia would have been an embarrassment, exposing rifts and contradictions in Soviet internationalism. Still, some of the ideas propagated in Czechoslovak media were considered revisionist in the Soviet context. Ukrainian-language publications posted to Ukraine from Czechoslovakia included *Druzhno vpered* and *Duklia*, which reprinted Vaculik's "2000 words" and commented extensively on the unfolding events. Czechoslovak media also reported on the revival of the Greek Catholic Church in Slovakia, "a true red flag for the Soviets," and questioned the need for collective farming. In addition, throughout the year, Prešov newspapers printed letters from Soviet citizens who protested against the suppression of Ukrainian culture in the USSR. They published an interview with the Ukrainian dissident Ivan Dziuba, as well as giving voice to a Ukrainian from Kyiv who wrote about the deaths of Ukrainian writers in Soviet concentration camps, and the loss of ten million lives in the famine of 1932-3.[14] The cross-border flow of what Soviet leaders deemed harmful information did not stop in August 1968. Participants in public gatherings were reportedly dismayed that official Czechoslovak radio and television, as well as underground radio stations, continued to propagate "counterrevolutionary" ideas after 21 August.[15]

Transnational contacts that Soviet leaders had been building in Eastern Europe since 1956, including cross-border travel between the USSR and Czechoslovakia, now became another source of concern for top apparatchiks in Kyiv. Petro Shelest, the first secretary of the Communist Party of Ukraine, raised alarm about the activities of Czechoslovak tourists who visited Soviet Ukraine as he confronted Dubček about illegal pamphlets that they allegedly spread in Transcarpathia.[16] Similarly, the Ukrainian KGB saw Soviet-Czechoslovak pen-pal programs as a source of "revisionist" ideas in the USSR, citing an intercepted letter that a student from Prague had posted to a ninth-grader in Odesa:

> What we have here is a real revolution. A great revolution … But there is one danger. It is possible that your armies, along with the Germans, will deal a bloody blow to our revolution. I cannot understand why your students have not done anything … Everyone wants a free and socialist Czechoslovakia. And we will get it. If your armies march into Czechoslovakia, many students, myself included, will form partisan units to fight against all those who want to destroy our freedom. I hope that you will be informing all students about this. Our freedom, our democracy is a little older than yours and we do not want anyone to teach us how to go about it.[17]

Transnational contacts with the near abroad thus challenged Soviet narratives of socialism and friendship among the population of Ukraine.

Notably, warning signals from Kyiv did not seem to affect Moscow's approach to cultural and public diplomacy before August 1968. When the Department of Propaganda and Agitation of the Communist Party of Ukraine Central Committee asked Moscow to decrease the amount of Czechoslovak publications in Ukraine in May, for example, they were informed that the issue would be considered after the Czechoslovak Communist Party Central Committee plenum.[18] Their request fell on deaf ears, or in any case it was never fully satisfied. Over two months after the CPU compiled their report, on 30 July 1968, the Czechoslovak press was still easily accessible in Ukraine by subscription and in retail outlets.[19] State and party officials in Ukraine were more determined to tighten the Soviet state border (both physical and cultural) than their superiors in Moscow.

From party leaders' point of view, the most pressing task was to make Soviet mass media more attractive than foreign broadcasts and unofficial sources of information. The Sumy region Communist Party secretary Kozyrev argued that local press, television, and radio should report on recent events before the news reached people from abroad in a distorted form.[20] Yet the authorities found it difficult to make Soviet broadcasts appealing, especially in western Ukraine, largely because the standard of Soviet programming did not compare well with East European media. In February 1968, the Propaganda and Agitation Department of the CPU Central Committee warned that the Uzhgorod television studio (the construction of which was already delayed by two years) produced a few trial broadcasts of poor quality, and still failed to come up with regular transmissions. The programs were "long-winded and pompous," resulting in inhabitants of the Transcarpathia lowlands tuning in to Czechoslovak, Hungarian, and Romanian television instead.[21] The need to improve the quality of Soviet programs in western Ukraine fuelled tensions between Petro Shelest in Kyiv, who was increasingly frustrated that foreign media affected popular opinion in the region, and state and party officials in Moscow, who did not seem to appreciate the gravity of the situation.[22]

To put it mildly, attempts to reduce the influence of foreign sources of information in Ukraine were amateurish. In the Chernivtsi oblast, for example, authorities worried about the influence of Romanian media, which sympathised with Dubček, and allegedly, encouraged Soviet citizens of Romanian origin to criticise Soviet policies. Consequently, officials in the borderlands conducted what they called "individual work" with local residents. This amounted to a door-to-door campaign in parts of western Ukraine with significant Romanian-speaking minorities. In the village of Gorbivs'k, for example, local agitators counted the number of television antennas turned towards Romania, concluding that twenty-five out of seventy families with televisions chose Romanian over Soviet broadcasts. After receiving a visit from party activists, fifteen families turned their antennas towards the Soviet broadcasting station in Chernivtsi. Travelling to the village, senior members of the regional party organisation sought to undermine the isolating and private nature of watching television: they convinced the villagers to choose the Soviet media and thereby to display their loyalty to the Soviet state and its policy.[23] Still, tactics adopted by the officials here could not assure that the public at large would follow the fifteen families in Gorbivs'k, reflecting the generally ambivalent attitudes of the political elites towards television.[24]

Gorbivs'k was not an isolated case. Party officials who organised agitation meetings in 1968 complained that the Romanian media constantly compromised their indoctrination work. As Romanian leader Nikolae Ceauşescu pursued more autonomy from Moscow and even made irredentist claims on Soviet territory,[25] the Romanian media condemned Warsaw Pact interference in the internal affairs of Czechoslovakia.[26] But unlike the Czechoslovak leadership, Romanian leaders never outlined an ambitious reform program that challenged Soviet visions of socialism, and in the months after the invasion of Czechoslovakia, became distinctly less confrontational (e.g., they advised Romanian travellers to the USSR to avoid provoking Soviet citizens). Moreover, in stark contrast to the military invasion of Czechoslovakia, Soviet reaction to the Romanian situation was much more restrained.[27] For these reasons, the Romanian crisis had less impact on Soviet popular opinion than the Prague Spring.

Ultimately, Soviet policies governing the flow of information across borders were jumbled and ineffective. Domestic mass media in the USSR did not provide a decisive rebuke to what the authorities considered to be "harmful" ideas from Eastern Europe. For one, pressures to maintain close cultural ties within the socialist camp led to some spectacular blunders. Although the Polish theatre evoked so much controversy in 1968, for example, officials in Moscow and Warsaw decided to show a selection of Polish plays on Soviet television.[28] Soon, however, the Central Committee complained that editors at Soviet central television took no account of the current international situation when planning their broadcasts: on 20 March, in the immediate aftermath of the Polish students' strikes, they ill-advisedly showed *The Mendicant Student*, an operetta about the struggle of Polish students "for their rights" in 1704. The program romanticized student strikes and led Communist Party Central Committee specialists on propaganda and communications – the former *Izvestiia* chief editor Vladimir Stepakov and the engineer Kirill Simonov – to conclude that Soviet television focused too much on light entertainment instead of producing educated viewers.[29]

But the problem was not just poor planning and management. Rather, the lack of a clear ideological stance in Soviet mass media reflected a deeper crisis of public and cultural diplomacy in the socialist camp. Tasked not only with shaping popular opinion at home, but also improving diplomatic relations in the socialist camp, Soviet journalists were careful not to step on Dubček's toes. Even when it became increasingly obvious that Prague was departing from the Soviet model, and the press began to depict reform communists as "revisionists" (a term used to designate unacceptable types of reform),[30] the Soviet media continued to present Dubček as a sovereign leader. As late as 18 July, *Pravda* and *Izvestiia* renounced military invasion as a possible solution to the crisis.[31] Soviet newspapers even offered a platform for Czechoslovak journalists, academics, and politicians to defend their right to pursue national reform. In June 1968, *Literaturnaia gazeta* printed a letter from the Czech writer Jan Procházka in which he criticized the newspaper's depictions of himself: "I regret that my interest in Czech and Slovak destiny is classified as bourgeois nationalism."[32] On another level, in rebuking Czechoslovak ideas, the Soviet media effectively informed citizens about new ideological trends in Prague.[33]

Managing the Soviet Information Sphere

The escalation of the Czechoslovak crisis transformed Soviet policies governing mass media and, more broadly, the flow of information across borders. The spread of Dubček's ideas in the USSR, followed by the brutal suppression of Czechoslovak reforms, exposed "socialist friendship" as a façade that masked fundamental differences between the Soviet Union and its satellite states. Unable to define a common bloc-wide outlook on key ideological, cultural, and political issues, Soviet media did not apply the slogan "national in form, socialist in content" to the people's democracies. Rather, it recast the USSR's relationship with Eastern Europe in terms of more traditional international relations, seeking to define the limits of national autonomy under Soviet control. From 1968, the goal of Soviet mass media was not to create a transnational socialist East European identity, but only to distinguish between forms of national expression that threatened Soviet state interests and those that helped strengthen the Soviet bloc. The nation was, for all intents and purposes, the most important locus of identity in the socialist camp.

In a conversation with his Polish colleagues in September 1968, Petr Nilovich Demichev, a CPSU Central Committee Secretary and future Soviet Minister of Culture, conceived of cultural diplomacy in terms of a competition over the proper definition of "independence": "We are currently preparing publications to celebrate the fiftieth anniversary of Czechoslovak independence. They are preparing this anniversary under nationalist slogans. The point is to get there first."[34] In effect, this meant that Soviet media outlined clear national hierarchies within the socialist camp, suggesting that East European nations owed a debt of gratitude to the Soviet big brother. In May 1968, for example, *Pravda Ukrainy* emphasised that Czechoslovak patriots expressed their "genuine gratitude for the heroic efforts of the Soviet people [*sovetskii narod*] who liberated Czechoslovak towns and villages from the fascist yoke."[35] By June 1968, newspapers wrote that Dubček's reforms undermined Czechoslovak respect for the USSR and its "great achievements."[36]

From this perspective, "revisionist" forces in Czechoslovakia were not only "antisocialist," but first and foremost "anti-Soviet."[37] The concept of a Soviet-led Eastern Europe thus helped to justify the invasion of Czechoslovakia and reinforced a broader campaign to create a Soviet people in the USSR itself. The press cast the Soviet-Czechoslovak relationship as a friendship between two distinct peoples, with Soviet citizens encouraged to take pride in their country's past, and to work for their homeland in the present.[38]

The Soviet bloc was defined in historical and geographical, not ideological terms. In line with this, the newspaper *Krasnaia Zvezda* described the concept of Central Europe as a hostile assault on natural affinities, produced by "Western specialists in ideological subversion" who sought to "tear Czechoslovakia away from the socialist commonwealth."[39] In order to justify Soviet sovereignty in the near abroad, Soviet opinion leaders evoked the idea of Eastern Europe as a territory that had historically developed in close alliance with Russia and the USSR.

A Soviet version of pan-Slavism helped to redefine the Soviet-East European friendship in explicitly national and ethnically exclusive terms. Describing the "defence of socialism" as "the highest international duty" on 22 August, *Pravda* also wrote about "the centuries old traditions of Slavic community."[40] This ethno-centric rhetoric echoed some of the statements published in the USSR in the aftermath of the Polish crisis earlier in the year, when *Pravda* and *Radians'ka Ukraina* printed Gomułka's speech about Polish-Soviet friendship, and the threat of "German imperialism," "Zionism," and "cosmopolitanism."[41] In Soviet propaganda, Eastern Europe was cast as a predominantly Slavic community, united against German and Jewish outsiders. History was a very important battleground in 1968, as attempts to cast the region's past in any competing terms (e.g. in the context of the "Central European" Habsburg Empire) undermined Soviet claims to shape politics in the satellite states.

The prominence of ethnic categories in Soviet coverage of East European affairs had wide-reaching implications for nationalities policy at home. For one, it built into the anti-Semitic rhetoric of the Soviet media, which identified enemies of the USSR with Jews in the aftermath of the 1967 Arab-Israeli conflict.[42] The Prague Spring also shook the foundations of the Ukrainian cultural revival of the 1960s. In line with the ambiguous status of Ukrainian cultural autonomy, the Soviet media variously defined residents of the republic as Soviet and Soviet Ukrainian people vis-à-vis the foreigners in Eastern Europe. For example, when *Literaturna Ukraina* printed an interview with the Czech scholar Václav Židlický on 19 April 1968, it wrote about both

Ukrainian-Czechoslovak and Soviet-Czechoslovak international cooperation.[43] More prominently, however, portrayals of the Prague Spring acted as a warning against framing Ukrainian identities without referencing the supposedly eternal Russo-Ukrainian friendship. Indeed, the Soviet Ukrainian press drew explicit links between Czechoslovak and Ukrainian "bourgeois nationalism." On 28 October 1969, *Radians'ka Ukraina* cited Slovak communist leader Vasil Bil'ak, who labelled the enemies of socialism in Czechoslovakia as "our Mazepas" who unsuccessfully tried to "undermine our friendship with the Soviet Union."[44] By comparing anti-Soviet nationalists to an early eighteenth-century Cossack leader who opposed the Russian Tsar, the article invoked the idea of a Russian-dominated Slavic community, suggesting that Ukrainian residents' loyalty to the Soviet Union was tantamount to a close Ukrainian-Russian political union.

It is also striking that federalism in Czechoslovakia was hardly discussed in the Soviet Ukrainian press in 1968 and 1969, and it did not figure at all in public anti-Czechoslovak polemics, even though reports from agitation meetings show that residents of the republic asked about the relationship between Czechs and Slovaks over and over again.[45] It seems likely that the subject was too sensitive to raise in the media.[46] With the Slovaks striving towards greater autonomy in Czechoslovakia, the authorities wanted to prevent inhabitants of Ukraine from questioning the position of their own republic in the USSR.

In this way, the crisis in Czechoslovakia played into high politics in the USSR. The first secretary of the Communist Party of Ukraine, Petro Shelest, generally recognized as giving new life to Ukrainian language and culture during the 1960s,[47] was very vocal in condemning developments in Czechoslovakia. Conceivably, he sought to demonstrate to Moscow that his limited endorsement of Ukrainian culture was different from Czechoslovak policies,[48] despite – or perhaps because of – his genuine fear of a potential spillover of the Prague Spring into Ukraine.[49] In his diaries, Shelest berated Brezhnev for his indecisiveness during the crisis, claiming that the Soviet leader fainted after the decision was made to invade Czechoslovakia.[50] Meanwhile, developments in Czechoslovakia helped to discredit Shelest's relatively liberal national policy. Volodymyr Shcherbyts'kyi had no scruples about subordinating the republic's interests to those of the Soviet state. As such, he was seen as more reliable by the Kremlin and his position in the CPU was strengthened during 1968.[51] Interestingly, Shcherbyts'kyi's evaluation of political stability in Czechoslovakia was much less alarmist than that of

Shelest, and he was less supportive of military intervention.[52] Because Dubček's "national road towards socialism" cast doubts on the extent to which ethno-national interests were compatible with existing Soviet-style regimes, the Czechoslovak crisis posed a potential challenge to Shelest's alliance with the Ukrainian cultural intelligentsia. By contrast, like Brezhnev, who initially took a more tolerant position towards Alexander Dubček's liberalisation than Shelest, Gomułka or Ulbricht,[53] Shcherbyts'kyi's political vision combined loyalty to Soviet institutions in return for political stability, social benefits, and economic growth.

Conservative Patriotism: Naming and Shaming Enemies

> I took part in the fight to liberate Czechoslovakia. I remember how ordinary, honest Czechoslovaks joyfully welcomed our armies. They are not to blame for the fact that counterrevolutionaries have now risen up in their country.[54]

This quote from K.P. Korshun, an accountant from the small town of Khust in the Transcarpathia region, echoed thousands of other participants in public meetings throughout Ukraine. Unsure about the influence of the mass media over the population, Soviet leaders resorted to the tried-and-tested party and agitation gatherings to shape public discussion in 1968 and 1969. In stark contrast to meetings that took place in the aftermath of the 1956 Polish and Hungarian crises, these gatherings were now extremely dull and formulaic.[55] Like Korshun, many participants whose statements were recorded were decorated war veterans and party members deemed to be reliable and active. Recalling the sacrifices of the Great Patriotic War, they spoke of their great concern for the future of the socialist camp. Unlike in 1956, numerous reports claimed that the local authorities registered "no undesirable opinions" during public meetings.[56] Yet, although agitation gatherings no longer provided a forum for meaningful discussion, they fulfilled an important function. Many inhabitants of Ukraine spoke in public to prove their patriotic credentials, and thereby improve their social standing in the USSR. The aspirational middle class came into its own during public discussion surrounding the Prague Spring.

Mass agitation meetings occurred in several waves over 1968. The first took place at collective farms, factories, and other institutions between 22 and 27 March, where participants expressed support for Gomułka's "decisive actions" in the aftermath of the student strikes in Poland.[57] Overseen by the regional party leader Vasilii Kutsevol,

3 Petro Shelest during a visit to school number 7 in Mukachevo, Transcarpathia. During the Prague Spring, authorities in Kyiv paid particular attention to popular opinion in the borderland region of Transcarpathia. Tsentral'nyi Derzhavnyi Arkhiv Hromads'kykh Ob"ednan' Ukrainy, Kyiv. Fond 330, op.1, d.21, l.15

agitation work was particularly intensive in the Lviv oblast.[58] Iurii Vasyliovych Il'nyts'kyi similarly set out to carefully monitor popular opinion in Transcarpathia, a region bordering on Czechoslovakia. The head of the Transcarpathian party organisation, and himself born in the region under Czechoslovak rule in the 1920s, Il'nyts'kyi was painfully aware of developments unfolding just across the border and raised alarm about a potential spillover of the Czechoslovak crisis.[59]

A wave of mass agitation meetings about Czechoslovakia geared towards party members and non-members alike took place between June and August 1968.[60] The meetings were ritualistic, with participants criticising foreign mass media and citing the Soviet press, radio, and television to publicly manifest their "correct" point of view.[61] As such, the gatherings were unlikely to provide participants with any more information than they could gather from the Soviet media – the agitators' role was often limited to reading TASS announcements and other press materials.[62] Nevertheless, through the very act of organising large meetings, the authorities showed that they expected residents of Ukraine to publicly manifest their support for Moscow's foreign policy.[63] The CPU leaders in Kyiv deemed the mass media an inadequate means of controlling popular opinion in the republic, concerned as they were by the influence of foreign broadcasts. It was through explicit condemnation of the "unorthodox" or "counterrevolutionary" East European media that citizens proved their loyalty to the Soviet state.

Active involvement in public meetings distinguished the most reliable citizens from the mass of participants. In late June of 1968, 791,747 people participated in public meetings devoted to Czechoslovakia, but only 9,415 actually spoke.[64] Party members on their way up the hierarchy (such as members and candidate members of raikoms, gorkoms, the obkoms, and the CPSU's regional branches) had more opportunities to publicly voice their "correct" views about Czechoslovakia than other members of society.[65] Speakers at public meetings typically acted as leaders of public opinion at home: "we must not lose control over the education of the masses, because [otherwise] … we might face negative consequences," underscored a manager and engineer from Odesa.[66] Like in 1956, it was also a common practice to speak on behalf of entire communities.[67]

Although public gatherings organised in the aftermath of the Czechoslovak crisis did not resemble the more open and conflict-ridden meetings of 1956, a public sphere that emerged during the Thaw survived the fall of Khrushchev. As Kristin Roth-Ey points out, the rise of television facilitated "the transformation of an active Soviet person into a passive and childlike viewer." Because of its location in the home, television provided room for the celebration of something resembling a Soviet "couch potato." Yet, at a time of crisis, Soviet apparatchiks still exerted pressure on residents of Ukraine to act as concerned citizens in public.[68] Commenting on the news they obtained from the mass media in various public forums, citizens did not engage in meaningful debate about the Prague Spring; still, they used the meetings to demonstrate a desire for middle-class custodianship of society. This was the conservative vision of citizenship in 1968 – proponents of conservative patriotism understood participatory citizenship not as meaningful public discussion of policy, but as the ability to claim a privileged status in Soviet society.

Conservative patriotism challenged the authorities in 1956, as citizens attacked Khrushchev's de-Stalinization for supposedly leading to violence and instability in the outer empire.[69] In contrast, with Stalin nostalgia and fear of war much weaker than in 1956, citizens who publicly condemned Dubček's reforms in Czechoslovakia refrained from criticising Soviet leadership in the late 1960s. Rather, they focused on identifying enemies of Soviet power among foreigners, members of non-titular ethnic minorities, and "bourgeois" nationalists who did not share the Soviet vision of what it meant to be Ukrainian. The making of enemies was a crucial part of the social hierarchies that emerged via ritualised politics.

Like in 1956, some residents of Ukraine's western oblasts feared the outbreak of a major war at the height of the Czechoslovak crisis. In preparation for war, some residents of Transcarpathia bought up great quantities of soap, salt, and matches, whilst others prepared to leave the region and escape east.[70] National tensions between Soviet Ukraine and Eastern Europe once again preoccupied residents of the borderlands. In this vein, after 21 August, two students from Uzhgorod wrote to their parents in Lviv and Kamianets-Podilskyi, relaying rumours to the effect that the Czechs wanted Transcarpathia back.[71] Whether out of fear or a sense of duty, citizens reported incidents that they considered important for their country's security to the local authorities. For example, Iurii Mykhailovych Karmanov, an amateur radio constructor from Chernihiv, informed the head of a local radio club that he had been contacted by a Czechoslovak underground broadcaster on 24 August. The broadcast was sharp and provocative: "Your army has occupied our country. The tanks and soldiers have killed ten unarmed citizens. Soviet aggressors – go home."[72]

The escalating crisis and the military invasion of Czechoslovakia evoked a form of Soviet patriotic fervour in Ukraine. According to KGB reports, numerous soldiers claimed that it was necessary to invade Czechoslovakia in various informal conversations.[73] It seems that Soviet policies in Czechoslovakia had a distinctly personal dimension for many citizens, as people spoke about their friends and relatives in the army during primary party cell meetings.[74] The public also seemed receptive to increasingly xenophobic official narratives in August 1968. In Chernivtsi alone, 100,000 people – more than half the local population – attended cinema screenings of documentaries devoted to Czechoslovakia. A particularly widespread film was *Counterrevolution Shall Not Succeed* (*Kontrrevoliutsiia ne proidet*), which was often screened before feature films. This eleven-minute long documentary portrayed everyday life in Czechoslovakia before and after the invasion. Foreigners across the border emerged as dangerous radicals, with the camera focusing on angry crowds of young "revisionists," West German tourists walking freely on the streets of Prague, crowds applauding anti-systemic speeches by Jan Procházka, and ordinary citizens buying anti-party newspapers. The movie had a clear message: the Czechs were gearing up for war (the camera showed piles of weapons that the enemies had supposedly stocked). The Soviet Union in contrast was represented by top statesmen seeking desperately to find a diplomatic solution to the crisis, as well as brave soldiers attacked brutally by "bandits" in the streets of Prague. *Counterrevolution Shall Not Succeed* had a happy ending, as the closing scenes showed young people cleaning anti-socialist slogans off building walls.[75] According to local officials, inhabitants of Chernivtsi watched the movie with great interest and often applauded the "heroic acts" of the Soviet army, and reacted very vocally to images of "sabotage" aimed at "our soldiers."[76]

Other sources also indicate that citizens publicly expressed support for Soviet policies in the near abroad and described foreigners as enemies during 1968. Their statements were sometimes framed in ideological terms. For example, participants in public gatherings expressed suspicion about the idea of "national independence" from the USSR, ascribing it to bourgeois influences and Western imperialism. "Independence from what and from whom?" exclaimed a participant of a public meeting in Donetsk – perhaps the Romanian media which claimed to defend Czechoslovak sovereignty referred to independence from "scientific communism and Marxism-Leninism," he charged.[77] Equally, however, citizens expressed a sense of great power pride that bore little explicit relation to the party's ideology. After the invasion, some believed that the USSR should adopt a still stricter policy in Eastern Europe, asking agitators to explain why the army did not invade Romania, too.[78] The way these citizens spoke about Eastern Europe reflected the apparent recognition and acceptance that Soviet-style socialism failed to take root in the near abroad, and that the USSR's control of its satellites was based on force. This did not necessarily reflect genuine belief, but it set the tone of public debates about the near abroad.

Speaking about Soviet national security, participants in public meetings quickly turned on internal enemies whom they accused of weakening the Soviet homeland. In late August 1968, for example, fifteen taxi drivers from Luhansk held a special meeting to discuss a forty-five-year-old non-party colleague who had spoken to his passengers about the high standard of living abroad, and what he referred to as the "occupation" of Czechoslovakia. They very aggressively branded I.K. Khudobin ungrateful and ignorant:

> I fought in the Finnish campaign and the Great Patriotic War. I took part in liberating Hungary, Poland, Romania, and Bulgaria. I have been to Germany. But there is no country better than our Homeland – remember this, Khudobin ... I am simply too disgusted to even look at you and your idiotic tongue.

In parallel with 1956, the language was hateful and uncompromising, suggesting that expressions of conservative patriotism were used to disparage dissent as unpatriotic. Sovietness was thus conceived as unquestioning allegiance to a territorially defined homeland. But precisely because belonging was defined in these terms, Khudobin found it relatively easy to retain his job. He admitted that he had made a mistake and publicly manifested his patriotic credentials as he promised to "go wherever the Motherland calls."[79]

The shaming of enemies was an important practice in the army, as soldiers publicly condemned their colleagues who spoke out against the invasion. On 28 August, the political department of the Kyiv military district wrote about a group of officers who listened to a Soviet radio program about "brotherly help" shown to Czechoslovakia in 1945. One of them commented that, unlike the Great Patriotic War, nobody asked the USSR for assistance now, and yet "we still marched in." His comment provoked lively protests among other officers present in the room, and he was later required to report to the commander of his unit. He explained that the comment was an ignorant joke.[80] Not only did the man seek to reinstate his conservative patriotic credentials by repudiating his earlier statements, but his case also offered an opportunity for other officers to prove that they remained committed to the Soviet cause.

The ritual of naming and shaming internal enemies acquired strong xenophobic undertones. Citizens who spoke in public talked of non-titular ethnic minorities – those that did not have ethnically designated republics in the USSR – as inherently suspect and disloyal. According to Polish diplomats in Moscow, Władysław Gomułka's anti-Semitic speech, in which he blamed "Zionists" for the trouble in Poland, found great resonance in the USSR itself:

> *Pravda* printed an extra two million copies of the issue in which the speech was published ... But the demand was even higher, and people asked after newspapers containing Władysław Gomułka's speech over the next few days. My old friends, Soviet citizens, told me that entire families spent the night reading the speech, with relatives sharing one copy among each other. I know of cases where extracts from the speech were read over the phone.[81]

To be sure, the Polish diplomats may well have been pandering to their superiors in Warsaw, but it appears that residents of the USSR and Soviet Ukraine specifically did find Gomułka's speech interesting. They asked many questions concerning the role of Jews in the Polish disturbances during agitation gatherings.[82]

Some members of ethnic minorities made an effort to defend themselves against popular suspicions of disloyalty, especially during informal conversations relayed by the KGB.[83] In early April, a sewing factory worker by the name of Zaltsman tried to distance himself from "Zionism," stating that Gomułka sounded so convinced about the Zionist plot that "it must be true," and concluded "the Jews must decide whose side they are on." For his part, a local rabbi Bronfenbrener went so far as to deny that the problem of anti-Semitism existed at all, claiming that Gomułka's speech was not anti-Semitic because it emphasised that most Jews were loyal to the Polish state. Consequently, he claimed, "we, the Jews, have no reason to worry."[84] Some Soviet citizens of Polish and Czech origin similarly highlighted their alienation from their rebellious external homelands.[85] Even as they emphasised loyalty to the USSR, these individuals identified explicitly with their ethnic communities by speaking of "Jews," "Poles," or "Czechs" as having particular obligations in the USSR. Members of non-titular minorities often took for granted that their relationship to the Soviet state was mediated through ethnic belonging.

At times, Soviet apparatchiks condemned some openly anti-Semitic statements in internal party correspondence.[86] The censure of anti-Semitism can partly be explained by Brezhnev's growing suspicion of Russian nationalism and the "Russian party" which had previously challenged his authority in the Politburo, and still preserved influence in journals such as *Molodaia gvardiia* and *Ogonek*.[87] During the second half of the 1960s, Brezhnev became suspicious of the "red patriots" who articulated a sense of Stalin nostalgia, and began to join forces with young "anti-communist" Russian nationalists, adopting some of their anti-Semitic views.[88] Still, as high-ranking Soviet officials such as Petr Demichev discussed both anti-Semitism and Zionism as a problem that transcended the Soviet-Polish border, they revealed their own anti-Semitic prejudice. "Zionist forces have become distinctly more active. The masses can feel it. In consequence, we can observe a backlash in the form of anti-Semitic moods," Demichev claimed in a conversation with a Polish diplomat in Moscow, blaming the rise of anti-Semitism on the Jews themselves.[89]

More broadly, in discussing the Czechoslovak crisis, participants in public meetings raised alarm about anti-Soviet nationalism. Expressions of Ukrainian national identity were now more constrained than during the early 1960s, as Soviet opinion leaders more frequently contrasted reliable citizens with "bourgeois nationalists."[90] The term was fluid and open to interpretation. It generally designated individuals who articulated an understanding of what it meant to be Ukrainian that differed from the official Soviet script. Still, it is striking that forms of national expression that were accepted as properly "Soviet" in previous months and years were deemed "bourgeois" at the height of the Prague Spring. In particular, the Czechoslovak crisis fuelled attacks on prominent Ukrainian cultural figures, with Oles' Honchar and his novel *Sobor* coming under especially harsh criticism. Although the novel initially gathered rather positive reviews, it became a target of a major "anti-nationalist" campaign by the summer of 1968.[91] In his diary, Honchar himself interpreted the attacks on his novel and the invasion of Czechoslovakia as part of the same global crisis: "They tortured [my novel] for four hours ... Our tanks are supposed to enter Czechoslovakia tomorrow morning. Events in the world are taking a dramatic turn."[92]

All in all, debates surrounding the events in Eastern Europe affected the discourse of ethno-cultural identities in Ukraine. For party leaders and KGB officers, ethnic minorities that did not have their own republics and communist parties in the USSR were the usual suspects that helped explain any manifestations of social discontent in Ukraine. Some members of non-titular ethnic groups challenged conceptions of rights defined in ethnically exclusive terms. However, the ideal of a multi-ethnic "Soviet people" – grounded in familiarity with the Russian language and culture, and frustrated by day-to-day xenophobia – was an ambition that was not so much unattainable, but ultimately unimaginable in a society where every citizen was assigned one ethnic identity ("Soviet" was not an option) in his or her internal passport.[93]

The point to be made here is not simply that residents of Soviet Ukraine developed ethnically based notions of nationhood, or that xenophobia was widespread in Soviet society. What is more surprising, particularly in a state founded as a "dictatorship of the proletariat," is that ethnicity shaped how citizens and representatives of the Soviet state related to each other in public. This was not unique to the USSR at all, but was in fact rooted in the Soviet political system. Assigning personal ethnic identity to each and every citizen, and yet claiming that nationality was a territorial and political concept expressed through such ethno-federal units as Ukraine, Soviet leaders created tensions between ethnic minorities and "nationalising" institutions designed to represent integral national communities.[94]

Reformist Patriotism

Freedom, equality, democracy – this is how a prisoner from the Donetsk oblast described the Prague Spring in a poem he wrote during 1968. His appeal to the "peoples of Russia" illustrated another trend in Soviet reactions to the Czechoslovak events when a small but very vocal group of Soviet citizens began to criticise the Soviet state for its betrayal of "socialist ideals."[95] Demanding a more tolerant nationalities policy in the USSR and calling for "openness" and "spiritual renewal" of Soviet society, they also criticised the Warsaw Pact invasion of Czechoslovakia. This was a generation that built on the ideas of reformist patriotism expressed in support of Gomułka's policies in 1956 (with his xenophobic policy and brutal suppression of student protests in 1968, Gomułka was no longer a reformist hero). Starting in the mid-1960s, supporters of these views insisted that many features of Stalinism in the USSR had not been eliminated, urging "popular vigilance and protest" should the authorities fail to make a fundamental break with the past.[96] Whereas conservative patriotism framed Soviet identities in ethnic terms, reformist patriotism held that commitment to socialism was a key part of what it meant to be Soviet. But they looked to Czechoslovakia and not the Soviet Party leadership to define what socialism meant or should mean.

Soviet citizens were more reluctant to criticise the authorities in 1968 than in 1956, and reformist patriotism never amounted to more than ad hoc questions and comments. As Nikolai Podgornyi put it in a conversation with the chair of the Polish Supreme Soviet, "during the Warsaw Pact operation in Czechoslovakia, even those people who had earlier distributed various pamphlets and declarations calmed down."[97] With Moscow's crackdown on Dubček's project and the increasing determination to root out dissent at home,[98] reformist ideas were increasingly pushed outside the boundaries of acceptable Soviet discourse. Proponents of reformist patriotism in 1968 mostly expressed their views in private conversations and underground publications. They faced prison sentences for "anti-Soviet agitation" and lost their jobs, party membership, and the right to study at university.[99]

Nevertheless, dissenting voices continued to trouble Soviet officials. The KGB's failures to identify the authors of illegal publications and anonymous letters, as well as their generic descriptions of the individuals who voiced "hostile views," make it difficult to determine who the proponents of reformist patriotism were. According to KGB statistics, most citizens who expressed "critical" views at the height of the Czechoslovak crisis were white collar workers, followed by blue collar workers, collective farmers, and students. The great majority of KGB reports concerned non-party members.[100]

As usual, university students came under suspicion. In a diary entry from early September 1968, Petro Shelest saw the Shevchenko University in Kyiv as a source of trouble:

> There was a meeting with students and professors ... The next day I received a libelous, offensive letter. What did I bother the students for, they say, why did I lie about Czechoslovakia and whitewash the state of affairs in the Union and in the republic? The tone of this note was not only cocky, but also offensive to me personally and to our system. I was deeply hurt and unsettled, it took me a long time to get over this cockiness. The note was written in Ukrainian, as a poem. It was signed: "Students listened to you."[101]

If KGB reports are to be trusted, the majority of students in cities such as Odesa sympathised with Dubček's ideas, which suggests that reformist patriotism was more geographically widespread than twelve years earlier when it concentrated in Kyiv and Moscow.[102]

Yet the extent to which the ideas of "reform socialism" permeated the universities was limited. Even the authorities were convinced that student complaints against the invasion of Czechoslovakia were primarily an expression of youth rebellion that did not automatically translate into a consistent effort to change Soviet foreign policy, or to copy Czechoslovak reforms in the USSR itself. Some KGB reports thus claimed that students found the very word "opposition" appealing.[103] At least in the authorities' view, young people's fascination with Czechoslovak reform ideas was tempered by a sense of Soviet distinctiveness from the near abroad. A report about university students, transmitted after the invasion of Czechoslovakia but completed sometime before then, highlighted young people's alienation from official ideology and their receptivity to Western culture, but also pointed towards the "resentment that most students felt toward the Soviet Union's 'fraternal' allies."[104] Just as in 1956, many students in 1968 saw Soviet tanks in Eastern Europe as "their" tanks.

Furthermore, both before and after 21 August, KGB reports suggested that anti-war sentiments spread among soldiers stationed in Ukraine and those sent to Czechoslovakia. Talking among colleagues, a few privates and officers claimed that the USSR should not interfere in Czechoslovak domestic affairs.[105] Doubts about the nature and consequences of the invasion, both personal and political, were particularly sharp among Soviet soldiers stationed in Czechoslovakia. In letters to relatives back in Ukraine, they often described their isolation and difficult living conditions. One soldier went so far as to threaten to "put a bullet through his head,"[106] and another wrote to his fiancée stating that there was a 99% chance he would not come back alive.[107] Moreover, according to the CPU Central Committee, the army was exposed to "hostile" opinions. Soviet soldiers in Czechoslovakia were reportedly shocked by the anti-Soviet propaganda in the country and the "bourgeois lifestyle" of the Czechoslovak youth.[108] In their letters home, soldiers often included "nationalist" and anti-Soviet pamphlets spread in Czechoslovakia – in late October, the KGB registered between ten and fifteen such instances every day.[109] However, it is difficult to determine whether this reflected any allegiance to the cause of reformist patriotism in the army, or merely showed that soldiers took an interest in the Prague Spring.

In trying to determine the source of trouble, numerous surveillance reports specified the ethnic background of the individuals who expressed dissenting views, especially when they were Jewish, even though the opinions in question did not often concern ethnic or religious issues.[110] Principally, this shows that KGB officers and party apparatchiks believed that there was a link between Jewishness and "anti-Soviet views." Yet it is conceivable, of course, that people of Jewish origin were more outspoken proponents of reformist patriotism than other Soviet citizens. Allegedly, some of them linked the Czechoslovak crisis to Soviet relations with Israel, a particularly thorny issue in the aftermath of the Six Day War,[111] as well as commented on the publication of Gomułka's speech in the Soviet press. In private conversations, some residents of Jewish origin in Odesa praised Warsaw's decision to allow the Jews to emigrate, claiming that the "swine" in the Soviet leadership would never agree to that.[112]

Yaacov Ro'i argues that Soviet support for the Arabs during the Six Day War and the rise of anti-Semitism in the USSR during the late 1960s convinced many Jews that "they were not and could not be an integral part of the Soviet body politic and of Soviet society."[113] However, it is striking that Jewish residents of Ukraine who commented on events in Eastern Europe were also outraged by the rise of anti-Semitism and wanted the authorities to reinstate a more tolerant nationalities policy in Soviet-style regimes, rather than simply claiming the right to leave the USSR.[114] These views were sometimes articulated in severe terms. In Odesa, the KGB recorded the opinion of a sixty-eight-year-old Jewish party member L.G. Lenskii who underlined that several tanks and thirty-seven servicemen burned to death in Czechoslovakia. He claimed that the Soviet and Polish governments were "fascists and not communists" as they occupied Czechoslovakia without proper justification, and following in the footsteps of Tsar Nicholas and Hitler, used Jews as a "scape goat."[115] Lenskii acted as a citizen concerned about Soviet soldiers and the failure of Soviet leaders to combat anti-Semitism. His views betrayed both faith in "communism" and rejection of the pronouncements by the CPSU Central Committee.

In sum, it is very difficult to define who supported reformist patriotism. While reform-minded patriots in 1956 had various attitudes towards the state – ranging from explicit support for Khrushchev's new course to protest and dissent – most supporters of reformist patriotism in 1968 harboured unambiguously negative feelings towards Brezhnev's leadership, especially after the military intervention in August. Disappointed as they were with the Soviet state's apparent reluctance to reform, they did not hope to pursue the interests of any particular social group, but rather focused on the need to force the leaders to become more responsive to reformist demands in the first place. Consequently, in contrast to the citizens who had openly spoken during public meetings in 1956 in the name of their student collectives, writers' unions, or workers' brigades, advocates of reformist patriotism now normally operated clandestinely and identified themselves by such pseudonyms as "voice of the people" or "revolutionary worker."[116]

Rather than ascribing dissenting views to particular social groups, it is easier to define reformist patriotism as a set of ideas. Most prominently, proponents of reformist patriotism defended the idea of participatory citizenship, understood as the ability to comment on and shape policy, at a time when public discussion of foreign and domestic affairs was increasingly constrained. For example, in a private conversation intercepted by the KGB, a fourth year student from Lviv University Natalia Zabolotna despaired that students in western Ukraine were less active than in Moscow, as she added that "something had to happen" here, too.[117] Her comment was underpinned by a sense of belonging in a Soviet community that included both western Ukraine and Russia. A Jewish worker from Dnipropetrovsk, previously expelled from the party, expressed a similar commitment to fixing Soviet society in a conversation that was subsequently reported to the authorities, as he claimed that the youth would provide the push necessary for reforming the corrupt Soviet system.[118]

Like Russian dissidents,[119] most proponents of reformist patriotism in Ukraine criticised the invasion of Czechoslovakia. In the first two and a half weeks after the invasion, the KGB registered 303 statements critical of the military intervention, as well as 209 cases where citizens referred to the events as an "occupation."[120] In attacking the military measures, some citizens claimed that Moscow violated "Soviet values," which they defined in several different ways. Many of them were rather vague when they articulated their support for "reform socialism," claiming that the USSR did not represent "the type of socialism for which I stood."[121] Four leaflets discovered in Chernihiv on 24 August read that the Soviet Union should learn how to build "socialism" from the Czechs, as the struggle in Czechoslovakia was not a fight between communism and capitalism, but rather a battle between new and old ideas within socialism.[122] One concrete means of demonstrating an active political stance in the aftermath of the Warsaw Pact invasion of Czechoslovakia was to spread illegal pamphlets and post anonymous letters to the authorities. Between 21 August and 12 September 1968, the KGB in Ukraine had registered twenty-three cases of citizens spreading anti-Soviet pamphlets about the invasion of Czechoslovakia, as well as ten examples of graffiti criticising Soviet foreign policy.[123] "Dear comrade, if you are a patriot of your country, make and distribute a few copies of this leaflet," read the back of one anti-invasion pamphlet found in Odesa in late August.[124]

At the same time, some other inhabitants of Ukraine were a little more specific about why they condemned the Soviet suppression of Dubček's reforms. For one, in various informal settings, citizens emphasised that the military intervention would weaken communist parties around the world and blur the division between socialist countries and the capitalist West.[125] The KGB thus claimed to relay *verbatim* the views of a young poet from Dnipropetrovsk, I.G. Sokul'skyi, whom they had been monitoring due to his supposed "nationalist views":

> Our army went into Czechoslovakia today, even though the situation there was not so threatening. This is what it means to follow old traditions and to cower before all that is new, advanced, and progressive. We can't sort things out in our own country, so we've stuck our noses in elsewhere. We have ridiculed ourselves as aggressors in front of the whole world.[126]

Sokul'skyi challenged Moscow-made notions of Eastern Europe as a Soviet near abroad where the USSR had the right to intervene, but also implied that a genuine threat to Soviet-style socialism could have justified an invasion. In a similar vein, a Jewish doctor from Luhansk and a student actor from Kyiv independently despaired that Soviet policies were now no different from US actions in Vietnam.[127] Views like these undermined Soviet leaders' attempts to present their country as the most progressive world power, which was particularly problematic at a time when Vietnamese resistance to the United States "made the Cold War in the Third World a central part of left-wing mobilisation within the pan-European world itself."[128] Yet these opinions were also underpinned by continuing faith in internationalism, and the drive to weaken capitalist influences around the world.

Furthermore, many supporters of reformist patriotism referred to the Prague Spring to argue that Soviet-style systems had to become more egalitarian. During informal conversations, some citizens suggested that the state's insensitivity to citizens' needs aggravated the population's living standards: "we have built socialism … and yet living becomes more and more difficult," despaired an inhabitant of the Odesa oblast. A few citizens came up with suggestions about how to make the Soviet system more equal. In Odesa, speaking among colleagues, a lecturer of political economics Bez'iablonskii applauded the Czechs and Slovaks for trying to create a multi-party system and free trade unions.[129]

Petro Shelest was especially frustrated by what he saw as vague and poorly articulated demands by some students and journalists for the USSR to embrace "unlimited democracy."[130] Not only did Soviet aggression in Czechoslovakia undermine socialism around the world, proponents of reformist patriotism suggested, but it also weakened Soviet institutions at home and led to the militarisation of Soviet society. For instance, local authorities in Chernivtsi found many leaflets spread at the university campus and stairwells around town which claimed that the Komsomol had turned from a youth organisation into an instrument of state control, whose role was now limited to dressing children in uniform and teaching them military discipline.[131] The authors of these materials were concerned that the Soviet authorities failed to mould citizens' attitudes and relied on force instead. The implication was that the Komsomol did not help create the kind of participatory society where distinctions between state and citizens would disappear. Instead of creating New Soviet People, much to the chagrin of the authors, the state relied on military-style discipline to hold society together.

At times, complaints about limited opportunities for political participation in the USSR took on the form of very concrete attacks against the local bureaucracy and even top CPSU apparatchiks. In Uzhgorod, the authorities wrote about S.N. Lendvai, a lawyer of Jewish background employed at the regional chamber of defence lawyers, who claimed among acquaintances that party members, inspired by the example of Czechoslovakia, would dismiss local factory managers.[132] The tone of complaints against corrupt officials was especially sharp after 21 August. As the anonymous residents of Zhdanov (Mariupol') in the Donetsk oblast put it in a letter sent to a Moscow newspaper, the "Soviet people" condemned the "bandit" invasion of Czechoslovakia and Brezhnev's "revisionist" system. The letter was underpinned by a sense of belonging in an imagined Russian nation, suggesting that both Russian and Ukrainian ethnic identities provided a platform for civil mobilization:

> And so the crime has been committed. Because of Brezhnev and his Central Committee the Russian people [*russkii narod*] is once again scorned as the "aggressor." We have not given you the right to justify your misdeeds in the name of the people ... Revisionists – out of Czechoslovakia! Hands off genuine socialism! Long live freedom of speech and freedom of the press! Down with red fascism! Out with Brezhnev! Long live Kosygin![133]

While the authorities characterised similar opinions as anti-Soviet, their proponents tried to claim that they would help to restore "Leninist principles."[134]

Soviet citizens who called for a more representative system in the USSR linked the problem to their ability to access information. Disbelief in the media coverage of Czechoslovakia was widespread.[135] A student calling the reception desk at the Central Committee in Kyiv thus boldly stated: "Tell comrade Shelest that we do not believe *Pravda* materials on Czechoslovakia."[136] In this respect, Ukraine's proponents of reformist patriotism expressed sentiments that underpinned dissent throughout the USSR. By publishing statements by Soviet intellectuals and translations of Czechoslovak documents, Soviet *samizdat* shed its predominantly literary character and turned into an illegal source of news about the unfolding events at home and abroad during 1968.[137] The search for more information encouraged some citizens to advocate reforming the entire media system. For example, leaflets distributed around several stairwells in Chernivtsi accused the Soviet media of "lying" about Czechoslovakia, and concluded that "the dissolution of censorship was the most important precondition for democratising the political system of our country."[138]

While many Soviet citizens were eager to access Czechoslovak mass media,[139] and complained about the quality of the Soviet press, radio, and television, it was only in isolated cases that this led them to engage in illegal activities and demand the entire Soviet system be made more transparent. It is not surprising, considering the harsh punishments the state was ready to dispense. On 22 August, a student from Uzhgorod who condemned the Warsaw Pact invasion decided to express his views by sending a letter to Prague radio. At the very height of the crisis, he manifested his faith in the Czechoslovak media as a reliable channel through which he could voice his concerns, implying that the Soviet media did not represent his interests. The authorities believed that this was a very incriminating act: on 23 March 1969, the court in Uzhgorod sentenced the twenty-four-year-old to three years in a hard labour colony.[140]

Indeed, some citizens still hoped to obtain information through legal channels, showing more loyalty to the Soviet system and its institutions as they called for change. As loyal consumers of the Soviet information market, they refused to be taken for fools. In late April, for example, V.A. Kozlov from Lviv stated in a letter to *Pravda* that the "Soviet people" were not idiots, and understood that their authorities did not trust them with all the available information (*"ved" sovetskii narod ne durak'*), even though people could obtain it from foreign radio stations anyway. His comments were echoed by A.P. Liashko from Dnipropetrovsk and V.M. Volynets from Kyiv, who stated that "regular communists" were concerned by the course of events, and enquired whether *Pravda* editors considered their readers unworthy of "the truth."[141] These letters were not anonymous, and their authors considered themselves to be loyal citizens and party members who had the right to understand how Soviet people should relate to the foreign crises.

The Prague Spring also encouraged advocates of reformist patriotism to discuss the national question. On the most basic level, some individuals distributed copies of the Ukrainian language journals from Czechoslovakia that discussed national issues – one resident of the Kolomyia region in western Ukraine received such publications in multiple copies by post from the Ukrainian minority in Czechoslovakia.[142] Moreover, throughout the latter half of the 1960s, "non-Russian *samizdat* championed 'genuine socialism' and 'the restoration of Lenin's norms'" as a guarantee of greater national autonomy for republics in the USSR.[143] In line with this, during and following the Prague Spring, some authors who published in the *samizdat* and *samvydav* sought to defend "Ukrainian rights," but also underlined their commitment to Soviet institutions. For example, an anonymous writer addressed a letter to Oles' Honchar and secretaries of the Ukrainian Writers' Union. Commenting at length on the situation in Czechoslovakia, the letter complained that Soviet authorities were prejudiced against Ukrainian culture, creating "artificial bureaucratic barriers" which halted its development.[144] Although the author was critical of Soviet nationalities policy, he still appealed to an official Soviet institution to rectify the problem.

Reformist views were underpinned by a sense of Soviet patriotism in 1968. Embarrassed about their country's actions in Czechoslovakia, proponents of reform were primarily concerned with the need to reinstate what they believed to be true participatory citizenship. Scholars have argued that certain groups (including residents of the western oblasts, the Jewish minority, and university students) were most likely to express support for Dubček's reforms,[145] but reformist patriotism as such was not defined by any geographical, ethnic, or social criteria. In fact, reformist patriotism represented a whole spectrum of interests: its advocates defended Ukrainian national rights, condemned anti-Semitism, called for the liberalisation of the Soviet media, and evoked socialist ideas to criticise Soviet repression at home and abroad. None of these concerns were specific to the western borderlands, which have traditionally been seen as the major source of dissenting views in Soviet Ukraine. Faced with an increasingly repressive state, citizens in different parts of Ukraine, from Lviv to Donetsk, claimed that the only way to reform the Soviet system was to introduce freedom of speech and more representative political institutions.

The Other Side of Illegal: Prague Spring and Anti-Soviet Views

Soviet reformist patriotism of 1968 was more openly challenging to the state than the reformist patriotism of 1956. Neither representatives of the state nor the proponents of reformist patriotism harboured many doubts that they were now in opposition to each other. Yet some forms of illegal protest were more radically anti-systemic, and as such do not fit the category of reformist patriotism. They did not represent more than a small minority of all the illegal statements the authorities identified in underground publications or private conversations, but they do show that some citizens did not believe that change could be achieved within the Soviet system. The most prominent among anti-Soviet citizens were Ukrainian nationalists who embraced the cause of independence and concentrated mostly, although not exclusively, in western Ukraine. However, the term "nationalist" does not accurately reflect the range of anti-Soviet opinions in the republic. Whilst commenting on the Prague Spring, inhabitants of Ukraine employed an anti-Soviet nationalist rhetoric to call for a radical restructuring of the economic system, to appeal for religious toleration, or simply to express anger and frustration with the Soviet bureaucracy.

Anti-Soviet opinions represented an explicit renunciation of the Soviet system and its institutions. Consequently, not all cases where citizens attacked the Soviet state and its institutions should be classified as anti-Soviet. The authorities frequently associated anti-state outbursts with "hooliganism" – a term that was often shorthand for public drunkenness and destruction of property. For example, one report informed party leaders about a worker from Melitopol who, upon being arrested for "hooliganism" in the city park one August evening, turned towards a group of youth standing nearby and encouraged them to "sort [the militia officers] out Czechoslovak style."[146] The man's outburst was spontaneous, though it is difficult to determine whether the report writers were accurate and sincere in ascribing it to

4 Vasyl Omelianovych Makukh with his family. Makukh's self-immolation in Kyiv in November 1968 was a protest against the Russification of Ukraine.

his momentary frustration with militia officers. In any case, it seems that for some Soviet citizens, the scope of media coverage surrounding the Prague Spring and the Warsaw Pact invasion turned Czechoslovakia into a symbol of anti-establishment attitudes, meaning that positive references to Dubček's reforms did not necessarily reflect support for altering the system, but rather anger with representatives of the state.[147]

In more radical cases, acts of "hooliganism" reflected a broader dissatisfaction with the Soviet order. Between 1967 and 1969, the KGB informed Shelest about eighty-eight incidents where citizens damaged state insignia, portraits of CPSU officials, and political posters, thus expressing their oppositional stance.[148] Although not necessarily inspired by the Prague Spring in the first instance, these anti-Soviet citizens were certainly fuelled by developments in Czechoslovakia. When a twenty-three-year-old non-party man named Trombak was found producing daggers at his work station in Uzhgorod in the immediate aftermath of the Warsaw Pact invasion, he explained that he was planning to use them to stab communists "like they did in Czechoslovakia."[149] His behaviour may well have simply represented momentary frustration, but it is also conceivable that he saw the Prague Spring as the beginning of an anti-Soviet war.

The Ukrainian authorities were certainly alarmed about the possibility of nationalist resistance to Soviet power in the western borderlands.[150] In other parts of Ukraine, they likewise raised alarm about citizens who made plans to resist the Soviet army. For instance, on 25 September 1968, the Kirovohrad KGB intercepted a letter to the Czechoslovak embassy in Moscow, which contained advice on how to fight against the Soviet army in Czechoslovakia. They managed to identify the author as T.O. Dubavov, a Russian non-party lecturer from the local pedagogical institute who would soon face trial.[151] Unfortunately, it is not clear what his motives were or how he justified his actions, but the letter could not be more anti-Soviet, as it basically amounted to treason.

Surveillance reports about anti-state outbursts did not concentrate exclusively in regions that authorities normally associated with anti-Soviet nationalism. They mostly came from Sumy, Cherkasy, Chernivtsi, Donetsk, Luhansk, Dnipropetrovsk, and Volhynia.[152] Nonetheless, the KGB often equated anti-Soviet views with nationalist influences, even when the opinions they cited did not explicitly concern national questions.[153] No doubt, the link between anti-Sovietness and nationalism was largely constructed by the reports themselves, reflecting the officials' distrust of Ukrainian nationalism defined in opposition to Russia and the USSR. At the same time, it seems that many anti-Soviet citizens employed a national rhetoric to show that they opposed the party and state. This is partly because Soviet leaders often branded their political adversaries in Ukraine as "bourgeois nationalists," and accused them of having cooperated with the Nazi occupiers during the Great Patriotic War.[154] Thus, they inadvertently turned fascist and nationalist symbols into signs of opposition to the Soviet regime. For example, on 9 May, "a fascist symbol" – possibly a swastika or tryzub – was drawn on a village council building in the Lviv oblast.[155]

At the height of the Prague Spring, the national solution was the most immediately obvious alternative to Soviet socialism for those who rejected existing state structures (as opposed to seeking reform within them). For instance, the KGB quoted a forty-four-year-old Gulag returnee from Stryi, Volodymyr Mykhailovych Dmytruk, who claimed that the only way to solve the Czechoslovak problem was to grant independence to everyone in Eastern Europe, including Ukraine.[156] Other anti-Soviet residents went further and took matters into their own hands. In the Sambir region of the Lviv oblast, the KGB discovered that "nationalists" had gone so far as to build a bunker in the woods in preparation for the seemingly impending civil war.[157] Even after the swift invasion, when opposition to Moscow's policy must have appeared more hopeless than before, the authorities suggested that some Ukrainian soldiers were reluctant to fight the "Russian" war.[158]

Inhabitants of Ukraine who reportedly voiced anti-Russian opinions often linked them to economic complaints. Immediately after the invasion, during a private conversation, a woman employed at the furniture factory in Chernivtsi stated that the "Moskali" (a pejorative term for Russians in Ukraine) prevented the people of Czechoslovakia from achieving high standards of living.[159] Echoing the same sentiments, a local twenty-eight-year-old I.I. Smuk claimed that the Ukrainians would also be richer had it not been for fifty years of "Muscovite oppression."[160] Cloaked in nationalist rhetoric, some material demands represented personal interest and ambition, at least according to the KGB. For instance, a metal worker from Lviv reportedly boasted that he had identified a house and a car belonging to a Russian and planned to take them during the coming war.[161]

In some cases, nationalism was very explicitly associated with anti-socialist views rather than just individual economic complaints. Talking to other workers during her shift at the bread factory in Uzhgorod, Mariia Fusko stated that "the Russians take everything away." At the suggestion that it was still better to live under the Russians than the Germans, she retorted that the Germans would "give people their land."[162] She thus echoed complaints against collective farming that had been more widespread in 1956. Likewise, Mykhailo Mykhailovych Demesh, a forty-five-year-old non-party manager at a sausage factory in Transcarpathia, hoped that the region would now be returned to Czechoslovakia and private property be reinstated: "I will be a large entrepreneur and I will show everyone what I am capable of."[163] The most tragic protest against the Soviet invasion of Czechoslovakia and the Russification of Ukraine was Vasyl Omelianovych Makukh's self-immolation in Kyiv on 5 November 1968.[164]

Anti-Soviet Ukrainian nationalism was also closely associated with support for the Greek Catholic church, which the authorities had criminalised in the 1940s. Historian Volodymyr Dmytruk shows that the legalisation of the church in Czechoslovakia in 1968 emboldened the faithful in Ukraine to call for similar measures at home.[165] Priests who still illegally held Greek Catholic services found the Czechoslovak example both inspiring and instructive. Discussing the TASS announcement about the August military intervention with other clerics of the illegal Uniate church (some of whom must have been KGB informers), Hodun'ko from Lviv criticised the clandestine Ukrainian Greek Catholics for focusing too much on the elderly, pointing out that Uniates in Czechoslovakia were in a much stronger position for having attracted young people to church.[166] At the same time, Uniate supporters had clear nationalist leanings, and according to official reports, they did not harbour many illusions that they would ever be able to profess their faith under the Soviet regime. The head of the Council for Religious Affairs of the USSR reported that Greek Catholic priests and the faithful listened to Vatican radio broadcasts, which encouraged them to support the cause of Ukrainian independence. Furthermore, Greek Catholic sympathisers associated religious intolerance with foreign occupation, and at times, the supposed Jewish domination of Ukraine. Kosylo, a cleric from the west Ukrainian city of Ivano-Frankivsk, reportedly encouraged the faithful to listen to the Pope rather that the "old Yid- the Patriarch of Moscow."[167]

Not all appeals for religious tolerance took on a Ukrainian nationalist form, of course. Some anti-Soviet residents who focused their energies on attacking the state's religious policy were more broadly "anti-communist," and they did not refer to the ethnic question. In late August, for example, the KGB wrote about an Orthodox priest from Kyiv who hoped that citizens in Ukraine would "oppose communist power, too."[168] The atheist state alienated religious citizens, including the handful of individuals who, during the mass mobilisation preceding the invasion of Czechoslovakia, refused to serve in the Soviet army on religious grounds.[169] In the view of a resident of Volodymyr-Volynskyi, communism was bound to fail precisely because it made God irate.[170]

Whereas advocates of reformist patriotism evoked Soviet values and called for democratising the USSR, anti-Soviet citizens had much more concrete hopes and expectations. In questioning the legitimacy of Soviet rule in Ukraine, they anticipated a war against the CPSU officials and the Russians. Some individuals were even preparing to fight, hoping to achieve Ukrainian independence. Most anti-Soviet citizens were Ukrainian nationalists who hoped to obtain economic independence for their republic, take their vengeance on the detested foreigners whom they blamed for all the evils that befell the country, and rehabilitate religious belief and the Greek Catholic church in particular. They did not, however, appeal to large audiences in the republic. It should be noted that KGB reports concerning anti-Soviet nationalism drew on long-standing stereotypes of radical, west Ukrainian Banderites. It seems likely that at least some surveillance reports caricatured or oversimplified anti-Soviet views, and perhaps exaggerated the extent to which residents of western Ukraine rejected Soviet power.

Conclusion

During a January 1968 meeting with the Soviet Premier Alexei Kosygin, the Polish leader Władysław Gomułka complained that the Catholic Church was still waging an open war on the socialist regime in Poland. "If only we had two or three religions, things would be better," Gomułka claimed, implying that different denominations could be played against each other. In response, Kosygin jokingly suggested that the USSR could "lend" its Muslim population to Poland to resolve the situation.[171] The joke offers an interesting insight into how party apparatchiks conceived of national (and religious) diversity in the USSR and the entire Soviet bloc during the late 1960s. Eastern Europe continued to diverge from the Soviet model of socialism, providing a source of reformist ideas: a Catholic Poland hardly fit the socialist camp. At the same time, as attempts to create a common socialist culture for the Soviet empire failed, communist apparatchiks throughout the bloc turned national tensions and prejudices that plagued the Soviet bloc to their advantage. Whether by pitting Soviet citizens against foreign countries in Eastern Europe or fuelling the flames of anti-Semitism and xenophobia at home, Soviet leaders also grounded their legitimacy in ethno-national and patriotic terms.

The events of 1968 made it clear that socialism had failed to create a new supranational community in Eastern Europe. More than twenty years after the Great Patriotic War, and without the violence and chaos of the Hungarian uprising, it was hard to blame the conflict in Czechoslovakia on legacies of fascism. For most citizens it was clear that the causes of the breakdown in Soviet-Czechoslovak relations were to be found within the state socialist system.

From the vantage point of conservative patriotism, it now seemed that "national roads" did not lead to "socialism." This encouraged some citizens to define their Soviet identity in opposition to certain ethno-national groups, particularly in the near abroad, but also in the USSR itself. Ultimately, advocates of conservative patriotism recognised and accepted that Moscow's control over the near abroad was based on the threat of force.

Conservative patriotism was less challenging to the CPSU leadership in 1968 than it was twelve years earlier. In order to prove their patriotic credentials, citizens contrasted themselves with imagined foreign and domestic enemies rather than the supposedly inefficient apparatchiks in the Kremlin. Members of the Soviet aspirational middle class were by far the most avid proponents of conservative patriotism. The formulaic meetings about Czechoslovakia and the ritual of naming and shaming enemies emerged as a means to recognise the special status of some party members, educated professionals, decorated workers, and other citizens who claimed the right to explain and justify Moscow's policies to members of their local communities. The conservative vision of Soviet participatory citizenship was deeply xenophobic. Self-appointed middle class opinion leaders claimed membership in Soviet society by contrasting themselves with foreigners in the near abroad and ethnic minorities at home.

Meanwhile, advocates of reformist patriotism bemoaned Moscow's suppression of national roads to socialism, arguing that national identities could act as a key vehicle for social mobilisation and the spread of socialism across borders. They called citizens to stand up against creeping re-Stalinization. Proponents of reformist patriotism had their own vision of Soviet participatory citizenship. For them, it meant the ability to deliberate and shape state policies at home and abroad, as well as to promote non-Russian languages and cultures (at the same time, some proponents of reformist patriotism in eastern Ukraine, like Nekrasov cited at the beginning of this chapter, mobilized Russian ethnic identities to call for change). Proponents of reformist patriotism were the only ones who still had the conviction that a shared belief in socialism could provide for peaceful international relations. But they did not see the Soviet Communist Party as a source of ideas about what socialism should become. Rather, they claimed that Brezhnev had betrayed the cause of internationalism by turning towards traditional great power politics.

With the emergence of the Soviet dissident movement, boundaries between what was permitted and what was illegal were now less fluid than in 1956.[172] During the trial of Andrei Sinavskii and Iulii Daniel in 1966, readers of Soviet newspapers had already witnessed a clash between state and party bureaucrats and representatives of the creative intelligentsia.[173] Boris Lewytzkyj shows that the growing rift between the state and the intelligentsia in Ukraine had erupted even earlier by the death of the young talented poet Vasyl Symonenko in December 1963.[174] However, it was the Prague Spring that compelled a small number of Soviet citizens to adopt a decidedly critical stance on such issues as the USSR's hegemony in Eastern Europe, access to information, and Soviet nationalities policy.

Finally, in the increasingly repressive atmosphere of the late 1960s, some inhabitants of Ukraine were convinced that national rights could not be defended within the USSR. This encouraged more people to express support for Ukrainian independence, though such explicitly anti-Soviet voices were few and far between. They were most popular among the clergy and the faithful of the underground Greek Catholic church and former members of Ukrainian nationalist movements.

All in all, the Prague Spring ended the Thaw in the USSR. Although Soviet citizens were rarely engaged in reinventing the socialist project after 1968, Soviet society did not come to a standstill. Soviet patriotism, with all its dark shades of prejudice and xenophobia, provided a new rhetorical device that animated social interactions and state-society dynamics in the late Soviet period.

4 Making Enemies: Historical Memory and the Ethnic Foundations of Soviet Patriotism in Ukraine, 1968–1980

School pupils in Brezhnev-era USSR spent many history classes learning about Russian and Ukrainian conflicts with their neighbours in Eastern Europe. Having studied ancient and medieval history in grades five and six, they moved on to explore how the "peoples of our country" defeated both foreign enemies and class oppressors to guide the rest of the world on the path to communism. They studied the past of Eastern Europe in a national framework, reading about Russians, Ukrainians, and Belarusians as the driving force behind socialist progress. The "tall, strong, and beautiful" East Slavs had inhabited the lands of the USSR since times immemorial, facing the destruction of the Galician-Volhynian kingdom by the Poles and Hungarians, defeating the Polish occupiers in Moscow, and fighting for the reunification of Ukraine with Russia during the seventeenth-century Cossack uprisings. The grade seven history textbook was meant to help students develop a sense of Soviet patriotism by playing on East Slavic ethnic identities: with pupils attending separate classes on the history of their republics, the introduction reminded them that their "national" past was "part of the wider history of our multinational homeland – the Soviet Union."[1]

These historical narratives suggested that a gulf separated the USSR from its allies in Eastern Europe. The implication was that Russians, Ukrainians, and Belarusians shared a natural bond and a common history that excluded Poles, Czechs, Hungarians, Jews, and other nations of the socialist bloc. Inhabitants of Eastern Europe, albeit socialist, were also inherently untrustworthy – their ethnic identity had always put them at odds with the founding East Slavic nations of the USSR.

During the 1970s, Soviet and East European public culture cast nations as primordial and even biological communities that had always existed and were there to stay. After the Prague Spring dealt a major blow to the idea of transnational friendship in the socialist camp, popular films, literature, school textbooks, and public anniversary commemorations depicted ethnic nations as the main actors in Eastern Europe's past and present. Irked by conflicts with their East European colleagues, Soviet party leaders, historians, and artists used history to draw a clear boundary between loyal Soviet citizens (Russians and Ukrainians in particular) and foreigners in Eastern Europe. Concerned about the growing influence of Western popular culture and unsure about the impact of television on Soviet citizens, party leaders supported these efforts in the hope that grand national narratives would capture popular imagination in eastern and western Ukraine alike.

This shift in Soviet public culture had far-reaching implications for interethnic relations and the evolution of Ukrainian identities in the USSR itself. Whereas domestic cultural policies exposed tensions between ethno-national (Ukrainian) and supranational (Soviet) identities in the 1970s, historical portrayals of Ukrainian-Polish relations in particular helped promote the vision of a united Soviet community composed of homogenous ethno-national groups. Although some forms of Ukrainian national expression were anathema after 1968, Soviet political and cultural elites encouraged inhabitants of Ukraine to think of the Ukrainian ethnic identity as an intrinsic part of their psyche. In the vision they promoted, Ukraine's age-old conflicts with its western neighbours placed it firmly within the Russian cultural and political sphere of influence.

In order to examine the meanings of borders and ethnic identities in Brezhnev-era Soviet bloc, this chapter first focuses on East European public and cultural diplomacy after the late 1960s. Showing that attempts to cultivate a transnational socialist identity for the Soviet bloc were now half-hearted at most, it proceeds to explore the evolution of Soviet, Soviet Ukrainian, and western Ukrainian identities under Brezhnev.

East European Public and Cultural Diplomacy After 1968

The late 1960s marked the end of an era in Soviet bloc public and cultural diplomacy. The small-scale exchanges of party apparatchiks and specialists that Soviet and East European leaders had promoted over the previous decade were no longer seen as a sufficient means of maintaining friendly relations in the socialist camp. Keen to appeal to the growing number of educated citizens, Soviet and East European officials searched for more attractive forms of cultural exchange. This was one more factor that helped ethnicity emerge as the most important identity category in the socialist camp.

Although transnational contacts in Eastern Europe became a major source of concern for Soviet leaders during the Prague Spring, cultural exchanges across borders expanded after 1968. For example, Polish diplomats at the consulate in Kyiv made it their ambition to attract millions of Soviet citizens to Polish films and TV shows during the 1970s.[2] Efforts to popularise Polish culture likely found a fertile ground among the Ukrainian establishment under Shcherbyts'kyi – a former Polish consul recalled that Schcherbyts'kyi was friendly towards Polish diplomats, and even claimed that his own grandmother was an avid consumer of Polish women's magazines.[3] Similarly, travel between the USSR and its satellite states that began in the mid-1950s continued to grow in the late 1960s.[4] By the 1970s, more than a million Soviet tourists visited Eastern Europe every year. Their trips were commonly organised through trade unions or Komsomol organizations, though it was also possible to travel without a tour group after 1967.[5]

From the perspective of party apparatchiks, the expansion of cultural exchanges and tourism in the socialist camp was a question of prestige. While Soviet and East European officials (particularly at the Ministries of Culture, as well as at the propaganda departments of their respective Central Committees) emphasised the need to present a united cultural front vis-à-vis the perceived onslaught of Western popular culture,[6] they also conceived of cultural diplomacy in terms of competition within the Soviet bloc. Polish diplomats in Moscow were thus disgruntled when East German programs on Soviet TV proved more popular than Polish shows.[7]

The search to win over foreign audiences was partly driven by financial considerations. Party officials closely monitored the import and export balance of books, theatre performances, and popular music records within the socialist camp.[8] Employees at the culture department of the Polish Central Committee complained that the number of Soviet films in Polish cinemas far exceeded that of Polish movies screened in the USSR.[9] The issue was in fact so important that international cultural cooperation was for the first time included on the agenda of the Sixth Congress of the Polish United Workers' Party in 1971, with Warsaw promising to lift limits on the export of Polish movies, books, and works of art.[10] On the Soviet side, diplomats such as the cultural attaché

5 & 6 (above and opposite) Sofiia Rotaru represented the Soviet record label "Melodiia" at the televised 1974 Sopot Intervision Festival in Poland. She performed Volodymyr Ivasyuk's Ukrainian-language "Vodohrai," a song inspired by Ukrainian folklore. The magazine *Przyjaźń*, published by the Polish-Soviet Friendship Society, emphasised that Ukrainian folklore was very popular in the USSR. More broadly, concerned about the commercial success of international cooperation, Soviet and East European officials increasingly turned to popular music and national cultures. Courtesy of the Chernivtsi oblast Volodymyr Ivasyuk Memorial Museum.

at the Warsaw embassy, O. Brykin, seemed as interested in what they called the "commercial success" of transnational cultural exchanges as they were in their ideological effects.[11]

Despite the upheavals of 1968, some party officials and members of the cultural elite continued to emphasise that cross-border travel and cultural exchanges could create a new socialist identity for the Soviet bloc.

magazyn ilustrowany
przyjaźń
nr 38 (1337) 22 września 1974 cena 5 zł

Dwoje popularnych

Fot. JANUSZ URBAN

filatelistyka

I MIĘDZYNARODOWY KONGRES TERIOLOGICZNY W MOSKWIE

Echoing earlier narratives, members of the Soviet and East European intelligentsia still promoted an idealised image of the socialist camp. For instance, popular non-fiction literature portrayed Soviet citizens and their friends in the people's democracies as educated, confident specialists – Soviet travel writers, including the Ukrainian journalist, poet, and secretary of the Soviet Writers' Union Vitalii Oleksiiovych Korotych, described their encounters with East European engineers in particular.[12] While notions of "communist morality" are normally associated with the Thaw of the late 1950s and the early 1960s,[13] they remained a prominent theme in Brezhnev-era travel literature as well. Apart from technical expertise and loyalty to the USSR, East European friends embodied such personal characteristics as daring, bravery, modesty, and industriousness. Describing a Polish engineer he met in Kraków's industrial suburb of Nowa Huta, for example, Iakov Ivanovich Makarenko did not shy away from pomp in his 1977 publication:

> Rushing, hot flames broke through one of the open-hearth furnaces somehow ... [He] raced down the stairs to examine the furnace ... Defying danger, he climbed up to the crack several times, facing the boiling and buzzing flames ... Get on with your work – he said calmly once the crack in the furnace was fixed.[14]

Soviet authors underlined that East European specialists were different from their colleagues in the capitalist West. Recruited as they were from the working class, they were modest and cultured.[15]

Still, Brezhnev-era public and cultural diplomacy was not about bridging national divisions or promoting internationalism in the Soviet bloc. The expansion of cross-border travel and cultural cooperation was in fact a source of anxiety for the Soviet bloc elites, as many party leaders and artists believed that the search to win over large audiences undermined the intelligentsia's task to educate the public about the building of socialism. For one, the rise of national televisions overshadowed any attempts at building a transnational, socialist culture in Eastern Europe. Already in the late 1960s, the Soviet Gosteleradio encountered Romanian resistance to the idea of building a transnational socialist equivalent to Eurovision, and they reassured their colleagues from the satellite states that cooperation in the field of television would not take away from the centrality of national television in each country of the socialist camp.[16] Moreover, just as Soviet TV professionals found it difficult to reconcile their ideological mission with the need to meet audience expectations,[17] apparatchiks in charge of cultural diplomacy struggled to engage Soviet and East European citizens in dialogue on contemporary social, political, and cultural issues. For example, the PUWP (Polish United Workers' Party) Central Committee Department of Culture despaired that Polish movies on contemporary themes, deemed important by film critics, bombed in Soviet cinemas.[18] In contrast, they found it much easier to involve the public in activities that they considered less educational or intellectually challenging, such as international pop music concerts, equestrian shows, and screenings of comedies and romantic dramas with gratuitous nudity.[19]

When it came to winning over foreign audiences, heroic national narratives sold. In the assessment of Warsaw officials, translations and screen adaptations of Polish classics, including nineteenth-century Romantic novels with strong nationalist undertones, were the surest way to attract Soviet audiences.[20] Jerzy Hoffman's film about the seventeenth-century Polish-Swedish wars pulled in some 30 million viewers in the USSR during the first half of the 1970s, whereas during the same period a mere 2.5 million Soviet citizens watched Andrzej Wajda's surreal portrayal of contemporary Polish cultural elites in *Everything for Sale*.[21] Riding the wave, bureaucrats in Moscow and Warsaw outlined a very important role for national histories in Soviet-Polish cultural cooperation: along with such internationalist events as anniversaries of the October Revolution, international cultural events would focus on celebrations of nineteenth-century national uprisings.[22]

Communist Party apparatchiks were themselves nationalists in that they saw ethnicity as a fundamental, biological characteristic that permeated all forms of cultural production. One Polish report went so far as to claim that Polish actors' education, psyche, and outward appearance made it virtually impossible for them to play Russian or Soviet people. With the notable exception of Barbara Brylska's role in *The Irony of Fate*, Soviet film studios hired them to play Poles, Germans, Frenchmen, Americans, and "as a last resort," Russian aristocrats. Film directors could only really understand "the reality of their own countries," continued the report, failing to produce meaningful films about their neighbours.[23]

In the 1970s, Soviet bloc cultural diplomacy celebrated the exotic at the expense of the familiar. In the USSR, the image of the satellite states as a socialist construction site, which was so prevalent in the late 1950s and early 1960s, was increasingly overshadowed by portrayals of

Eastern Europe as a fun and exotic tourist destination. Soviet tourists were encouraged to enjoy monuments to the pre-socialist past in Eastern Europe.[24] Partly in order to make travel more exciting, no doubt, Soviet travel literature revelled in stories about missing Hungarian crown jewels, and tempted readers with descriptions of Budapest's Turkish baths, Gothic churches, and ancient castles and palaces.[25] Official descriptions of Eastern Europe were underpinned by a primordial understanding of nationhood. The introduction to a Soviet book about Czechoslovakia thus praised the author for finding a way to understand "the soul of the country and its people, the very heart of its history … its national identity."[26] The implication was that inhabitants of the outer empire had always had distinct national identities that shaped their views and attitudes. In mainstream Soviet publications, the supposedly inborn ethnic characteristics that made each East European nation distinct were at least as prominent as the political and ideological similarities that brought the socialist bloc together.

In Brezhnev-era publications, the Soviet bloc was increasingly portrayed not simply as a socialist commonwealth, but also a confederation of closely related ethnic groups. Just as calls for Slavic unity resounded at the height of the Czechoslovak crisis in 1968, a Soviet version of pan-Slavism was especially important in justifying the USSR's control over the near abroad. Already in the 1950s, the Central Committee put pressure on the Slavic Studies Institute at the Soviet Academy of Sciences to write a "transnational" history of Slavs.[27] By the early 1970s, the celebration of Slavdom acquired a very wide scope. The idea was that the friendship between Slavs in the USSR and its satellite states predated the establishment of socialism. In 1983, for example, the Lviv-based journal *Zhovten'* celebrated the early twentieth-century Czech writer Jaroslav Hašek for deserting the Habsburg army during the First World War. The article claimed that Hašek took a keen interest in Galicia and did not want to fight against his fellow Slavs in the Imperial Russian army, though it was only after the February and October Revolutions of 1917 that he fully understood the plight of the Ukrainian nation.[28] Similarly, during a conference of the Soviet-Czechoslovak Friendship Society in which activists celebrated the restoration of cultural cooperation after the upheavals of 1968, the Ukrainian representative Stetsenko cited the nineteenth-century poet Taras Shevchenko to outline the society's mission as enriching "Slavic lands stretching from sea to sea."[29] East European friendship was thus defined in ethnic (and ethnically exclusive) terms.

Diplomatic Tensions

As cross-border contacts and cultural exchanges acquired an increasingly popular character, national and ideological tensions between the USSR and its satellite states intensified.

Diplomatic tensions in the Soviet bloc were partly caused by overgrown bureaucracies and economic difficulties. Cultural exchanges between Poland and the USSR, for example, were subject to long-term planning. Every year, Warsaw and Moscow would conclude agreements specifying exactly how many writers, composers, and actors would travel over the next twelve months,[30] which made for a very inflexible system. "Must not exceed what we agreed on with the USSR," stated a hand-written note dousing the ambitions of Warsaw apparatchiks planning Polish Culture Days in the USSR in 1974.[31] To make matters worse, economic cuts hit cultural diplomacy in the second half of the 1970s. "I was one against three," bemoaned Eugeniusz Kabatc, a writer and translator of Soviet literature who represented the Polish Ministry of Culture and Arts at a meeting in Moscow in January 1976. The Soviets did not accept any Polish proposals to expand cross-border travel, he complained in an internal report compiled upon returning to Warsaw, and even cut the numbers of professional exchanges that Warsaw and Moscow had agreed on before for economic reasons. The general atmosphere of the meeting was "cold," Kabatc said, "perhaps because they felt guilty about limiting cooperation that had been developing so well."[32] Paying lip service to "the constantly developing Polish-Soviet friendship," Polish and Soviet apparatchiks spent a lot of time and energy negotiating exactly how to control the amount that Polish citizens bought in the USSR and what Soviet citizens were allowed to transport out of Poland, reflecting worsening shortages in both countries during the late 1970s.[33]

Cultural relations between the USSR and its allies were also strained because Communist Party elites in the USSR and Eastern Europe did not share a common vision of cultural diplomacy during the 1970s and 1980s. On the Soviet side, concerns about the lack of unity in the socialist camp led the Central Committee to impose strict central control over cultural diplomacy. As the Soviet Minister of Culture Petr Demichev reminded the Poles in 1972, "the management of culture [in the USSR] should be centralised."[34] Yet Warsaw continued to seek direct contacts with Kyiv and other republican centres. The PUWP Central Committee bemoaned the fact that Ukrainian literature was often translated into Polish through the medium of Russian.[35]

Seeing the USSR's western borderlands as a fertile ground for the promotion of Polish culture, Poland maintained a very active consulate in Kyiv.[36] The consuls travelled around Ukraine to establish personal contacts with leading intellectuals, which was partly driven by a desire to support Polish language in the republic. For example, the consuls Wanda Michalewska and Władysław Kruk paid special attention to the two Polish-language high schools and the Polish-language amateur theatre in Lviv, claiming that a rising number of local inhabitants expressed an interest in learning Polish.[37] On another level, Polish diplomacy focused on Ukrainian language and culture. In the 1960s, for example, Michalewska facilitated contacts between local intelligentsia and students who came from Poland to study Ukrainian language and literature. Florian Nieuważny and Mirosław Werbowy thus studied at the Shevchenko University in Kyiv, and later during the Brezhnev era, worked as translators of Ukrainian literature in Poland. As activists of the Society for the Friends of Kyiv in Warsaw, these men gave a very Ukrainian dimension to the Polish-Soviet Friendship Society.[38] Polish consuls in Ukraine sought allies among the leadership of the Ukrainian Writers' Union, and to attract them to Polish-led cultural initiatives, put pressure on Warsaw to name streets and schools in Poland after famous Ukrainian cultural figures (this was met with some resistance, especially in Poland's eastern borderlands). The consulate also encouraged forms of cultural exchange that fostered memories of a common Polish-Ukrainian history, such as the 325th anniversary of the founding of Lviv University.[39]

While Moscow sought to articulate a strong Soviet position on cultural cooperation in Eastern Europe, therefore, Warsaw treated the USSR not as a unitary state but a multi-ethnic federation. Tellingly, as Soviet documents mentioned the need to increase cooperation between the peoples (*narody*) of the USSR and Eastern Europe, the Polish versions of the same documents used the term nations (*narody*) and not peoples (*ludy*).[40]

Most importantly, Soviet-East European tensions arose because cultural exchanges in the 1970s involved not only the relatively reliable friendship society activists and outstanding communist party members who had previously dominated international cooperation, but also representatives of other cultural and social organizations who often proved more provocative. In 1972, for example, to mark the fiftieth anniversary of the USSR, Polish TV professionals proposed to interview "Soviet citizens of Polish origin." Their list consisted of individuals who, in the words of alarmed Central Committee apparatchiks in Warsaw, had "very complicated political vicissitudes." This was probably code for victims of Stalinist deportations and members of the Polish minority in the USSR's western borderlands. In the end, the idea was too controversial, and Polish political leaders ordered journalists to interview Soviet war veterans instead, apparently recognising their special middle class status in society. Despite such close ideological control, Polish TV crews who covered the anniversary celebrations in 1972 produced shows that made Soviet apparatchiks distinctly uncomfortable. In particular, Moscow complained that Polish journalists focused on "exotic regions and spheres of life" in the Soviet Union.[41] As an attaché of the Soviet embassy in the GDR (German Democratic Republic) explained on another occasion and with reference to East German television, Soviet exotic regions that interested East European television crews were far-flung provinces (*glubinki*) such as Sakhalin and Kamchatka that offered opportunities to observe rare species and natural phenomena.[42] Television professionals were more interested in creating original programming than in exploring ideological questions, which pushed them to emphasise differences between the USSR and its satellite states.

More broadly, Polish and Soviet apparatchiks in charge of cultural diplomacy found the Polish intelligentsia rather uncooperative. Repeating pompous slogans about the successes of cultural cooperation, they were nevertheless frustrated that few contemporary writers in Poland wrote the kind of prose that "promoted a constructive image of reality." Because of this, one Polish report claimed in 1975, the number of Soviet translations of Polish literature into Russian, Ukrainian, and other languages of the USSR had been in constant decline since 1959.[43]

East European writers, journalists, and social activists alienated Soviet apparatchiks especially because their work contributed to the growth of dissent in the USSR. The samizdat *Chronicle of Current Events*, for example, drew on the Polish weekly *Polityka* to comment on cultural politics in the USSR itself.[44] From the perspective of Soviet officials, citizens' contacts with sanctioned East European organizations were sometimes incriminating, especially in cases of individuals already considered suspect or unreliable. The fact that the east Ukrainian poet Volodymyr Syrenko posted his works to Ukrainian cultural organisations in Poland and Czechoslovakia was thus used against him during his 1976 trial.[45] Personal contacts with citizens of the satellite states were likewise suspect. In 1978, *The Chronicle of Current Events* reported that the authorities had cut off the phone line at the apartment of a friend of the dissident scholar Aleksandr Zinoviev, simply because his wife had used it to contact her sister in Hungary.[46]

On the Soviet side of the border, members of the cultural intelligentsia claimed the right to shape and evaluate cultural relations with Poland. This exposed divisions within Soviet society as well as Polish-Ukrainian tensions. The controversial nature of cultural exchanges in the socialist camp became apparent in 1984, for example, after the Goskomizdat publishing house in Moscow released the first Soviet edition of Henryk Sienkiewicz's *Ognem i mechom* (*With Fire and Sword*),[47] with a large print run of 200,000 copies. The nineteenth-century Polish epic forms part of a trilogy that was very popular in socialist Poland. It tells the story of a seventeenth-century Polish nobleman who seeks to rescue his beloved from Cossack captivity. Written from a very Polono-centric point of view, the novel portrays the Ukrainian hetman Khmel'nyts'kyi and the Cossacks as barbaric bandits who weaken the Polish-Lithuanian Commonwealth. While Sienkiewicz's other works (including two segments of a trilogy set against the background of the Commonwealth's wars against Sweden and the Ottoman Empire) had been published in the Soviet Union, *Ognem i mechom* did not come out until 1983.

In May 1984, a group of four Ukrainian historians and one literary scholar from Lviv complained about the publication. Arguing that the book would undermine the population's "class understanding" of the past, the director of the historical archive in Lviv, N.F. Vradyi, as well as doctors Iu. Iu. Slyvka, Iu. G. Toshko, K.K. Trofimovich, and D.D. Nizovyi, pointed out that as early as 1884 the Polish writer Bolesław Prus attacked Sienkiewicz for idealising the elites and ignoring the cause of the "oppressed people." Supported by the local communist boss Viktor Dobryk who was particularly sensitive to any manifestations of Polish nationalism, the Lviv scholars alleged that Sienkiewicz represented the Ukrainian masses as "hordes of dogs," mistaking social struggle for national conflict. The novel described the Ukrainian war of liberation, the academics continued, from the point of view of the Catholic magnates who sought to enslave the Ukrainians and break their ties with the brotherly Russian people. Although the report admitted that the introduction to the Soviet edition placed *Ognem i mechom* in the appropriate context, it also questioned how much influence this would have on readers, and lobbied for the large-scale publication of Marxist academic studies of the novel.[48] In their appeal to the CPSU Central Committee, the scholars talked of Ukrainian national liberation and reunification with Russia, all the while attacking the novel for emphasising the national rather than the class question. They evoked both national and class identities to advance their professional interests, suggesting in particular that a wide audience should read their analysis of Sienkiewicz's work. The nationalism so apparent in Sienkiewicz's nineteenth-century novel brought scholarly attention to the importance of ethnic divisions and borders at the end of the twentieth century.

However, other scholars and bureaucrats in both Russia and Ukraine defended the publication in correspondence with party apparatchiks in Moscow. A.N. Sakharov, the chief literary editor at the publishing house Goskomizdat, pointed out that *Ognem i Mechom* had received the approval of the Central Committee and the Institutes of World Literature and Slavic and Balkan Studies at the USSR Academy of Sciences.[49] The hope was that the publication of Sienkiewicz's novels in the USSR would help strengthen Polish-Soviet friendship.[50] Unlike the scholars who protested against the publication of *Ognem i Mechom*, other members of the Soviet literary establishment were at peace with Polish nationalism in the novel. The head of Goskomizdat's section for literatures of the socialist countries, P.M. Toper, whose job it was to cultivate lively literary relations between Poland and the USSR, defended the translation. He claimed that the novel not only allowed Soviet audiences to "feel the poetry of the Ukrainian landscape," but also expressed progressive nineteenth-century ideas of the Polish national movement. True, Sienkiewicz resorted to hyperbole and idealised the Poles who had fought against the Cossacks, but he did this to create strong characters and contrast them with his imperfect contemporaries, praising the ideals of soldiers' camaraderie, friendship, as well as loyalty and stability in love. To support his views, Toper cited the Ukrainian writer and Lenin prizewinner Mykola Bazhan, who voiced his views about Sienkiewicz in December 1979: the history of Polish-Ukrainian relations was complex and bloody, but while Soviet people could understand the class background of the mutual conflicts, they should not expect the same of Sienkiewicz.[51] As the chief editor of the Soviet Ukrainian Encyclopaedia, former head of the Ukrainian Writers' Union, and the author of works about Russo-Ukrainian friendship, Bazhan offered a model Soviet Ukrainian perspective on history and literature. He advocated the use of sweeping national narratives that essentialised notions of "Russian," "Ukrainian," and "Polish" in Soviet public culture. At the same time, he evoked the concepts of class struggle and proletarian internationalism to justify this approach.

The exchange of ideas about *Ognem i mechom* exposed conflicting approaches to cultural diplomacy among intellectuals and cultural bureaucrats, both on the all-Soviet and Ukrainian-republican stage. Undoubtedly, their opinions were conditioned by the institutions they represented, and the need to defend the decisions they had taken earlier. The scholars from Lviv, as well as Viktor Dobryk, were most adamant that academics should protect Soviet Ukrainians from harmful foreign ideas. In contrast, their opponents were moved by nineteenth-century Romantic portrayals of national heroes, national landscapes, and national struggles in Eastern Europe. But in all these accounts, class and national struggles went hand-in-hand: nationalism was progressive in that it mobilised Ukrainians against their Polish overlords, or else imbued positive values in Polish nineteenth-century society and helped to build friendly relations between Poland and the USSR in the 1980s. Opponents and advocates of *Ognem i Mechom* alike took it for granted that ethnically-defined national communities were the most important driving forces in history.

Soviet Patriotism in the 1970s

As cultural exchanges continued through the 1970s, Soviet political and cultural leaders grew increasingly uneasy about the transfer of ideas across borders, and articulated strong Soviet and Soviet Ukrainian identities that distinguished inhabitants of the USSR from socialist Eastern Europe. Commemorations of the Second World War provided the most important forum where Soviet citizens celebrated friendship in the socialist camp, all the while articulating a distinct Soviet identity. During the 1970s, Soviet and East European citizens regularly marked anniversaries of Soviet victories over Nazi Germany, laid flowers at monuments to Soviet soldiers during tourist trips to Eastern Europe, and watched Soviet and East European war films. These popular forms of commemoration outlined a clear hierarchy in the socialist camp: the idea was that all nations in Eastern Europe that had fallen victim to German Nazism owed their liberation to the Soviet people.

Commemorations of the Second World War provided a degree of cultural homogeneity to the socialist camp. For example, the Polish television series *Four Tank Drivers and a Dog*, which portrayed the Soviet-Polish brotherhood in arms, was very popular in both Poland and the USSR (reportedly, the program was so popular that Soviet power plants had to work at extra capacity to provide electricity for all the television sets that people switched on when it was broadcast). Narratives of war suggested that Soviet and East European citizens had been brought together in a common struggle against external enemies from further west. Soviet war veterans published memoirs about the cooperation between Polish and Soviet partisans in occupied Ukraine, and Polish and Soviet citizens met to lay flowers and plant "trees of friendship" at the Soviet cemetery in Poznań.[52] Meanwhile, most organised Soviet tourist groups travelling around Eastern Europe in the 1970s visited sites of battles against the Nazi forces.[53]

These narratives of friendship were underpinned by a strong degree of anti-Western (and especially anti-German) sentiment. Although Soviet officials were careful to describe the wartime enemy as "fascists" rather than "Germans," they also fanned anti-German sentiment by suggesting in various public forums that Bonn would jump at the first opportunity to dominate Eastern Europe all over again should the USSR relax controls over its satellite states.[54] The Second World War was commemorated as a conflict between different nations rather than just an ideological clash between fascism and communism. The authorities sponsored celebrations not only of the ultimate defeat of the Nazis in May 1945, but also the Soviet liberation of each individual ethnonational group on the way from Moscow to Berlin.[55] Links between the "fascist" and "German" threat to Eastern Europe were drawn by such prominent Soviet Ukrainian cultural figures as Oles' Honchar who, in describing trips to Eastern Europe in his diary, claimed that national cultures and languages helped East Europeans resist Germanisation and to progress towards socialism.[56]

East European officials were even less subtle in playing on fears of German nationalism. Struggling against a strong anti-Soviet and anti-Russian current in Polish popular opinion during the early 1980s, the Polish leadership under General Wojciech Jaruzelski sponsored press articles which suggested that Poland's membership in the Warsaw Pact was necessary to guarantee the inviolability of its western borders.[57] In 1975, the Polish Ministry of Arts and Culture wrote about the "Polish-Soviet brotherhood in arms" as the most important theme for literary and cinematic cooperation with Soviet artists.[58] For Polish officials, the war was perhaps the most useful context in which to discuss their friendship with the USSR. It offered an opportunity to avoid more contemporary problems of intra-bloc relations and to overshadow émigré and dissident-produced memories of wartime violence that divided Poland and the USSR (such as the Nazi-Soviet Pact, the Soviet massacre of Polish elites at Katyn', and ethnic cleansing in Volhynia). The critique of Ukrainian émigré publications that glorified wartime nationalist resistance turned into the most important platform that united Polish and Soviet Ukrainian establishment historians.[59]

Meanwhile, from the Soviet perspective, as the cult of war grew under Brezhnev in particular, memories of Eastern Europe's liberation took on a different dimension. They were used to strengthen a sense of Soviet patriotism that provided a moral justification for Soviet domination of the near abroad. Soviet publications thus suggested that inhabitants of the people's democracies were indebted to the Soviet people: "And we owe this to you, Soviet Man, to the Soviet Army, to the Soviet Union … which bore the greatest burden in the war against fascism and made the decisive contribution to the liberation of many peoples, including the Czechoslovak."[60] The Czech author of this introduction to a Soviet book about Czechoslovakia left his readers in no doubt about his admiration for the USSR. Similarly, Soviet travel literature of the 1970s portrayed Soviet army cemeteries as important sites of memory in the outer empire.

> How many times have I seen this! A modest tomb of a soldier under the chestnut trees, next to it an old woman deep in her grief … If you ask whom she's mourning, you will hear a voice full of sorrow: - Vaniusha! … His mother is old, like me. He died from his wounds in my arms. And now I am another mother to him … There are many monuments in the ancient Polish lands. But none of them are more sacred than the graves of Soviet soldiers who died for the freedom and happiness of the people.[61]

Playing on emotions, these forms of commemoration did not allow for a sober reflection on the history of Soviet relations with Eastern Europe, and marginalized any criticism of Soviet policies in the socialist camp, past or present, as unpatriotic and even sacrosanct.

Narratives that questioned the idea of Soviet noble suffering during the Second World War were confined to the sphere of dissent. In line with the broader marginalisation of non-titular ethnic groups in Soviet Ukraine, the idea that Slavs of the USSR had been not simply victims of Nazi aggression but also oppressors was taboo. Ivan Dziuba's September 1966 speech at Babyn Yar, in which he spoke about complicated Ukrainian-Jewish relations and Jewish victims of the Holocaust, could not be published in the USSR as it undermined the idea that all peoples of the USSR suffered equally during the German occupation.[62] While Polly Jones demonstrates that Thaw-era literature contained some limited criticism of Stalin's leadership that contributed to the massive death toll during the Second World War,[63] this was about the extent to which wartime history was re-evaluated in Soviet public culture after the 1950s. Soviet collaboration with the Nazis and violence committed by Soviet soldiers against civilian populations at home and abroad were only discussed in samizdat.[64]

In Ukraine, memories of nationalist resistance to Soviet rule underpinned some of these dissident narratives. A group of self-identified Ukrainian patriots thus appealed to Radio Liberty to debunk Soviet claims that the USSR had singlehandedly defeated the Nazis, to speak of the Nazi-Soviet Pact and the enormous human costs of the Soviet victory caused by the army command, and to commemorate such "people's heroes" as Stepan Bandera.[65] In other cases, however, Ukrainian dissident narratives drew on sanctioned Soviet visions of history and contained no positive references to the wartime nationalist underground. In 1972, for example, Ivan Dziuba (who had earlier called for a return to Leninist nationalities policy in Ukraine) touched on the controversial issue of annexing western Ukraine into the USSR in the underground *Ukrains'kyi visnyk*:

> The historic fact of the reunification of Western Ukraine with Soviet Ukraine is known to all, but here are some details of the event, as related by the participants in the reunification ... As soon as the Red Army divisions arrived, they would surround a village, call out the activists on their lists, load them on trains and send them off to Siberia. Tens of thousands were deported. They took the literate and the illiterate, peasants, townspeople, the intelligentsia, anyone who at anytime, anywhere had expressed doubts as to the necessity for reunification.[66]

Dziuba agreed that Soviet occupation of eastern Poland in 1939 amounted to a "reunification of Western Ukraine with Soviet Ukraine," but also called for more openness in discussing the brutality of the Soviet army. This stood in stark contrast to official narratives, in which the Great Patriotic War and the establishment of the socialist camp emerged as the most progressive events in East European history that helped justify the USSR's control over the near abroad.

Soviet Ukrainian Patriotism in the 1970s

Scholars and party leaders in Kyiv and Moscow also used history to promote strong ethnic identities in the USSR. In particular, the history of Polish-Ukrainian relations helped promote Soviet Ukrainian patriotism that combined loyalty to the Soviet state with a Ukrainian identity defined in opposition to Eastern Europe. In other words, though the 1970s are normally seen as a time when the authorities cracked down on expressions of Ukrainianness,[67] history was in fact used to promote a distinct Soviet Ukrainian identity under Brezhnev.

Brezhnev-era historians commemorated Ukrainian resistance to Polonisation. Long in the making, *Istoriia Ukrains'koi RSR: Korotkyi narys* (*History of the Ukrainian SSR: A Short Course*) was finally published in 1981, helping to entrench in public rhetoric the idea that Ukrainians defended the common interests of East Slavs and Soviet people against the Poles. Aimed at a "wide circle of readers," as chief editor Iurii Iuriiovych Kondufor stated, it described the "long history of the Ukrainian people, and its struggle for social and national liberation." The introduction emphasised that Russians, Ukrainians, and Belarusians all sprang up from Kievan Rus, setting out a clear teleological structure of history: through working together against class enemies and foreign tormentors, the "brotherly peoples" gradually developed into a new Soviet community. The editors underlined that internationalism did not preclude, but actually encouraged the love for one's ethnic nation (*natsiia*), though it seemed that "internationalism" was effectively limited to friendship between titular ethnic groups of the USSR.[68] This statement summed up the theses outlined in the eight-volume history of the Ukrainian SSR.

Volodymyr Shcherbtyts'kyi and other Soviet Ukrainian leaders of the 1970s spread this ethnocentric vision of history far and wide. In commemorating Ukrainian uprisings against Poland and struggles for "reunification" with Russia, they drew on postwar narratives developed in preparation for the 300th anniversary of the Pereiaslav Treaty in 1954,[69] and departed from the more diverse portrayals of East European history promoted during the late 1950s. This was particularly evident in 1979 when the authorities organised the 325th anniversary of Ukraine's "reunification" with Russia. While the celebrations were mostly concentrated in Ukraine itself, Shcherbyts'kyi was adamant that the anniversary should be an all-Soviet holiday. He went so far as to equate Ukrainian resistance against social and national exploitation by Poles to other founding events in Soviet history, including the October Revolution itself.[70] Accordingly, the party, the ministries of education and culture, the writers' union, amateur book clubs, and various professional associations prepared for the celebrations. Architects were instructed to design a monument to mark the anniversary – the "Friendship Arch" constructed in 1982 still stands in Kyiv's Khreshchatyk Park today.[71] Anniversary celebrations acquired a mass appeal, with half a million people attending 180 special concerts in Kyiv alone.[72] Underlining Ukraine's alienation from Poland and Kyiv's special relationship with Moscow, Shcherbyts'kyi used the events to portray the Ukrainian nation as a key agent in Soviet history.

His emphasis on the centrality of Ukraine and Ukrainians in Soviet history reflected important shifts in academic approaches towards the past that occurred over the 1970s. Establishment historians had earlier argued that the Ukrainian nation had developed after the Russian nation (and after Ukraine's incorporation into the Russian Empire). Without questioning the master narrative of Russo-Ukrainian reunification, scholars such as Olena Apanovych now popularised the notion that Ukrainians had developed a national identity much earlier and much more independently from Russia in their struggle against Polish-Lithuanian rule from the sixteenth century onward.[73]

Soviet leaders' fixation on the Ukrainian past was largely driven by the need to debunk foreign-produced historical narratives that questioned the supposed unity of Ukrainians and Russians. For Shcherbyts'kyi, commemoration of the Pereiaslav Treaty in 1979 was meant to strengthen Soviet patriotism in the face of "bourgeois, bourgeois-nationalist, Maoist, Zionist and other" distortions of history.[74] More specifically, the Ukrainian Central Committee instructed historians in the republic to counteract Austrian attempts to popularise the historical paradigm of Central Europe, in which Ukraine was portrayed as part of the Habsburg cultural and political world. Historians were also to discredit Ukrainian émigré publications that framed Ukrainian history in terms outlined by the famous Mykhailo Hrushevs'kyi (these publications undermined the official Soviet vision of three brotherly Slavic peoples, as they suggested that Kyivan Rus' was part of Ukrainian, not Russian history, as well as presented Russian imperial and Soviet rule in Ukraine as unremitting foreign occupation).[75]

In order to resist these narratives, Ukrainian leaders also planned to translate the short history of Ukraine into English in order "to show the historical links and brotherly unity between [the Ukrainian people] and the great Russian people [and] their common struggle against foreign and domestic enemies," including the Polish-sponsored Uniate church and NATO. The task would not be easy. In August 1980, A. Merkulov at the Ukrainian Central Committee Foreign Relations Department complained that the first draft was dry and incomprehensible, failing to provide convincing arguments against Ukrainian émigré historians who rejected the paradigm of Russo-Ukrainian friendship.[76] The CPSU Politburo also instructed Soviet historians to work with the Poles on very delicate issues. For example, A.M. Shlepakov at the Ukrainian Academy of Sciences specified that scholars should denounce publications about the "Soviet occupation" of western Ukraine in 1939.[77]

Tensions among academics in the socialist bloc further provoked Ukrainian historians to reaffirm the master narrative of Russo-Ukrainian unity. Unlike their Soviet colleagues, for example, Polish historians studied the national movement in Tsarist and Habsburg Ukraine as part of the broader European phenomenon of nationalism.[78] Soviet state officials informed Warsaw about their anger at similar shortcomings in literary studies, as well as instructed Ukrainian scholars to criticise the Poles who supposedly brought out a non-Soviet character of Ukraine in their work. In February 1974, Volodymyr Shcherbyts'kyi complained about two collections of Ukrainian poetry published in Poland two years earlier. Their chief flaw consisted in confusing officially sanctioned forms of Ukrainianness with other notions of what it meant to be Ukrainian. Among the authors included in the publications that were palatable for the first secretary of the Communist Party of Ukraine was Ivan Franko, whom Shcherbyts'kyi classified as part of the Ukrainian canon. Franko's life had been colourful and his political choices complex, but Soviet propaganda presented him as a Ukrainian national hero, a Marxist, and a founder of socialist realism.[79] Notably, Shcherbyts'kyi was also happy that Polish publishers included poet Volodymyr Sosiura in their compilation, which shows that the limits of permissible national expression had somewhat expanded since the death of Stalin. Although Sosiura had been part of the Soviet Ukrainian literary establishment and even received the Stalin prize in 1948, he was also accused of nationalist deviations for his famous poem "To Love Ukraine" in 1951.[80] Still, other poets did not fit the party vision of what constituted Soviet Ukrainian culture. In his criticism, Shcherbyts'kyi distinguished between ideologically immature "nationalist" authors such Bohdan Lepkyi, who had supposedly ignored important social problems and committed "art for art's sake,"[81] and explicitly "anti-Soviet" poets such as the OUN activist Oleh Olzhych. The Ukrainian Party First Secretary was also alarmed that the Poles published works by poets from the Thaw-era that had "compromised themselves" through "anti-social behaviour" – or in

7 The "Friendship Arch" commemorating the "reunification of Russia and Ukraine," or in other words the transfer of right-bank Ukraine from Polish to Russian rule in 1654, became one of Kyiv's landmarks in the late Soviet era. Wikipedia, creative commons licence.

other words, dissidents (Shcherbyts'kyi named the famous Sixtier poet Lina Kostenko in particular).[82] Shcherbyts'kyi ordered *Voprosy literatury* (*Issues of Literature*) or *Radians'ke literaturoznavstvo* (*Soviet Literary Studies*) to publish critical reviews of the Polish publications.[83]

As the early modern history of Ukraine was discussed very widely, some portrayals diverged from the master narrative of "reunification." For one, blunders and inconsistencies occurred. For example, the CPU leadership voiced serious concerns regarding a publication by M.F. Kotliar. Historian I.F. Kuras, who was in charge of Ukraine's social sciences at the Central Committee in Kyiv, alleged that Kotliar's article in *Vsesvit* (*Universe*) effectively publicised the views of scholars who denied that 1654 amounted to a "reunification" of Ukraine and Russia. In arguing against them, Kotliar's work allegedly quoted at length the views of such historians as Hrushevs'kyi, Kostomarov, Antonych, and Doroshenko who presented Russia as a foreign force in Ukraine.[84] More frequently, fiction literature produced ambiguous depictions of Khmel'nyts'kyi's role in Ukrainian history. Due to the blatant manipulation of historical accounts in Ukraine, artistic renditions of historical events (which could more easily slip by the censors than purely scholarly texts) "were often seen as more truthful" than academic studies.[85]

Because of this, fiction evoked some heated debates about history. This was evident after Pavlo Zahrebel'nyi published his novel *Ia, Bohdan* (*I, Bohdan*) in 1983, which presented a more complex psychological portrait of the hetman than inhabitants of Ukraine were accustomed to. It called into question Khmel'nyts'kyi's motivations in staging the uprising against Polish rule and signing the Pereiaslav agreement. Public reactions to the novel were symptomatic of the status quo in Soviet Ukraine's politics of memory during the early 1980s. As many reviewers criticised the book for undermining the idea of Russian-Ukrainian unity, even the dissident historian Volodymyr Serhiichuk spoke of the work's potentially negative influence on Ukrainian youth. This "Ukrainian patriot," as Frank Sysyn describes him, believed that national myths should not be challenged, especially "under foreign occupation": however distorted his image, Khmel'nyts'kyi constituted one of the few sanctioned symbols helping to foster a separate Ukrainian identity in the USSR.[86] In this sense, commitment to promoting Ukrainian national identity provided a platform that went some way towards bridging the gap between party leaders, establishment historians, and prominent dissident figures.

Only a few samizdat publications questioned the grand narrative of Russo-Ukrainian unity promoted in school history textbooks, the Soviet press, and bombastic anniversary celebrations. These underground publications showed that some members of the cultural intelligentsia grew frustrated with the highly ritualised historical narratives that set the tone for Soviet Ukraine. Writing of the "Soviet occupation" of Ukraine, for example, editors of the Ukrainian-language samizdat *Ukrains'kyi visnyk* (*The Ukrainian Herald*) insisted on using the Russian word for "Soviet" (*sovetskii*) instead of the Ukrainian (*radians'kyi*), as the latter implied that Soviet rule in the republic was home-grown and representative of Ukrainian language and culture. They effectively equated Sovietness with Russianness and implied that Soviet rule in

Ukraine amounted to Russian domination.[87] Similarly, in contrast to other dissidents such as Ivan Dziuba (who called for increased Ukrainian cultural autonomy within the USSR), Valentyn Moroz refused to recognise the legitimacy of Soviet rule in Ukraine and thus celebrated historical examples of resistance to foreign domination in the western borderlands. In particular, he wrote about the survival of the Hutsul identity in the Carpathian Mountains.[88]

Other non-conformists were less concerned with the national question as such, but mocked the pompousness of state-sponsored historical anniversaries, claiming that they obscured real problems plaguing Soviet society. A pamphlet discovered in Kyiv during the early 1980s addressed tourists who came to celebrate the city's anniversary:

> You have come to celebrate 1500 years of a city which is currently ruled by communists. They even made up the date – 1500 years – because scholars have not established how old Kyiv really is … They will try to convince you that the city has flourished under communism. They will show you monuments that they constructed in haste and for which they bled local inhabitants dry … They will bring groceries [during the anniversary celebrations] to pretend that they can actually be found in Kyiv. They want to turn you into propagandists of the Soviet way of life.[89]

The pamphlet expressed frustration with Soviet politics of memory, in which Kyiv was celebrated as the cradle of East Slavic nations. At the same time, it testified to the central role that history played in late Soviet public culture. The massive scale of the celebrations that the authors criticised stood in stark contrast to the small pamphlet that likely reached very few people.

Because nations turned into the most important agents in Soviet accounts of East European history, both Sovietness and Ukrainianness were defined against the Poles and other ethnic groups of the socialist bloc. The national paradigm thus overshadowed the narrative of a common socialist identity that some Soviet and East European officials in charge of cultural and public diplomacy had promoted in the late 1950s and early 1960s. Under Brezhnev, history was used to show that to be Soviet meant to belong to one of the USSR's titular ethnic groups – to be Soviet meant to be Ukrainian or Russian, and not Polish or Jewish. These narratives had a special significance for western Ukrainian regions incorporated into the USSR during the Second World War. Because of the Holocaust and postwar deportations, the formerly multi-ethnic borderlands had acquired an unambiguously Ukrainian ethnic identity.[90] And it was this Ukrainian identity that turned the western regions into an unlikely bulwark of Sovietness.

Soviet Patriotism and Western Ukraine

While the great majority of Soviet historians looked towards narrow topics of regional or local history to keep out of trouble,[91] histories of the western borderlands did not offer such an escape from controversial issues. The region had been part of the Habsburg Empire in the nineteenth century, and had been divided between Poland, Czechoslovakia, Hungary, and Romania in the first half of the twentieth century. Party leaders were concerned that memories of exclusion from Russian rule could encourage residents of the western oblasts to articulate a Ukrainian identity defined in non-Soviet terms.[92] But with increasing state control over the intelligentsia, local bureaucrats in west Ukraine began to promote a cult of specifically local historical events and heroes that fit into the master narrative of Soviet history, thus claiming for their region an equal status within the wider Soviet community. They mobilized Ukrainian ethnic identities to Sovietise the western borderlands.

History of the territories incorporated into the USSR in 1939 was widely discussed in Soviet Ukraine throughout the postwar period. In particular, scholars were to write about "foreign occupation" of the region prior to its incorporation in the USSR.[93] Campaigns to discredit Greek Catholicism that began in the 1940s continued into the Brezhnev era. In order to combat what the authorities labelled "Uniate propaganda" (which normally referred to Ukrainian émigré publications), the Lviv obkom opened a museum of the history of religion and atheism. This reflected pressures from officials who otherwise promoted Ukrainian identities in the USSR, including the same Petro Tron'ko who had been so instrumental in establishing Ukrainian-Polish transnational cooperation during the Thaw, encouraged the writing of Ukrainian history in the USSR,[94] and now oversaw Soviet Ukraine's propaganda. According to Soviet statistics, the museum attracted 30,000 visitors between its opening in April and December 1970. Housed in the former Dominican monastery in Lviv, the exhibition was designed to educate citizens about the socio-political context in which "foreign occupiers" created the Uniate church, thus "spiritually enslaving the working masses of Ukraine and Belarus." In designing the exhibition, historians made a special effort to bring out the alleged links between Greek

Catholics, anti-Soviet Ukrainian nationalists, and German fascists, both before and after the imposition of Soviet power in the region.[95]

Just as portrayals of the past underlined the evils of foreign occupation in the borderlands, the "reunification" of the western oblasts with Soviet Ukraine in 1939 emerged as the most celebrated event in the region's history. In August 1979, *Pravda Ukrainy* wrote that the Soviet Union helped western Ukraine during the Polish, Romanian, and Czechoslovak occupation of the 1920s and 1930s, which culminated in the incorporation of Galicia into the USSR in September 1939.[96] On numerous occasions, party leaders and historians such as G. Ia. Serhienko emphasised that foreign ruling classes of Poland, Czechoslovakia, Romania, and Hungary oppressed the "hungry and illiterate" west Ukrainians, who subsequently achieved great progress under Soviet tutelage.[97] In this way, celebrating the events of 1939, Soviet officials highlighted the role that other parts of Ukraine had played in modernising the borderlands.[98] Historians and party apparatchiks presented the indigenous inhabitants of west Ukraine as passive victims, saved by their heroic Slavic brothers from further east.

Although the Ukrainian authorities in Kyiv established a strong degree of central control over memory politics in the western regions, regional party and state leaders also showed some initiative in shaping historical narratives. Yet it is striking that, in contrast to the Ukrainian Party Central Committee, regional leaders from Lviv often used history to present residents of western Ukraine as full-fledged Soviet citizens who had defeated foreign occupiers through their own efforts. This was not an easy task in the 1950s and 1960s. For example, in the aftermath of the Polish and Hungarian unrest in 1956, Mykhailo Konstanovych Lazurenko who headed the regional party organisation under Khrushchev lobbied for the CPU Central Committee to award the Order of Lenin to the city of Lviv. In his appeal, Lazurenko argued that the people of Lviv had long resisted Polish feudal oppression and the Austro-Hungarian occupation, fighting for "national freedom" and the "reunification of Ukraine with Russia."[99] He portrayed residents of the west as part of both the all-Soviet and Ukrainian communities in order to claim an equal status for the region over which he presided. However, despite repeated appeals, his request was denied. The central authorities in Kyiv were reluctant to commemorate western Ukraine as a distinguished segment of the Soviet Ukrainian people at a time when Khrushchev's Secret Speech, the return of former nationalist activists from the Gulag, and the events in Poland and Hungary destabilised the region. At the CPU Central Committee, Iukhym Antonovych Lazebnyk (otherwise recognised as a strong supporter of cultural liberalisation and a critic of Russification in Soviet Ukraine) was very cautious in his response to Lazurenko.[100] Rejecting the appeal, Lazebnyk argued in Ukrainian that major industrial centres such as Kharkiv, Odesa, Stalino (Donetsk), and Dnipropetrovsk "had a glorious history" and revolutionary traditions. There was no good reason to suggest that Lviv was in any way 'more important than them.[101] While Lazurenko tried to mobilise regional history to emphasise Lviv's belonging the wider Soviet Ukrainian community, it seems that his superiors feared it would have the opposite effect, fueling a sense of distinctiveness and superiority among local inhabitants. [102]

These fears were not entirely unfounded. Although the authorities in Lviv were careful not to overemphasise Galicia's non-Russian and non-Soviet path of development, their efforts were often undermined by academics and lower level bureaucrats.[103] Museum directors were a particularly uncooperative group, devoting little attention to the region's links with other parts of the USSR when they designed historical exhibitions. In 1967, D. Slobodaniuk from the Lviv region Communist Party leadership reprimanded museums for failing to present local history as part of a broader Soviet story. The museums displayed few materials relating to western Ukraine's development during the Soviet period and the spread of Leninist ideas in Polish-ruled western Ukraine before 1939. Moreover, while the open-air ethnographical museum in Lviv enjoyed the status of a republican institution, the architecture it displayed was predominantly representative of west Ukraine, with the eastern banks of the Dnipro River ignored almost entirely.[104] Low-level officials in Lviv presented the Ukrainian nation outside the Soviet, party-approved framework.

Literary narratives of the village further contributed to undermining the image of western Ukraine as part of the Soviet and Soviet Ukrainian community during the 1960s. In his study of Russian village prose, Geoffrey Hosking demonstrates that many writers explored folk traditions, thus portraying the village "in the grip of an alien bureaucracy and losing its values and culture in the face of the encroachments of urban and industrial civilisation." This evoked contradictory responses among Soviet officials and literary critics, some of whom believed that the static village characters provided no model for Soviet people who lived in a fast changing world, with others retorting that men in the modern urban environment had the most need for "moral guidance."[105]

While the village prose movement caused controversy because it fed into wider debates about de-Stalinization and subjectivity in Soviet society,[106] officials at the CPU Central Committee department of culture gave a very negative assessment to literary descriptions of the countryside in the western borderlands, in particular asserting that they put into question the Soviet status of the western regions. This explains why, when Roman Andryiashyk sent his novel *Zelenyi klyn* (*The Green Wedge*) to be published in the journal *Dnipro* in 1967, the editors refused to publish it, pointing out that the Hutsuls were not shown to have strong links with other "Soviet peoples."[107] Charging that the Hutsul fight against the colonial politics of Austria-Hungary, Germany, Tsarist Russia, and Romania was treated in an artificial manner, as if it bore no relation to the revolutionary uprisings in the east and west, the journal sent the manuscript back to the author for corrections. However, Andryiashyk's work was eventually published in *Dnipro* in 1969 under the title *Dodomu nema vorottia* (*There Is No Return Home*), furthering the impression that western Ukraine was different from other parts of the USSR. Apparatchiks at the culture department at the CPU Central Committee were outraged because the author had made few changes to the original.[108]

Under Brezhnev, local officials in the borderlands became more efficient in censoring depictions of west Ukraine's history that downplayed its links with other parts of Ukraine and the USSR. In 1972, just as Brezhnev and Schcherbyts'kyi staged a full-blown attack on Ukrainian dissidents,[109] they also stressed that west Ukrainian leaders had to do a better job of explaining the evils of Ukrainian nationalism defined in opposition to Russia and the USSR. In practice, they were to prevent the publication of press articles that commemorated pre-Soviet times as anything other than a period of constant strife and suffering.[110] This pressure seemed to work. The vicious and often personal conflicts that rocked academia in western Ukraine came to an end around 1973.[111] On 11 March 1975, the head of the Glavlit's Ukrainian branch, M. Pozdniakov, was happy to report that censors had strengthened control over publishing in the republic over the course of the preceding two years. Under increased pressure from the CPU, editors approached their work more carefully and committed fewer "mistakes" than before. The editorial board of *Vitchyzna* had thus removed Hutsal's short story *Zustrich z Karpatamy* (*A Meeting with the Carpathians*) from the May issue of the journal, due to its focus on old architecture, customs, and traditions.[112]

Notably, the space for the articulation of western Ukrainian regional peculiarities shrank just as the expression of national identities among titular ethnic groups came to define Soviet public culture.[113] This was no coincidence. Local heroes and major historical events from the borderlands were increasingly commemorated only to the extent that they were written into the Soviet Ukrainian master narrative.

Because it took so long to bring the history of western Ukraine under control, it was only very gradually that party leaders in Kyiv allowed scholars and regional apparatchiks to portray residents of western Ukraine as historical agents in their own right. Instead of stressing the region's peculiarities, new histories emphasized how residents of the western borderlands contributed to broader Soviet and Soviet Ukrainian communities. Stories about socialist struggle in the region emerged first. Exaggerated, de-Polonised, and Ukrainianised histories of communist resistance in the shape of the Ivan Franko National Guard (Narodna Hvardia) were published from 1957.[114] From the mid-1950s, scholars at the Institute of Party History in Kyiv, supported by the CPU secretary Stepan Vasiliovych Chervonenko, talked about the importance of rehabilitating the Communist Party of Western Ukraine (CPWU).[115] The scholars demanded that the central party archives in Moscow send photocopies of relevant documents to Ukraine.[116] The process was painfully slow, partly because it took until 1966 before the archivists at the USSR Council of Ministers found many materials relating to the CPWU.[117]

Meanwhile, Lviv party members active in western Ukraine's pre-Soviet communist movement continued to exert pressure on historians to explore the history of the CPWU in more depth. In a 1962 appeal to the Institute of History in Kyiv, a senior party activist, historian, and former member of the CPWU Mykhailo Tesliuk still found it necessary to underline that the party should be rehabilitated and its history published. Persecuted in interwar Poland and critical of Moscow's nationalities policy in Ukraine during the interwar period, Tesliuk spent twenty years in the Stalinist Gulag after moving from Polish-ruled Galicia to Soviet Ukraine in the early 1930s. It is hardly surprising that, after his rehabilitation in 1956, he did not see prewar Soviet Ukraine and its elites as the only source of progress. His version of Soviet Ukrainian history was much more favourable to indigenous inhabitants of Lviv – Tesliuk suggested that veterans of the CPWU should be given state pensions.[118] More broadly, as Tarik Cyril Amar argues, the idea that the communist movement was not imported into western Ukraine resonated among

CPWU veterans.[119] These narratives found support among the local political elite.[120]

Shortcomings of cultural diplomacy in the socialist camp go a long way towards explaining the shift in Soviet politics of memory whereby western Ukraine emerged as an important historical agent. Soviet historians of the western oblasts grounded the legitimacy of their research by explicitly rebuking the claims of their colleagues in the satellite states, whom they accused of trying to undermine the Ukrainian, East Slavic, and Soviet character of the region. It was the historian's duty, claimed the Ukrainian press, to expose any such "falsifications."[121] From the mid-1960s, the Romanians were especially provocative, publishing books and atlases that claimed that Northern Bukovyna was an ethnically Romanian land.[122] Similarly, Polish historical representations of Lviv put pressure on Soviet scholars to integrate Galicia into the broader framework of Soviet and Ukrainian history. As early as 1956, the head of Lviv's regional executive council, Semen Vasilovych Stefanyk, born and bred in Habsburg and Polish-ruled western Ukraine, noted that the Polish press used the 700th anniversary of Lviv to portray it as a Polish town. He suggested that Soviet scholars retort by portraying Lviv as a city where Ukrainians lived side-by-side with other nations of the USSR, or "a city of the friendship of the peoples" (this slogan was normally reserved for describing relations between titular ethnic groups of the USSR).[123]

The need to respond to foreign accounts inspired party apparatchiks to sponsor more historical images of the borderlands, which permitted residents of the western regions to introduce west Ukrainians as positive historical protagonists. The first secretary of the Lviv regional party committee, Vasilii Kutsevol, though originally from eastern Ukraine, sought a more prominent role for the borderlands and their inhabitants in Soviet Ukrainian public culture during the 1960s. In 1965, he appealed for the authorities in Kyiv to recognise the heroism of Lviv's inhabitants during the Great Patriotic War.[124] The "search for a usable Galician past," to use William Risch's term, gathered pace in the late 1960s. Published in 1968 and highly controversial, the collectively written *Triumph of Historic Justice* was a "cautious, diplomatic reassessment of Galicia's historical record" that "refused to call Ukrainians'" national movement a product of German-Austrian intrigue, a notion historians and publicists insinuated before the Thaw. Historians of west Ukraine were still subject to repression as limits of the permissible continued to shift.[125] Still, it was precisely because communist party apparatchiks got a firmer hold over public culture that they felt comfortable enough to cultivate memories of west Ukrainian history and its heroes. Iurii Kondufor's 1981 history of Ukraine finally conceded that the accusations leveled against the CPWU in the 1930s were fabricated.[126]

Kutsevol's successor at the post of the first secretary of Lviv's communist party organization, Viktor Dobryk, is normally associated with the Brezhnev-era crackdown on Ukrainian national expression.[127] Yet even he was a very eager advocate of local histories in the borderlands, especially because he was keen to condemn Polish accounts at the height of the Solidarity crisis in the early 1980s.[128] The Polish crisis provided a context in which Soviet scholars lobbied party authorities to let them write more about western Ukraine's past, though strictly within the confines of the broader Soviet Ukrainian narrative. As Soviet-Polish tensions heightened, the Social Sciences Institute of the Ukrainian Academy of Sciences received instructions from the CPU Central Committee to analyse how Polish academic periodicals presented west Ukraine's history.[129] Responding to Polish claims that Lviv had been a thoroughly Polish city before 1939, Soviet Ukrainian scholars projected twentieth-century concepts of ethnicity into the past. For example, the Lviv-based journal *Zhovten'* claimed that Galicia had a clear East Slavic identity at least since the middle ages, tracing the genesis of Lviv as a city of Ancient Rus that came under Polish occupation in the fourteenth century.[130]

In line with these developments, Kyiv agreed to honour the memory of the medieval Lviv Prince Danylo Halyts'kyi in September 1981, though the central Ukrainian authorities had rejected Lviv's appeal to commemorate his resistance to Polonisation in 1956.[131] In June 1981, the CPU Central Committee and Ukraine's Council of Ministers received a petition from Lviv. Viktor Dobryk asked for permission to erect a new monument honouring Prince Danylo, the founder of Lviv, and thus to commemorate the city's history before a long period of Polish domination. Memory politics in the western borderlands was clearly shaped by rising tensions in the socialist camp: Dobryk did not mince his words, arguing that the monument to Prince Danylo had to be built in order to provide a counterpoint to the "Polish chauvinist" monuments that still littered the streets of Lviv.[132] Appealing to his superiors in Kyiv, Dobryk played on fears of foreign domination, underlining that Danylo Halyts'kyi had led the popular struggle against Tatar-Mongol, Hungarian, Polish, and German invasions. After Danylo's death, the report continued, when Lviv fell under Polish feudal rule in 1349, the Ukrainian people in the region strove for social and national liberation for almost 600 years, which culminated in the glorious reunification of 1939. Dobryk despaired that Polish historians deviated from this version of history, portraying Lviv as a Polish city with only coincidental links to Kyivan Rus.[133] As a result, the Ministry of Culture in Kyiv agreed to include the monument in the plan of new constructions for the period between 1981 and 1985.[134]

Like Kutsevol before him, Dobryk hailed from eastern Ukraine and yet, keen to undermine Polish claims to Lviv, sought a prominent place for Ukrainian historical heroes from west Ukraine in Soviet public culture. This suggests that the distinction between indigenous and non-indigenous leaders in the borderlands had become blurred after the death of Stalin. Party apparatchiks of eastern Ukrainian origin cast themselves as western Ukrainian leaders by cultivating the memory of specifically local heroes. This was possible because western Ukrainian history was now firmly conceived of as part of a larger Ukrainian, Soviet, and East Slavic story.

Language, customs, and memories of recent history made the western borderlands, and especially Galicia, distinct from other parts of the republic. This has led many observers to conclude that the region was the "least Soviet" part of the USSR. But, in the words of Caroline Ford, to suggest that the persistence of regional identities amounted to the failure of nation building projects in the peripheries "is to fail to confront local articulations of the national identity." In nineteenth century Britanny, Ford shows, regional clergy participated in national politics to promote social reform and weaken the Breton nobility, but also to defend regional institutions and practices.[135] In parallel with the Breton clergy, scholars and political leaders in the USSR's borderlands presented west Ukrainian traditions as key aspects of what it meant to be Soviet Ukrainian, seeking thereby to earn social capital and shape policy through Soviet Ukrainian institutions. They presented west Ukraine as an unlikely bulwark of East Slavdom defined in opposition to the (very) near abroad.

Conclusion

Soviet bloc public and cultural diplomacy of the 1970s was part of a new "socialist way of life" that emerged after the Prague Spring. Transnational cultural exchanges and international travel were no longer the domain of a few educated specialists charged with the task of "building socialism" and overcoming nationalist prejudices in the socialist camp; rather, they were part of popular culture whose movers and shakers sought to provide avenues for fun and self-realisation under state socialism. As Paulina Bren argues in her study of Czechoslovakia, "the opportunity to live a life not merely – in fact, not at all – defined by work became a common trope of normalisation and the silver bullet of late communism."[136] Both in the USSR and its satellite states, officials in charge of public and cultural diplomacy aimed to make international travel, as well as the cinema, literature, and television programs of the socialist camp, attractive and popular throughout the Soviet bloc. Although this gave Eastern Europe and the USSR a degree of cultural coherence, it also undermined the Thaw-era ideological mission to create a socialist culture that would overshadow national differences. Largely in order to meet audience demands, but also reflecting their own ethnic prejudices and loss of faith in internationalist ideals, Soviet bloc political and cultural elites promoted forms of popular culture that played on national stereotypes and contained few references to the party's ideological pronouncements. In this vision, ethnic differences in the socialist camp mattered more than political and ideological similarities.

Whereas Bren argues that the Czechoslovak leadership of the 1970s used popular culture to turn citizens' attention away from public affairs and towards the private world of consumption, family, and friends,[137] the forms of international travel and cultural exchanges that emerged in the Soviet bloc under Brezhnev explicitly highlighted questions of public interests (and national identity in particular). Tensions among the political, cultural, and academic elites of the socialist camp, coupled with their desire to tap into ethnic sentiments among the population, fuelled the growth of such forms of cultural expression that defined Sovietness in opposition to East European nations. The Brezhnev era was not about encouraging people to escape into the private sphere as faith in state socialism crumbled after 1968. Rather, particularly as the economic crisis hit in the late 1970s and early 1980s, Soviet and East European leaders turned towards ethnic nationalism as a means of social and political mobilisation.

The centrality of borders and national identities in Brezhnev-era Soviet culture had a strong impact on the development of Soviet and Ukrainian identities. On one level, cultural and scholarly exchanges within the Soviet bloc helped promote a vision of Soviet patriotism focused on celebrations of the Second World War. Suggesting that inhabitants of Eastern Europe owed a debt of gratitude to Soviet citizens who had liberated them from Nazi oppression, Soviet officials justified Soviet domination of the region, as well as presented the Soviet community as the unblemished "good guys." This silenced dissidents who criticised the Soviet political system, foreign policy, and social relations, presenting their views as unpatriotic and marginal.

Soviet patriotism in Ukraine was intimately linked with the promotion of strong ethnic identities. Official publications and cross-border travel helped promote the vision of a united Soviet community composed of homogenous ethno-national groups, with Ukrainian national identities defined in opposition to Eastern Europe. This helped to propagate the idea of Ukraine as part of a world dominated by Russia, and made it difficult even for self-identified Ukrainians to speak of Ukraine as part of the same cultural and political community as Hungary, Czechoslovakia, or Poland. Most surprisingly, it was in western regions that the starkest articulations of a Soviet Ukrainian identity emerged during the 1970s. Party leaders in the borderlands encouraged historians to highlight popular resistance to Polish national and class oppression in western Ukraine. They thus tapped into and fanned anti-Polish sentiment in order to present western Ukraine as part of a wider East Slavic community.

Ironically, although the idea of East European friendship was a product of Soviet and East European party leaders, it was mostly dissidents who still took it seriously under Brezhnev. To be sure, however, they infused it with their own meanings as they sought to establish transnational opposition networks in the Soviet bloc. Soviet dissidents and Polish opposition activists thus issued common appeals in defence of Czechoslovak intellectuals put on trial in the late 1970s.[138] The Soviet *samizdat* also emphasised that the Czechoslovak dissident manifesto, Charter 77, along with other East European dissident statements issued after the signing of the Helsinki Agreements, touched on issues relevant in the USSR itself: the right to fair trial, freedom of movement, and freedom of speech and belief.[139] Most importantly for Polish-Ukrainian relations, as Khrystyna Chushak demonstrates, the vast majority of Polish dissidents made every effort to bridge national divides: they recognised Ukraine's sovereignty in formerly Polish-ruled territories, supported the notion of Ukrainian independence, and stressed that the future Polish-Ukrainian border should be easy to cross.[140]

It was also in the 1970s that the seeds of cooperation between illegal trade unions in the USSR and Eastern Europe were laid. In 1976, Andrei Sakharov issued an appeal to the newly formed Workers' Defence Committee in Poland, emphasising that the Soviet bloc intelligentsia should defend the rights of blue-collar workers.[141] This question became more pressing during the early 1980s.

5 A Prelude to Perestroika: Solidarity and Soviet Patriotism, 1980–1985

"We feed these dirty scum … and they want to go over to the West."[1] According to an émigré who left Kyiv for the West in early 1982, anti-Polish ethnic slurs like this one proliferated among his friends and colleagues back home as strikes swept through Poland in the early 1980s. Soviet patriotism with its anti-Polish undertones that had become so prominent in the 1970s provided a powerful legitimating discourse for the late Brezhnev regime, helping to insulate the USSR from the Solidarity crisis in Poland. For most Soviet citizens, the rise of the Solidarity trade union appeared not as a challenge to state socialism and a potential source of inspiration for the entire bloc, but rather as a Polish national upheaval that threatened the USSR and East Slavs in particular.

In August 1980, in the midst of an enormous wave of strikes, the Polish state recognised the twenty-one demands of the newly formed independent trade union, Solidarity. In contrast to earlier workers' protests, the demands of the union were distinctly political: freedom of association, freedom of conscience, freedom of the press, social autonomy and self-government, and equality of rights and duties. As such, the demands reflected the alliance among workers, intellectuals, students, and the Catholic Church that had been developing since the mid-1970s; they combined a commitment to civil activism with the ideas of the democratic opposition and the moral views of the church. The rise of Solidarity "indicated the collapse of a definite concept of social and political order" in Poland.[2] With some ten million members, the movement "presented a mighty political force that was able to threaten not only the domestic order but the entire political stability of the region."[3] As Solidarity grew over the course of 1981, Soviet criticism of the independent trade unions became increasingly sharp, and Warsaw adopted a more confrontational attitude towards the opposition. This culminated in the imposition of martial law on 13 December 1981, which demonstrated the regime's ability to survive a major challenge from below, but also Solidarity's "self-limiting" demands and non-violent tactics. While the stalemate between the state and society was not broken, the regime weakened the opposition and forced Solidarity underground.[4]

There was no Soviet equivalent to Solidarity. To be sure, Soviet workers faced very similar problems and frustrations as their Polish colleagues, and Solidarity leaders sought to reach out to them in the early 1980s.[5] That Solidarity held very limited appeal in the USSR can largely be attributed to the USSR's brutal suppressions of working class dissent, but this is only part of the story. Equally important, anti-Polish ethnic slurs and apprehensions about the political and economic consequences of the Solidarity strikes were very widespread in the USSR between the autumn of 1980 and the end of 1981, especially among self-identified Ukrainians and Belorussians.[6] In the early 1980s, residents of Soviet Ukraine were more concerned about the Polish nationalist threat than domestic social and political dynamics.

Yet the Polish events inspired Soviet citizens to reflect on the relationship between socialist states and blue-collar workers. As Solidarity shook the foundations of the regime in Warsaw, Soviet citizens spoke about the deep socio-political problems that plagued the USSR and its satellites. In various public settings, including queues outside shops and public transport, they blamed the Poles for economic shortages. At the same time, however, they claimed that Soviet citizens deserved more than what they were getting from the state in the early 1980s.

Perhaps more surprisingly, the late Soviet regime, widely regarded as stagnant and inefficient, appeared to listen. A desire to transform the Soviet polity that began to manifest itself in the early to mid-1980s was founded not in dissenting ideas for reform, nor, as Stephen Kotkin claims, in the socialist ideology that held little popular appeal.[7] Rather, it was grounded in ethnically and geographically defined Soviet patriotism. Keen to discredit Solidarity among Soviet society and to retain close control over Eastern Europe, leaders of the USSR fanned anti-Polish sentiment at home, while seeking new ways to promote Soviet and Soviet Ukrainian culture in the near abroad. The rise of a workers' opposition in Poland further pushed Soviet leaders to confront popular economic discontent at home, as residents of Ukraine complained that the state failed to protect its own nations from foreign exploitation. In the short term, this led to improved consumer goods supplies. In the long term, Soviet leaders embarked on very cautious institutional and legal reforms that were supposed not only to strengthen the USSR's international standing, but also, through combatting the second economy, to create more transparent rules to govern state-society relations at home. The early 1980s was not yet a time of fundamental reform, but rather a prelude to perestroika – cautious, incomplete, and half-hearted. Still, Soviet Ukrainian patriotism underpinned a widespread commitment to change before the onset of Gorbachev's reforms.

The Weakness of Reformist Patriotism

Solidarity attracted considerable interest among the Soviet population, particularly in Ukraine and the western borderlands, where residents encountered numerous Polish tourists, received Polish radio and television broadcasts, and recalled Ukraine's historical ties with Poland. Some contemporary observers saw this as a threat to Soviet stability.[8] Ultimately, however, those who sympathised with Solidarity's agenda were crushed under the weight of the authoritarian regime.

Like in 1956 and 1968, curiosity about the major crisis in Soviet-controlled Eastern Europe fuelled demands for more information. Some citizens, such as a Ukrainian engineer interviewed during a trip to the West, complained that the Soviet mass media did not provide enough truthful information about Poland, which forced him to turn to Radio Liberty. "In our broadcasts, the only information we get on the subject is the official version, which is on the side of the authorities. But Solidarity has the support of many workers in Poland."[9] Noting that jamming had intensified since the outbreak of the Polish crisis, many citizens questioned by Radio Liberty researchers nevertheless echoed the twenty-eight-year-old man from the Odesa oblast who emphasised that "because of the events in Poland, I am even more eager to listen to Western radio."[10]

Residents of Soviet Ukraine also accessed news directly from Polish sources. Mainstream Polish mass media provided more information about the unfolding events than Soviet leaders were comfortable with.[11] Moreover, Solidarity activists tried to appeal to citizens of the USSR and other East European countries through less official channels. Most famously, in September 1981 they issued a "Message to the Working People of Eastern Europe" that included "all the nations of the Soviet Union," in which they wrote about "the community of our fates."[12] Such contraband literature reached at least some residents of the

USSR's western oblasts. In the first five months of 1981, the authorities caught 130 Polish travellers smuggling over 2,000 issues of "ideologically hostile literature."[13] During the early 1980s, the first secretary of the Lviv party organization, Viktor Dobryk, was especially concerned that contacts between Soviet dissidents and members of Solidarity who distributed illegal newspapers and leaflets in the region would strengthen Ukrainian separatism.[14] The authorities perceived religion as another potential source of contagion because members of the Polish clergy transported not only Polish religious literature to Ukraine, but also Ukrainian émigré publications such as *Suchasnist*.[15]

More broadly, in party officials' view, smuggling and trade created contexts where visitors from Poland expressed "anti-Soviet" and "anti-socialist" views. Soon after the outbreak of strikes on the Polish coast, for example, party leaders in Lviv wrote about a group of tourists travelling on a Polish tour bus from Lviv to Ternopil. One woman reportedly took out a pair of Polish jeans from her bag and started sewing on a western label (probably in order to sell them at a higher price than Polish jeans would fetch in the USSR). The Soviet guide reproached her, but the Polish tour group leader intervened to say that the Poles "were not ashamed to trade and that, in general, their government gave unofficial approval to Polish citizens who supported themselves in this way, because they believe that rich individuals make for a rich country."[16] Party-produced reports further suggested that customs controls turned into a forum of confrontation between Soviet citizens and Polish travellers. A Polish train conductor attacked Soviet customs officers in explicitly national terms: he yelled at them, claimed that the train was "Polish property" which Soviet officials had no right to search, and charged that the "Russians treated the Poles badly."[17]

Solidarity inspired the expression of new types of dissenting opinions in Soviet Ukraine and other parts of the USSR. According to KBG reports from Lviv, a handful of citizens voiced support for the idea of strikes under the influence of western radio stations, the Polish media, and tourist trips to Poland. In November 1980, for example, informers relayed the views of a man queuing outside a shop:

> Our government's policy is wrong. We send everything abroad, and leave nothing for ourselves. Nobody is happy with this policy and strikes could break out here like they have in Poland, where the workers will get their way.[18]

8 Soviet-Hungarian border crossing, 1976. As cross-border travel expanded after 1968, customs controls became a site of confrontation. Courtesy of the Hungarian Museum of Photography.

Meanwhile, the Polish crisis seemed to spur some Soviet workers to action. Describing a two-hour strike held by Odesa dock workers, a Ukrainian sailor visiting a Western port claimed that "they did this as a token of solidarity with the Polish people."[19]

In fact, apart from such seemingly ad hoc comments and initiatives, Solidarity inspired some more sustained forms of dissent. Illegal trade unions and groups devoted specifically to protecting workers' rights were especially affected by the rise of Solidarity. The most prominent among these organizations was the Free Interprofessional Union of Workers (SMOT), which was a small and fragmented group. "Since SMOT was founded under extremely difficult circumstances," explained one member during an interview in the West, it "consist[ed] of separate autonomous groups ... No one [knew] – neither the KGB, nor SMOT itself – how many SMOT chapters exist[ed]." In his estimation, there were about ten to fifteen SMOT units in total.[20] The group attracted blue and white-collar workers from various professional groups who had been unfairly dismissed from their jobs, and some dissidents saw this eclectic membership as a source of weakness.[21] The underground SMOT bulletin further publicized bureaucratic abuses that exposed the weakness of Soviet institutions. In September 1980, for example, the bulletin featured an article about a fifty-eight-year-old widow from Kyiv who had filed a complaint with the local administration. Her upstairs neighbour regularly flooded her apartment, but the woman's complaints were ignored. It so happened that the neighbour was a traffic militia officer, well connected in the region. She appealed to higher authorities in both Kyiv and Moscow, and getting nowhere, refused to take part in elections. Her neighbour's friend soon checked her into a local psychiatric hospital, where she was subjected to shock therapy.[22]

Highlighting similar abuses, activists of underground workers' movements in the USSR operated under the assumption that the Soviet regime was not responsive to their grievances. They argued that an effective opposition movement could not be confined to intellectuals, but had to involve the supposedly more "extreme" blue-collar workers as well: "Workers engage in active dissent; intellectuals in passive dissent."[23] In this way, their vision of participatory citizenship differed significantly from that advocated by proponents of reformist patriotism in 1968. Whereas proponents of reformist patriotism in 1968 called for reforming Soviet institutions to involve more citizens in the deliberation and implementation of policy, SMOT activists saw further discussion as futile and hoped that the involvement of blue-collar workers in opposition would lead to a more fundamental shake-up of the Soviet system.

Although SMOT and other underground workers' groups had appeared before the outbreak of the Polish crisis, new chapters were set up in late 1980.[24] In an interview with Charles Allen, a founding member of SMOT Vladimir Borisov claimed that the Polish events gave his organization a new lease of life:

> I think its influence is going to grow. For one thing, there is Poland. What is happening there is valuable experience for the members of our organisation. I find the whole course of events in Poland extremely encouraging. And at home now, there are stirrings among the workers. Some are turning to Western radio, while others are getting involved in samizdat. Of course, a lot is going to depend on government policy, and how people see their standard of living and the economic situation in general.[25]

Dissidents in various parts of the USSR cited the example of independent trade unions in Poland in an attempt to reach out to blue-collar workers at home, too. This was true among members of the Helsinki groups, who had previously expressed support for the Polish Workers' Defence Committee in underground publications (this was a Polish organization formed to protect workers' rights after the 1976 strikes in Radom).[26] In 1980 and 1981, dissidents such as Andrei Sakharov and even some individual blue-collar workers published articles in *samizdat*, outlining plans to encourage workers to "draw conclusions from the Polish experience."[27]

Yet it is impossible to draw a direct link between the Polish crisis and the sporadic and de-politicised strikes that took place in the USSR. In Kyiv, for example, two strikes were said to have taken place in response to increased production norms, while a third protested against the lack of water supply. However, as Elizabeth Teague points out, these strikes did not resemble the Polish events, as they included no political demands and were said to have ended as soon as the authorities gave in to the workers' demands.[28]

Dissent was ultimately weak in Soviet Ukraine and the USSR as a whole. In the long run, rather than strengthening Soviet dissident groups, Solidarity evoked a spirit of fatalism among Soviet dissidents who commented on just how different their society was from Poland. With the Soviet dissident movement in tatters,[29] the few *samizdat* authors despaired that the Polish events would not find their equivalent in the USSR itself. They contrasted the activism of the Polish trade unions with Soviet workers' apathy and dissidents' failure to work with "the masses."[30] Similarly, when a group of Moscow dissidents attempted to conduct an independent opinion poll about Poland between September and December 1981, they concluded that Soviet citizens were "certainly under a strong influence of official propaganda." Although they claimed that twenty per cent of blue-collar workers were "sympathetic" towards Solidarity, only two respondents considered the Polish crisis a "vital concern" (*krovnoe delo*). In contrast, many of the fifty per cent of blue-collar workers holding "negative" views were described as outright "aggressive and hostile."[31] Members of illegal trade unions were especially suspicious that the Soviet intelligentsia would stab them in the back: "If you remember, during the Novocherkassk uprising of 1962, students were armed and used to quell the striking workers."[32] Dissidents who called for the establishment of a workers' opposition in the USSR recognized that their views were marginal and referred to themselves as "extremists" and "revolutionaries."[33]

More broadly, other inhabitants of the USSR who did not publish in *samizdat* but voiced support for Solidarity experienced a sense of hopelessness and alienation. Even as some Soviet citizens believed that their compatriots supported free trade unions in Poland, they did not see Solidarity as a serious challenge to the status quo. In this vein, during an interview conducted in the West, a Chişinău blue-collar worker in his twenties emphasised that most of his colleagues voiced support for Solidarity, but also claimed that they "realised that the Poles would not be given the chance to work things out quietly in their own way." Meanwhile, other interviewees claimed that their positive view of Solidarity distinguished them from society at large. As an engineer from Moscow put it, "the majority believed Soviet information and thought that the Poles had gone mad."[34] This sense of isolation seemed to permeate even family relations. Soon after emigrating to the West, a retired railroad technician from Kharkiv remembered his colleagues saying, "God taught the Poles how to raise their children, but we missed the opportunity with ours, and now they believe the authorities and the newspapers more than they believe us."[35]

Pessimism about any prospects of reform was particularly widespread after the introduction of martial law in Poland. In early 1982, for example, a recent Jewish émigré from the west Ukrainian town of Rivne suggested that the rise of Solidarity helped fuel nationalist sentiment in the borderlands, but the introduction of martial law destroyed the spirit of those who sought change.[36] Although Polish and Soviet leaders claimed in public that Warsaw would correct the mistakes that had led to the crisis in the first place, some people did not take these promises seriously. A popular joke held that Leningrad's Solidarity Avenue would be renamed Jaruzelski's Dead End.[37]

To be sure, it was largely the repressive policies of the Soviet state that made it very difficult for citizens to voice ideas for change. After the outbreak of the Polish strikes, members of illegal workers' organizations came under intensified attack. The blue-collar worker Mikhail Kukobaka, involved in underground trade union activity since 1968 (when he sent a letter protesting the Warsaw Pact invasion of Czechoslovakia to the Czechoslovak consul in Kyiv), had already spent approximately ten years in prisons and mental institutions between 1970 and 1981. Despite reaching the end of a three year sentence in October 1981, he was not released from prison. "All things considered," wrote SMOT activists in an appeal to the International Labour Organization, "because of the recent events in Poland the authorities will be ten-times more cruel in dealing with an activist of the Russian workers' movement."[38] Further arrests and apartment searches followed in 1982.[39]

But the decline of reformist patriotism, whose proponents in 1956 and 1968 had claimed that dissidents and non-conformists could improve Soviet-style regimes, cannot be explained only with reference to state repression. Because ethnicity had become so central in Soviet public culture by the early 1980s, and since internationalism had not obliterated the importance of the Soviet-Polish border, Polish ideas for reform were ultimately seen as either irrelevant for Russians and Ukrainians in the USSR, or as a threat to Soviet stability. Some residents of Ukraine interviewed by Radio Liberty researchers went so far as to deny the Poles the right to strike. As an accountant from Odesa emphasised, "the Poles have always been privileged compared to other socialist countries, but even so they never stop complaining. I wonder what they would do if they were in our shoes."[40] As a SMOT activist explained with reference to Soviet workers:

> Their feelings are certainly contradictory. On the one hand, they are a bit envious. They know that, while Romanian and Bulgarian workers live no better than they do, the reverse is true of the Germans and the Czechoslovaks. But at the same time, some Soviet workers feel that they are being taken for a ride by the East Europeans. Not realising that the USSR takes far more than it gives, they wonder why the Soviet Union should be feeding all these people – the Cubans, the Czechoslovaks, and so on. Besides this, the authorities encourage world power chauvinism in an attempt to diminish people's resentment at being exploited.[41]

Anti-Polish sentiments in Ukraine prevented even the usual suspects, such as Greek Catholics, from commenting positively on social and cultural transformations of the Solidarity period. Viktor Dobryk in Lviv was relieved to find that many members of the illegal Uniate church did not become more active during Pope John Paul II's 1983 visit to Poland, alienated as they were by what they saw as his "Polish nationalism."[42] Albeit frustrated with the Soviet regime, many inhabitants of the USSR were seemingly even more resentful of foreigners whom they blamed for deepening the economic crisis in the socialist bloc.

A Veneer of Conformity

At the height of the Solidarity crisis, Soviet leaders believed that most citizens toed the sanctioned line, repeating slogans about foreigners' ungratefulness to the USSR and Polish anarchy and chaos. Soviet apparatchiks underlined that they registered hardly any "undesirable" attitudes among the population.[43]

To be sure, party leaders faced numerous difficulties in gauging citizens' views, which skews the historian's view of popular opinion in Ukraine. Still, it seems that Soviet society remained remarkably stable in the early 1980s.[44] In the western regions, local party officials looked for trouble, but were surprised to find a largely complacent population. In November 1980, for example, the Volhynia region party secretary Leonid Ivanovych Palazhchenko stressed that even former OUN members voiced "no negative views" about the socio-political changes in Poland.[45] Similarly, just after Wojciech Jaruzelski introduced martial law in Poland, Soviet officials from Lviv surveyed popular opinion in every region and every village, at industrial enterprises and collective farms, educational institutions, halls of residence, as well as market places, bus and railway stations, and on public transport.They nevertheless concluded that the population, including the Polish minority, voiced "no negative opinions" in relation to the Polish crisis.[46] It may be surprising that the KGB reported everything was fine. In the view of at least one dissident who commented on the Polish crisis in an open letter to American railroad workers, KGB officers were likely to exaggerate problems in their areas of jurisdiction: "Of course, if an agent, a group of agents, or an entire department report that there are no anti-statist elements in their area, their organization will in the end be dissolved."[47] Almost despite themselves, the authorities found few signs of trouble in the early 1980s.

Popular acquiescence in the early 1980s was underpinned by widespread fear of war. During public meetings across Ukraine, residents of the republic openly admitted that they were afraid of the Polish crisis escalating into a military conflict and asked lecturers and agitators to discuss the possibility of war.[48] The spectre of war seemed most threatening in the borderlands. Reporting on conversations in public spaces around Lviv, the KGB concluded that many people were happy to bear the shortages as long as they would help to avoid war.[49] Viktor Dobryk believed that the desire to avoid bloodshed was also behind the relative acquiescence of the Polish minority in the region.[50]

Outward manifestations of conformity ruled the day. In all likelihood, they did at times mask more confrontational attitudes. As an ethnically Polish blue-collar worker from the Belarusian town of Hrodna explained during a visit to the West, "the sympathy of Soviet Poles was clearly with Solidarity during recent events in Poland, although people kept their feelings to themselves and even spoke out against 'counter-revolution' at meetings."[51] While it is virtually impossible to assess levels of "genuine belief," it is striking that Soviet citizens learned to justify their criticism of Solidarity by employing a fixed canon of propaganda slogans in various public forums. The press repeatedly emphasised that Poland threatened the peace and economic stability of the entire socialist bloc, and particularly after spring 1981, claimed that the Poles were nationalist and anti-Soviet, challenging the USSR's territorial integrity.[52] Speaking in public, residents of Ukraine stuck to this script very closely.[53] Public statements about Solidarity became very hostile in the course of 1981. In May, for example, it was reported that "workers of the republic" asked why the Polish leadership failed to destroy "nationalist and chauvinist" forces in their country.[54]

Proponents of conservative patriotism in the 1980s posed the greatest challenge to the Soviet authorities not because of what they said, but because of how they said it. Eastern Europe functioned much like Yurchak's "imaginary West," forming a Soviet "internal elsewhere." Just as it was possible to represent the wearing of jeans as "bad cosmopolitanism" or "good internationalism," inhabitants of the USSR could also speak about economic complaints as legitimate demands voiced by the Soviet people who worked hard for the benefit of their "socialist brothers" abroad, or as panic-mongering that disgusted responsible citizens.[55] Following Yurchak's idea that "the more the immutable forms of the system's authoritative discourse were reproduced everywhere, the more the system was experiencing a profound internal displacement," I call these "correct" ways of speaking and behaving "staging patriotism."[56]

The term staging patriotism refers to the practice of using a set of slogans or clichés to express different social identities and opinions; it helps to make sense of the seemingly conformist types of public speech and behaviour that characterized the late Soviet period. Like actors who had been practicing one play for a few decades, inhabitants of Ukraine repeated the same lines about "Soviet sacrifices in the Great Patriotic War" and "imperialist threats" over and over again. Like participants in a staged performance, many people did not necessarily believe these slogans, which is not to deny that Soviet patriotism may well have carried a real meaning for some of them. In any case, the very act of speaking or behaving in a patriotic way mattered more than what was actually said. Official surveillance reports specify who spoke about Solidarity or travelled to Eastern Europe, showing which categories of citizens were most successful at manifesting their "correct" point of view, thereby improving their social standing and claiming material benefits and other perks from the Soviet state in return for their loyalty. Furthermore, as they shifted emphasis from one line to another, Soviet citizens could give a different spin to the same formulaic slogans about the outer empire, aiming to evoke different reactions among their audiences. Without deviating from the general script about the need to maintain Soviet control over Eastern Europe, they sometimes even introduced elements of improvisation into the performance, asserting their right to voice limited criticism of the Soviet leadership and the mass media. For example, repeating slogans about Soviet aid to Eastern Europe along with formulaic condemnations of East European departures from the Soviet model of socialism, some citizens who staged patriotism claimed the USSR should no longer subsidise Eastern Europe, and focus on economic improvements at home instead.

Staging Patriotism and Middle Class Aspirations

Mirroring earlier patterns from 1968, many citizens of Ukraine staged patriotism to perform middle class identities. It appears that war veterans, university professors, leading workers, and party members with some managerial responsibilities were once again the most outspoken participants in various public meetings, claiming to be better citizens than Poles abroad and more important than other residents of the USSR.

War veterans in particular stated that they were personally offended by the rise of Polish nationalism, recalling Soviet feats during the Great Patriotic War. During an agitation meeting in June 1981, for instance, a lieutenant from Zaporizhzhia and honorary citizen of the Polish town of Racibórz, H.A. Zhyl'ko, criticised the Warsaw leadership: "As someone who fought for the liberation of Poland, I am well aware of the high price that the Soviet people paid for the honour and independence of this country ... I would like the Polish leadership to act more decisively."[57] Residents of Ukraine who enjoyed a high status in Soviet society were expected to repeat propaganda slogans in various heavily controlled public forums. Volodymyr Iosypovych Zdoroveha, a senior professor of philology and journalism from Lviv, thus stated that foreign-inspired forces should not be allowed to undermine the foundations of socialism in Poland for which "such a high price had been paid."[58] These statements were painfully jingoistic, repeating the idea that the USSR had earned Poland's loyalty.

For the Soviet aspirational middle class, little had changed since 1968. If anything, middle class patriotic rhetoric had become even more xenophobic. Soviet tourists in the West, no doubt a privileged and select group, emphasised their loyalty to the Soviet state as they referred to the "idiot Poles" as a "race of hooligans."[59] After emigrating to the West, a Kyiv hairdresser described a troubling conversation with an old client:

> In the autumn of 1981, the wife of a military officer told me that her husband's section was being sent to Poland. She spoke of the Poles with such hatred that I couldn't understand it. "They ought to send a few million of them to Siberia," she said. "They should cut them down, the way you cut down a forest. That way they wouldn't strike any more."[60]

To belong to the aspirational middle class in the early 1980s meant to make strong statements about Soviet foreign policy, and even to voice tacit criticism of the authorities for being too soft.

Party activists and other members of the aspirational middle class in Soviet Ukraine grew concerned about social tensions across the border during this period. Therefore, attacks on Solidarity made during public gatherings acted as a means through which this group reaffirmed their special status in Soviet society and underscored their links with the "masses." Once again, speaking on behalf of entire communities during public meetings was a common rhetorical device used by the aspirational middle class. This allowed a brigade leader from Kharkiv to prove that he was well informed about developments across the border, and to claim that he represented the workers at his factory: "We, the workers, find it difficult to understand the position of the Polish leadership ... It is time to use force and put an end to the counterrevolution."[61] Middle class claims to guide and control other citizens were more important than ever as a mass working class movement threatened established social structures just across the border.

The middle class nature of Soviet patriotism was most palpable during international travel in the early 1980s. In the first half of 1981, the number of Soviet people travelling to Poland was cut by 44 per cent, from 45,400 to 24,500.[62] This is partly explained by financial difficulties that had already affected international exchanges before the outbreak of the Polish crisis.[63] However, travel became much more constrained after August 1980, turning into an important marker of social differentiation in 1981. While mass tourism was halted, it was mainly war veterans, leading workers, friendship society and trade union activists, and amateur artists who continued to visit Poland to influence the situation there.[64] In contrast to the late 1970s, and reflecting earlier patterns from the late 1950s, travel became more strictly defined as a means to promote Soviet values abroad.[65] From 1 April 1981, Soviet officials shaped travel in such a way as to ensure Soviet citizens (and not their foreign guests and hosts) set the agenda. Organized trips from the USSR to Poland were temporarily discontinued.[66] Meanwhile, Polish citizens still visited the USSR, where the hosts confined discussions to culture and swept political questions under the carpet.[67] In the assessment of the PUWP Central Committee, the USSR's new policies on travel reflected the resentment that Soviet specialists, activists, and artists had long felt towards Polish colleagues' assertions to cultural superiority.[68]

Admittedly, blunders did occur, and some members of the aspirational middle class failed to prove their patriotic credentials upon encountering the Poles.[69] More often, however, party officials praised members of Soviet delegations for trying to maintain close contacts with Polish workers, despite the latter's positive assessment of Solidarity, reluctance to socialise, and preponderance to criticize Soviet policies.[70] In this sense, international travel and exchanges of workers' collectives in particular were a means for a large section of Ukraine's population to reaffirm their status as the most reliable Soviet citizens. Practices that had long been helping some citizens claim a middle class status ran strong in the late Brezhnev era.

Soviet Patriotism and Rowdy Polish Tourists

In the western borderlands, staging patriotism was not confined to the aspirational middle class. This is largely because the region hosted many more Polish tourists than other parts of Ukraine. During their visits, Polish-Ukrainian conflicts came to the fore, which inspired public articulations of Soviet and Soviet Ukrainian patriotism among the local population.

According to Polish historian Paweł Sowiński, smuggling across the Polish-Soviet border exploded in the 1970s. It was a common practice even on friendship trains, which was facilitated by the propagandistic nature of such tourist exchanges, as customs officers were reluctant to search trains decorated with red flags and the hammer and sickle.[71] The problem was so prominent that the Soviet Ukrainian radio broadcast a regular program called "Tourists and pseudo-tourists," in which they exposed smuggling across the Soviet border.[72] People's interests in travel seemed to revolve around trade. This goes some way towards explaining why the number of Polish citizens travelling across the border fell after changes in Soviet customs law made it more difficult to buy gold in the USSR in April 1978. It was through engaging in illegal activities that Soviet and East European citizens satisfied some very simple consumer needs. In October 1977, for example, the Soviet customs charged 990 Polish citizens with smuggling. These travellers tended to smuggle gold from the USSR to Poland, whilst commonly transporting blue jeans, wigs, head scarves, and even plastic bags into the Soviet Union (in 1977, the monetary value of the wigs alone exceeded that of any other product). Likewise, Polish customs officers in Terespol discovered 51 pairs of jeans hidden between the ceiling and roof of a Warsaw-Moscow train; notably, they found 83 boxes of cosmetics and 11,000 "devotional articles" on another train, suggesting that illegal economic activity was sometimes associated with other, more ideological acts of rebellion.[73]

The authorities were concerned that some of the most prominent members of Soviet and East European societies engaged in smuggling. The KGB reported that a large number of Soviet sportsmen travelling to the people's democracies and other countries were complicit in "speculation."[74] The Polish Central Customs Office even produced special reports on pop music stars smuggling currency, jewellery, and various other products upon returning from tours in the USSR. In April 1972, for example, they found fourteen icons concealed in the hand luggage and loudspeakers of the popular band Czerwone Gitary, with one band member landing a 5,000 zloty fine.[75]

These problems were brought into sharp relief during the early 1980s. Western Ukraine lay between Poland and the Black Sea resorts in Bulgaria and Romania. Between January and May 1981, 110,000 Polish citizens passed through the Chernivtsi oblast in transit to those countries,[76] and even though they were supposed to merely drive through the region and leave Soviet territory as soon as possible, many of the so-called "transit tourists" made stops to trade and see the sites of Lviv. In addition, about 5,000 Poles visited the Lviv region between October and December 1980 as part of organised tour groups, although their numbers were significantly slashed in 1981.[77] These visitors talked to Soviet people about Solidarity, spread rumours about the Polish and Ukrainian resistance to Soviet rule, and openly called for the local people to organise Polish-style strikes in the USSR.[78] Moreover, some members of Polish tour groups in the region voiced views critical not only of the Polish party, but also the USSR. They warned their Soviet interlocutors that "blood would flow" if the USSR invaded Poland.[79] The Poles behaved in a provocative manner as they walked around shops and market places in Lviv, asking people to name prices for milk, meat, sugar, and butter. The driver of a Polish tour bus was particularly confrontational: "You don't have freedom here. In Poland … when we don't like something, we simply go out on the streets and strike … The government listens to our demands and suggestions, and then gradually implements them."[80]

Contacts between local inhabitants and visitors from Poland brought Polish-Ukrainian national tensions to the fore. Visitors from Poland were especially outspoken when the USSR celebrated the 42nd anniversary of the Ukrainian "reunification" on 17 September 1981. They claimed that the Soviet army had occupied western Ukraine (or eastern Poland) in 1939, and that Lviv would once again return to Poland. Allegedly, some tourists became very aggressive, threatening that "the Poles would slaughter the Russians."[81] Ignoring approved plans for borderland travel, Polish tourists also challenged their Soviet guides and interpreters. For instance, one group demanded that the program of their excursion around Lviv be changed. Instead of visiting new regions constructed after 1944, they wanted to go to the *Orlęta* cemetery. Their guide claimed not to know what that was, but one Polish woman explained it was where Józef Piłsudski's soldiers were buried who had fought for a "Polish Lwów" after the First World War. The guide apparently defended the Ukrainian character of Lviv as she asked, tongue-in-cheek, whom the Poles were fighting against, only to hear that they battled "the Reds."[82] The Polish tourist thus threw west Ukrainians into one basket with all Soviet people.

It is not surprising that these types of behaviour encouraged residents of west Ukraine to distance themselves from the near abroad. Encounters with Polish tourists who visited west Ukraine provided a context where many locals articulated ideas of Soviet patriotism. According to surveillance reports, most locals resisted Polish travellers' provocative statements. Local citizens were infuriated by the shopping trips during which Polish tourists traded, drank, and claimed that Lviv was Polish.[83] When a group of Polish citizens addressed a long queue of local residents in a shop in Lviv, encouraging them to protest against poor supplies just as people did in Poland, Soviet citizens reportedly retorted that economic problems only arose because they had to feed "lazy, speculative" Poles. The tourists left the shop in a hurry and did not try to speak to anyone else.[84] The Polish tourists clearly expected to find a sympathetic audience among local Ukrainians, but locals contrasted themselves with Polish "wreckers and reactionaries," evoking ethnic identities to distance themselves from the crisis that unfolded across the border.

Other citizens spoke more explicitly about the need to protect Ukrainian national rights against Poland. During agitation meetings, for instance, members of workers' collectives from Volhynia, a region with a predominantly Ukrainian-speaking population, complained that anti-Soviet attitudes in Poland forced them to use Russian and not Ukrainian when they visited their relatives across the border.[85] Moreover, throughout the Solidarity period, inhabitants of Galicia appealed to the authorities to limit the number of Poles in the region,[86] and they continued to complain about the behaviour of Polish tourists in western Ukraine even after the imposition of martial law.[87] They thus posed a challenge to the local authorities. In 1980, for example, an anonymous letter sent to Viktor Dobryk expressed a sense of frustration, xenophobia, and Soviet pride that was specific to west Ukraine:

> If only you knew, comrade Dobryk, what goes on in Lviv, especially after dark. Clearly, we have to strengthen state security and send out more plain clothes officers to catch those bandits quickly … Illegal trade is flourishing … opposite the opera house and in public toilets. Who are these people? The people who come here, are they not provocateurs,

> especially the Poles? After all, they are a hopeless bunch, even though they are our allies. We think it would be better to cut the number of tourists coming here.[88]

Although the man wrote about "enemies of Soviet power" in western Ukraine and may well have been referring to some local residents as he wrote about "bandits,"[89] he also identified foreigners as the main source of trouble, implying that most residents of western Ukraine were essentially loyal to the Soviet system. It was on this basis that he claimed the right to shape policy.

Confronting Polish citizens, numerous inhabitants of west Ukraine exposed Soviet-Polish tensions whilst obscuring differences in Ukrainian society. According to Viktor Dobryk, in letters to relatives across the border, some citizens in the region recalled the horrors of interwar Poland and expressed concern about Polish forces that allegedly laid claims to western Ukraine.[90] They made references to the history of Ukrainian-Polish conflicts in the region to show their alienation from the near abroad. Other citizens suggested that residents of the borderlands were particularly keen to protect the Soviet community from harmful Polish influences, which helped challenge stereotypical perceptions of the borderlands as the "least Soviet" part of the republic:

> I am from Polissia. This year we had a proper flood. And we receive many kinds of products from other oblasts and republics. Oblasts and republics help each other. And the Poles, instead of working, are raising a fuss, going on strike. We feed them, and yet they are unhappy. This is especially worrying, as it is taking place right across the border from us.[91]

Voicing these views during a workers' meeting, Lutsk factory worker Liudmyla Trots' evoked a distinctly local, borderland identity, all the while highlighting her loyalty to the USSR as a whole. The claim that Poles were lazy while Soviet people worked hard for everyone's benefit was a common trope throughout Ukraine. However, according to surveillance reports and accounts of public meetings, such ethnic diatribes were particularly widespread in the borderlands.[92] More than ever before, inhabitants of the borderlands mobilized Ukrainian identities defined in opposition to Poland to write themselves into the broader Soviet and Soviet Ukrainian community during the early 1980s.

Staging Patriotism and Citizenship in the Borderlands

As residents of western Ukraine underlined their loyalty to the Soviet homeland, they also challenged the Soviet apparatchiks and their policies as loyal and engaged members of society, particularly in the sphere of economics. It was in the west of Ukraine that people discussed the Polish events not only during public agitation meetings, but also in unofficial conversations outside shops, on public transport, and in anonymous letters. These forums allowed for more creative interpretations of what it meant to be Soviet during the early 1980s.

Members of the western Ukrainian population suggested different solutions to the mounting crisis. For example, residents of Lviv who spoke in various public spaces offered solutions to the problem of shortages. Addressing colleagues at work, one inhabitant of the region suggested that the authorities should quickly introduce rationing so that people would not have to waste their time in queues.[93] More challenging were citizens' comments about Soviet mass media that sometimes accompanied complaints about economic shortages. While members of the aspirational middle class claimed that they needed to mediate important information to counteract potentially subversive rumours, many residents of western Ukraine suggested that all citizens were entitled to information. In this vein, discussing social and economic problems plaguing the Lviv oblast, the author of an anonymous letter to the obkom first secretary wrote:

> Why is all this concealed? A bitter truth is always better than sweet lies … And then the people will have more trust in you. We believe in you and respect you as an honest communist and principled leader, but we are also concerned about our Motherland … we do not want for the Polish fire to spread here.[94]

Citizens also demanded more information during public agitation gatherings. In the autumn of 1980, party members and non-party members alike expected party activists who addressed them in public to explain what conclusions were being drawn from the Polish experience in the USSR itself.[95] In the spring of 1981, they continued to ask whether the USSR had foreign debts like Poland, and demanded to know how it would pay them off.[96]

Apart from complaints about the Soviet information sphere, it was common for the west Ukrainian advocates of Soviet patriotism to criticise Soviet economic policies and subsidies to Poland in particular. Some were very circumspect about it, especially when speaking in public. During an agitation meeting in October 1980, a driver and party member from west Ukraine expressed a sense of Soviet pride as he subtly criticised the USSR's foreign policy:

> Why is it that, in a short space of time, our hard work allowed us to build a strong industry, create normal living conditions in this country, and defeat fascism? Meanwhile, thirty years down the line, they are not even able to feed themselves. We have to help our brothers at a difficult time, but we must not harm them with our selfless help.[97]

Citizens also expressed more radical views in spontaneous outbursts. At a fishmonger's store in Lviv, for example, "two people around the age of forty, probably a husband and wife," raised a fuss about the lack of fish. The man pointed out that that "we catch more fish now than ever before," and the woman shouted that "we send it all to our friends abroad."[98] People in queues likewise claimed that the Soviet authorities must take care of their own citizens before sending aid elsewhere.[99]

At the same time, with the escalation of the crisis, residents of the borderlands began to address the Soviet leadership more directly. Many recognized their comments as a challenge to the Soviet state, and therefore confined their criticism of Soviet aid to Poland to anonymous notes passed to lecturers during agitation meetings.[100] At the same time, other citizens did not conceive of their complaints as acts of defiance, expecting Soviet officials to address their grievances. They openly asked agitators who addressed them at public meetings to confirm the rumours that the USSR paid off Polish debts with its own natural resources.[101] Inhabitants of the west focused their attacks on local institutions rather than top CPSU leaders or the Soviet system itself. For instance, two elderly men travelling on a tram in Lviv complained about queues and corruption in shops, blaming the municipal authorities for all economic problems.[102] Similarly, an anonymous letter blamed the local leaders for potato shortages in Lviv, asking, "is it true that our potatoes have gone to Poland?"[103] Residents of the borderlands thus confronted Soviet bureaucrats whom they suspected of ignoring the population's material needs by presenting themselves as citizens concerned about the welfare of Soviet nations. The rhetoric of Motherland resounded in one anonymous letter: "As the saying goes: 'The Mother should feed her children before she eats.' And it is the other way round here ... The USSR has turned into a dairy cow."[104]

Inhabitants of western Ukraine staged patriotism by condemning Polish disobedience of the USSR and attempts at reforming Soviet-style socialism. In doing so, they also criticized local party officials in Soviet Ukraine, and Soviet domestic and foreign policies more broadly.

Official Reactions

Although Soviet leaders did not indulge all the demands made through staging patriotism, and cracked down brutally on dissent, the Polish crisis pushed them to pay more attention to citizens' needs, rights, and duties.

Violent protests in Poland had already inspired party officials in Ukraine to reflect on their relationship with blue-collar workers in the aftermath of the riots in Gdańsk, Gdynia, and Szczecin in December 1970. The first secretary of the Central Committee in Kyiv, Petro Shelest, telephoned all regional-level party leaders with instructions to improve the functioning of communal canteens, shops, and public transport. "People can get tired off constant promises of a brighter future," he stated.[105] The example of unrest in the near abroad fed into broader Brezhnev-era concerns about guaranteeing decent standards of living immediately, rather than relying on utopian visions of vaguely defined future "communism" to mobilise the population. Consequently, during closed party meetings, local apparatchiks throughout Ukraine spoke about workers as a potentially explosive force that must be controlled by party activists, drawing explicit links between Poland and the USSR.[106] In this context, many CPSU members in Ukraine inquired whether prices would be raised at home like they had been in Poland.[107] Because the importance of mobilizing the public behind the project of building communism had declined since the Khrushchev years, party leaders seemed less bothered about citizens who withdrew into the private sphere, and much more worried about the potential for private grievances to translate into organized, public action. For this reason, perhaps, Vasilii Kutsevol was particularly apprehensive about the influence of the Polish events on students and blue-collar workers who lived in Lviv's communal halls of residence.[108]

The overwhelming majority of reports concerning reactions to the Polish disturbances in 1970 only refer to discussions among party leaders in Kyiv and the regional centres. This could suggest that there was relatively little public debate about the events, owing perhaps to the short duration of the crisis. In contrast, as Solidarity brought out tensions between the "rulers" and the "ruled" in a Soviet-style regime ten years later, top CPSU officials broached the topic of workers' rights much more openly. They instructed the mass media to condemn Warsaw's neglect of the working class,[109] they publicized Soviet workers' grievances in the press, and they put pressure on factory managers and party and trade union activists within the USSR to highlight their concern for blue-collar workers.[110]

Party apparatchiks in Ukraine were confident in dealing with the Solidarity crisis, organising agitation meetings and answering questions about events across the border.[111] Such meetings offered citizens an opportunity to speak and ask about the relationship between socialist regimes and workers. In autumn 1980, the Volhynia regional party leadership went so far as to set up a special commission that regularly met with secretaries of primary party organisations from large factories, held seminars for agitators, and analysed local residents' questions about the Polish crisis.[112] The bulk of agitation gatherings devoted to Solidarity took place in September and October 1980 in parts of western Ukraine, Belarus, Lithuania, and Latvia with significant Polish minorities.[113] Organised public discussions about Poland, geared for party members and non-members alike, continued in March and June 1981.[114]

As these meetings slowly raised the spectre of workers' unrest in Soviet-style regimes, top party officials called on the aspirational middle class to become more attuned to the mood among blue-collar workers. Describing the influence of the Polish crisis in Ukraine, the CPU Central Committee Secretary Ivan Zakharovych Sokolov identified numerous cases where managers enterprises and building sites proved unresponsive to the pressing demands of the population, particularly concerning the supplies of meat and potatoes, as well as bed linen, threads, soap, and washing powder.[115] Similarly, the CPSU Central Committee Secretary Ivan Vasil'evich Kapitonov complained that trade union officials were unfriendly and indifferent towards Soviet blue-collar workers, rarely visiting them at factories to better their working environment.[116] Consequently, top party apparatchiks in Ukraine held meetings with the republic's trade union council to improve labour conditions and health services at large enterprises.[117]

Alarming reports about the need to improve workers' living conditions were especially frequent during the autumn of 1980, with leaders then turning towards more repressive measures among blue-collar workers.

Party activists, trade union officials, and bureaucrats in charge of trade, among others, were again very concerned about improving the well-being of blue-collar workers and the vaguely defined "masses" at the end of 1981 (immediately after General Jaruzelski introduced martial law in Poland on 13 December). In Kyiv, the head of the city's party organization Iurii Nykyforovych El'chenko, formerly in charge of propaganda and agitation in the republic, called on his subordinates to "increase political alertness" and act decisively against any "negative phenomena." Undoubtedly, this implied that the authorities would closely monitor popular opinion to crack down on anyone who dared to criticise Jaruzelski's actions. The local administration introduced more positive measures to assure calm and stability. They made a special effort to monitor public transport and other services in the city, while seeking to guarantee reliable food and fuel supplies, as well as making sure that central heating functioned properly.[118] Likewise, in the Zhytomyr oblast, a region with a sizable Polish minority, officials in all the primary party committees and managers at large industrial enterprises were on a twenty-four hour call to help control the state of affairs.[119]

Between August 1980 and December 1981, Soviet apparatchiks became more alert to blue-collar workers' opinions and needs. They addressed their most pressing economic grievances to avoid the spread of the Solidarity crisis into the USSR itself. Elizabeth Teague claims that these were "short-term, stop-gap measures" that the authorities used "to 'appease' a workforce they perceived as likely to exhibit a dangerous degree of discontent," especially before autumn 1981.[120] However, Communist Party responses to popular opinion went beyond mere lip service and short-lived material handouts, as debates about reform extended beyond the demise of Solidarity.

A Prelude to Perestroika: Reform Politics, 1981–1985

Between 1981 and 1985, Soviet and East European officials developed new policies on travel and cultural exchange. This served not only to isolate the population of the USSR from destabilising foreign influences, but also to channel cross-border contacts in such a way as to encourage gradual and very limited changes in cultural politics. The shifts in Soviet-Polish relations had important implications for Soviet domestic politics, as party leaders concluded that they had failed to control their citizens' relations with the outside world. In particular, the Solidarity crisis pushed Soviet leaders to crack down on the second economy in Ukraine. CPSU apparatchiks encouraged residents of Ukraine to publicly talk about their needs and grievances, and began to reform the legal system in an attempt to more clearly define citizens' rights and obligations vis-à-vis the state.

Soviet policies governing transnational contacts changed very slowly before 1985. Officials continued to impose strict controls on international travel to and from Poland after the outbreak of Solidarity and well into the mid-1980s. Although a few professional delegations crossed the Polish-Soviet border a mere few months after the introduction of martial law,[121] and local branches of the Soviet-Polish Friendship Society throughout Ukraine held meetings and book fairs to celebrate the Polish national holiday in July 1982,[122] the mass tourism seen in the 1970s did not pick up in the early 1980s.[123]

For party officials and citizens accustomed to travel in the 1970s, it was obvious that the Soviet bloc had changed and the USSR's relations with the near abroad were more tense than ever. As a recent émigré from the Transcarpathia town of Mukachevo stated during an interview in the West in 1983:

> It was formerly possible to buy things from Poland and Hungary, since a lot of tourists from those countries came to Transcarpathia oblast. Ukrainians were allowed to go abroad too, and a lot of stuff was shipped in by people's relatives and acquaintances. All this has now ceased. There is talk of a new law about border restrictions being under preparation, and rumours that we are about to return to Stalinist-type regimentation of trips abroad.[124]

While Stalinist restrictions on travel were not imposed during the 1980s, cultural exchanges and tourism became more conservative than they had been before Solidarity. Even as the number of people crossing the Soviet-Polish border increased in 1984, party apparatchiks promoted forms of cultural exchange that left travellers little room to depart from a rigid program of activities celebrating the achievements of the USSR and national cultures of the socialist bloc.[125] Keen to appease their colleagues in the USSR, the foreign affairs department of the PUWP Central Committee promised not to expose Soviet audiences to edgy art or controversial ideas that they had sometimes promoted before the outbreak of Solidarity. In fact, they would not even try to convince Soviet officials to invite Polish artists "of whom they were rightly suspicious," sending only "party-minded artists" across the eastern border.[126]

At the same time, some apparatchiks in both Eastern Europe and the USSR saw General Jaruzelski's suppression of Solidarity as a sign that the 1970s would eventually be back. In diplomatic correspondence, the emphasis was on restoring cyclical events that Petr Demichev and other officials at the Soviet Ministry of Culture had got used to before the Solidarity crisis, rather than inventing new forms of cooperation.[127] After a three-year freeze in Polish-Soviet cultural relations, for example, the USSR hosted Polish Culture Days in 1984, modelled on similar events in the 1970s.[128] A year later, Soviet-Polish cultural cooperation proceeded almost as if Solidarity had never happened. Soviet Culture Days in Poland took on a massive scale, and the fortieth anniversary of the Soviet-Polish Agreement on Friendship, Cooperation, and Mutual Assistance was celebrated with pomp.[129] Polish diplomats in Moscow hoped that this would demonstrate that Poland was firmly back within the socialist camp.[130] In practice, Polish culture in the USSR was now largely represented by such classic composers as Chopin and Moniuszko, as well as by conventional popular music (especially records and concerts devoted to the late Anna German, a Polish performer with Soviet roots who sang in Russian with no accent). Transnational exchanges also focused on light comedies and children's movies, such as Juliusz Machulski's *Seksmisja* and Krzysztof Gradowski's Soviet-Polish coproduction *Akademia Pana Kleksa*. The most prominent manifestation of Polish-Soviet friendship in the 1980s was a festival of Soviet pop music in the Polish city of Zielona Góra.[131] In this way, Soviet and Polish officials in charge of cultural exchange focused on entertainment, and largely avoided controversial political and ideological questions.

Still, after Solidarity, officials in charge of travel and cultural diplomacy reflected on their apparent failure to promote friendly relations between the USSR and Poland. Especially on the Polish side, party leaders openly acknowledged important problems in international cooperation. Members of a PUWP Central Committee team charged with examining young people's problems in Poland in 1984 claimed that the youth did not support the Warsaw Pact's foreign policy.[132] Polish apparatchiks also pointed to economic and organisational problems that hindered successful transnational cooperation. Travel in the USSR was less than pleasant, with one report emphasising that all members of a Polish rock band caught a cold in a Rostov hotel – their Soviet hosts reportedly did not respond to complaints about the lack of heating.[133]

Warsaw therefore pushed for reforming Soviet-Polish cultural relations in the first half of the 1980s. Polish officials believed that audiences in the Soviet bloc had become more autonomous and demanding over the preceding decades. This made it imperative to work out a "new model of cultural exchange between socialist countries … appropriate for the culturally aware audiences that show initiative in seeking out highest quality art, for audiences that cannot be 'organised' anymore." In translation from newspeak, they argued that residents of the Soviet bloc would no longer attend the poor-quality concerts and exhibitions that entire factories or collectives had been herded into. Cultural exchanges could be scaled down, but should still include a genuinely attractive program and involve such prominent figures as the Polish classical composer Krzysztof Penderecki.[134] "Today it is not enough to voice vague wishes for widening cooperation," R. Paciorkowski at the PUWP Central Committee stressed, apparently tired of old slogans. "We should put forward more concrete proposals (what, where, and when)."[135] Warsaw therefore looked for new forms of transnational exchange that would translate into more prolonged and intense contacts between Polish and Soviet partners. For example, in 1985, instead of simply visiting each other and watching each other's productions, actors at the Tbilisi Drama Theatre and the Targówek Theatre in Warsaw prepared a play together.[136]

The need to improve transnational contacts between Poland and the USSR took on a particular urgency in Ukraine. As the Polish consuls in Kyiv travelled around provincial centres to encourage more direct Polish-Ukrainian cooperation,[137] they relayed complaints voiced by Roman Lubkiv'skyi, Pavlo Zahrebel'nyi, and other members of the Ukrainian Writers' Union Presidium. The writers were reportedly concerned about Moscow-centrism in Soviet cultural policy, claiming that Ukraine was often bypassed by Polish artists visiting the USSR, even though the local intelligentsia knew Polish literature better than anyone else in the USSR.[138] Like other forms of transnational contacts, the issue of Polish-Ukrainian cultural cooperation brought out the urgent need to reform the economy. Whereas in the late 1970s the value of Polish books sold in Ukraine exceeded 400,000 roubles per year, in 1985 the total dropped to 200,000 roubles. This was partly because Polish publishing houses made no effort to prepare new, contemporary titles for the Soviet market; the Polish consul in Kyiv, Władysław Kruk, was painfully aware of the need to train new cadres and overcome bureaucratic complacency among publishers. More importantly, however, Polish publishers were simply too poor to help improve Polish-Ukrainian relations. They did not print enough books to satisfy the demand of Ukrainian bookshops, and while raising prices to the level of Yugoslav publications, they continued to print unnattractive books on poor quality paper.[139]

For their part, Soviet officials also pointed to the urgent need to reform social and cultural institutions in the satellite states. Viktor Maksimovich Mishin at the Komsomol Central Committee complained that Polish youth organizations exerted little to no influence over university students who participated in international exchanges with the USSR.[140] According to Soviet reports, young Poles visiting the USSR drank too much, spoke about the "undemocratic character of socialism," and showed unhealthy interest in the role that religion played in Soviet society.[141] During the early 1980s, senior party apparatchiks from the western regions of Ukraine, as well as Ukrainian state officials in charge of foreign tourism, likewise complained about anti-Soviet nationalism among Romanian tourists and the rising problem of smuggling among the new generation of Hungarians, Czechoslovaks, and Bulgarians. Apart from criticising Soviet policies in Afghanistan, these groups sold blue jeans and pornographic pictures in Lviv and Kyiv, as well as purchased large quantities of electronic equipment and other goods during their visits in Soviet Ukraine. Viktor Dobryk was especially outspoken and fearful of such harmful foreign influences in Ukraine's borderlands, probably because Lviv and other western regions were most exposed to smuggling. Clearly outraged, officials in charge of international travel claimed that trips to the Soviet Union were actually advertised as "shopping trips" or "business tourism" in Hungary.[142]

Soviet apparatchiks were more reluctant to criticise their own institutions and citizens. Volodymyr Shcherbyts'kyi blamed the low productivity of mixed Polish-Soviet workers' brigades in the USSR on the Poles' inability to keep up with their Soviet comrades.[143] Yet some Soviet bureaucrats, including Dobryk himself, believed that Soviet institutions failed to control the ways citizens (and young people in particular) approached foreigners and the outside world. Soviet surveillance reports offer only occasional glimpses into Soviet citizens' role in illegal trade, but they do suggest the Ukrainian borderlands became a site of shady activities and somewhat chaotic attempts to meet and trade with visiting East Europeans. For instance, Soviet citizens boarded trains that had cleared the customs in Chop to buy what one report helpfully described as "things" from Hungarian tourists. Some Soviet citizens even took the long train ride from Chop to Lviv in order to buy foreign currency from Hungarian tourists along the way.[144]

Some members of the Soviet cultural elite seemed to share their Polish comrades' concerns about the quality of cultural exchanges in the socialist camp. For instance, Soviet writers travelling in Poland in February 1983, including Borys Illich Oliinyk who headed the Kyiv writers' party organisation, inquired about the production value of Soviet-published books on sale in Eastern Europe.[145] To give Polish-Ukrainian cultural events more resonance, Soviet apparatchiks began to rely more heavily on television – the Gosteleradio in Ukraine pledged to record Polish-Ukrainian cultural events on tape so they could be showcased to a larger audience, particularly in Poland.[146] On another level, for all the talk of maintaining intense cultural contacts with Eastern Europe, the Soviet Ministry of Culture in Moscow grew evermore concerned about the financial viability of cultural exchanges in the mid-1980s. In fact, deemed too expensive, exchanges between the USSR and Hungary, the GDR, and Bulgaria were therefore scaled down in 1985. These cuts were presented as an attempt to improve the political effectiveness of cultural cooperation: because too many Soviet events were organised in Eastern Europe, the ministry officials reasoned, attendance was poor, which created a very bad impression on everyone involved.[147]

The drive to reform Soviet and East European policies on travel and cultural diplomacy shaped Soviet domestic policies. On one level, the perceived need to improve the quality of transnational cultural exchanges led Soviet leaders to confront institutional and financial problems at home. Shortcomings in the transnational work of Goskontsert, an institution responsible for organising concerts for Soviet performers abroad and inviting foreign performers to the USSR, did not escape the attention of the deputy Minister of Culture in Moscow, Iurii Iakovlevich Barabash, who complained that the organisation's "bureaucratism" frustrated attempts to strengthen cultural ties with countries of the socialist camp.[148] The need to reform the organisation was particularly pressing because Western music proved more successful in Eastern Europe than Soviet pop. Soviet Ministry of Culture officials believed this was the result of Goskontsert's complacency, as the organisation had repeatedly sent the same artists (such as Zhanna Bichevskaia) to tour the satellite states.[149] At the same time, Soviet and East European citizens who coordinated cultural exchanges were painfully aware that no real improvement would be achieved without substantial financial investments. For example, Goskontsert employees (as well as their Polish counterparts at Pagart) knew full well that the equipment they used left much to be desired.[150]

Notably, it is easier to gauge Soviet apparatchiks' concerns from Polish reports than their own accounts intended for internal use. Officials in the USSR clearly found it easier to speak about problems in conversations with foreigners than to write about them to their superiors at home. In a July 1984 conversation with the Polish consul in Kyiv, the first secretary of the Ukrainian Komsomol, Viktor Mironenko, lamented that Soviet youth organizations were largely ineffective:

> We are concerned about the petit-bourgeois attitudes and political naivety that we observe among some groups. A part of our youth, fascinated with the West, does not participate in our struggle to improve the functioning of the economy. They voice baseless criticisms of the changes being made and of our efforts, uncritically following a lifestyle alien to our system.[151]

The awkward and opaque language may suggest that Mironenko was unable to identify problems in a straightforward and unambiguous manner, which would no doubt make reform difficult, but this prominent political activist nonetheless spoke about the need to find more efficient ways of shaping young people's views of their own society and the rest of the world. This signified rising support for reform among the younger generation of Ukraine's political leaders.

By 1985, partly under the influence of transnational exchanges in the socialist camp, Soviet leaders talked more openly about the need to reform the mass media. According to the Polish embassy press attaché, apparatchiks in Moscow despaired that their domestic mass media were too formulaic. Although Moscow still insisted that more Polish journalists come to the USSR to learn from Soviet experiences than the other way round, some Soviet journalists (especially at the newspaper *Vecherniaia Moskva*) began to copy new approaches to journalism developed in Poland over the previous few years.[152]

Most importantly, reflecting on the roots of the Polish crisis and responding to problems created by Polish tourists who traded illegally in Soviet Ukraine, party leaders took more seriously the need to enforce the Soviet law and combat the second economy. Lviv in particular turned into a fortress of sorts. In 1981, the all-Ukrainian and Lviv branches of the KGB implemented special measures to prevent Polish transit tourists from entering the city, which they hoped would help combat crime and illegal trade. Accordingly, the traffic police established fourteen specially dedicated posts on roads leading into Lviv, eight of which operated twenty-four hours a day. Militia officers at the railway station would also prevent Polish citizens from getting off the Warsaw-Bucharest train, and would travel on the trains themselves to make sure the Poles did not pull the emergency stop to get off in the middle of a field. Overall, this was a major effort involving six operational groups, 1,589 people, six cars, and four motorcycles. Indeed, it seems that this grand scale was justified by the scope of illegal travel to Lviv. From the end of May to mid-July, the authorities prevented 21,000 attempts by Polish citizens to enter Lviv without permission (*samovol'no*).[153]

These policies continued after the imposition of martial law in Poland. In particular, Soviet authorities cracked down on the kinds of black market dealings that some local residents of western Ukraine complained about at the height of the Solidarity crisis. They discovered and investigated eighty cases where local citizens rented private flats to Polish tourists.[154] Just as in the late 1950s, party apparatchiks were also determined to limit personal contacts between residents of western Ukraine and Odesa on the one hand, and their relatives in the people's democracies and the capitalist West on the other. From the perspective of senior officials responsible for propaganda and ideological work in Ukraine, including the future President of independent Ukraine, Leonid Kravchuk, uncontrolled contacts between family members allowed citizens to escape state control. Kravchuk, himself hailing from formerly Polish-ruled territories, emphasised that controls over state borders established after the Second World War must be tightened. Reports mentioned 47,800 inhabitants of Ukraine who visited relatives abroad in 1982 (with 45,400 of them going to socialist countries). Party activists failed to keep track of these citizens, to prepare them for their family visits, or even to check that they did in fact have relatives across the border. Neither did they prepare Soviet citizens to host their family members in the USSR: as the visitors stayed with their families, they did not register with the local police or Inturist, and sometimes used private cars and public transport to reach regions that were out of bounds for foreigners. Kravchuk and his colleagues were particularly frustrated that many citizens obtained forged medical notes to get off work, and then used formal trade union channels to travel abroad on "private business" (*po chastnym delam*).[155]

Contemporary Western observers noted a broader shift in Soviet official understandings of legality after the death of Brezhnev. George Kolankiewicz went so far as to argue that, largely under the influence of the Solidarity crisis, Iurii Andropov tried to increase societal discipline and promote the idea of "law and order," hoping to use judicial means to increase labour efficiency and "exact obligations from managers and managed alike." Andropov had had extensive experience with East European unrest, having played a central role in the suppression of the Hungarian uprising as the Soviet ambassador in 1956. During the early 1980s, partly because of the ongoing war in Afghanistan, he no longer supported the use of military measures to maintain Soviet control in Eastern Europe.[156] He appeared to believe that Poland was an extreme example of societal disobedience, and the militarisation of its society was necessary to strengthen work discipline and bring back order. The USSR itself, while not nearly as unstable, needed "militarisation at one remove" to combat absenteeism, high labour mobility, work indiscipline, as well as laxity in management and plan fulfilment. Thus, Andropov's reforms aimed to encourage Soviet citizens to work more efficiently through imposing a strict and well-defined system of rights and responsibilities. They aimed to inspire blue-collar workers in the USSR to think of themselves as Soviet (in the sense that they were subject to a Soviet law, as distinct from Poland with its own legal and social system). Appreciative of the dangers of mutual over-identification which discredited the Soviet system at home and encouraged anti-Soviet feelings in Poland, Soviet journalists began to emphasise that Warsaw, lagging behind on the road towards communism, should follow its own policies, albeit within the confines of "a clearly defined set of legal and political norms."[157]

Conclusion

Whereas comparisons with the West fuelled some dissatisfaction with the Soviet economic system among the population of the USSR,[158] perceptions of Poland during the early 1980s reinforced a popular sense of belonging to the imagined Soviet political community in Ukraine. It seems that conflicts between Soviet citizens and Polish tourists in western Ukraine and the belief that Solidarity's strikes led to economic chaos in Poland made some inhabitants of Ukraine distrustful of the "anti-Soviet" opposition across the border. At the same time, debates about Solidarity provided an important forum for staging patriotism in Soviet Ukraine. Speaking about the Polish crisis in a patriotic manner, residents proved their loyalty, but also voiced limited criticism of the Soviet leadership.

Anxious about the Polish developments, many citizens articulated an elitist vision of Soviet patriotism, suggesting that some individuals made a special contribution to the Soviet Motherland. These people were very adept at staging patriotism, hardened not only by the earlier crises in 1956 and 1968, but also by experiences of international travel in the post-Stalinist period. In the early 1980s, they once again spoke publicly in various heavily controlled contexts and declared their readiness to back Soviet policies in Eastern Europe. They thereby claimed a middle class status, presenting themselves as important activists and community leaders. Such views were particularly widespread among party and Komsomol activists, "leading workers," and war veterans who, it appears, grew more conscious of forming a separate class in the USSR.

At the same time, however, many inhabitants of the western borderlands challenged the elitist vision of patriotism and the nature of Ukraine's social and geographical divisions. In contrast to 1956 and 1968, they did this not by voicing support for far-reaching reform, but rather by themselves rallying behind ideas of conservative patriotism. Inhabitants of the borderlands thus condemned attempts to reform the system in Poland and supported repressive Soviet policies in the outer empire. At the same time, however, they voiced views that differed from the aspirational middle class. Particularly in Lviv, many people escaped the narrow context of public agitation gatherings to suggest that residents of west Ukraine formed a crucial part of the wider Soviet community. Having established their patriotic credentials, they articulated hopes that the Solidarity crisis would not escalate into a military conflict, as well as demanded more information from the Soviet mass media. More prominently, many inhabitants of west Ukraine were emboldened to criticise state and party leaders for helping ungrateful Poles instead of taking care of their own citizens.

Popular reactions to events and developments in Eastern Europe do not therefore fit the stereotypical divide into an "anti-Soviet" west and "pro-Soviet" east. It would rather appear that many inhabitants of western Ukraine staged patriotism by claiming that their exposure to the "Polish threat" increased their loyalty towards the USSR. In this way, transnational interactions in Eastern Europe strengthened Soviet patriotism in Ukraine during the early 1980s, contributing to the Sovietisation of the western borderlands.

On the eve of perestroika, the system had proven its ability to react to a major crisis and survive. Soviet society was remarkably stable in the early 1980s, largely because the outer empire was an important source of legitimacy for Brezhnev's regime. Yet Solidarity also inspired new ideas for reform that were to shape the dynamics of perestroika in the late 1980s. In particular, reflecting on the Polish experience, Soviet apparatchiks talked about the need to improve the functioning of state and party institutions, to combat bureaucratism, and to enforce the rule of law.

Epilogue: The Legacies of Soviet Patriotism in Ukraine

Kyiv was tense in March 2014. I arrived in the city a few days after the disgraced president Yanukovych fled to Russia. Protesters from across the country still camped out in tents lining the city's central streets while normal life continued in the suburbs. The police were nowhere to be seen and citizens' militias patrolled the city centre. The Maidan, a large square that had witnessed months of protests after president Yanukovych refused to sign an association agreement with the European Union, was still buzzing with activity. Posters of Russian president Vladimir Putin with a Hitler moustache read "hands off Ukraine!" and photographs of the "Heavenly Hundred," the Maidan activists shot by snipers a few weeks before, helped boost morale among protesters opposed to Russia's invasion of Ukraine.

Yet the Maidan embodied differing ideas about Ukraine's past and future. A huge poster of Stepan Bandera, leader of the Organisation of Ukrainian Nationalists in the 1930s and 1940s, was by far the most divisive. Celebrated by some as a symbol of resistance to the Soviet annexation of western Ukraine and brutal Stalinist repressions, Bandera is seen by many others (and not only in eastern Ukraine) as the embodiment of the Ukrainian ethnic nationalism that fuelled the mass murder of Jews, Poles, Ukrainians, and Soviet soldiers during the Second World War. For some Maidan activists in 2014, Bandera stood for a Ukraine united by the Ukrainian language and culture, defined in opposition to Putin's Russia but also to "Western" liberal ideas. An equally large poster of Viacheslav Chornovil, a prominent Soviet Ukrainian dissident, looked upon the Maidan. It evoked memories of civil activism and protests against human rights abuses in the USSR. In contrast to Bandera, Chornovil stood for a more inclusive vision of Ukraine, unambiguously pro-European and united by commitment to the rule of law and parliamentary democracy.

It took only a short walk from the Maidan to discover a third Ukraine. Trying to sleep at a friend's apartment on Red Army Street,[1] I overheard two women arguing across the wall, who I gathered were mother and daughter. "It is your Yanukovych that is to blame. He abandoned the Ukrainian people and fled to Russia!" yelled the younger woman in Russian. But her mother was convinced that the ouster of Yanukovych and Ukraine's break from Putin's "Russian world" would only lead to poverty and violence, accusing her daughter of playing fast and loose with her own children's future. She embodied a Putin vision of Ukraine, underpinned by acute fear of change and commitment to close relations with the "East Slavic brothers" in Russia.[2]

The Bandera, Chornovil, and Putin notions of Ukraine are of course ideal types that obscure a much more complex web of identities. As Mykola Riabchuk argued at the beginning of the twenty-first century, contrasting notions of what it means to be Ukrainian, Russian, Soviet, and European "permeate each other so deeply that even in Lviv one may find many remnants of sovietism, while in Donetsk some signs of 'Ukrainianness' and 'Europeanness' may equally be discerned" (though in the highly politicized atmosphere of 2014 it was difficult to uncover the "invisible, mute, uncertain" majority that Riabchuk identified).[3] For all their limitations, the three ideal types provide a useful prism for understanding ideological divisions among the current population of Ukraine. The history of Soviet Ukraine offered in this book helps to illuminate the political claims and geopolitical choices associated with these differing visions of Ukrainianness today, for all three were shaped in the second half of the twentieth century.

The Bandera Ukraine and Legacies of Anti-Soviet Nationalism

During the Second World War and in the late 1940s, Ukrainian ethnic nationalism defined in opposition to Russia and Poland provided an ideological basis for widespread ethnic cleansing campaigns. After the war, however, it acquired new forms, becoming more anti-Russian and less anti-Polish. The notion that Soviet rule in Ukraine represented foreign (Russian) domination was sustained by examples of East European resistance movements which inspired some residents of Ukraine's western borderlands to believe the USSR would collapse and Ukraine, along with its western neighbours, would shake off Moscow's dominance.

But these ideas were relatively unpopular in the post-Stalinist period. Leaders of the USSR effectively fanned popular fears of both East European and Ukrainian anti-Soviet nationalisms, convincing many inhabitants of Ukraine that these forces threatened the USSR's economic stability and territorial integrity.

The Bandera concept of Ukraine as an ethnically Ukrainian and Ukrainian-speaking territory gained some more traction during the late 1980s and early 1990s, particularly in western Ukraine. The far-right Ukrainian National Assembly – Ukrainian People's Self Defence, headed by long-time political prisoner Hryhorii Prykhod'ko, categorically claimed that "Soviet rule in Ukraine [was] illegitimate."[4] Similarly, Roman Koval' and his radical wing of the Ukrainian Republican Party made no secret of their desire to destabilise the political situation in Soviet Ukraine, because for them stability meant the perpetuation of the political status quo.[5] These tactics effectively limited the spread of Ukrainian identities defined in opposition to Russia at a time when most people's priorities "remained conservative and practical."[6]

After 1991, some of the former anti-Soviet Ukrainian nationalists argued that Russian language and culture had no place in Ukraine.[7] They also adopted an anti-Western rhetoric, suggesting that religion must provide a buffer against what they perceived as negative features of the West, including violence, pornography, and homosexuality.[8] Their vision of Ukraine united by common language and descent was never likely to find much appeal among liberally minded citizens and self-identified Ukrainians who spoke Russian or *surzhyk* (a mixture of Russian and Ukrainian), not to mention self-identified Russians and other ethnic groups. At the same time, the fear of far-right nationalism served important political purposes. The first two presidents of independent Ukraine, Leonid Kravchuk and Leonid Kuchma, fuelled the popular phobia of Bandera-brand nationalism in order to discredit moderate political opponents. In 2002, for example, Ukrainian mass media linked Viktor Yushchenko to an alleged decision by the Ivano-Frankivsk city council to grant former combatants in the wartime SS-Galicia division the status of war veterans.[9]

Ukrainian nationalism grounded in anti-Soviet traditions, intolerant of Ukraine's Russians and Russian-speakers as well as Western liberal ideas, is still unpopular today. Far-right parties thus failed to attract significant support in the 2014 parliamentary elections.[10] At the same time, in a striking parallel with the Soviet period, perceptions of the far right continue to underpin popular fears of change. Opponents of the

Maidan in Russia and Ukraine disparage reformist groups as "fascists" and "Banderites," evoking Soviet-era stereotypes that equated any sign of resistance with far-right nationalism. Equally important, and with more reason, some supporters of the Maidan fear that well-organised far right groups may gain disproportionate influence over politics in the absence of strong state institutions in Ukraine.

To be sure, the image of Bandera carries many connotations in modern-day Ukraine. Citizens who carried his posters in 2014 hardly ever acknowledged the role that the Organisation of Ukrainian Nationalists (OUN) and the Ukrainian Insurgent Army (UPA) played in wartime ethnic cleansing campaigns. They did not even necessarily associate Bandera's image with far-right ideologies. In staging massive propaganda campaigns to discredit Bandera and the OUN-UPA during the second half of the twentieth century, the Soviet authorities effectively turned them into broader symbols of resistance. As Grzegorz Rossoliński-Liebe writes, "Khrushchev and other Soviet politicians used the term 'Banderites' to label all kinds of political opponents. This entirely changed the meaning of the term, which had originally been used by the victims of OUN-UPA mass violence to define its perpetrators." Furthermore, Ukrainian diaspora publications disassociated Bandera from wartime violence. Some post-Soviet public intellectuals and museums in Ukraine have likewise sought to portray Bandera and the OUN-UPA as only the victims and never the perpetrators of wartime crimes. To put it bluntly, carrying a poster of Bandera in today's Ukraine is not the same as supporting far-right ideas.[11]

At the same time, however, Bandera is associated with the rise of the far right. For one, many citizens of Ukraine, particularly in the east, still believe that people who mobilise symbols of Bandera and the OUN-UPA support fascism. Moreover, denying or ignoring OUN-UPA wartime crimes in post-Soviet Ukraine helps legitimise far-right ideologies, as it complicates any meaningful discussion of far-right threats, past or present. The construction of Bandera monuments and the waving of OUN's red-and-black flags have been largely sponsored by the far-right party Svoboda. Svoboda does not condone (indeed denies) UPA's wartime crimes, and yet promotes many of the ideas that once underpinned violent ethnic cleansing campaigns. Svoboda's political program calls for distinguishing Ukraine's citizens on the basis of nationality (nationality is to be written in every citizen's passport and birth certificate). It further suggests criminalising "any displays of Ukrainophobia" and the "promotion of sexual perversions," and calls for setting up "a special investigative structure for tracing criminals who were destroying the Ukrainian nation."[12]

Chornovil Ukraine and Legacies of Soviet Reformist Patriotism

A Chornovil vision of Ukraine as a multi-ethnic and multi-lingual space is much more widespread than Bandera-brand nationalism. It is founded in the notions of Soviet and Soviet Ukrainian reformist patriotism developed in dialogue with East European satellite states after the death of Stalin. In the 1950s and 1960s, proponents of reformist patriotism rejected Soviet-made notions of the near abroad by criticising Moscow's interventionist policies in Eastern Europe. They further emphasised that East European reforms, particularly relaxation of censorship and attempts to expand political participation, should be emulated in the USSR itself. While advocating for Ukrainian language to occupy a more important role in Soviet public culture, they also supported the preservation of a multi-ethnic Soviet state and defended the cultural and civic rights of Ukraine's non-titular minorities.

Although reformist patriotism was suppressed after 1968, it got a new lease of life under Gorbachev. Just as reformist patriotism had earlier advocated change in the USSR, Ukraine's proponents of reform in the last years of Soviet rule did not at first attack the Soviet state as such. Early perestroika-era reformism was largely limited to cultural and linguistic questions. The underground Lion Society, for example, "avoided antagonising the authorities in its efforts to preserve the Ukraine's national and cultural heritage" in the late 1980s.[13] Even as reformist patriotism acquired more politicised forms, its advocates presented themselves as supporters of Gorbachev's policies concerned about the future of their Soviet and Soviet Ukrainian homeland. The biggest Ukrainian opposition movement of the late Soviet era, Rukh, "saw Ukraine as part of a revamped Soviet federation as late as 1990."[14] It thus sought to "force the [Soviet] state to honour its commitments to the rule of law, and individual and national rights."[15]

Yet Rukh and other reformist activists gradually came to the conclusion that change could only be achieved outside the Soviet state. Disappointment with the slow pace of change under Gorbachev convinced reformists that problems plaguing Soviet Ukraine were systemic, inherent in the Soviet state and its founding ideology. For example, a member of the Ukrainian Helsinki Union Iurii Zhyzhkoin remarked in 1990 that citizens had to be won over to the cause of Ukrainian independence because the deep economic crisis that had overtaken the USSR was an outcome of the Soviet social system and "communism."[16]

Largely because of state repression, the spread of reformist ideas before 1991 was limited to west Ukraine and the creative intelligentsia. The use of force frustrated Rukh's attempts to create a Popular Front in 1988,[17] while the refusal to officially register Rukh until February 1990 made it impossible for the party to stand in the March 1990 elections.[18] Coupled with censorship, this made it difficult for reformist patriotism to capture popular imagination outside Ukrainian-speaking regions. In 1989, deputy head of the Donbas Strike Committee Petro Pohreznyi told the Rukh congress that miners in the eastern regions knew next to nothing about the movement's activities.[19]

Independent Ukraine was hardly a more fertile ground for the spread of reformist ideas propagated by Chornovil and his supporters. True, some citizens during the 1990s drew on legacies of reformist patriotism as they recalled Ukraine's historical links with Central and Eastern Europe, especially the Habsburg Empire, and claimed that the country should follow the "European" path of reform pursued in the former Soviet satellite states. Mirroring earlier patterns, these attitudes were especially widespread among the creative intelligentsia.[20] But former CPU apparatchiks enjoyed an unbroken hold on power across the 1991 divide, which gave them a major advantage over Rukh and other reformist forces.[21] In addition, Rukh was tainted by cooperation with the corrupt elites of the Kuchma era, particularly as they joined forces against the Communist Party in parliament.[22]

It was the Orange Revolution of 2004 that finally gave a significant boost to reformist ideas in Ukraine. It witnessed the rise of a civil society that bridged linguistic, and to some extent, regional divides in a manner resembling Soviet-era reformist patriotism. Crowds who supported Yushchenko in 2004 gave him a clear mandate for political and economic reform.[23] But the years of political infighting and economic recession that followed facilitated the return of Yanukovych in 2010. Proponents of reform who identified with Chornovil-brand Ukraine found themselves without credible political representation.

During the Maidan protests in 2013 and 2014, reformist patriotism was no longer associated with a particular party or an individual leader. Just as advocates of Soviet reformist patriotism called for expanding participatory citizenship to undermine authoritarian practices, Ukraine now witnessed the explosion of civil activism that did not find effective political expression or translate into institutional change. In the absence of a strong state today, it is still civil society that holds Ukraine together. For example, as the authorities struggle to deal with over a million internally displaced persons in 2015,[24] a special group on the social network "V kontakte" provides a forum where residents of Ukraine offer jobs and accommodation to refugees from Crimea and the Donbas.[25] Even the Ukrainian army relies on civil society initiatives such as the Kharkiv-based group "Help Army" to obtain basic supplies and equipment.[26]

Advocates of reformist patriotism questioned the idea of Eastern Europe as a Soviet near abroad, and their successors today reject Kremlin-made notions of Ukraine as Russia's near abroad. At the same time, they stay clear of the aggressive and conservative rhetoric of the former anti-Soviet nationalists who see Ukraine as a Ukrainian nation space. In their ranks are Russian speakers and members of ethnic minorities, such as Crimean Tatars. A reformist understanding of what it means to be Ukrainian today translates into popular support for broadly understood democratisation of public life. At the same time, successors to reformist patriotism do not entirely reject Soviet-made identities – they hark back to Soviet promises of social equality, and in calling for closer ties with the European Union, draw in part on Soviet-era narratives of transnational friendship.

Putin Ukraine and Legacies of Soviet Conservative Patriotism

Just as reformist patriotism was seriously undermined by conservative concerns in the Soviet era, fears of change fuelled widespread opposition to the Maidan in 2014. Anti-reformist views and support for close ties with Putin's Russia should not be dismissed as signs of ignorance, national indifference, or political passivity. Rather, they are better understood as products of Soviet conservative patriotism that still provides a powerful source of political and social mobilization in the country. While the Bandera-brand Ukrainian nationalists have rightly attracted much criticism for their aggressive deeds and rhetoric, it is important to remember that Soviet conservative patriotism that underlies the Putin vision of modern Ukraine has also been an ethnocentric and xenophobic ideology that demonized dissent and cultural diversity.

In the second half of the twentieth century, conservative patriotism was widespread among the population of Soviet Ukraine. Proponents of conservative patriotism claimed that Ukraine was inherently different from socialist Eastern Europe. Far from a force of Russification, Soviet conservative patriotism was underpinned by the idea that Ukrainians were a proud and ancient people who had long resisted Polish, German, and to a lesser extent, Hungarian, Romanian, and Czechoslovak domination. Advocates of conservative patriotism saw Ukraine as an East Slavic nation space, a home to Russians and Ukrainians threatened by foreigners across the western border as well as ethnic minorities at home. This was a deeply intolerant ideology, underpinned by the unquestioning assumption that Ukraine's western neighbours, backed by their supposed German, American, and Jewish allies, were out to grab Ukrainian land and resources. In this world view, popular protest and political liberalization were tantamount to war and economic instability.

But conservative patriotism was more than just fear of change. Evoking notions of conservative patriotism allowed many residents of Ukraine to build political capital and claim perks and privileges in return for their loyalty. It further fuelled new types of citizenship, encouraging citizens to publicly comment on and criticize the USSR's foreign and domestic policies as engaged and loyal members of Soviet society. Because conservative patriotism was such a useful tool for many residents of Ukraine, it continued to shape popular opinion in the late 1980s and the 1990s. In line with the conservative suspicion of "anti-Russian" and "anti-Soviet" nationalism, few inhabitants of Ukraine showed interest in the cause of protecting Ukrainian culture against Russification during the Gorbachev era.[27]

At the same time, residents of Ukraine (including Crimea and the Donbas) voted overwhelmingly in favour of Ukrainian independence in December 1991.[28] This was partly because important pillars of conservative patriotism collapsed during the late 1980s. In particular, Gorbachev's loss of Eastern Europe in 1989 discredited the Soviet state at home, undermining the sense of imperial pride that had underpinned patriotic attitudes throughout the post-war period.[29]

More importantly, Soviet conservative patriotism itself helped rally citizens against Gorbachev's far-reaching reforms, and thus fuelled support for the emergence of an independent Ukraine. Whereas citizens had earlier offered obedience in return for material rewards and economic stability, Gorbachev failed to deliver the kind of living conditions the state promised to loyal citizens. Faced with growing popular unrest, keen to preserve political power and control over Ukraine's economic resources, and concerned that Moscow would crack down on the autonomy they had gained over previous decades, republican-level communist leaders in Kyiv fled the sinking ship.[30] Members of the Soviet political elite provided the most decisive push towards independence in 1991. They promised that they would fix the economy as leaders of an independent Ukraine.[31] This strategy worked, as Soviet citizens grew frustrated with Moscow's economic policies. They hoped that a sovereign Ukrainian state would fulfil citizens' material expectations better than the USSR.[32]

Therefore, popular legitimacy of the Ukrainian state in 1991 was largely founded in the ideas of Soviet conservative patriotism. Leaders of Ukraine were the old Soviet elites who promised to restore the old Soviet social contract. This acted as an important limit on reform during the 1990s. In line with earlier claims of conservative patriotism, many citizens of Ukraine defined themselves in opposition to their western neighbours and expressed negative attitudes towards the political and economic reforms undertaken in former East European satellite states.[33] Likewise, they still perceived NATO as an enemy.[34] All in all, as Andrew Wilson argues, "patrimonial communism and its characteristic features – the suppression of civil society, clientelism and authority worship" had strong roots in 1990s Ukraine.[35]

Because Soviet conservative patriotism thrived in Ukraine across the 1991 divide, official and popular notions of what it meant to be Ukrainian were still often informed by Soviet concepts of East Slavic brotherhood. Just as Soviet conservative patriotism was often articulated through the means of Ukrainian language, history, and culture defined in opposition to Eastern Europe, leaders of independent Ukraine who hailed from the old CPU apparat were quite at ease promoting Ukrainian patriotism in the 1990s. Leonid Kravchuk, formerly in charge of propaganda at the CPU Central Committee during the Brezhnev era, stressed the need to protect Ukrainian linguistic rights and even confined Russian to the status of a minority language.[36] Leonid Kuchma's policies were much more favourable towards Russian language and culture, yet his administration also engaged in Ukrainian nation building.[37] Leaders of independent Ukraine lent support to Ukrainian national expression to the extent that it was still largely defined within the confines of old Soviet narratives. In 1995, for example, the authorities attended the funeral of Oles' Honchar, a prominent member of the Soviet Ukrainian literary establishment, but not the funeral of the former OUN member and political prisoner, the Ukrainian Orthodox Church bishop Volodymyr Romaniuk.[38]

Soviet notions of Ukrainianness defined in East Slavic terms ran even stronger on the popular level, especially in the east and south of Ukraine. Many people in Ukraine were not supportive of the cultural changes that privileged the Ukrainian over the Russian language during the 1990s.[39] From the conservative patriotic standpoint, it did not make sense to define Russian language and culture as a threat to Ukraine – Ukrainians were cast in opposition to the world outside their western border and not against Russia. Moreover, the sense of material entitlement that underpinned conservative patriotic support for Ukrainian independence resulted in much disappointment after 1991, fuelling a strong current of Soviet nostalgia and popular calls for a closer union with Russia.[40] During the 2000s, Yanukovych's Party of Regions capitalized on Soviet conservative visions of Ukraine to gain popular support. Echoing Soviet-era fear mongering, they fanned conspiracy theories about American imperialism and anti-Russian Ukrainian nationalism that supposedly threatened Ukraine's stability.[41]

In 2014, legacies of Soviet conservative patriotism ran strong in Ukraine. This manifested itself very starkly as I arrived in Donetsk the weekend before the Crimean "referendum" in March 2014. Anti-Maidan protesters in the streets echoed Soviet-made stereotypes about German fascists, American imperialists, Ukrainian Banderites, and Crimean Tatar traitors. These crude statements justified violence in the streets of Donetsk. As about a hundred pro-Maidan demonstrators gathered at the city's cathedral to express support for Ukraine's territorial integrity, they were soon surrounded by several thousand anti-Maidan activists. The police made little effort to separate the two sides. The anti-Maidan crowd threw firecrackers at their opponents, and a young man standing by my side was punched in the face as he pulled a blue and yellow Ukrainian flag from his backpack.

Mirroring Soviet-era patterns, expressions of conservative patriotism in the Donbas of 2014 conveyed a sense of entitlement and fear of economic reform. Evoking Soviet-made notions of status, local miners and engineers claimed the right to set the economic agenda for the whole country, holding on to the mistaken Soviet-era view that their resource-rich region subsidized the rest of Ukraine.[42] Added to this was a deeply felt sense of disenfranchisement. After the ouster of president Yanukovych, who had enjoyed great electoral success in the region, many locals felt that their voices were simply not heard. Association with the European Union was widely seen as a prelude to deep economic reforms that would cut right to the heart of the post-Soviet welfare state. "I heard the new prime minister has already announced pension cuts. I can help my mum, but what about the old people who don't have children?" asked a taxi driver as I arrived in Donetsk on a train from Kyiv. All told, occupational differences mattered more than regional and ethnic divisions in fuelling opposition to the Maidan. Many citizens employed in eastern Ukraine's steel industry knew that their factories depended on the Russian market, and therefore saw the Euromaidan as out of touch with their needs. As Russian orders and supplies dried out after the Maidan began, Ukrainian citizens in the Donbas feared for their jobs.

To be sure, legacies of Soviet patriotism shaped not only internal political dynamics in 2014 Ukraine, but also Russian foreign and domestic policy. Just as Soviet leaders feared a potential spillover of dissent from socialist Eastern Europe to the USSR, Kremlin leaders in 2014 realized that the Ukrainian challenge to the post-Soviet oligarchic system invited obvious comparisons with Russia. Soviet conservative patriotism was an effective rallying call for opponents of the Maidan in Russia. Russian mass media thus drew on Soviet-era myths of East Slavic brotherhood, fanned popular fears of Western plots to dominate the region, and tapped into memories of the Great Patriotic War that had helped turn Soviet citizens against anti-authoritarian movements in Eastern Europe before 1989. These myths were based on an uncritical approach to history that defined nationhood in primordial terms (modern-day Russian and Ukrainian identities were projected into the Middle Ages, as mass media stressed the supposedly inborn affinities between East Slavs), and did not allow for any critical reflection on the USSR's role during the Second World War. They echoed on a popular level, as many Russian citizens refused to see Ukraine as a legitimate state whose inhabitants had the right to shape their own future.

The Putin vision of Ukraine that built on Soviet notions of conservative patriotism had further implications throughout the former socialist camp. In 2014, the Kremlin played on anti-American, xenophobic, and homophobic sentiment to garner support in former Soviet republics, particularly among the Orthodox faithful, as well as in former East European satellite states including Viktor Orbán's Hungary and Miloš Zeman's Czech Republic.[43] Putin's ethnocentric, anti-liberal, and anti-Western rhetoric even attracted some very limited support in Poland as a group of intellectuals, including professors at Kraków's Jagiellonian University, signed a letter claiming that only "the great Christian Russia" could stop the onslaught of "satanic Western" ideas in Slavic lands.[44]

Soviet-era reformist patriotism lies at the root of pro-European political movements in modern-day Ukraine, which combine protests against state officials' abuses of power with a commitment to the welfare state. At the same time, conservative patriotism in Ukraine has helped create politically engaged citizens committed to maintaining close relations with Russia and suspicious of Western liberal ideas. Legacies of Soviet patriotism therefore exert a very ambiguous impact on Ukrainian political culture today. Although it was inconceivable that socialist Eastern Europe would leave Moscow's sphere of influence before the mid-1980s, Russia has now seemingly come to terms with Hungary, Czechoslovakia, and Poland as part of NATO and the European Union. Myths of Ukraine as an inseparable part of the "Russian World" can likewise crumble. But for now, the widespread belief that Russia has the moral right to control and protect former Soviet republics from Western domination helps justify Moscow's aggressive foreign policy in the post-Soviet near abroad, both in Russia and in Ukraine.

Notes

Introduction

1 W. Risch, "Soviet 'Flower Children': Hippies and the Youth Counter-Culture in 1970s Lviv," *Journal of Contemporary History* 40:3 (2005): 565–84. *Tsentral'nyi derzhavnyi arkhiv hromads'kykh ob"ednan' Ukrainy* (TsDAHOU) (Central State Archive of Social Organizations of Ukraine), f.1, op.24, s.6313, ark.36.

2 Risch, "Soviet 'Flower Children,'" 565–84.

3 K. Farmer, *Ukrainian Nationalism in the Post-Stalin Era: Myth, Symbols, and Ideology in Soviet Nationalities Policy* (The Hague: Hijhoff, 1980), 8.

4 A. Yurchak, *Everything Was Forever, Until It Was No More: The Last Soviet Generation* (Princeton: Princeton University Press, 2006), 1–33.

5 As Westad puts it, after the death of Stalin, "Washington and Moscow needed to change the world in order to prove the universal applicability of their ideologies." Odd Arne Westad, *The Global Cold War: Third World Interventions and the Making of Our Times* (Cambridge: Cambridge University Press, 2005), 4–5.

6 Unlike in the Arab-Israeli conflict or any of the localised conflicts in Africa, and in parallel with the Soviet interventions in Hungary and Czechoslovakia, Soviet troops in Afghanistan were involved en masse. In addition, the scale of resistance in Afghanistan was much larger than in Eastern Europe. This fuelled very widespread discussion of the war, particularly during *glasnost*. A. Kalinovsky, *A Long Goodbye: The Soviet Withdrawal from Afghanistan* (Cambridge, MA: Harvard University Press, 2011), 86, 214.

7 In contrast, although the USSR shared a 2,000 kilometre-long border with Afghanistan, "Soviet leaders did not worry much about a spillover effect." Kalinovsky, *A Long Goodbye*, 45–9, 214–15.

8 Soviet leaders maintained stricter control over Eastern Europe than client states further afield. For example, the Cuban Missile Crisis "reminded Moscow leaders of the dangers involved in intervening in conflicts that could not be easily controlled far from home." Westad, *The Global Cold War*, 168.

9 I do not mean to imply that the term "near abroad," which has been used to describe Russia's post-Soviet neighbours since 1991, was in use during the Soviet period. But I want to suggest that contemporary notions of "near abroad" build on tropes developed during Soviet interactions with Eastern Europe.

10 S. Kotkin, "Mongol Commonwealth? Exchange and Governance across the Post-Mongol Space," *Kritika: Explorations in Russian and Eurasian History* 8:3 (2007), 525.

11 R. Szporluk, "Introduction," in Roman Szporluk, ed., *The Influence of Eastern Europe and the Soviet West on the USSR* (New York: Praeger, 1976), 2.

12 P. Babiracki, "Interfacing the Soviet Bloc: Recent Literature and New Paradigms," *Ab Imperio* 4 (2011): 376–407.

13 While nation and empire building are often seen as conflicting processes, Terry Martin has famously called the USSR "an affirmative action empire," in which state-controlled nation-building projects were used to disarm anti-Soviet nationalism, to facilitate the USSR's territorial expansion, to promote political and economic centralisation, and to classify the population into "friends" and "enemies." T. Martin, *The Affirmative Action Empire: Nations and Nationalism in the Soviet Union, 1923–1939* (Ithaca: Cornell University Press, 2001), 1–27. Although Martin focuses on the importance of the Bolshevik Party to explain this process, the belief that nation and empire building went together was not new in the USSR. Scott Bailey shows that some ethnographers in Tsarist Russia saw non-Russian nation building as both a product and source of support for Russian rule in Asia. S.C.M. Bailey, "A Biography in Motion: Chokan Valikhanov and His Travels in Central Eurasia," *Ab Imperio* 1 (2009), 165–90. Hirsch suggests that it was Soviet ethnographers, trained in Tsarist Russia, who promoted the view that nation and empire building were mutually constitutive. Francine Hirsch, "Towards an Empire of Nations: Border-Making and the Formation of Soviet National Identities," *Russian Review* 59:2 (2000), 225. At the same time, however, Soviet leaders claimed that the USSR was not an "empire" like France or Britain. Edgar argues that this belief indeed differentiated Soviet policies from European imperial practices. In its approach to non-Russian populations in Central Asia, the USSR rather resembled nation states such as Turkey and Iran. Adrienne Edgar,

"Bolshevism, Patriarchy, and the Nation: The Soviet 'Emancipation' of Muslim Women in Pan-Islamic Perspective," *Slavic Review* 65:2 (2006), 255.

14 Hirsch, "Towards and Empire of Nations," 202.

15 The few studies of Soviet interactions with Eastern Europe concentrate on the spillover of reformist ideas from the satellite states to the USSR. For example, Prizel sees Poland in particular as a source of inspiration for Ukrainian intellectuals striving for more autonomy and independence for their republic. Ilya Prizel, *National Identity and Foreign Policy: Nationalism and Leadership in Poland, Russia, and Ukraine* (Cambridge: Cambridge University Press, 1998), 353.

16 Westad writes of "a long period of uncertainty in Soviet Third World policy – a time of euphoric engagement between 1958 and 1962, followed by an era of doubts and disappointments up to the end of the 1960s, leading to a renewed activism from around 1970 onwards." Westad, *The Global Cold War*, 159.

17 Anne Gorsuch, *All This Is Your World: Soviet Tourism at Home and Abroad after Stalin* (Oxford: Oxford University Press, 2011), 87, 106, 148.

18 M. Kirasirova, "Sons of Muslims in Moscow: Soviet Central Asian Mediators to the Foreign East, 1955–1962," *Ab Imperio* 4 (2011), 106–32.

19 As Anne Gorsuch and Diane Koenker put it, "socialist authorities did not encourage all forms of internationalism." "Introduction: The Socialist 1960s in Global Perspective" in Anne Gorsuch and Diane Koenker, ed., *The Socialist Sixties: Crossing Borders in the Second World* (Bloomington: Indiana University Press, 2013), 8. Roth-Ey demonstrates that Soviet cultural elites came under increased pressure to create forms of entertainment that would prove popular and competitive on the world market, which undermined their mission to create a new type of Soviet person. Kristin Roth-Ey, *Moscow Prime Time: How the Soviet Union Built the Media Empire that Lost the Cultural Cold War* (Ithaca: Cornell University Press, 2011), 1-24.

20 Gorsuch and Koenker, "Introduction," 9.

21 S. Lovell, "In Search of an Ending: *Seventeen Moments* and the Seventies," in Gorsuch and Koenker, ed., *Socialist Sixties*, 317.

22 I use the term "nation" to refer to an "imagined political community – and imagined as both inherently limited and sovereign." Benedict Anderson, *Imagined Communities: Reflections on the Origins and Spread of Nationalism* (London: Verso, 2006), 6.

23 Sheila Fitzpatrick, "Ascribing Class: The Construction of Social Identity in Soviet Russia," *Journal of Modern History*, 65:4 (1993), 745–70. Class was not a political category among the non-Russians of the USSR for most of the 1920s, but it became an important marker of social and political distinction

with the onset of collectivisation. Yuri Slezkine, "The USSR as Communal Apartment, or How a Socialist State Promoted Ethnic Particularism," *Slavic Review* 53:2 (1994), 414–52.

24 The party systematically encouraged Soviet intellectuals to cultivate ties with left-leaning public opinion leaders and institutions around the world. M. David-Fox, *Showcasing the Great Experiment: Cultural Diplomacy and Western Visitors to the Soviet Union, 1921-1941* (New York: Oxford University Press, 2011), 1–27, 41–2.

25 Creating cultures that were to be "national in form and socialist in content," Soviet leaders in Moscow aimed to undermine regional, religious, and clan identities, and more broadly, to create what they defined as modern societies in the non-Russian regions of the USSR. Slezkine, "The USSR as a Communal Apartment," 417–21.

26 Martin, *The Affirmative Action Empire*, 450.

27 In this vein, they allowed mass media from the socialist camp to circulate in the USSR. R. Szporluk, "The Role of the Press in Polish-Ukrainian Relations," in P. Potichnyj, ed., *Poland and Ukraine: Past and Present* (Edmonton: Canadian Institute of Ukrainian Studies, 1980), 219-20.

28 See R. Applebaum, "A Test of Friendship: Soviet-Czechoslovak Tourism and the Prague Spring," in Anne Gorsuch and Diane Koenker, ed., *Socialist Sixties*, 213–32.

29 Gorsuch, *All This Is Your World*, 79–110.

30 M. Pauly, "Soviet Polonophobia and the Formulation of Nationalities Policy in the Ukrainian SSR 1927-1934," in David Ransel and Bożena Shallcross, ed., *Polish Encounters, Russian Identity* (Bloomington: Indiana University Press, 2005), 172–85 ; Lars Peder Haga, "Coming to Terms with Europe: Konstantin Simonov and Oles' Honchar's Literary Conquest of East Central Europe at the End of World War II," in Patryk Babiracki and Austin Jersild, ed., *Socialist Internationalism in the Cold War: Exploring the Second World* (New York: Palgrave Macmillan, 2016), 20; Patryk Babiracki argues that Soviet journalists, writers, and activists played an important role in spreading Soviet culture in Poland during postwar Stalinism. Meanwhile, attempts to establish a more reciprocal cultural relationship between the two countries were "abortive," getting a new lease of life only after the death of Stalin. Patryk Babiracki, *Soviet Soft Power in Poland: Culture and the Making of Stalin's New Empire, 1943–1957* (Chapel Hill: The University of North Carolina Press, 2015), 186, 221–3.

31 K. Brown, *A Biography of No Place: From Ethnic Borderland to Soviet Heartland* (Cambridge, MA: Harvard University Press, 2004), 223–5.

32 T. Snyder, "'To Resolve the Ukrainian Problem Once and For All': The Ethnic Cleansing of Ukrainians in Poland, 1943–1947," *Journal of Cold War Studies* 1:2 (1999), 86–120.

33 During the 1970s, for example, "the Ethiopian regime was an experiment that on a gigantic scale attempted to prove the validity of the Soviet experience for Africa, in a manner similar to the US civilian effort in Vietnam." Westad, *The Global Cold War*, 253.

34 Ethnicisation of Soviet public culture was driven by failures of Soviet policy elsewhere, too. The Sino-Soviet split and the resulting failure of the dream to build socialism "from Berlin to Shanghai" fuelled racist rhetoric in the USSR. Many Soviet leaders claimed that "the Soviet effort in China was failing because of the inborn deviousness and selfishness of the Chinese." Hanoi's pro-Chinese leanings were also rationalised in racial terms. Westad, *The Global Cold War*, 70, 183–4.

35 On the far left, the Communist Party of Western Ukraine called for the destruction of Poland and the incorporation of its south-eastern territories into Soviet Ukraine. The CPWU was dissolved by Comintern in 1938. In contrast, the major centrist party in Poland's Ukrainian territories, the Ukrainian National Democratic Union, pledged loyalty to the Polish state in return for promises of local reform. But Polish interwar political elites did not consistently cooperate with the Ukrainian centre, and attacked Ukrainian institutions such as the Orthodox Church in Volhynia. Meanwhile, Soviet propaganda fanned anti-Polish sentiments among Poland's ethnic minorities in the east. Consequently, attempts by Polish statesmen such as Henryk Józewski to build a Ukrainian society loyal to the Polish state were quickly undone in 1939. The Soviet occupation of eastern Galicia and Volhynia in 1939 and the German invasion of the USSR in 1941 dealt a decisive blow to west Ukrainian centrists. T. Snyder, *Sketches from a Secret War: A Polish Artist's Mission to Liberate Soviet Ukraine* (New Haven: Yale University Press, 2007), 167; T. Snyder, "The Causes of Ukrainian-Polish Ethnic Cleansing 1943," *Past and Present* 179 (2003), 203–5.

36 The OUN, founded in 1929, anticipated that the removal of enemies would take place through the means of a violent conflict. The younger generation of OUN leaders, including Stepan Bandera, was strongly influenced by the ideas of Dmytro Dontsov who argued that "all deeds that would help Ukrainians to achieve a Ukrainian state, regardless of their nature, were moral and right." G. Rossoliński-Liebe, *Stepan Bandera, The Life and Afterlife of a Ukrainian Nationalist: Fascism, Genocide, and Cult* (Stuttgart: Ibidem-Verlag, 2014), 28, 56, 67, 77.

37 Soviet policies between 1939 and 1941 brought public attention to the importance of ethnic divisions in Ukraine's borderlands. As Christoph Mick argues, "during the Soviet occupation, class theoretically mattered more than ethnicity, but in everyday life class and ethnicity were interlinked and ethnic categories played an important role … The Ukrainians were the titular nationality, which meant that they took precedence in the administration,

and in culture and education over Poles and Jews." In addition, partly due to long-standing anti-Semitic stereotypes and also because "Poles, Ukrainians and Jews were affected differently and at different points in time by the waves of [Soviet] repression," UPA activists, Polish underground leaders, and the gentile population more commonly linked Jews to Soviet rule. C. Mick, "Incompatible Experiences: Poles, Ukrainians and Jews in Lviv under Soviet and German Occupation, 1939–44," *Journal of Contemporary History* 46:2 (2011), 340–5. Deep social divisions in west Ukraine were partly caused by Soviet attempts to radicalise the local youth and to destroy old sources of authority, including the predominantly Polish elites. J.T. Gross, *Revolution from Abroad: The Soviet Conquest of Poland's Western Ukraine and Western Belorussia* (Princeton: Princeton University Press, 2002), 125–43. For a comprehensive overview of the first Soviet occupation in Lviv, see Tarik Cyril Amar, *The Paradox of Ukrainian Lviv: A Borderland City between Stalinists, Nazis, and Nationalists* (Ithaca: Cornell University Press, 2015), 44–87.

38 In a study of wartime Vinnytsia (a region under Soviet rule in the 1920s and the 1930s), Amir Weiner argues that "the exposure to a lengthy, relentless barrage of Nazi anti-Semitic policies left unmistakable imprints on various segments of the local population," including Soviet officials and army officers. A. Weiner, *Making Sense of War: The Second World War and the Fate of the Bolshevik Revolution* (Princeton: Princeton University Press, 2001), 287–9.

39 As Tarik Cyril Amar puts it, German instigation and local initiative contributed "to a wave of assaults [against Jews] from the Baltic to the Black Sea." Amar, *The Paradox of Ukrainian Lviv*, 96–7. The bulk of UPA recruits in 1943 had served in the German auxiliary police. In this capacity, they collaborated in the Final Solution. T. Snyder, "The Causes of Ukrainian-Polish Ethnic Cleansing 1943," *Past and Present* 179 (2003), 211. Ukrainian society further east had likewise been polarised along overlapping ethnic and social lines during the 1930s, particularly during the famine of 1932–1933. This helped the Nazi occupation regime recruit Ukrainians to kill Jews. T. Snyder, "The Causes of the Holocaust," *Contemporary European History* 21:2 (2012), 167. The Polish Home Army leadership harboured anti-Semitic stereotypes but condemned the Holocaust. Mick, "Incompatible experiences," 354. Nevertheless, some self-identified Poles murdered their Jewish neighbours after the Soviet occupation regime in Galicia and Volhynia gave way to Nazi rule in 1941. For instance, in his study of the Galician town of Buczacz (Buchach), Omer Bartov argues that Poles and Ukrainians alike collaborated and profited from the Holocaust. At the same time, "most Jews who survived the genocide in this area were helped by their gentile neighbours for a variety of reasons, which included greed and altruism." O. Bartov, "Wartime Lies and Other Testimonies: Jewish-Christian

Relationships in Buczacz, 1939–44," *East European Politics and Societies* 25:3 (2011), 491.

40 Snyder, "Causes of Ukrainian-Polish Ethnic Cleansing," 217–28.

41 At the same time, only a minority of the UPA rank and file fully shared the ideals of their leaders. A. Statiev, *The Soviet Counterinsurgency in the Western Borderlands* (Cambridge: Cambridge University Press, 2010), 137.

42 J.P. Himka, "The Greek Catholic Church and Nation-Building in GaliciRisca, 1772–1918," *Harvard Ukrainian Studies* 8:3–4 (1984), 426–52. For a detailed account of the Soviet suppression of the Greek Catholic Church, see B. Bociurkiw, *The Ukrainian Greek Catholic Church and the Soviet State (1939–1950)* (Edmonton: Canadian Institute of Ukrainian Studies Press, 1996). It should be noted that, contrary to Soviet propaganda, the Greek Catholic Church provided the most important alternative to OUN's vision of what it meant to be Ukrainian in Galicia. During the interwar period, the Church demonstrated its loyalty to the Polish republic. Metropolitan Sheptyts'kyi generally supported Ukrainian nationalism, but was uneasy about the radicalisation of the younger generation of nationalist activists. Rossoliński-Liebe, *Stepan Bandera*, 86, 366.

43 Statiev, *Soviet Counterinsurgency*, 208, 228, 270–1.

44 W. Risch, *The Ukrainian West: Culture and the Fate of Empire in Soviet Lviv* (Cambridge, MA: Harvard University Press, 2011), 29–49, 70–81.

45 S. Yekelchyk, "The Early 1960s as a Cultural Space: A Microhistory of Ukraine's Generation of Cultural Rebels," *Nationalities Papers* 43:1 (2015), 46–7.

46 Zisserman-Brodsky argues that "the primary and most relevant resource for the study of the crystallisation of ethnic politics can be found in ethnic samizdat." Dina Zisserman-Brodsky, *Constructing Ethnopolitics in the Soviet Union: Samizdat, Deprivation, and the Rise of Ethnic Nationalism* (New York: Palgrave Macmillan, 2003), 10.

47 Y. Bilinsky, *The Second Soviet Republic: The Ukraine after World War II* (New Brunswick: Rutgers University Press, 1964), 303.

48 Yekelchyk argues that Ukrainian republic-level bureaucrats and intellectuals played a decisive role in determining everyday cultural policies. Sticking to the party line, they nevertheless used republican institutions to rehabilitate Ukrainian national heroes. S. Yekelchyk, *Stalin's Empire of Memory: Russian-Ukrainian Relations in the Soviet Historical Imagination* (Toronto: University of Toronto Press, 2004), 5, 6–9, 19.

49 As Yekelchyk puts it, "the Moscow authorities sought to achieve total control over cultural production, but their efforts were frustrated by the relative autonomy of the local bureaucracy and intellectuals." S. Yekelchyk, "Diktat and Dialogue in Stalinist Culture: Staging Patriotic Historical Opera in Soviet Ukraine, 1936–1954," *Slavic Review* 59:3 (2000),

624. In William Risch's words, "the western borderlands represented compromises with Soviet power that could come apart quickly." W. Risch, "A Soviet West: Nationhood, Regionalism, and Empire in the Annexed Western Borderlands," *Nationalities Papers* 43:1 (2015), 64.

50 For instance, Lewytzkyj suggests that the Soviet and the Ukrainian clashed in the USSR's public culture, and that Petro Shelest himself promoted the idea that Ukraine was oppressed in the USSR. He also presents economic reforms as a conflict between the Soviet-Russian centre and the Ukrainian periphery. B. Lewytzkyj, *Politics and Society in Soviet Ukraine, 1953–1980* (Edmonton: Canadian Institute of Ukrainian Studies, 1984), 95, 100, 139, 151–6.

51 N. Shlikhta, *Tserkva tykh, khto vyzhyv. Radians'ka Ukraina, seredyna 1940x – pochatok 1970x rr.* (Kharkiv: Akta, 2011), 386–8.

52 In his words, "Soviet Lviv was not Russified but Ukrainianized, while the Soviet idea of Ukrainian identity presupposed a subordinate relationship to a Soviet version of Russian culture." Amar, *The Paradox of Ukrainian Lviv*, 13.

53 At the same time, "the definition of the local as synonymous with Ukrainian also marked a crucial excision in Lviv's postwar memory, erasing both Poles and Jews." Ibid., 21, 182, 217, 259, 282–317.

54 "Outsiders were either those 'political amphibians' who abused the possibilities of choosing different identities in the borderland or … [communities] across the boundary." P. Sahlins, *Boundaries: The Making of France and Spain in the Pyrenees* (Berkeley: University of California Press, 1991), 8–9, 220, 269–70.

55 During the eighteenth century, for example, Spain and France cooperated in suppressing cross-border smuggling. Sahlins, *Boundaries*, 89–90.

56 O. Zimmer, *A Contested Nation: History, Memory and Nationalism in Switzerland, 1761–1891* (Cambridge: Cambridge University Press, 2003), 14.

57 Though wary of nationalist potential to disrupt the empire's power structures, the authorities "recognised the potential of the Little Russian idea to contest Polish claims on the southwestern borderlands," especially after 1831. The pressure to redefine the population in ethnic and linguistic terms came from local governors who distrusted the Polish population and grew to believe that the region was composed of discrete nations, each with their own interests. F. Hillis, *Children of Rus': Right-Bank Ukraine and the Invention of a Russian Nation* (Ithaca: Cornell University Press, 2013), 2, 7, 10, 12–13, 22, 71–2. Little Russian patriotism in left-bank Ukraine, incorporated into the Russian Empire in mid-seventeenth century, was weaker. Although Orthodox nobles, church leadership, and (to a much lesser extent) burghers, low-level clergy, and ordinary Cossacks supported Little Russian autonomy, they did not present a common Little Russian front to oppose Catherine's reforms. Because Little Russian privileges in the region came under attack from St. Petersburg, Little Russian patriotism

on the left-bank was often defined in political terms: in opposition to the Tsarist state and as an alternative to assimilation in Russian society. It was not an ethnic category defined in opposition to Poles and Jews. Z. Kohut, *Rosiis'kyi tsentralizm i ukrains'ka avtonomiia: Likvidatsiia Het'manshchyny, 1760–1830* (Kyiv: Osnovy, 1996), 108–13, 167–8, 208, 217, 226–33.

58 In the 1870s, Drahomanov came to see the imperial "Russian" state as an oppressor, rather than a protector, of the local "Ukrainian" population. Hillis, *Children*, 44–5, 88–9, 118–19.

59 This was despite Tsarist repression of Ukrainian language. As Hillis explains, "'truly Russian' commentators" hostility toward Ukrainian national separatism should not be read as disdain for the peculiarities of the southwest and its culture. Hillis, *Children*, 66–70, 193.

60 T. Snyder, *The Reconstruction of Nations: Poland, Ukraine, Lithuania, Belarus, 1569–1999* (New Haven: Yale University Press, 2003), 127.

61 J. Hrycak, *Prorok we własnym kraju: Iwan Franko i jego Ukraina (1856–1886)* (Warsaw: Wydawnictwo Krytyki Politycznej, 2011), 167–71. This was especially because Drahomanov, who hailed from left-bank Ukraine and initially did not perceive the Poles as an obstacle to Ukrainians' social liberation, developed increasingly anti-Polish views that chimed with social concerns in right bank Ukraine and Galicia. Hillis, *Children*, 52.

62 After 1905, Ukrainophiles in Kyiv joined forces with non-Orthodox mercantile elites and socialists in calling for an equal rights regime in Tsarist Russia. They were opposed by the self-identified "truly Russian" activists who insisted that this "would only reward and embolden the putative exploiters" of the Orthodox population. Hillis, *Children*, 150, 181–2, 235–6.

63 The tension between nation-building and anti-nationalist campaigns was especially pronounced in Ukraine. As Francine Hirsch argues, "the Ukrainian case illustrates how Soviet authorities responded when they perceived nationalities as too nationalistic." Hirsch, "Towards an Empire of Nations," 211.

64 It should be noted, however, that Breuilly dates the emergence of nationalisms in the USSR to the late twentieth century. J. Breuilly, *Nationalism and the State* (Manchester: Manchester University Press, 1993), 34, 382.

65 As Lowell Tillett points out, propaganda celebrated the friendship of "peoples" rather than governments or leaders. Propaganda projected Old Russian nationality into the Middle Ages to emphasise that Russians, Ukrainians, and Belarusians shared common roots. *The Great Friendship: Soviet Historians on the non-Russian Nationalities* (Chapel Hill: University of North Carolina Press, 1969), 6–7.

66 S. Frunchak, "Commemorating the Future in Postwar Chernivtsi," *East European Politics and Societies* 24:3 (2010), 435–63; Brown, *Biography*, 230. The national "consolidation" of the borderlands was of course not unique to the

USSR. Polish and Czechoslovak borderlands were cleansed and nationalised in very similar ways. Although ethnic cleansing has often been studied with reference to East-Central European borderlands, it was also widespread in Western Europe. T. Zahra, "The 'Minority Problem' and National Classification in the French and Czechoslovak Borderlands," *Contemporary European History* 17:2 (2008), 137–65; M. Venken, "Nationalization Campaigns and Teachers' Practices in Belgian-German and Polish-German Border Regions (1945–56)," *Nationalities Papers* 42:2 (2014), 223–41.

67 The war was commemorated as a Soviet effort, but ethnic Russians were singled out as having made the most important contribution to victory. Meanwhile, some ethnic groups such as Crimean Tatars were branded as collaborators. Stephen Lovell, *The Shadow of War: Russia and the USSR, 1941 to the Present* (Oxford: Wiley-Blackwell, 2010), 207–13. At the same time, Ukraine and Ukrainian Red Army servicemen occupied a special place in the Soviet commemoration of the war. Weiner, *Making Sense of War*, 362. Roman Serbyn wrote about the emergence of a distinct Ukrainian national rhetoric in commemorations of the Great Patriotic War. R. Serbyn, "Managing Memory in Post-Soviet Ukraine: 'Victory Day' or 'Remembrance Day'" in S. Velychenko, ed., *Ukraine, the EU and Russia: History, Culture and International Relations* (Basingstoke: Palgrave Macmillan, 2007), 116–18.

68 Hosking argues that important aspects of Russian culture came under attack in the USSR. Yet after Ukraine exposed a "crisis of *korenizatsiia*" in the early 1930s, Russian language and culture came to occupy the central place in Stalinist USSR. Geoffrey Hosking, *Rulers and Victims: The Russians in the Soviet Union* (Cambridge, MA: Bellknap, 2006), 143-54.

69 D. Gorenburg, "Soviet Nationalities Policy and Assimilation," in Dominique Arel and Blair A. Ruble, ed., *Rebounding Identities: The Politics of Identity in Russia and Ukraine* (Washington, DC: Woodrow Wilson Center Press, 2006), 288.

70 This mirrored developments in other western Soviet republics. Elisa Bemporad argues that a "Jewish Soviet patriotism" developed in Belarus during the 1920s and remained strong through the late 1930s. Soviet leaders did not seek to "de-nationalise" Belarus, but rather mobilised ethnic identities to fuel support for the Soviet project. Soviet Jewish patriotism was underpinned by the notion that life for Jews in the USSR was better than under the Tsar, and in the 1930s, better than life in European countries further west. Jewishness in prewar USSR was defined in ethnic and territorial (Belarusian) terms, with religious identities suppressed by the Soviet state. At the same time, Soviet officials began to see Jewish and Polish communities in Minsk as a potential fifth column, which spurred attacks on Soviet Jewish culture in the late 1930s. After the war, Minsk's Jewish past was erased from public memory and Belarus

was increasingly portrayed as an Eastern Slavic nation space. Elisa Bemporad, *Becoming Soviet Jews: The Bolshevik Experiment in Minsk* (Bloomington: Indiana University Press, 2013), 2–11, 104–5, 177, 195–9, 202–3, 216.

71 O. Subtelny, *Ukraine: A History* (Toronto: University of Toronto Press, 2000), 483.

72 *Derzhavnyi arkhiv L'vivs'koi oblasti* (DALO) (State Archive of L'viv Oblast), f.P3, op.5, s.402, ark. 220–2.

73 Snyder, *Reconstruction*, 188.

74 Weiner, "Empires," 353.

75 For example, *Rossiiskii gosudarstvennyi arkhiv noveishei istorii* (RGANI) (Russian State Archive of Contemporary History), f.5, op.75, d.243, ll. 48–59.

76 This reflected broader tendencies in other republics. Kate Brown, "Securing the Nuclear Nation," *Nationalities Papers* 43:1 (2015), 8–26; Krista Goff, "Why Not Love Our Language and Our Culture: National Rights and Citizenship in Khrushchev's Soviet Union," *Nationalities Papers* 43:1 (2015), 27–44.

77 V. Dunham, *In Stalin's Time: Middleclass Values in Soviet Fiction* (Durham: Duke University Press, 1990), 13–14, 17.

78 Dunham claims that the leadership now valued skill, productivity, and performance over ideological orthodoxy. Dunham, *In Stalin's Time*, 5.

79 M. Lewin, *The Soviet Century* (London: Verso, 2005), 320–1, 325.

80 T.H. Rigby, "Soviet Communist Party Membership Under Brezhnev," *Soviet Studies* 28:3 (1976), 319–20, 322, 327, 330.

81 For example, Hyder Patterson identified a "New Class" in his study of Yugoslavia as "an ascendant, consumerist social grouping distinct not for its social or economic status, but defined primarily through conspicuous consumption." Patrick Hyder Patterson, *Bought and Sold: Living and Losing the Good Life in Yugoslavia* (Ithaca: Cornell University Press, 2011), 297–8.

82 Lovell, *Shadow of War*, 116–26.

83 Brown demonstrates that perks associated with belonging to the "middle class" were promised to blue-collar workers in the closed city of Ozersk in the late 1940s. This was driven by specific local concerns about maintaining stability among workers of plutonium processing plants, but at the same time reflected a growing recognition that "middle class" perks and privileges offered a way to keep important workers acquiescent. Kate Brown, *Plutopia: Nuclear Families, Atomic Cities, and the Great Soviet and American Plutonium Disasters* (Oxford: Oxford University Press, 2013), 135–6.

84 J. Millar, "The Little Deal: Brezhnev's Contribution to Acquisitive Socialism," *Slavic Review* 44:4 (1985), 694–706.

85 J. Brooks, "Socialist Realism in Pravda: Read All About It!" *Slavic Review* 53:4 (1994), 986–7.

86 The post-Stalinist middle class defined in dialogue with Eastern European satellite states did not correspond to the official Soviet tripartite division of society into workers, agricultural workers, and the intelligentsia. While many members of the middle class were indeed the Soviet intelligentsia, the post-Stalin elite was more heterogeneous than Sheila Fitzpatrick's generation of *vydvizhentsy*, and considerably larger than Dunham's middle class of High Stalinism. S. Fitzpatrick, "Stalin and the Making of a New Elite, 1928–1939," *Slavic Review* 38:3 (1979), 377–402. Dunham argues that the concept of middle class excluded workers to the benefit of professional groups during high Stalinism. However, she also claims that, after 1953, the Big Deal facilitated "the upward mobility of more and more people." Dunham, *In Stalin's Time*, 15, 244.

87 In contrast, John Bushnell claims that "middle class" optimism about the USSR's economic prospects was an important source of legitimacy for the Soviet state in the first two decades after the Second World War, but was then overshadowed by "doubts as to whether the gap with the West would ever be filled." Notably, Bushnell equates the "middle class" with Soviet intelligentsia. "The 'New Soviet Man' Turns Pessimist," in S.F. Cohen, A. Rabinowitch and R. Sharlet, ed., *The Soviet Union since Stalin* (Bloomington: Indiana University Press, 1980), 180–90.

88 Yanni Kotsonis, *States of Obligation: Taxes and Citizenship in the Russian Empire and Early Soviet Republic* (Toronto: University of Toronto Press, 2014), 297–9. As O'Keeffe puts it, "Soviet citizenship was predicated on the notion that the individual's participation in the state – no matter how coerced – inescapably compelled the embodiment of the state in the self." Bridget O'Keeffe, *New Soviet Gypsies: Nationality, Performance, and Selfhood in the Early Soviet Union* (Toronto: University of Toronto Press, 2013), 9.

89 Kotsonis, *States of Obligation*, 14.

90 Serhy Yekelchyk, *Stalin's Citizens: Everyday Politics in the Wake of Total War* (Oxford: Oxford University Press, 2014), 5–6, 153–63, 177.

91 In her analysis of amateur theatres of the Khrushchev period, Susan Costanzo argues that "the use of *grazhdanstvennost* to legitimise controversial artistic content and to encourage members of the public to support it reveals a changing role for citizens in the post-Stalin era ... The environment of the Thaw led amateur publics to present a model of an engaged citizen ... This alternative suggested not an oppositional stance but an interest in cooperation with existing institutions." S. Costanzo, "Amateur Theatres and Amateur Publics in the Russian Republic, 1958–71," *Slavonic and East European Review* 86:2 (2008), 394.

92 Other studies that show new types of political mobilization emerged under Brezhnev focus on Russian nationalism, concerns about environmental degradation, and consumerism. For example, Parthé shows that village prose authors evoked Russian nationalism to highlight the costs of Soviet industrialisation and modernisation. Kathleen Parthé, *Russian Village Prose: The Radiant Past* (Princeton: Princeton University Press, 1992), 48–63. Chernyshova argues that new types of "active engagement with the state and society" were underpinned by Soviet citizens' awareness of their rights as consumers. Natalia Chernyshova, *Soviet Consumer Culture in the Brezhnev Era* (London: Routledge, 2013), 101.

93 Yurchak, *Everything Was Forever*, 128–31.

94 S. Kotkin, *Magnetic Mountain: Stalinism as a Civilization* (Berkeley: University of California Press, 1995), 42, 294.

95 S. Kotkin, "Modern Times: The Soviet Union and the Interwar Conjuncture," *Kritika: Explorations in Russian and Eurasian History* 2:1 (2001), 113.

96 Kotkin, *Magnetic Mountain*, 355–6.

97 Kotkin, *Magnetic Mountain*, 91–2, 267–8.

98 S. Davies, *Popular Opinion in Stalin's Russia: Terror, Propaganda, and Dissent, 1934 –1941* (Cambridge: Cambridge University Press, 1997), 183.

99 S. Kotkin, review of *Popular Opinion in Stalin's Russia: Terror, Propaganda, and Dissent, 1934–41*, by Sarah Davies. *Europe-Asia Studies* 50:4 (1998), 739–42. Similarly, Jochen Hellbeck argues that it would be a mistake to view opinions expressed in relatively uncontrolled settings as more "genuine" than citizens' more public pronouncements. Based on the examination of personal diaries from the 1930s, Hellbeck claims that individuals did at times express ideas that they regarded as "non-Soviet," but also tried to purge themselves of those "private" thoughts and attitudes which did not correspond with their "public" Soviet personae. Jochen Hellbeck, *Revolution on My Mind: Writing a Diary under Stalin* (Cambridge, MA: Harvard University Press, 2006), 165–222.

100 Matthew Pauly, *Breaking the Tounge: Language, Education, and Power in Soviet Ukraine, 1923–1934* (Toronto: Toronto University Press, 2014), 7.

101 Fitzpatrick argues that the end of Stalin's "cultural revolution" in the early 1930s "was almost the end of serious intellectual-political debate within a Marxist framework in the Soviet Union." This was partly because there was no clear "Bolshevik" rhetoric – Stalin was reluctant to clearly formulate policy and relied instead of ambiguous "signals" that could be repudiated and reinterpreted in a myriad of ways. Sheila Fitzpatrick, *Everyday Stalinism: Ordinary Life in Extraordinary Times, Soviet Russia in the 1930s* (New York: Oxford University Press, 1999), 17, 27. It seems that Stalinist master narratives were not always informed by revolutionary, "socialist" ideas, but rather

harked back to pre-1917 notions of right and wrong. Especially in rural areas, the Soviet state judged the behaviour of local officials not only against the party's ideological pronouncements, but first and foremost against peasants' "sense of fairness and propriety." S. Fitzpatrick, "How the Mice Buried the Cat: Scenes from the Great Purges of 1937 in the Russian Provinces," *The Russian Review* 52:3 (1993), 307.

102 Kotkin argues that Bolshevik "anti-liberal" visions gave rise to a "new socialist city" with its unique architecture. Yet Kate Brown shows that the urban layouts of Soviet Karaganda and American Billings were almost the same, reflecting similar goals and concerns that cannot be explained with reference to the USSR's peculiar political and ideological structure. In Kotkin's view, such similarities are essentially unimportant because, unlike in the USSR, the life of a worker in an American company town was not the only option available to American citizens. For her part, Brown points out that workers in Billings did not always have the freedom to choose a different life. Kotkin, *Magnetic Mountain*, 108, 223; K. Brown, "Gridded Lives: Why Kazakhstan and Montana are Nearly the Same Place," *The American Historical Review* 106:1 (2001), 17–48.

103 As Martin puts it, "the Soviet nationalities policy of the mid-1930s was both more practical and less coherent than the utopian but logically coherent policy of the 1920s." Terry Martin, *Affirmative Action Empire*, 448.

104 Krylova argues that "Bolshevik ideology" was never a fixed set of fundamental tenets. Already in the 1930s, Stalinist discourse was far from coherent. After the war, "the dramatic transformation of Soviet routines of work, leisure and private life" further changed the key values of Soviet socialist imagination, undermining the early Bolshevik cultural mantra of anti-individualism. Because of this, Krylova claims, it is problematic to view "Bolshevism" as a single ideology that mediated state-society relations in the USSR. Krylova levels similar criticism at Alexei Yurchak. Yurchak examines how Soviet citizens positioned themselves vis-à-vis the "'fixed and normalised discursive system' of Marxism-Leninism. What is left unexplored is the question of how Yurchak's historical subjects related to those vast terrains of post-war Soviet culture that did not make it into the book. The varied worlds of Soviet journalism, literature, film, popularised social sciences did not speak the language of the 'authoritative discourse' while they did inform the way Soviet citizens got to know themselves and their socialist contemporaneity." A. Krylova, "Soviet Modernity: Stephen Kotkin and the Bolshevik Predicament," *Contemporary European History* 23:2 (2014), 171, 178, 182–4, 187–8; A. Krylova, "Identity, Agency, and the 'First Soviet Generation'" in S. Lovell,

ed., *Generations in Twentieth-Century Europe* (Basingstoke: Palgrave Macmillan, 2007), 111.

105 Weiner acknowledges his indebtedness to Kotkin's ideas as he describes the post-Stalinist system as a "Soviet revolution" that approached middle age. A. Weiner, "Robust Revolution to Retiring Revolution: The Life Cycle of the Soviet Revolution, 1945–1968," *The Slavonic and East European Review* 86:2 (2008), 227–8.

106 As Weiner puts it, "with thousands involved in the public legal process [of anti-Soviet Ukrainian nationalists], as active spectators or aspiring executioners, the totalitarian dream (or nightmare) of entire communities policing themselves under the auspices of an all-powerful party-state was becoming a reality." For Khrushchev, "class was the guiding principle in restructuring the Soviet landscape and 'drawing all the people' into the process of 'molding the New Man and building communism.'" A. Weiner, "The Empires Pay a Visit: Gulag Returnees, East European Rebellions, and Soviet Frontier Politics," *The Journal of Modern History* 78, 2 (2006), 371, 374.

107 Weiner, "Empires," 365–7.

108 Analysing reactions to East European unrest in 1956, for example, Weiner throws the young Jewish activists "who viewed the developments in Poland as a revival of the very democratic socialism that the Soviets had abandoned" into one basket with amnestied Ukrainian nationalists who longed for the establishment of independent Ukraine. He discusses both groups in the context of the "agitation" that engulfed the borderlands. Weiner, "Empires," 354.

109 Weiner, "Robust Revolution," 226.

110 A. Weiner, "Déjà Vu All Over Again: Prague Spring, Romanian Summer, and Soviet Autumn on Russia's Western Frontier," *Contemporary European History* 15:2 (2006), 186.

111 Kotkin defines "speaking Bolshevik" as the "barometer of one's political allegiance to the cause." Stephen Kotkin, *Magnetic Mountain*, 220.

112 Krylova, "Soviet Modernity," 171.

113 As Sheila Fitzpatrick argues, "for all the similarities between popular sedition in the Stalin and the post-Stalin periods, there were two very important differences. The first was the level of risk and the likely degree of punishment, which were far higher in the Stalin period. The second was that by the 1950s and 1960s, Soviet society was no longer as isolated from the outside world as it had been before the Second World War." S. Fitzpatrick, "Popular Sedition in the Post-Stalin Soviet Union," in V.A. Kozlov, S. Fitzpatrick, and S.V. Mironenko, eds., *Sedition: Everyday*

Resistance in the Soviet Union under Khrushchev and Brezhnev (New Haven: Yale University Press, 2011), 3.

114 Focusing mostly on the late Stalinist era, Tarik Cyril Amar argues that "national identities were indispensable, but also subordinate and historically transitory." Amar, *The Paradox of Ukrainian Lviv*, 86.

115 Here I build on the ideas of Ethan Pollock, whose study of the immediate postwar years distinguishes between articulations of loyalty to the Soviet homeland and expressions of allegiance to the party. Ethan Pollock, "'Real Men Go to the Bania': Postwar Soviet Masculinities and the Bathhouse," *Kritika: Explorations in Russian and Eurasian History* 11:1 (2010). In his history of the 1940s, Weiner argues that the war paved the way for people to advance conflicting visions of who was properly "Soviet." With ordinary citizens invoking the myth of war as an "autobiographical point of reference," social origin became considerably less important for classifying reliable citizens and enemies than it had been before 1941. Weiner, *Making Sense*, 20–1, 59.

116 To be sure, patriotic sentiment was sometimes filtered through communist ideology. For example, Susan Reid shows that Soviet citizens' responses to the American National Exhibition in 1959 were often underpinned by a sense that the Soviet system was superior to American capitalism. Susan Reid, "Who Will Beat Whom? Soviet Popular Reception of the American National Exhibition in Moscow, 1959," *Kritika: Explorations in Russian and Eurasian History* 9:4 (2008), 855–904.

117 J. Hellbeck, "Speaking Out: Languages of Affirmation and Dissent in Stalinist Russia," in Michael David-Fox, Peter Holquist, and Marshall Poe, eds., *The Resistance Debate in Russian and Soviet History* (Bloomington: Slavica Publishers, 2003), 134–5.

118 Notably, Weiner's conclusion that troubling questions about the future of the Soviet project were most evident on the western frontier during 1968 is a self-fulfilling prophecy, based as it is on an examination of materials concerning the borderlands only. Weiner, "Déjà Vu."

119 P. Bren, *The Greengrocer and His TV: The Culture of Communism after the 1968 Prague Spring* (Ithaca: Cornell University Press, 2010), 105; J. Bolton, *Worlds of Dissent: Charter 77, the Plastic People of the Universe, and Czech Culture under Communism* (Cambridge, MA: Harvard University Press, 2012), 175–6.

120 Bren, *The Greengrocer*, 107.

121 Thompson defines "the moral economy of the poor" as the consistent, traditional view of social norms, roles, and obligations. E.P. Thompson, "The Moral Economy of the English Crowd in the Eighteenth Century," *Past and Present* 50 (1971), 79, 88, 98–9. James Scott's study of twentieth-century Vietnam similarly reveals that subsistence farmers were "risk-averse." He argues that peasants opposed capitalist ideas and

supported strong, paternalist states as long as they guaranteed them the minimum subsistence levels. Yet Scott raises further questions about the role of welfare states in changing popular attitudes to reform. The rise of welfare states, he suggests, guarantees people a degree of stability that eventually makes them less risk-averse. But it appears that most Soviet citizens never believed they reached a level of stability that would insure them against the possible negative effects of anti-authoritarian reform. J. Scott, *The Moral Economy of the Peasant: Rebellion and Subsistence in Southeast Asia* (New Haven: Yale University Press, 1976), 1–10.

122 Complaints about export were especially common, and not just in relation to Eastern Europe. During the Six Days War in 1967, for example, many Soviet citizens claimed that their country's support for the Arabs drained the USSR's resources "that should be directed first and foremost to domestic development and consumption." Y. Ro'i, "The Soviet Jewish Reaction to the Six Day War," in Y. Ro'i and B. Morozov, eds., *The Soviet Union and the June 1967 Six Day War* (Washington, DC: Woodrow Wilson Center Press, 2008), 252–3. While demands to improve supplies of basic goods abounded at times of crisis, Brezhnev-era consumers became increasingly concerned with quality, too. Chernyshova, *Soviet Consumer Culture*, 189.

123 "If the state was indiscriminate in the targets of its repression, many of its opponents and critics were just as arbitrary in choosing the form of their opposition," Kozlov writes. Ed. Kozlov, Fitzpatrick, and Mironenko, *Sedition*, 26–8.

124 To gauge top party leaders' approaches to managing popular opinion during the Khrushchev era, I draw on the rich collection of CPSU Central Committee Presidium meeting transcripts compiled by A. Fursenko and other historians at the Russian State Archive of Contemporary History in Moscow (RGANI). The multi-volume collection reveals conflicts, tensions, and contradictions among senior political leadership of the USSR. A. Fursenko, *Prezidium TsK KPSS 1954–1964: chernovye protokol'nye zapisi zasedanii, stenogrammy, postanovleniia: v 3 tomakh* (Moscow: ROSSPEN, 2003–8). In order to further analyse the evolution of official narratives about the near abroad, I have examined not only newspapers and official publications such as guidebooks to Eastern Europe and school history textbooks, but also internal party correspondence. I have drawn on English-language collections of Soviet press materials compiled by the American Association for the Advancement of Slavic Studies. *The Current Digest of the Soviet Press*, vols. 8–27. I have also used English-language collections of Soviet Ukrainian press published in New York by the "Prolog" Research and Publishing Association. *Digest of the Soviet Ukrainian Press*, vols. 5–13 (New York, 1961–9).

125 Many Soviet underground materials have been collected and published by the Radio Free Europe/Radio Liberty research unit. *Sobranie dokumentov samizdata*, vols. 1–16 (Munich: Radio Liberty, 1973) and *Materialy samizdata* (Munich: Radio Liberty, 1972–91). In addition, the samizdat *Chronicle of Current Events* (*Khronika Tekushchikh Sobytyi*) which appeared irregularly between the 1960s and 1980s and was published outside the USSR, offers a useful overview of other illegal publications from various parts of the USSR. See *Khronika tekushchikh sobytii*, issues 1–27 (Amsterdam: Fond im. Gertsena, 1979); *Khronika tekushchikh sobytii*, issues 28–63 (New York: Khronika, 1974–83).

126 Drawing on KGB reports, Dmytruk and Bazhan focus almost exclusively on non-conformist opinions. For example, see O. Bazhan (ed.), "Praz'ka Vesna' u dokumentakh Galuzevoho derzhavnoho arkhivu Sluzhby Bezpeky Ukrainy," *Z arkhiviv VUChK-GPU-NKVD-KGB* 1/2 (2008); O. Bazhan, "Zovnishn'o-politychni aktsii SRSR u 50– 80-ti rr. ta ikh vplyv na rozvytok opozytsiinoho rukhu v Ukraini," *Z arkhiviv VUChK-HPU-NKVD-KHB* 2/4 (2000); V. Dmytruk, *Ukraina ne movchala: Reaktsiia ukrains'koho suspil'stva na podii 1968 roku v Chekhoslovachchyni* (Kyiv: Instytut Istorii Ukrainy NAN Ukrainy, 2004).

127 Davies, *Popular Opinion*, 9.

128 Needless to say, the Soviet system did not allow for the rise of public opinion understood in Habermas' framework, for it left few spaces for the open exchange of ideas. At the same time, Habermas' binary division of modern cultures into "informal, personal, non-public opinion" and "formal, institutionally authorised opinion" does not apply in the context of the USSR either. For one, many dissidents explicitly rejected official ideas, but claimed that their opinions should become the new "public" norm. Moreover, even as people reflected upon their relationship to the regime without engaging in rational public debate on political or ideological questions, their views acquired a public significance. The authorities endeavoured to monitor all forms of communication, praising citizens who articulated "correct" views about the near abroad, and expressing alarm about "incorrect" opinions voiced in both formal and informal contexts. All citizens' attitudes – whether expressed in official public meetings or in less controlled settings such as conversations with friends – were therefore a matter of public concern. For definition of "public," "authorised," and "individualised" opinion, see J. Habermas, *The Structural Transformation of the Public Sphere: An Inquiry into a Category of Bourgeois Society* (Cambridge, MA: MIT Press, 1989), 89–102, 245.

129 J. Plamper, "Beyond Binaries: Popular Opinion in Stalinism," in *Popular Opinion in Totalitarian Regimes: Fascism, Nazism, Communism*, ed. Paul

Corner (Oxford: Oxford University Press, 2009), 72. In socialist Poland, the first centre for investigating public opinion was originally supposed to monitor only official radio broadcasts. M. Kula, "Poland: The Silence of Those Deprived of Voice," in *Popular Opinion*, Corner, 149–50.

130 In this sense, they were similar to the Tsar's subjects who engaged in debates about the meaning of "hooliganism." J. Neuberger, *Hooliganism: Crime, Culture and Power in St. Petersburg, 1900–1914* (Berkeley: University of California Press, 1993), 13.

1 De-Stalinization and Soviet Patriotism

1 Paweł Machcewicz, *Polski rok 1956* (Warsaw: Mowią wieki, 1993), 13–27.

2 Wojciech Roszkowski, *Najnowsza historia Polski 1945–1980* (Warsaw: Świat książki, 2003), 339–47.

3 Johanna Granville, "Poland and Hungary, 1956: A Comparative Essay Based on New Archival Findings," *The Australian Journal of Politics and History* 48:3 (2002), 369–95.

4 Weiner, "Empires"; Mark Kramer, "Soviet Policy during the Polish and Hungarian Crises of 1956: Reassessments and New Findings," *Journal of Contemporary History* 33:2 (1998): 163–214.

5 P. Jones, "From the Secret Speech to the Burial of Stalin: Real and Ideal Responses to De-Stalinisation," in Polly Jones, ed., *The Dilemmas of De-Stalinisation: Negotiating Cultural and Social Change in the Khrushchev Era* (London: Routledge, 2005), 43.

6 Little evidence suggests that Soviet citizens talked extensively about the workers' riots in Poznań in June 1956, at least not in any public forum.

7 "Hostile Provocation by Imperialist Agents in Poland," *Pravda* and *Izvestiia*, 30 June 1956, from the *Current Digest of the Soviet Press* (*CDSP*) 8:26, 8 August 1956; "Polish People Brand Organizers of Provocation," *Pravda*, 1 July 1956, from *CDSP* 8:26, 8 August 1956; "International Forces of Peace, Democracy and Socialism are Growing and Gaining in Strength," *Pravda*, 16 July 1956, from *CDSP* 8:29, 29 August 1956; "Report by Ernö Gerö at Plenary Session of Hungarian Workers' Party Central Committee," *Pravda*, 20 July 1956, from *CDSP* 8:29, 29 August 1956; "On Political and Economic Situation and Main Tasks of PUWP," *Pravda*, 21 July 1956, from *CDSP* 8:29, 29 August 1956.

8 Fursenko, *Prezidium* 2. Document 74.7.1, 449–51.

9 Fursenko, *Prezidium* 1. Document 74, 170; 2. Document 74.7.2, 452; Fursenko, *Prezidium* 2. Document 74.7.3, 454.

10 "Antisocialist pronouncements in the Polish press," *Pravda*, 20 October 1956, from *CDSP* 8:40, 14 November 1956.

11 Fursenko, *Prezidium* 1. Document 77, 175.
12 Władysław Gomułka, "Przemówienie na wiecu w Warszawie," *Trybuna ludu*, 25 October 1956.
13 Fursenko, *Prezidium* 1. Document 78, 177.
14 "The Working Class Must Resolutely Rebuff Alien Slogans – Newspaper *Trybuna ludu* Urges the Working People to be Vigilant," *Pravda*, 24 October 1956, from *CDSP* 8:41, 21 November 1956; "Pure Stream and Dirty Scum – Editorial in *Trybuna ludu*," *Pravda*, 25 October 1956, from *CDSP* 8:41, 21 November 1956; "From the Resolution of the Eighth Plenary Session of the Central Committee of the Polish United Workers' Party 'On the Current Political and Economic Tasks of the Party,'" *Pravda*, 28 October 1956, from *CDSP* 8:41, 21 November 1956; "This is Warsaw," *Pravda*, 29 October 1956, from *CDSP* 8:42, 28 November 1956; "Soviet Musicians Perform in Poland," *Pravda*, 30 October 1956, from *CDSP* 8:42, 28 November 1956; "Appeal of Central Committee of the Polish United Workers' Party," *Pravda* and *Izvestiia*, 3 November 1956, from *CDSP* 8:43, 5 December 1956.
15 "The Downfall of an Antipopular Venture in Budapest," *Pravda* and *Izvestiia*, 25 October 1956, from *CDSP* 8:41, 21 November 1956.
16 "Situation in Hungary," *Pravda* and *Izvestiia*, 3 November 1956, from *CDSP* 8:43, 5 December 1956.
17 Fursenko, *Prezidium* 1. Document 84, 202.
18 Fursenko, *Prezidium* 2. Document 84.0.1, 478.
19 "Hungarian Working People Will Defend Their Socialist Achievements," *Pravda*, 5 November 1956, from *CDSP* 8:43, 5 December 1956.
20 Iuzef Khachin'skii, "A *dekada* of Ukrainian Culture in Poland," *Pravda Ukrainy*, 4 October 1956.
21 "Festival dopomozhe ednanniu," *Literaturna hazeta*, 26 July 1957; "Govoriat uchastniki festivalia," *Pravda Ukrainy*, 28 July 1957.
22 TsDAHOU f.1, op.24, s.4265, ark.51–8, 79–86, 87–98, 99–112.
23 Kyiv summarised the effects of the agitation work in the localities for the CPSU Central Committee on 3 November, 12 November, and 16 November 1956. TsDAHOU, f.1, op.24, s.4265, ark. 73–7, 156–65, 227–35.
24 TsDAHOU, f.1, op.24, s.4265, ark. 208–12.
25 TsDAHOU, f.1, op.24, s.4377, ark. 86–9.
26 TsDAHOU, f.1, op.24, s.4265, ark. 208–12.
27 DALO, f.P3, op.5, s.443, ark. 23–7.
28 TsDAHOU, f.1, op.24, s.4265, 30–1, 99–112.
29 Fursenko, *Prezidium* 2. Document 84.0.1, 478.
30 Weiner, "Empires," 362–3.
31 Fursenko, *Prezidium* 2. Document 93.0.2, 503.

32 Fursenko, *Prezidium* 2. Document 93.0.2, 506–7.

33 Fursenko, *Prezidium* 2. Document 93.0.2, 498, 501.

34 Fursenko, *Prezidium* 2. Document 93.0.2, 503–4.

35 RGANI, f.5, op.31, d.79, ll.1–7.

36 *Derzhavnyi arkhiv Odes'koi oblasti* (DAOO) (State Archive of Odesa Oblast), f.P11, op.15, s.467, ark. 1–2.

37 In the aftermath of the Twentieth Party Congress, as Jones claims, speeches, questions and notes diverged seriously from the official script of de-Stalinisation. Polly Jones, "From the Secret Speech," 43, 46–7.

38 TsDAHOU, f.1, op.24, s.4377, ark.102–5.

39 *Derzhavnyi arkhiv Kyivs'koi oblasti* (DAKO) (State Archive of Kyiv Oblast), f.P5, op.6, s.712, ark. 9–20.

40 M. Edele, *Soviet Veterans of the Second World War: A Popular Movement in an Authoritarian Society, 1941–1991* (Oxford: Oxford University Press 2008), 162.

41 Ibid., 181.

42 DAKO, Kyiv, f.5, op.6, s.712, ark. 9–20.

43 RGANI, f.5, op.31, d.62, ll.81–7.

44 Miriam Dobson, *Khrushchev's Cold Summer: Gulag Returnees, Crime, and the Fate of Reform after Stalin* (Ithaca, NY: Cornell University Press, 2009), 100.

45 It should be noted that the officers seemed to differ from younger soldiers in their assessment of the Hungarian crisis. Individual soldiers expressed doubts about the USSR's repressive policies in Eastern Europe. See TsDAHOU f.1, op.24, s.4265, ark. 51–8.

46 TsDAHOU, f.1, op.24, s.4265, ark. 124–31. Similarly, a local engineer from Kyiv pointed out that Soviet leaders had recently enjoyed "parties and banquets," instead of working hard to resolve the problems that arose in Eastern Europe. Had Batia been alive, he said referring to Stalin, things would never have gone as far as they had. TsDAHOU, f.1, op.24, s.4265, ark. 236–45.

47 TsDAHOU, f.1, op.24, s.4265, ark. 124–31.

48 TsDAHOU, f.1, op.24, s.4265, ark. 267–8. W. Michalewska, *Sercem i czynem* (Warsaw: Książka i Wiedza, 1981), 411.

49 TsDAHOU, f.1, op.24, s.4265, ark. 2–14.

50 TsDAHOU, f.1, op.24, s.4377, ark. 86–9.

51 This was especially because the authorities promised to extend welfare to a greater number of citizens, particularly the elderly. Several years in the making, a new comprehensive pension law was unveiled in 1956. S. Lovell, "Soviet Russia's Older Generations," in S. Lovell, ed., *Generations in Twentieth-Century Europe* (Basingstoke: Palgrave Macmillan 2007), 217.

52 TsDAHOU, f.1, op.24, s.4377, ark. 90–3; TsDAHOU, f.1, op.24, s.4265, ark. 120–3, 151–4.
53 DALO, f.P3, op.5, s.443, ark. 23–7.
54 TsDAHOU, f.1, op.24, s.4265, ark. 120–3.
55 DAKO, f.P5, op.6, s.712, ark. 31–2.
56 TsDAHOU, f.1, op.24, s.4377, ark. 90–3. In Lviv, the apparatchiks reported that after the Soviet armies marched into Budapest and a new Hungarian government was formed, demand for basic products subsided and reached "almost normal" levels. A similar report arrived from the Khmelnytskyi region. DALO, f.P3, op.5, s.402, ark. 194–8; TsDAHOU, f.1, op.24, s.4265, ark. 151–4.
57 TsDAHOU, f.1, op.24, s.4265, ark. 274–8.
58 V.A. Kozlov, *Mass Uprisings in the USSR: Protest and Rebellion in the Post-Stalin Years* (Armonk, NY: M.E. Sharpe, 2002), 155.
59 DAKO, f.P5, op.6, s.712, ark. 28–30.
60 DAKO, f.P5, op.6, s.712, ark. 21–2.
61 See TsDAHOU, f.1, op.24, s.4377, ark. 90–3.
62 Brian LaPierre, "Making Hooliganism on a Mass Scale: The Campaign Against Petty Hooliganism in the Soviet Union, 1956–1964," *Cahiers du monde russe* 47:1–2 (2006): 349–52, 356–7.
63 TsDAHOU, f.1, op.24, s.4265, ark. 99–112.
64 TsDAHOU, f.1, op.24, s.4265, ark. 156–65.
65 Christine Varga-Harris, "Forging Citizenship on the Home Front: Reviving the Socialist Contract and Constructing Soviet Identity During the Thaw," in Jones, ed., *Dilemmas*, 104, 111.
66 DALO, f.P3, op.5, s.406, ark. 83–5.
67 TsDAHOU, f.1, op.24, s.4265, ark. 87–98; DALO f.P3, op.5, s.443, ark. 23–7.
68 TsDAHOU, f.1, op.24, s.4265, ark. 87–98.
69 See Chapter 5.
70 D. Kozlov, "Naming the Social Evil: The Readers of *Novyi mir* and Vladimir Dudintsev's *Not by Bread Alone*, 1956–59 and Beyond," in Jones, ed., *Dilemmas*, 83, 87.
71 D. Filtzer, "From Mobilised to Free Labour: De-Stalinisation and the Changing Legal Status of Workers," in Jones, ed., *Dilemmas*, 157.
72 DALO, f.P3, op.5, s.418, ark. 58–9.
73 DALO, f.P3, op.5, s.418, ark. 62–3.
74 Amar, *The Paradox of Ukrainian Lviv*, 183.
75 Outward expression of support for Soviet rule cost the west Ukrainian writer and journalist Yaroslav Halan his life. For a discussion of Halan's murder and its consequences, see Ibid., 243.

76 For many local Ukrainians, urban modernity was synonymous with Sovietization. "By the 1959 census, nearly a third of Lviv's total population of approximately 411,000 consisted of Ukrainians from the territory of the former Galicia but not from Lviv." Ibid., 200.
77 Amir Weiner states that local state and party organs in the west were "gradually being indigenised," and mentions tensions between "indigenous members and outsiders within the party organization in the western frontier." Weiner, "Empires," 336, 342–3. William Risch points out that migrants from further east sometimes saw themselves as bearers of Ukrainian culture in Lviv. Risch, *The Ukrainian West*, 60–2.
78 TsDAHOU, f.1, op.24, s.4265, ark. 99–112.
79 TsDAHOU, f.1, op.24, s.4265, ark. 87–98.
80 TsDAHOU, f.1, op.24, s.4265, ark. 87–98.
81 TsDAHOU, f.1, op.24, s.4265, ark. 2–14.
82 TsDAHOU, f.1, op.24, s.4265, ark. 87–98.
83 DALO, f.P3, op.5, s.443, ark. 23–7.
84 DALO, f.P3, op.5, s.402, ark. 194–8.
85 DALO, f.P3, op.5, s.443, ark. 28–31.
86 TsDAHOU, f.1, op.24, s.4265, ark. 79–86.
87 TsDAHOU, f.1, op.24, s.4265, ark. 151–4.
88 Ibid.
89 TsDAHOU, f.1, op.24, s.4265, ark. 79–86.
90 DALO, f.P3, op.5, s.406, ark. 78–82.
91 TsDAHOU, f.1, op.24, s.4265, ark. 73–7.
92 TsDAHOU, f.1, op.24, s.4377, ark. 86–9.
93 Szporluk, "Introduction" in *The Influence of Eastern Europe*, 2.
94 Kenneth Farmer writes about "reformist" challengers to the Soviet status quo who often sought a better implementation of Leninist nationalities policy in the USSR. He further describes "revolutionary" challengers to the USSR, who rejected any authority of Moscow over Ukraine. Farmer, *Ukrainian Nationalism*, 208–9.
95 Dina Zisserman-Brodsky, *Constructing Ethnopolitics in the Soviet Union: Samizdat, Deprivation, and the Rise of Ethnic Nationalism* (New York: Palgrave Macmillan, 2003), 197.
96 TsDAHOU, f.1, op.24, s.4265, ark. 156–65.
97 TsDAHOU, f.1, op.24, s.4265, ark. 87–98.
98 TsDAHOU, f.1, op.24, s.4265, ark. 156–65. Interestingly, the draft of Kyrychenko's document was more direct here, stating that the local administration should operate in "Ukrainian, especially in the western oblasts." See TsDAHOU, f.1, op.24, s.4265, ark. 145–54.

99 TsDAHOU, f.1, op.24, s.4265, ark. 156–65.
100 See Chapter 3.
101 C. Hooper, "What Can and Cannot be Said: Between the Stalinist Past and New Soviet Future," *The Slavonic and East European Review* 86:2 (2008), 316–17.
102 RGANI, f.5, op.31, d.79, ll. 11–15; DALO, f.P3, op.5, s.443, ark. 23–7; TsDAHOU, f.1, op.24, s.4265, ark. 208–12.
103 DAKO, f.P5, op.6, s.712, ark. 9–20; TsDAHOU, f.1, op.24, s.4265, ark. 208–12.
104 Leonid Pliushch, *History's Carnival: A Dissident's Autobiography* (London: Collins, 1979), 16–17.
105 DAKO, f.P5, op.6, s.712, ark. 9–20.
106 TsDAHOU, f.1, op.24, s.4265, ark. 99–112.
107 TsDAHOU, f.1, op.24, s.4265, ark. 37–9.
108 TsDAHOU, f.1, op.24, s.4265, ark. 73–7.
109 TsDAHOU, f.1, op.24, s.4265, ark. 87–98.
110 Bazhan, "Zovnishn'o-politychni aktsii," 52, 54.
111 Kramer, "Soviet Policy During the Polish and Hungarian Crises of 1956', 196.
112 RGANI, f.5, op.31, d.79, ll. 65–7.
113 TsDAHOU, f.1, op.24, s.4265, ark. 2–14.
114 TsDAHOU, f.1, op.24, s.4302, ark.155–6.
115 TsDAHOU, f.1, op.24, s.4265, ark. 87–98.
116 E.R. Drachman, *Challenging the Kremlin: The Soviet Jewish Movement for Freedom, 1967–1990* (New York: Paragon House, 1991), 30.
117 Z. Gitelman, *Bespokoinyi vek: Evrei Rossii i Sovetskogo Soiuza s 1881 g. do nashikh dnei* (Moscow: Novoe literaturnoe obozrenie, 2008), 232–3.
118 Lewytzkyj, *Politics and Society*, 70.
119 DAOO, f.P11, op.15, s.446, ark. 114–17.
120 TsDAHOU, f.1, op.24, s.4265, ark. 236–45.
121 Ibid.
122 TsDAHOU, f.1, op.24, s.4537, ark. 48–9.
123 TsDAHOU, f.1, op.24, s.4265, ark. 236–45.
124 Gitelman, *Bespokoinyi*, 234.
125 Anatoly Rusnachenko, "Sprotyv robitnytstva ta robitnychi protesty v Ukraini (kin. 50kh- poch. 80kh rr)', *Rozbudova derzhavy* 4 (1996), 55.
126 TsDAHOU, f.1, op.24, s.4537, ark. 52.
127 TsDAHOU, f.1, op.24, s.4265, ark. 79–86.
128 TsDAHOU, f.1, op.24, s.4265, ark. 236–45.
129 DALO, f.P3, op.5, s.402, ark. 194–8.

130 TsDAHOU, f.1, op.24, s.4377, ark. 86–9.
131 TsDAHOU, f.1, op.24, s.4265, ark. 236–45.
132 TsDAHOU, f.1, s.4265, ark.73–7, 156–65, 236–45. For a discussion of the term "bandits," see Miriam Dobson, "'Show the Bandits No Mercy!': Amnesty, Criminality and Public Response in 1953," in *Dilemmas*, ed. Jones, 21–40.
133 Weiner, "Empires," 337–8.
134 Bociurkiw, *The Ukrainian Greek Catholic Church*, 107–27; V. Markus, "Religion and Nationality: The Uniates of Ukraine," in Bohdan R. Bociurkiw and John W. Strong, ed., *Religion and Atheism in the USSR and Eastern Europe* (London: Macmillan, 1975), 106–9.
135 For example, Petro Shelest informed the CPU Central Committee about a Kyivan who claimed that the "Ukrainian *narod*" would follow the Hungarian example and put an end to the Soviet regime. TsDAHOU, f.1, op.24, s.4265, ark. 236–45.
136 A Transcarpathian miner claimed that a world war was about to begin, which would give "us" a chance to chase the Russians out of Transcarpathia. The report did not actually specify the man's ethnicity, and he could well have been Hungarian. RGANI, f.5, op.31, d.62, ll. 92–5.
137 DALO, f.P3, op.5, s.406, ark. 78–82.
138 TsDAHOU, f.1, op.24, s.4265, ark. 223–6.
139 For example, the language used in the liturgical functions was "a Ukrainianised variant of Old Church Slavonic; the language of the sermon and of local administration [was] standard Ukrainian." Markus, "Religion and Nationality," 145–7.
140 Bociurkiw, *The Ukrainian Greek Catholic Church*, 108.
141 F. Burlachenko, "Vatican Forgers," *Voiovnychyi ateist*, 6 June 1962. Digest of Soviet Ukrainian Press 6:7, July 1961.
142 TsDAHOU, f.1, op.31, s. 1458, ark. 20.
143 TsDAHOU, f.1, op.24, s.4302, ark. 125; TsDAHOU, f.1, op.24, s.4265, ark.73–7.
144 DALO, f.P3, op.5, s.402, ark. 220–2.
145 TsDAHOU, f.1, op.24, s.4265, ark.124–31.
146 TsDAHOU, f.1, op.24, s.4265, ark. 73–7.
147 Weiner, "Empires," 353.
148 TsDAHOU, f.1, op.24, s.4265, ark. 73–7.
149 DALO, f.P3, op.5, s.402, ark. 220–2.
150 TsDAHOU, f.1, op.24, s.4265, ark. 99–112.
151 TsDAHOU, f.1, op.24, s.4265, ark. 73–7.
152 TsDAHOU, f.1, op.24, s.4265, ark. 79–86.
153 DALO, f.P3, op.5, s.402, ark. 220–2.

154 Weiner, *Making Sense*, 251. See also chapters 4 and 5, which consider Ukrainian-Polish relations in more depth.
155 TsDAHOU, f.1, op.24, s.4265, ark. 79–86.
156 TsDAHOU, f.1, op.24, s.4265, ark. 73–7.
157 A Hungarian woman employed at the Uzhgorod passport office had a peculiar interpretation of the dramatic developments across the border, stating that "the Hungarians" took down the old Jewish prime minister and chose "a Magyar" in his stead. TsDAHOU, f.1, op.24, s.4265, ark. 73–7. The authorities also registered anti-Semitic outbursts in other parts of Ukraine. For instance, officials in Mykolaiv discovered eight handwritten anti-Semitic leaflets, posted around Lenin Street in the regional centre of Bol'shaia Bradievka on 6 November, which called for the "working people" to "beat up the Jews" to avenge the war in Egypt. TsDAHOU, f.1, op.24, s.4302, ark. 126; TsDAHOU, f.1, op.24, s.4265, ark. 73–7.
158 S. Zhuk, *Rock and Roll in the Rocket City: The West, Identity, and Ideology in Soviet Dniepropetrovsk, 1960–1985* (Washington DC: Woodrow Wilson Center Press, 2010), 31–52, 60–2.
159 Vladislav Zubok, *Zhivago's Children: The Last Russian Intelligentsia* (Cambridge, MA: Belknap, 2009), 78.

2 Friendship in the Soviet Empire

1 *Achiwum Akt Nowych* (AAN) (Archive of Contemporary Files), z.1354, s.XIA, t.75, ark. 238–9.
2 A.E. Gorsuch, "Time Travellers: Soviet Tourists to Eastern Europe," in A.E. Gorsuch and D. Koenker, ed., *Turizm: The Russian and East European Tourist under Capitalism and Socialism* (Ithaca: Cornell University Press, 2006), 208.
3 Gorsuch, "Time Travellers," 206, 212.
4 Gorsuch, "Time Travellers," 211.
5 AAN, z.1354, s.XIA, t.75, ark. 220–2.
6 AAN, z.1354, s.XIA, t.75, ark. 241.
7 AAN, z.1354, s.XIA, t.78, ark. 150–2.
8 AAN, z.1354, s.XIA, t.78, ark. 406.
9 AAN, z.1354, s.XIA, t.76 ("Extracts from an information note sent by comrade Gede," 5 February 1957).
10 In line with this, Khrushchev's regime implemented a variety of measures aimed at attracting more students from working class and peasant backgrounds to university. Lovell, *The Shadow of War*, 119.
11 AAN, z.1354, s.XIA, t. 74 ("Letter to the CPSU Politburo members sent in 1959").

12 AAN, z. 1354, s.XIA, t.77 ("Text of Khrushchev's conversation with Polish journalists").
13 AAN, z.1354, s.XIA, t.75, ark. 222.
14 AAN, z.1354, s.XIA, t. 78 ark. 409–10.
15 RGANI, f.5, op.33, d.66, ll. 31–4.
16 RGANI, f.5, op.33, d.202, ll. 150–5.
17 RGANI, f.5, op.33, d.66, ll. 60–3.
18 *Gosudarstvennyi arkhiv Rossiiskoi Federatsii* (GARF) (State Archive of the Russian Federation), f.6903, op.2, d.218b, ll. 1–26; RGANI, f.5, op.73, d.274, ll. 57–9.
19 RGANI, f.5, op.33, d.17, ll. 36–44.
20 RGANI, f.5, op.33, d.17, l. 45.
21 RGANI, f.5, op.33, d.7, ll. 176–7.
22 RGANI, f.5, op.62, d.41, ll. 241–52.
23 RGANI, f.5, op.33, d.66, ll. 60–3.
24 RGANI, f.5, op.33, d.235, ll. 189–95.
25 RGANI, f.5, op.33, d.235, ll. 203–4.
26 P. Shelest, *Spravzhnii sud istorii shche poperedu. Spohady, shchodennyky, dokumenty, materialy*, ed. Iurii Shapoval. (Kyiv: ADEF Ukraina, 2003), 118–19.
27 A.K. Timashev, *Ot Karpat do Baltiki: Zametki geografa o Pol'skoi Narodnoi Respublike* (Moscow: Geografgiz, 1959), 18.
28 Applebaum, "A Test of Friendship," 216.
29 Ibid.
30 Inturist, *Posetite Vengriiu* (Moscow: Inturist, no date), 6.
31 P.N. Burlaka, *Mezh Tissoi i Dunaem* (Moscow: Geografgiz, 1959), 25.
32 AAN, z.1354, s.XIA, t.76, ark. 34.
33 N. Ravich, *Po dorogam Evropy* (Moscow: Sovetskaia Rossiia, 1964), 147–8.
34 Ravich, *Po dorogam*, 128–9.
35 K.S. Ivanova, Iu. V. Pomortseva, E.A. Orlianskii, "Istoricheskoe znachenie pravozashchitnogo dvizheniia v SSSR," *Sibirskii torgovo-ekonomicheskii zhurnal* 3 (2011), 25–30.
36 L. Slavin, *Portrety i zapiski* (Moscow: Sovetskii pisatel, 1965), 196, 207, 209–10, 212.
37 A.L. Litvin, *Writing History in Twentieth-Century Russia: A View from Within* (Basingstoke: Palgrave, 2001), 22.
38 G.D. Alekseeva, *Istoricheskaia nauka v Rossii. Ideologiia. Politika (60-80-e gody XX veka)* (Moscow: Institut rossiiskoi istorii RAN, 2003), 50–1; Litvin, *Writing History*, 25; R.D. Markwick, *Rewriting History in Soviet Russia: The Politics of Revisionist Historiography, 1956–1974* (Basingstoke: Palgrave, 2001), 69, 71.

39 Alekseeva, *Istoricheskaia nauka*, 40–1.
40 Markwick, *Rewriting History*, 45.
41 Ibid., 68.
42 By the late Stalinist period, official narratives stressed that "Russians" and "Ukrainians," led by powerful leaders such as Bohdan Khmel'nyts'kyi, had always striven towards "reunification," which laid the foundation for the establishment of the USSR. F. Sysyn, "The Changing Image of the Hetman: On the 350th Anniversary of the Khmel'nyts'kyi Uprising," *Jahrbucher fur Geschichte Osteuropas* 46:4 (1998), 531–45.
43 V. Yaremchuk, "Ukrains"ka radians'ka istoriohrafiia 50x–80x rokiv pro ukrains'ke natsiietvorennia: ofitsiina ta al'ternatyvni kontseptsii'," *Naukovi zapysky. Seriia "Istorychni nauky"* 17 (2011), 267.
44 J. Basarab, *Pereiaslav 1654: A Historiographical Study* (Edmonton: University of Alberta Canadian Institute of Ukrainian Studies, 1982), 179–80, 182.
45 Michalewska, *Sercem*, 407–8.
46 TsDAHOU, f.1, op.31, s.1458 ("Popravki i dopolneniia k knige N. Nashkovskogo").
47 S. Yekelchyk, *Stalin's Empire of Memory*, 123–4.
48 TsDAHOU, f.1, op.31. s.1212, ark. 7–10.
49 In 1967, literary scholars employed at the Ministry of Culture library in Lviv, supported by the first secretary of the regional party organisation Vasilii Kutsevol, commemorated another nineteenth-century writer. They celebrated Aleksander Fredro for ridiculing the gentry and advancing the revolutionary cause in Ukraine. TsDAHOU, f.1, op.24, s.6373, ark. 10–11.
50 Michalewska, *Sercem*, 416, 423–4, 444, 476–92.
51 AAN, z.1354, s.XIA, t.78, ark. 442–3.
52 AAN, z.1354, s.LVI, t.1109 ("Note on conversation with comrade Furtseva that took place on 11 March 1968," 11 March 1968).
53 *Zhovten'*, October 1957.
54 Alekseeva, *Istoricheskaia nauka*, 15–19, 59–60; Markwick, *Rewriting History*, 68.
55 Litvin, *Writing History*, 23.
56 Alekseeva, *Istoricheskaia nauka*, 23.
57 The journal printed articles about such topics as "Soviet patriotism and internationalism," the development of Russo-Ukrainian friendship, and Ukrainian relations with the people's democracies. TsDAHOU, f.1, op.31, s. 1458, ark. 34–8.
58 Children aged fourteen and fifteen would first study the "Soviet" past, which basically amounted to Russian history, and then focus on how the same social and political developments occurred on the territory of their own republic. TsDAHOU, f.1, op.31, s.1463, ark. 3–6.

59 TsDAHOU, f.1, op.31, s. 1665, ark. 3–7. Similar views were echoed in Transcarpathia, where the local intelligentsia complained about distortions of regional history. TsDAHOU, f.1, op.31, s. 1665, ark. 40–3.

60 TsDAHOU, f.1, op.31, s. 1665, ark. 30–2.

61 Yaremchuk, "Ukrain'ska radians'ka istoriohrafiia," 268–9.

62 TsDAHOU, f.1, op.31, s. 1463, ark. 36–45.

63 TsDAHOU, f.1, op.31, s. 1463, ark. 3–6; TsDAHOU, f.1, op.31, s. 1665, ark. 30–2; TsDAHOU, f.1, op.31, s.1463, ark. 90–4; TsDAHOU, f.1, op.31, s. 1463, ark. 46–8.

64 TsDAHOU, f.1, op.31, s. 1463, ark. 27–35.

65 TsDAHOU, f.1, op.31, s. 1463, ark. 73–8.

66 TsDAHOU, f.1, op.31, s. 1665, ark. 8–12.

67 For example, immediately after the war, Soviet authorities encouraged the official cult of Ivan Franko in western Ukraine in order to displace the "nationalist tradition of revering Mazepa, Hrushevs'kyi, and the Ukrainian Galician Army." Franko was presented as both a proto-socialist and "the father of the nation." For a while, Ukrainians were even described as "great," a label normally reserved for the Russians. When the Institute of Ukrainian History finally published a collectively written *History of Ukraine: A Short Course* in 1940, socialist deeds were described in an unmistakably national rhetoric. The apogee of Ukrainian history came in 1939 with the Soviet annexation of Eastern Poland and "the great Ukrainian people's reunification within a single Ukrainian socialist state." Yekelchyk, *Stalin's Empire*, 24, 52.

68 TsDAHOU, f.1, op.31, s.1458 ("Dovydka do lysta sekretaria Zakarpats'koho obkomu partii," December 1960).

69 AAN, z.1354, s.XIA, t.78, ark. 147, 159–60.

70 Borys Oliinyk, "Ukrainians live in Poland," *Literaturna Ukraina*, 12 April 1968, from the *Digest of the Soviet Ukrainian Press* (*DSUP*), 12:5, May 1968.

71 AAN, z.1354, s.LVI, t.1116 ("Notatka służbowa dotycząca udzielenia pomocy polskiemu amatorskiemu zespołowi teatralnemu we Lwowie," March 1986).

72 The institutions involved in organising travel included Inturist, the central, republican, and local branches of the Society for Cultural Relations with the Abroad and its successor, the Union of Soviet Friendship Societies (SSOD), its constituent organisations such as the Soviet-Czechoslovak, and Soviet-Hungarian and Soviet-Polish Friendship Societies. It also included trade unions, gorkoms, obkoms, and the central committees in Moscow and Kyiv, individual factories and universities, and state and party organisations in the people's democracies.

73 V.V. Dvornichenko, *Turizm v SSSR i deiatel'nost' sovetskikh profsoiuzov po ego razvitiiu (1917–1984 gg.)* Moscow: Vysshaia shkola profsoiuznogo dvizheniia VTsSPS im. N.M. Shvernika, 1985), 132–3. In 1963 alone, more than 60,000 Soviet tourists travelled to Eastern Europe via Inturist, trade union organisations, or the Komsomol. Gorsuch, "Time Travellers," 206.
74 Dvornichenko, *Turizm*, 133, 139.
75 AAN, z.1354, s.XIA, t.75, ark. 148–9.
76 DAKO, f.P5, op.6, s.1060, ark. 1–6.
77 Michalewska, *Sercem*, 383–4.
78 Ibid., 372–4, 414.
79 GARF, f.9576, op.4, d.212a, ll. 1–49.
80 GARF, f.9576, op.4, d.58, ll. 325–6.
81 GARF, f.9576, op.4, d.58, ll. 183–9.
82 DAKO, f.P5, op.7, s.561, ark. 73–8.
83 GARF, f. 9612, op.3, d. 873, ll. 85–94. The idea to exchange friendship trains (*poezda druzhby*) between the USSR and Poland originated in 1959; from 1964 to 1969, 18 trains and over 60 buses of friendship travelled between the two countries. Stowarzyszenie współpracy Polska-Wschód (SWPW) (Union for Cooperation between Poland and the East), t.41/219 ("Information on TPPR Tourist Travel. Data for the end of December 1966"); DAKO, f.P5, op.7, s.1003, ark. 12–23; GARF, f.9576, op.4, d.350a, l. 3.
84 DAKO, f.P5, op.7, s.1003, ark. 12–23.
85 On average, the Soviet side organised thirty meetings between specialists per each friendship train from Poland, and significantly more for trains from the mining region of Katowice which visited the Donetsk oblast. SWPW, t.41/219 ("Information on TPPR Tourist Travel. Data for the end of December 1966").
86 DAKO, f.P5, op.7, s.1003, ark. 12–23.
87 R. Applebaum, "A Test of Friendship."
88 RGANI, f.5, op.33, d.235, ll. 189–95.
89 TsDAHOU, f.1, op.31, s.1458, ark. 43–4; TsDAHOU, f.1, op.32, s.46, ark. 15–22; DAKO, f.P5, op.6, s.1835, ark. 21–4; GARF, f.9576, op.4, d.58, ll. 89–92.
90 RGANI, f.5, op.28, d. 400, l. 54.
91 AAN, z.1354, s.XIA, t.78, ark. 149–54.
92 GARF, f.9576, op.4, d.58, ll. 105–13.
93 GARF, f.9576, op.4, d.58, ll. 267–80.
94 GARF, f.9576, op.4, d.58, ll. 3–4.
95 Ibid., 3–4, 5–12, 89–92, 267–80.
96 Travellers in the borderlands would have to "represent their factories," as official reports put it, as well as celebrate 1 May and the October Revolution anniversary. GARF, f.9576, op.4, d.58, ll. 3–4.

97 GARF, f.9576, op.4, d.58, ll. 89–92.
98 A. White, *De-Stalinization and the House of Culture: Declining State Control Over Leisure in the USSR, Poland, and Hungary, 1953–1989* (London: Routledge, 1990), 36–7.
99 GARF, f.9576, op.4, d.58, ll. 5–12.
100 GARF, f.9576, op.4, d.58, ll. 267–80.
101 Ibid.
102 Ibid., 105–13, 267–80.
103 SWPW, t.41/180 ("Letter from the Polish Consul in Kyiv to the Polish-Soviet Friendship Society," 8 July 1960).
104 Michalewska later recalled that she had chosen the post in Kyiv because she had already been familiar with "Soviet customs" and the nature of diplomatic work in the USSR. Michalewska, *Sercem*, 372.
105 AAN, z.1354, s.LVI, t.1112 ("A Note on Regional Cultural Exchanges Between Poland and the USSR," 7 April 1976).
106 SWPW, t.41/180 ("Letter from the Polish Consul in Kyiv to the Polish-Soviet Friendship Society," 8 July 1960); Michalewska, *Sercem*, 381.
107 AAN, z.1354, s.XIA, t.84. 279.
108 AAN, z.1354, s. LVI, t. 739 ("New Problems in Borderland Contacts," October 1979).
109 Michalewska, *Sercem*, 440–5.
110 GARF, f.9576, op.4, d.58, ll. 105–13.
111 For a discussion of "communist morality," see D. Field, "Irreconcilable Differences: Divorce and Conceptions of Private Life in the Khrushchev Era," *Russian Review* 57:4 (1998), 599–613.
112 GARF, f.9576, op.4, d.58, ll. 105–13.
113 Ibid., 267–80.
114 For example, see GARF, f.9612, op.3, d.10, ll. 101–16.
115 GARF, f.9612, op.3, d.10, ll. 27–36.
116 Many Soviet tourists were likely to travel along the same route. DAKO, f.P5, op.6, s.2576, ark. 12–16.
117 DAKO, f.P5, op.6, s.1835, ark. 9–18. Kyiv obkom officials staying in Kraków seven years later pointed to the same issues. DAKO, f.P5, op.7, s.561, ark. 63–71.
118 GARF, f.9576, op.4, d.58, ll. 267–80.
119 AAN, z.1354, s.XIA, t.75, ark. 322–3.
120 RGANI, f.5, op.58, d.20, ll. 25–9.
121 Lewytzkyj, *Politics and Society*, 67–8.
122 RGANI, f.5, op.33, d.7, ll. 36–44.
123 RGANI, f.5, op.55, d. 45, ll. 57–61.

124 G. Hodnett and P. Potichnyj, *The Ukraine and the Czechoslovak Crisis* (Canberra: Australian National University, 1970), 119.
125 O. Bazhan, "Suspil'ni nastroi," 40.
126 TsDAHOU, f.1, op.25, s. 255, ark. 41–4.
127 TsDAHOU, f.1, op.25, s.28, ark. 161.
128 TsDAHOU, f.1, op.25, s.30, ark. 119–33.
129 TsDAHOU, f.1, op.25, s.255, ark. 126–47; TsDAHOU, f.1, op.25, s.30, ark. 33–9; TsDAHOU, f.1, op.25, s.31, ark. 132–7.
130 Apart from concerts organised by the Czechoslovak-Soviet Friendship Society, Ukrainian artists in Czechoslovakia had to perform in poor conditions, mostly in the open air, and the Ministry of Culture in Prague failed to advertise their recitals. Reportedly, Soviet citizens were also appalled that the microphones were switched off during an official meeting with Ludvik Svoboda precisely at those moments of his speech when he talked about sacrifices the USSR made to liberate Czechoslovakia. TsDAHOU, f.1, op.25, s.30, ark. 33–9.
131 TsDAHOU, f.1, op.25, s.255, ark. 2–5.
132 While one Czechoslovak tourist in the USSR claimed some "socialist initiatives" were worthwhile, and people supported such projects as the building of nursery schools by volunteer brigades, the Czechoslovak workers were outraged that they were forced to follow the Soviet practice and help farmers dig for potatoes during harvest time. This created anti-Soviet feelings in Czechoslovakia, the tourist concluded. TsDAHOU, f.1, op.25, s.30, ark. 139–48.
133 TsDAHOU, f.1, op.25, s.31, ark. 132–7.
134 TsDAHOU, f.1, op.25, s.255, ark. 41–4, 126–47.
135 GARF, f.9576, op.4, d.330a, ll. 1–23.
136 Ibid., 24–47.
137 TsDAHOU, f.1, op.25, s.30, ark. 33–9.

3 The Limits of De-Stalinization

1 RGANI, f.5, op.61, d.35, ll. 57–61.
2 W. Rozenbaum, "The March Events: Targeting the Jews," *Polin: Studies in Polish Jewry* 21 (2009); W. Roszkowski, *Najnowsza Historia Polski 1945–1980* (Warsaw: Świat Książki, 2003), 531–47.
3 J. Suri, "The Promise and Failure of 'Developed Socialism': The Soviet 'Thaw' and the Crucible of the Prague Spring, 1964–1972," *Contemporary European History* 15:2 (2006), 156.
4 Suri, "The Promise," 138, 148, 150–3.

5 Ibid., 146–7.
6 Ibid., 153.
7 Ibid., 102.
8 This was partly because the Prague Spring affected the situation of the Ukrainian minority in Czechoslovakia, and cultural relations between the USSR and Czechoslovakia were the closest out of the entire socialist camp. Hodnett and Potichnyj, *The Ukraine*, 45; S. Yekelchyk, *Ukraine: Birth of a Modern Nation* (New York: Oxford University Press, 2007), 169.
9 Weiner, "Déjà Vu," 172–6.
10 Kramer, "The Czechoslovak Crisis," 144.
11 TsDAHOU, f.1, op.25, s.14, ark. 26–30.
12 Dmytruk, *Ukraina*, 96.
13 TsDAHOU, f.1, op.25, s.32, ark. 15–20.
14 Weiner, "Déjà Vu," 172–4.
15 DAKO, f.P5, op.7, s.822, ark. 42–3. TsDAHOU, f.1, op.25, s.39, ark. 10–14.
16 Shelest, *Spravzhnii sud*, 275.
17 Bazhan, "Praz'ka Vesna," 55–6.
18 TsDAHOU, f.1, op.25, s.28, ark. 98.
19 RGANI, f.5, op.60, d.20, ll. 58–75.
20 TsDAHOU, f.1, op.25, s.14, ark. 26–30.
21 TsDAHOU, f.1, op.31, s.3607, ark. 1–9.
22 On 1 July, for example, the Ukrainian first secretary alerted his superiors to the fact that broadcasting stations in Chernivtsi, Odesa, and Transcarpathia regions did not assure good quality reception for Soviet programmes, which increased the popularity of foreign broadcasts. However, just over a month later, the propaganda department of the CPSU Central Committee concluded that international agreements did not allow for the building of more powerful television broadcasting stations in those regions. RGANI, f.1, op.60, d.28, ll. 65–7.
23 TsDAHOU, f.1, op.31, s.3604, ark. 129–32.
24 K.J. Roth-Ey, "Finding a Home for Television in the USSR, 1950–1970," *Slavic Review* 66:2 (2007), 290.
25 Weiner, "Déjà Vu," 164–71.
26 TsDAHOU, f.1, op.25, s.27, ark. 47–9.
27 Weiner, "Déjà Vu," 191–2.
28 AAN, z.1354, s.LVI, t.1109 ("Current Problems in Polish-Soviet Cooperation in the Sphere of Theatre," no date, but probably February 1968).
29 The country needed an institute to train professional television journalists, producers and engineers, they claimed. RGANI, f.5, op.60, d.28, ll. 23–30.
30 B. Lewytzkyj, *Politics and Society*, 119.

31 The open letter of East European leaders to the Czechoslovak Party stated that "the reactionaries' offensive, supported by imperialism" threatened not only the interests of socialism in Czechoslovakia, but also imperilled "the entire socialist system"; at the same time, however, the letter assured that the Warsaw Pact states had "no intention of interfering in your internal affairs." "To the Czechoslovak Communist Party Central Committee," *Pravda* and *Izvestiia*, 18 July 1968, from *CDSP* 20:29, 7 August 1968. Similarly, the otherwise alarmist "statement of communist and workers" parties of socialist countries' published on 4 August emphasised that "each fraternal party takes into account national characteristics and conditions." "Statement of Communist and Workers' Parties of Socialist Countries," *Pravda* and *Izvestiia*, 4 August 1968, from *CDSP* 30:31, 21 August 1968.

32 Jan Procházka, "To Comrades," *Literaturnaia gazeta*, 26 June 1968, from *CDSP* 20:26, 17 July 1968.

33 V. Platkovsky, "The Chief Force in the Struggle for Communism," *Izvestiia*, 26 June 1968, from *CDSP* 20:26, 17 July 1968.

34 AAN, z.1354, s.XIA, t.84, s. 306.

35 *Pravda Ukrainy*, "Bratstvo," 15 May 1968.

36 Soviet newspapers compared the Prague Spring to the 1956 crisis in Hungary, despaired that "some Czechoslovak press organs … have attempted to belittle the significance of the Soviet people's glorious exploit during the Second World War," and cast "veiled aspersions" on Czechoslovakia's economic cooperation with the Soviet Union, as well as informed readers about the inherently suspicious inflow of West German tourists into Czechoslovakia. "Plenary Session of the Czechoslovak Communist Party Central Committee," *Pravda*, 8 June 1968, from *CDSP* 20:23, 26 June 1968; A. Nedorov, "Contrary to the Facts," *Izvestiia*, 29 June 1968, from *CDSP* 20:26, 17 July 1968; I. Aleksandrov, "Attack on the Socialist Foundations of Czechoslovakia," *Pravda*, 11 July 1968, from *CDSP* 20:28, 31 July 1968; V. Mikhailov, "In the Revanchists' Sights," *Pravda*, 22 July 1968, from *CDSP* 20:30, 14 August 1968; B. Aleksandrovskii, "Fruitful Cooperation," *Pravda*, 29 July 1968, from *CDSP* 20:31, 21 August 1968; Iurii Zhukov, "Concerning a False Slogan," *Pravda*, 26 July 1968, from *CDSP* 20:31, 21 August 1968.

37 "One Goal and Common Interests," *Pravda* 25 June 1968, from *CDSP* 20:26, 17 July 1968.

38 For instance, *Pravda Ukrainy* described a peace rally race organised to celebrate Soviet-Czechoslovak friendship: "The route follows those places where patriots of Czechoslovakia fought back-to-back with Soviet soldiers during the terrible years of anti-fascist struggle. Places where Soviet people [*sovetskie liudi*] continue the peaceful construction to strengthen their Homeland [*Rodina*], to strengthen peace in the world." "The

Unbreakable Friendship of the Peoples of the USSR and Czechoslovakia," *Pravda Ukrainy*, 15 May 1968.

39 V. Kozyakov, "What the American Policy of 'Building Bridges' Aims At," *Krasnaia Zvezda*, 24 May 1968, from *CDSP* 20:21, 12 June 1968.

40 "Defence of Socialism is the Highest Internationalist Duty," *Pravda*, 22 August 1968, from *CDSP* 20:34, 11 September 1968.

41 "Speech by Comrade W. Gomułka at Meeting with Warsaw Party Aktiv," *Pravda*, 22 March 1968, from *CDSP* 20:14, 24 April 1968; Bolesław Kowalski, "On Certain Theses of Israeli and West German Propaganda," *Literaturnaia gazeta*, 3 April 1968, from *CDSP* 20:14, 24 April 1968; "An Address by Comrade W. Gomułka at the Meeting with the Party Active," *Radians'ka Ukraina*, 23 March 1968, from *DSUP* 12:5, May 1968.

42 Zvi Gitelman shows that the "anti-Zionist" campaign employed stereotypical images of Jews, and it became virtually impossible to distinguish between "Zionists" and Jews. Gitelman, *Bespokoinyi vek*, 244. As Amir Weiner points out, "Jews seemed to antagonise the party and the KGB, especially in western Ukraine": the "visible role of several Jewish figures in the Prague Spring," demands for restoring relations with Israel, and the Polish anti-Semitic events "fuelled the anti-Jewish campaign already under way inside the Soviet Union." Weiner, "Déjà Vu," 180.

43 Václav Židlický, "Achievements of Ukrainian Studies in Czechoslovakia," *Literaturna Ukraina*, 19 April 1968, from *DSUP* 12:6, June 1968.

44 "Eternal Friendship! A Meeting of Soviet-Czechoslovak Friendship in the Illich Kolhosp on Vasylkiv Rayon, Kyiv Oblast," *Radians'ka Ukraina*, 28 October 1969, from *DSUP* 13:12.

45 TsDAHOU, f.1, op.25, s.14, ark. 131–3; TsDAHOU, f.1, op.25, s.35, ark. 6–7; TsDAHOU, f.1, op.25, s.39, ark. 10–14.

46 Hodnett and Potichnyj, *The Ukraine*, 116–17.

47 Prizel, *National Identity*, 349–50.

48 Hodnett and Potichnyj, *The Ukraine*, 78; Yekelchyk, *Ukraine*, 161.

49 Lewytzkyj, *Politics and Society*, 119; M. Kramer, "The Czechoslovak Crisis and the Brezhnev Doctrine," in *1968: The World Transformed*, ed. Carol Fink, Philipp Gassert, and Detlef Junker (Cambridge: Cambridge University Press, 1998), 144.

50 Shelest, *Spravzhnii sud*, 331.

51 Lewytzkyj, *Politics and Society*, 204.

52 Hodnett and Potichnyj, *The Ukraine*, 123.

53 Prizel, *National Identity*, 350.

54 TsDAHOU, f.1, op.25, s.37, ark. 99–101.

55 Dmytruk, *Ukraina*, 43, 225.

56 TsDAHOU, f.1, op.25, s.37, ark. 9–12; TsDAHOU, f.1, op.25, s.37, ark. 17–18; TsDAHOU, f.1, op.25, s.35, ark. 101–4; TsDAHOU, f.1, op.25, s.37, ark. 114.
57 TsDAHOU, f.1, op.25, s.27, ark. 47–9.
58 DALO, f.P3, op.10, s.248, ark. 1–2.
59 TsDAHOU, f.1, op.25, s.29, ark. 53–5; s.37, ark. 99–101; s.65, ark. 28–39.
60 For example, once a week, 25,355 agitators gave short lectures to workers at local factories in the Donetsk oblast. They normally spoke between two shifts to assure maximum attendance, describing the current situation and discussing the results of the meeting of world communist parties in Budapest. See TsDAHOU, f.1, op.31, s.3604, ark. 180–6. Between March and June 1968, and then again between September 1968 and April 1969, non-party members and rank-and-file communists in Ukraine were largely excluded from public discussion about the Prague Spring. TsDAHOU, f.1, op.25, s.29, ark. 37–8; TsDAHOU, f.1, op.25, s.29, ark. 53–5; TsDAHOU, f.1, op.25, s.37, ark. 99–100; TsDAHOU, f.1, op.25, s.14, ark. 26–30.
61 DAOO, f.11, op.19, s.702, ark. 4–11; TsDAHOU, f.1, op.25, s.27, ark. 47–9; TsDAHOU, f.1, op.25, s.14, ark. 131–3; TsDAHOU, f.1, op.25, s.29, ark. 93–6. TsDAHOU, f.1, op.25, s.29, ark. 37–8; TsDAHOU, f.1, op.25, s.35, ark. 18–19. TsDAHOU, f.1, op.25, s.39, ark. 10–14; DAKO, f.P5, op.7, s.822, ark. 42–3.
62 TsDAHOU, f.1, op.25, s.38, ark. 14–16.
63 The press publicised examples of good behaviour of citizens who attended mass meetings devoted to the crisis. H. Nikol'nikov, "The Struggle of V.I. Lenin and the CPSU for Consolidating the Principles of Proletarian Internationalism," *Radians'ka Ukraina*, 3 September 1968, from *DSUP* 12:10.
64 TsDAHOU, f.1, op.25, s.30, ark. 190–3.
65 Even at the ostensibly open gatherings during the summer, it was party members with some managerial roles who predominated. The order in which participants spoke at the meetings was telling: during a gathering of an Odesa weavers' collective on 21 August, two senior managers spoke first, only then followed by two women from the shop floor. DALO, f.P3, op.10. s.248, ark. 49–50; DAOO, f.P11, op.19, s.724, ark. 106–7.
66 DAOO, f.P11, op.19, s.702, ark. 4–11.
67 TsDAHOU, f.1, op.31, s.3817, ark. 1–3. Calling for Prague to combat "hostile elements" in Czechoslovakia, a shoe factory worker and member of the Ivano-Frankivsk gorkom likewise claimed to speak in the name of "the thousands of workers" of the west Ukrainian region. TsDAHOU, f.1, op.25, s.35, ark. 18–19.
68 In fact, by the late 1960s, the press began to criticise the "hypnotic effect" of television and the practice of watching indiscriminately. Roth-Ey, "Finding a Home," 296, 298, 330.

69 See chapter 1.
70 Bazhan, "Praz'ka Vesna," 70–1, 73, 105.
71 TsDAHOU, f.1, op.25, s.28, ark. 102–12.
72 TsDAHOU, f.1, op.25, s.32, ark. 123–5.
73 TsDAHOU, f.1, op.25, s.31, ark. 141–3; DAOO, f.P11, op.20, s.88, ark. 15–26.
74 DALO, f.3, op.10, s.248, ark. 20–3.
75 "*Kontrrevolutsiia ne proidet* (1968)," *Arkhiv kinokhroniki i dokumental'nykh fil'mov 'Netfilm.'* Accessed 21 October 2015, http://www.net-film.ru/film-6571/.
76 TsDAHOU, f.1, op.25, s.33, ark. 111–15.
77 TsDAHOU, f.1, op.25, s.38, ark. 154–5.
78 TsDAHOU, f.1, op.25, s.39, ark. 10–14.
79 TsDAHOU, f.1, op.25, s. 32, ark. 199–202.
80 Ibid., 141–5.
81 AAN, z.1354, s.XIA, t.84, ss. 269–70.
82 TsDAHOU, f.1, op.25, s.14, ark. 131–3.
83 As Yaacov Ro'i argues in his study of Soviet Jewish reactions to the 1967 Six Days War, statements like these were likely underpinned by Jewish fear of anti-Semitism. "It is reasonable to assume that many Jews, especially older ones who remembered the propaganda campaigns of early 1949 and early 1953, genuinely feared the negative results of the Six Day War might have on them and made every effort to dissociate Soviet Jewry from the activity and policy of the Israeli government and to condemn them." Ro'i, "The Soviet Jewish Reaction," 258.
84 DAOO, f.P11, op.19, s.702, ark. 4–11.
85 DAOO, f.P11, op.20. s.88, ark. 15–26; TsDAHOU, f.1, op.25, s.37, ark. 93.
86 For instance, when an unnamed individual from Minsk wrote a letter to *Pravda*, claiming that "political diversion conducted by people of Jewish origin" threatened the national (*natsional'nye*) interests of our country and the building of communism, the chief editor branded him an anti-Semite. RGANI, f.5, op.60, d.26, ll. 68–70.
87 N. Mitrokhin, *Russkaia partiia: Dvizhenie russkikh natsionalistov v SSSR 1953–1985* (Moscow: Novoe literaturnoe obozrenie, 2003), 255–6.
88 Mitrokhin, *Russkaia partiia*, 340–1.
89 AAN, z.1354, s.XIA, t.84, s. 308.
90 TsDAHOU, f.1, op.25, s.40, ark. 97–9; TsDAHOU, f.1, op.25, s.14, ark. 124–5.
91 The campaign was particularly fierce because the story was based on a real event, which struck a raw nerve with party apparatchiks in Dnipropetrovsk. Zhuk, *Rock and Roll*, 53–4.
92 O. Honchar, *Shchodennyky*, ed. Valentyna Honchar, vol. 2 (Kyiv: Veselka, 2002–4), 31.

93 Adrienne Edgar, "Marriage, Modernity, and the 'Friendship of Nations': Interethnic Intimacy in Postwar Central Asia in Comparative Perspective," *Central Asian Survey* 26 (4): 581–600.
94 Brubaker shows that the USSR was a "nationalising state," intolerant of ethnic diversity within its ethno-federal units. R. Brubaker, *Nationalism Reframed: Nationhood and the National Question in the New Europe* (Cambridge: Cambridge University Press, 1996), 38–40, 83–4.
95 Bazhan, "Suspil'ni nastroi," 45.
96 D. Spechler, *Permitted Dissent in the USSR:* Novyi Mir *and the Soviet Regime* (New York: Praeger, 1982), 242.
97 AAN, z.1354, s.XIA, t.84, s. 292.
98 H. Kasianov, *Nezhodni: ukrains'ka intelihentsiia v rusi oporu 1960x–80x rokiv* (Kyiv: Lybid, 1995), 64.
99 Dmytruk, *Ukraina*, 227–8.
100 See Bazhan, "Praz'ka vesna," 111–16.
101 Shelest, *Spravzhnii sud*, 291.
102 Kramer, "Spill Over from the Prague Spring," 67–8.
103 Suri, "The Promise," 154–5.
104 Kramer, "Spill-Over from the Prague Spring," 67.
105 TsDAHOU, f.1, op.25, s.31, ark. 138–40.
106 TsDAHOU, f.1, op.25, s.33, ark. 131–5.
107 Bazhan, "Praz'ka Vesna," 129–32.
108 Ibid., 125–7.
109 Ibid., 129–32.
110 Ibid., 88, 94–6, 105.
111 Weiner, "Déjà Vu," 181.
112 DAOO, f.P11, op.19, s.702, ark. 4–11.
113 This fuelled interest in non-Soviet sources of information among the Jewish population, facilitated the rise of Jewish samizdat, and gave rise to the movement for the right to emigrate. Ro'i, "The Soviet Jewish Reaction," 254, 262, 267.
114 DAOO, f.P11, op.19, s.702, ark. 4–11.
115 DAOO, f.P11, op.20, s.88, ark. 48–51.
116 TsDAHOU, f.1, op.25, s.31, ark. 141–3.
117 DALO, f.P3, op.10, s. 248, ark. 1–2.
118 Bazhan, "Praz'ka Vesna," 95–8.
119 The most famous example of protest against the Soviet crackdown in Czechoslovakia was the demonstration of a few brave individuals on Red Square on 25 August. *KhTS*, 30 August 1968.
120 Bazhan, "Praz'ka Vesna." 111–16.

121 Ibid., 105.
122 TsDAHOU, f.1, op.25, s.31, ark. 141–3.
123 Bazhan, "Praz'ka Vesna." 111–16.
124 Ibid., 103–4.
125 Ibid., 84, 94–6, 111–16.
126 Ibid., 83–6.
127 Ibid., 88, 94.
128 Notably, some West European socialists such as the German author Günter Grass also drew parallels between Soviet and American foreign policies, but with the aim of criticising left-wing activists in the West. Grass "accused the [Western] students of solidarising themselves with the Third World while forgetting Communist oppression inside Europe itself. Protesting the Soviet invasion of Czechoslovakia in August 1968 was less attractive to the students that attacking US behaviour in Vietnam, he argued." *The Global Cold War*, 192–3.
129 DAOO, f.P11, op.20, s. 88, ark. 15–26.
130 Shelest, *Spravzhnii sud*, 260.
131 TsDAHOU, f.1, op.25. s.64, ark. 56–8.
132 TsDAHOU, f.1, op.25, s.28, ark. 102–12.
133 It is not clear why the authors praised Kosygin. Bazhan, 'Praz'ka Vesna," 93.
134 TsDAHOU, f.1, op.25, s.28, ark. 102–12.
135 Bazhan, "Praz'ka Vesna," 105.
136 Shelest, *Spravzhnii sud*, 284–5.
137 *KhTS*, 31 December 1968.
138 TsDAHOU, f.1, op.25, s.64, ark. 56–8.
139 Three years later, *samizdat* authors recalled that it was difficult to buy Czechoslovak newspapers in the USSR, even though they continued to be distributed through official channels before 21 August 1968. *KhTS*, 5 March 1971.
140 V. Dmytruk, "Nelehal'na informatsiina merezha v Chekhoslovachchyni ta ii vplyv na formuvannia opozytsiinykh nastroiv v Ukraini (kinets 60x – pochatok 70-x rr.)," *Z arkhiviv VUChK-GPU-NKVD-KGB* 2-4 (2000), 71.
141 RGANI, f.5, op.60, d.26, ll. 43–9, 64–5.
142 TsDAHOU, Kyiv, f.1, op.25, s.28, ark. 169–70.
143 Zisserman-Brodsky, *Constructing Ethnopolitics*, 197.
144 The letter subsequently circulated in the *samvydav*. Sobranie dokumentov samizdata (Collection of Samizdat Documents), AS970: A member of the Writers' Union of Ukraine, "Letter to Oles' Honchar and secretaries of the

Writers' Union of Ukraine, concerning cultural relations between Ukraine and Czechoslovakia," 1968.

145 Weiner, "Déjà Vu," 174–5, 183.

146 Bazhan, "Praz'ka Vesna," 96.

147 On the other hand, the extent to which such outbursts could become politicised is uncertain. For the 1950s, Vladimir Kozlov shows that a blatant political mistake or an obvious abuse of power could pull the "typical urban bystander" into mass urban riots and encourage them to "support hooligans against the police." Kozlov, *Mass Uprisings*, 161.

148 Bazhan, "Suspil'ni nastroi," 43.

149 Bazhan, "Praz'ka Vesna," 97.

150 Shelest, *Spravzhnii sud*, 254.

151 TsDAHOU, f.1, op.25, s.64, ark. 133–8; TsDAHOU, Kyiv, f.1, op.25, s.64, ark. 71–2.

152 Bazhan, "Suspil'ni nastroi," 43.

153 On 27 August, for example, the Lviv obkom secretary claimed that "nationalist" and "anti-Soviet" elements intensified their hostile activities in the oblast after the Warsaw Pact invasion of Czechoslovakia. DALO, f.P3, op.10, s.248, ark. 87–9.

154 A. Wilson, *The Ukrainians: Unexpected Nation* (New Haven: Yale University Press, 2002), 143.

155 TsDAHOU, f.1, op.25, s.29, ark. 97.

156 Bazhan, "Praz'ka Vesna," 90.

157 Ibid., 99–100.

158 Ibid., 90.

159 TsDAHOU, f.1, op.25, s.38, ark. 141–3.

160 Bazhan, "Praz'ka Vesna," 90.

161 Ibid., 71–2.

162 Ibid., 97–8.

163 TsDAHOU, f.1, op.25, s.28, ark. 12–13.

164 Bohdan Krasavtsev, "Vasyl Makukh: liudyna, iaka zhorila za Ukrainu", Radio Free Europe – Radio Liberty, accessed 28 October 2015, http://www.radiosvoboda.org/content/article/24770217.html.

165 Dmytruk, *Ukraina*, 228.

166 TsDAHOU, f.1, op.25, s.33, ark. 82–7.

167 RGANI, f.5, op.60, d.24, ll. 151–6.

168 Bazhan, "Praz'ka Vesna," 97–8.

169 Ibid., 71–2.

170 Ibid., 71.

171 AAN, z.1354, s.XIA, t.84, s. 212.

172 Spechler, *Permitted Dissent*, 264.

173 While top apparatchiks condemned the two writers for "anti-Soviet propaganda," some intellectuals refuted the accusations of disloyalty levelled against Daniel and Sinavskii, defended the right to free speech, and began to publish in the *samizdat*. M. Hayward, "Introduction" in Leopold Labedz and Max Hayward, ed., *On Trial. The Case of Siniavskii-Tertz and Daniel-Arzhak* (London: Collins and Harvill Press, 1967), 34–9.

174 Despite his young age, Symonenko left a rich literary legacy and an unpublished journal that testified to state persecution of the Ukrainian intelligentsia. He acquired popularity among émigré Ukrainians. Although the authorities initially tolerated Symonenko's posthumous popularity in Ukraine, they subsequently made "every effort to minimise his importance," clashing with some members of the republic's cultural intelligentsia. Lewytzkyj, *Politics and Society*, 66–7.

4 Making Enemies

1 M.V. Nechkina, S. Leibengrub, *Istoriia SSSR: Uchebnik dlia 7-go klassa* (Moscow: Prosveshcheniie, 1982), 5–7, 24, 62, 80, 83, 128, 141–3, 146, 173, 207–8.

2 AAN, z.1354, s.LVI, t.824 ("A Note on the Polish Cultural Days in Ukraine," The Consulate General of Poland in Kyiv, 31 May 1979).

3 Michalewska, *Sercem*, 499.

4 In the 1960s and 1970s, about 60 per cent of foreign travellers visiting the USSR came from socialist countries, while 55 per cent of Soviet citizens going abroad went to socialist states. Most of them travelled as part of organised groups. V.V. Dvornichenko, *Turizm v SSSR i deiatel'nost' sovetskikh profsoiuzov po ego razvitiiu (1917–1984 gg.)* (Moscow : Vyshaia shkola profsoiuznogo dvizheniia VTsSPS im. N.M. Shvernika, 1985), 129–30.

5 Gorsuch, *All This is Your World*, 19, 79–105.

6 AAN, z.1354, s.XI, t.462, ark. 46.

7 AAN, z.1354, s.LVI, t.608 (T. Biegański, "The Effectiveness of Information about Polish culture in the USSR," no date, probably 1971).

8 AAN, z.1354, s.LVI, t.1238 ("PAGART financial results for 1975").

9 AAN, z.1354, s.LVI, t.981 ("Polish movies in the USSR").

10 AAN, z.1354, s.LVI, t.710 ("Plan for cultural cooperation with foreign countries for 1972").

11 RGANI, f.5, op.76, d.295, ll. 5–19.

12 V. Korotich, *Most: Razmyshleniia o puteshestviiakh s piatnadtsat'iu otstupleniiami* (Moscow: Sovetskii pisatel', 1981), 17; N. Ravich, *Po dorogam Evropy* (Moscow: Sovetskaia Rossiia, 1964), 8; I. Biriukov, *Chekhoslovakiia:*

liudi i gody (Moscow: Izdatel'stvo politicheskoi literatury, 1986), 93; Ia. Makarenko, *Korni i vetvi* (Moscow: Sovetskaia Rossiia, 1977), 33.

13 D. Field, "Irreconcilable Differences: Divorce and Conceptions of Private Life in the Khrushchev Era," *Russian Review* 57:4 (1998), 599–613.

14 Makarenko, *Korni*, 172–3.

15 Korotich, *Most*, 131.

16 GARF, f.6903, op.2, d.500, ll. 102–10.

17 Roth-Ey, *Moscow Prime Time*, 225–77.

18 AAN, z.1354, s.LVI, t.981 ("Polish movies in the USSR").

19 AAN, z.1354, s.LVI, t.981 ("Polish movies in the USSR"); AAN, z.1354, s.LVI, t.1110 ("Information about cooperation between Poland and the USSR between 1976 and 1980," 11 February 1981).

20 AAN, z.1354, s.LVI, t.608 (T. Biegański, "The effectiveness of information about Polish culture in the USSR," no date, probably 1971).

21 AAN, z.1354, s.LVI, t.981 ("Polish movies in the USSR").

22 AAN, z.1354, s.LVI, t.710 (Stanisław Wroński, "Report from a trip to Moscow that took place from 20 to 24 April 1972").

23 AAN, z.1354, s.LVI, t.981 ("An assessment of the work conducted by Polish diretors, script writers, and film actors in Soviet movies, and of Soviet artists in Polish movies").

24 Travel guidebooks similarly described Warsaw's old town as a real point of pride for the Poles. Ravich, *Po dorogam*, 12, 125–6.

25 Gerasimov and Gerasimova, *Servus*, 207; Biriukov, *Chekhoslovakiia*, 62.

26 Z. Gorzeni, "Foreword" in Biriukov, *Chekhoslovakiia*, 4.

27 Soviet scholars and their colleagues in Poland and Czechoslovakia thus strove to expose the common "ethnogenesis of Slavs," and Slavicists from the Ukrainian and Soviet Academy of Sciences participated in celebrations devoted to "socialist friendship" in Eastern Europe in the late 1950s. Dudzinskaia, *Mezhdunarodnye nauchnye sviazi sovetskikh istorikov* (Moscow: Nauka, 1978), 107–8; RGANI, f.5, op.33, d. 66, l. 1.

28 *Zhovten'*, April 1983.

29 GARF, f.9576, op.4, d.431a, ll. 24–34.

30 AAN, z.1354, s.LVI, t.1112 ("Agreements on cooperation and exchanges between creative unions and institutions").

31 AAN, z.1354, s.LVI, t.712 ("A note on Polish Cultural Days in the USSR, 2 April 1974–11 April 1974").

32 AAN, z.1354, s.LVI, t.714 ("Report by a delegation of Polish Writers' Union from a trip to Moscow, 5–9 January 1976").

33 AAN, z.1354, s.XL, t.216 ("Note on planned customs regulations for Polish and Soviet tourists travelling between Poland and the USSR," 14 February

1978); AAN, z.1354, s.XL, t.217 ("Agreement between governments of the Polish People's Republic and the USSR on regulating certain customs issues").

34 AAN, z.1354, s.LVI, t.710 (Stanisław Wroński, "Report from a trip to Moscow, 20 to 24 April 1972").

35 AAN, z.1354, s.LVI, t.981 ("Russian and Soviet literary works translated into Polish and published in book form between 1965 and 1975").

36 AAN, z.1354, s.LVI, t.824 ("Note on the Polish Culture Days in the Ukrainian SSR," 31 May 1979).

37 In the 1950s and 1960s, Wanda Michalewska devoted much of her time to dealing with Soviet citizens of Polish origin who were now applying for repatriation to Poland. This involved navigating Soviet archives to determine Soviet citizens' "Polishness." Michalewska, *Sercem*, 381, 390–6, 399.

38 Michalewka, *Sercem*, 403.

39 AAN, z.1354, s.LVI, t.1116 (Włodzimierz Woskowski, "Note from a trip to Lviv," 4 November 1985).

40 AAN, z.1354, s.XIB, t.131, ark. 85–6.

41 AAN, z.1354, s.XI, t.460, ark. 98.

42 RGANI, f.1, op.5, d.69, ll. 4–8.

43 AAN, z.1354, s.LVI, t.981 ("Russian and Soviet literary works translated into Polish and published in book form between 1965 and 1975").

44 *KhTS*, 3 August 1976.

45 *KhTS*, 31 December 1976.

46 *KhTS*, 14 March 1978.

47 *Ogniem i mieczem* in the Polish original.

48 RGANI, f.5, op.90, d. 139, ll. 10–15.

49 Ibid., 25–9.

50 Ibid., 16–24.

51 Ibid., 16–24.

52 AAN, z.1354, s.LVI, t.608 (T. Biegański, "The Effectiveness of Information about Polish culture in the USSR," no date, probably 1971).

53 GARF, f. 9612, op.3, d. 873, ll. 85–94.

54 In this vein, the Prague Spring was portrayed as an American, German, and Zionist plot – see chapter 3.

55 TsDAHOU, f.1, op.25, s. 1963, ark. 5–7, 9–11, 25–8.

56 Honchar, *Shchodennyky* 2, 488.

57 Z. Wojnowski, "Communism and Nationalism: Poles' Perceptions of the West and Legitimacy of the Jaruzelski Regime, 1980–83," *Slovo* 19:1 (Spring 2007).

58 AAN, z.1354, s.XI, t.465, ark. 252.

59 Western scholars who argued that the UPA had not cooperated with the Nazis were a favourite target of Soviet Ukrainian historians. Lewytzkyj,

Politics and Society, 43. The Institute of History in Kyiv even established a special unit tasked with counteracting émigré historical narratives. Grzegorz Motyka argues that the KGB was directly involved in producing anti-émigré publications. "Polsko-ukraińskie stosunki w XX wieku w ocenie ukraińskiej historiografii emigracyjnej," *Warszawskie zeszyty ukrainoznawcze* 25–6 (2008), 123. Meanwhile, access to émigré publications was highly restricted for most historians. A. Atamanenko, "Ukrains'ka zarubizhna istoriohrafiia druhoi polovyny XX stolittia u svitovomu istoriohrafichnomu protsesi: perspektyvy doslidzhennia," *Warszawskie zeszyty ukrainoznawcze* 25–6 (2008), 121.

60 Z. Gorzeni, "Foreword" in Biriukov, *Chekhoslovakiia*, 5.

61 Makarenko, *Korni*, 119.

62 OSA, f.300, sf.85, s.44, c.9, file 17 (Ivan Dziuba's speech at Babyn Yar).

63 Even this caused controversy among the literary establishment and Soviet readers. Polly Jones, *Myth, Memory, Trauma: Rethinking Stalinist Past in the Soviet Union, 1953–70* New Haven: Yale University Press, 2013), 173–211.

64 *Ukrains'kyi visnyk* (Paris: Smoloskyp), vol 6, March 1972.

65 OSA, f300, sf.85, s.44. c.9, file 17 ("Letter from Ukrainian patriots").

66 *Ukrains'kyi visnyk*, vol 6, March 1972.

67 Boris Lewytzkyj claims that Russification made it difficult for historians to propagate Ukrainian history after the early 1970s. Volodymyr Shcherbyts'kyi insisted that even those parts of Ukrainian history that have nothing to do with nationalism should not be glorified, implying that Petro Shelest had violated this principle by eulogising the democratic Cossack state. B. Lewytzkyj, *Politics and Society in Soviet Ukraine, 1953–1980* (Edmonton: Canadian Institute of Ukrainian Studies, 1984), 150.

68 Iu. Iu. Kondufor, et al., *Istoriia Ukrains'koi RSR: Korotkyi narys* (Kyiv: Naukova dumka, 1981), 2–6.

69 F. Sysyn, "The Changing Image," 531–45.

70 TsDAHOU, f.1, op.25, s.1679, ark. 9–10.

71 TsDAHOU, Kyiv, f.1, op.25, s.1679, ark. 15–24.

72 TsDAHOU, Kyiv, f.1, op.25, s.1880, ark. 9–12.

73 Yaremchuk, "Ukrains'ka radians'ka istoriohrafiia," 271–2.

74 TsDAHOU, f.1, op.25, s.1679, ark. 9–10.

75 TsDAHO, f.1, op.25, s.575, ark. 102–7; Atamanenko, "Ukrains'ka zarubizhna istoriohrafiia," 108.

76 TsDAHOU, f.1, op.25, s.2052, ll. 34–40.

77 RGANI, f. 89, 14, d. 11, ll. 1–6; TsDAHOU, f.1, op.25, s.1880, ark. 32–4.

78 S. Velychenko, *Shaping Identity in Eastern Europe and Russia: Soviet-Russian and Polish Accounts of Ukrainian History, 1914–1991* (New York: St. Martin's Press, 1993), 203.

79 Franko's stories set in the Habsburg industrial town of Boryslav were especially important in proving his "socialist realist" credentials. Soviet literary scholars presented Franko as a "Ukrainian" writer by largely ignoring themes in his works that did not fit the Soviet vision of what it meant to be Ukrainian, including his writings about Jews in Galicia. Notably, prewar Soviet scholars had promoted a much more negative assessment of Franko. Hrycak, *Prorok we własnym kraju*, 210, 221, 230, 238, 278.

80 After the death of Stalin, Sosiura toed the official line. See Lewytzkyj, *Politics and Society*, 62.

81 Notably, Taras Koznarsky states that Lepkyi, along with other poets who worked outside Soviet Ukraine, "expressed staunch anti-Soviet, nationalist, anti-colonial views in their work." T. Koznarsky, "Ukrainian Literary Scholarship in Ukraine Since Independence," *Canadian Slavonic Papers* 54:1–2 (2012): 169.

82 For a discussion of the Ukrainian sixtiers generation, see S. Yekelchyk, "The Early 1960s as a Cultural Space," 45–62.

83 The report concerned *Z poezji ukraińskiej*, published by Czytelnik in 1972 in Tadeusz Hollender's translation, and Kazimierz Jaworski's book, *Przekłady poezji ukraińskiej, białoruskiej i ludów kaukaskich*, published by Wydawnictwo Lublin in 1972. TsDAHOU, f.1, op.25, s.1036, ark. 40–2.

84 TsDAHOU, f.1, op.25, s.1880, ark. 16–17.

85 C. Wanner, *Burden of Dreams: History and Identity in post-Soviet Ukraine* (University Park, Pennsylvania: Pennsylvania State University Press, 1998), 205.

86 Sysyn, "The Changing Image," 543–4.

87 *Ukrains'kyi visnyk*, vols. 7–8, no date, but probably spring 1974.

88 *KhTS* 14, 30 June 1970.

89 OSA, f.300, sf.85, s.44, c.10, file 12 ("Guests of Kyiv").

90 As William Risch puts it, "being part of a Soviet Ukrainian nation [in west Ukraine] thus emphasised an important element of what it meant to be Soviet." Risch, *The Ukrainian West*, 29.

91 Litvin, *Writing History*, 22.

92 R. Solchanyk, "Polska a sowiecki zachód," *Suchasnist: Zeszyt w języku polskim* 1–2 (1985), 82, 86.

93 For instance, the CPU Central Committee instructed the obkom authorities in Uzhgorod to search the local archives for documents about the activity of "American imperialists" in Transcarpathia during the interwar period. TsDAHOU, f.1, op.24, s.5111, ark. 4, 9–10.

94 Tron'ko was the chief editor of the multi-volume *Istoriia mist i sil Ukrains'koi RSR* (*The History of the Towns and Villages of the Ukrainian SSR*).

95 TsDAHOU, f.1, op.25, s. 369, ark. 14–23.
96 *Pravda Ukrainy*, 8 August 1979.
97 TsDAHOU, f.1, op.32, s.51, ark. 11–42; TsDAHOU, f.1, op.31, s.2370, ark. 18–20; TsDAHOU, f.1, op.25, s.1880, ark. 16–17, 21–2. For Il'nytskyi's key role in 1968, see A. Weiner, "Déjà Vu," 174–6. As Kondufor's *Istoriia Ukrainy* put it, all peoples of the USSR helped western Ukraine defeat illiteracy and economic backwardness in the aftermath of 1939. Kondufor, *Istoriia*, 418–21.
98 As William Risch shows, Ukrainians from other parts of the republic even saw themselves as the bearers of the "true" Ukrainian culture in the borderlands. Risch, *The Ukrainian West*, 60–2.
99 TsDAHOU, f.1, op.31, s.335, ark. 56–8.
100 I.M. Baranovs'ka, "Ukrains'ke zhurnalistykoznavstvo 1950–1980x rr.," *Visnyk Kyivs'koho natsional'noho universytetu imeni Tarasa Shevchenka* 13 (2005), 52. For Lazurenko's critique of Shcherbyt'skyi's policies targeted against Ukrainian language and culture, see O.A. Iakubets', "V. Shcherbyts'kyi ta ideolohiia: do pytannia shchodo prychyn 'Malanchukivshchyny,'" *Ukrain'skyi istorychnyi zhurnal* 5 (2014), 108–11.
101 TsDAHOU, f.1, op.31, s.335, ark. 55.
102 The CPU Central Committee was still in the process of working out the politics of memory in the borderlands. The Order of Lenin was eventually granted to Lviv in 1958. Risch, *The Ukrainian West*, 29.
103 The academic community and political elites in Lviv did not agree on a common vision of the past. Risch, *The Ukrainian West*, 160.
104 DALO, f.P3, op.13, s.142, ark. 11–15.
105 G. Hosking, *Beyond Socialist Realism: Soviet fiction since Ivan Denisovich* (London: Granada Publishing 1980), 81–2.
106 Ibid., 198.
107 The novel is about the life of Hutsuls during the First World War.
108 They also emphasised that editors of the journal should have known better: Andryiashyk had previously been convicted for "hooliganism," and he was generally considered to be an unreliable individual. At the same time, the authorities continued to send mixed signals about how to represent Ukraine's past: a positive review of the story had been published. TsDAHOU, f.1, op.25, s.363, ark. 55–7.
109 Farmer, *Ukrainian Nationalism*, 210, 213, 121.
110 RGANI, f.5, op.66, d.106, ll. 27–33.
111 Risch, *The Ukrainian West*, 164–5.
112 TsDAHOU, f.1, op.25, s.1036, ark. 5–13.
113 Apart from the ethnicisation of Ukrainian culture that I discuss above, the 1970s witnessed the emergence of new ethnocentric narratives in

other Soviet republics. For instance, romantic portrayals of the Kazakh nomadic past gained great popularity in Brezhnev-era Kazakhstan. D. Kudaibergenova, '"Imagining Community' in Soviet Kazakhstan. An Historical Analysis of Narrative on Nationalism in Kazakh-Soviet Literature," *Nationalities Papers* 41:5 (2013), 839–54.

114 Amar, *The Paradox of Ukrainian Lviv*, 297.

115 The CPWU had been an autonomous unit in the Communist Party of Poland dissolved by Stalin in 1938.

116 TsDAHOU, f.1, op.24, s.4259, ark. 42.

117 TsDAHOU, f.1, op.24, s.6140, ark. 3–11.

118 TsDAHOU, f.1, op.31, s.1949, ark. 101–5.

119 Amar, *The Paradox of Ukrainian Lviv*, 307.

120 TsDAHOU, f.1, op.24, s.6060, ark. 46–8.

121 Author unknown, "Not One Day...," *Pravda Ukrainy*, 25 June 1968, from *DSUP* 12:8, August 1968; author unknown, "Soviet Bukovyna Celebrates," *Robitnycha hazeta*, 3 August 1968, from *DSUP* 12:8, August 1968.

122 A. Hlushovs'kyi, I. Kompaniyets', "Against Bourgeois Falsification of Bukovyna's History," *Komunist Ukrainy* 1, January 1968, from *DSUP* 12:5, May 1968; TsDAHOU, f.1, op.32, s.631, ark. 24.

123 TsDAHOU, f.1, op.31, s.335, ark. 70–1.

124 TsDAHOU, f.1, op.24, s.6060, ark. 51–4.

125 Risch, *The Ukrainian West*, 151–5.

126 Kondufor, *Istoriia*, 344.

127 Lewytzkyj, *Politics and Society*, 147–8.

128 TsDAHOU, f.1, op.25, s.2295, ark. 37–50.

129 TsDAHOU, f.1, op.25, s.2287, ark. 70.

130 *Zhovten'*, October 1980.

131 TsDAHOU, f.1, op.31, s.335, ark. 56–8.

132 TsDAHOU, f.1, op.25, s.2221, ark. 139, 144.

133 DALO, f.P3, op.46, s. 99, ark. 22–3.

134 Ibid., 15. However, the monument standing in Lviv today was not built until after 1991.

135 C. Ford, *Creating the Nation in Provincial France: Religion and Political Identity in Brittany* (Princeton: Princeton University Press, 1993), 9, 220–5. The case of western Ukraine was of course very different – local institutions such as the Greek Catholic Church or the Communist Party of Western Ukraine were destroyed under Stalin.

136 Bren, *The Greengrocer*, 187.

137 Ibid., 149.

138 OSA, f.300, sf.85, s.44, c.25, file 4 (Polish-Soviet appeal, July 1979).

139 OSA, f.300, sf.85, s.44, c.25, file 4 (Statement, 19 October 1977); OSA, f.300, sf.85, s.11, c.12, file 30 (Public statement in support of Charter 77, 12 February 1977).

140 At the same time, however, Polish underground publications frequently expressed "sentimental" feelings about Lviv and other cities that Poland lost at the end of the Second World War. Kh. Chushak, "Shliakhy vrehuliuvannia problemy pol's'ko-ukrains'koho kordonu v publikatsiiakh pol's'kykh opozytsioneriv (1976–1989)." In M. Lytvyn, ed., *Ukraina-Pol'shcha: istorychna spadshchyna i suspil'na svidomist,'* 3–4 (2010–2011), 199, 202, 210.

141 *KhTS*, 31 December 1976.

5 A Prelude to Perestroika

1 OSA, f.300, sf.6, s.3, c.2 (Unevaluated comments by recent emigrants, August 1982).

2 Grzegorz Ekiert, *The State against Society: Political Crises and Their Aftermath in East Central Europe* (Princeton: Princeton University Press, 1996), 11.

3 D. Mason, "Solidarity as a New Social Movement," *Political Science Quarterly* 104:1 (1989): 41; G. Ekiert, "Rebellious Poles: Political Crises and Popular Protest Under State Socialism, 1945–89," *East European Politics and Societies* 11:2 (1997): 325–7.

4 Ekiert, "Rebellious Poles," 331.

5 To be sure, the Soviet Union and other East European countries did not share the structural features that facilitated the emergence of Solidarity in Poland (such as a strong Catholic Church and a private agricultural sector). See György Schöpflin, "Poland and Eastern Europe," in Abraham Brumberg, ed., *Poland, Genesis of a Revolution* (New York: Random House, 1983), 132–3.

6 OSA, f.300, sf.6, s.3, c.1 ("Attitudes in the USSR Toward the Right to Strike," January 1981; "Attitudes of Soviet citizens to the Strike Movement in Poland, September 1980–February 1981," May 1981; "Developing Soviet Citizen Attitudes Towards Poland," October 1981); OSA, f.3, sf.6, s.3, c.1 ("Attitudes of Some Soviet citizens to the Solidarity Trade Union Movement, Comparison of SAAOR Data with Unofficial Soviet Poll," May 1982).

7 Kotkin claims that perestroika was rooted in "a deeply felt urge to make socialism live up to its promises." But support for change slowly began to emerge among a much wider section of the population than Stephen Kotkin's reformists seeking to "return to the imagined ideals of October" in the second half of the 1980s. S. Kotkin, *Armageddon Averted: The Soviet Collapse, 1970–2000* (Oxford: Oxford University Press, 2008), 30.

8 Solchanyk, "*Polska a sowiecki zachód*," 79, 82, 86.

9 OSA, f.300, sf.6, s.3, c.3 ("Nationality Listener Report, Ukrainian and Belorussian Services, 1982 Data," May 1983). Another engineer from Kyiv seemed to entirely give up on Soviet sources of information, though he may well have geared his response to compliment the Radio Liberty researchers that he spoke with: "Foreign stations have replaced our press, parliament and university. It is very important to report on the events in Poland as much as possible." OSA, f.300, sf.6, s.3, c.1 ("Monthly Summary of Listener Reactions to Radio Liberty," December 1980).
10 OSA, f.300, sf.6, s.3, c.1 ("Monthly Summary of Listener Reactions to Radio Liberty," January 1981).
11 DALO, f.P3, op.46, s.85, ark. 84–6.
12 G. Ekiert, *The State Against Society: Political Crises and Their Aftermath in East-Central Europe* (Princeton: Princeton University Press, 1996), 12.
13 TsDAHOU, f.1, op.25, s.2287, ark. 8–10.
14 Ibid., 43.
15 I. Zaitsev, "Pol's'ka opozytsiia 1970–80-kh rokiv pro zasady ukrains'ko-pol's'koho porozuminnia," in Iurii Slyvka, ed., *Deportatsii ukraintsiv ta poliakiv: kinets 1939- pochatok 50-kh rokiv* (Lviv: Instytut ukrainoznavstva im. Kryp'iakevycha, 1998), 57.
16 DALO, f.3, op.44, s.85, ark. 21–6.
17 TsDAHOU, f.1, op.25, s.2287, ark. 8–10.
18 TsDAHOU, f.1, op.25, s.2048, ark. 114–17.
19 OSA, f.300, sf.6, s.3, c.2 ("Unevaluated Comments by Recent Emigrants," January 1983).
20 OSA, f.300, sf.6, s.3, c.1 (Charles Allen, "Interview with Vladimir Borisov, Founding Member of Soviet Independent Trade Union" August 1981).
21 OSA, f.300, sf.85, c.46, b.5, t.2 ("Writers' trade union").
22 OSA, f.300, sf.85, c.44, b.14, t.25 ("Ukrainian Helsinki Group Informational Bulletin," September 1980).
23 OSA, f.300, sf.6, s.3, c.1 (Charles Allen, "Interview with Vladimir Borisov, Founding Member of Soviet Independent Trade Union," August 1981).
24 OSA, f.300, sf.85, c.46, b.5, t.2 ("Writers' trade union").
25 OSA, f.300, sf.6, s.3, c.1 (Charles Allen, "Interview with Vladimir Borisov, Founding Member of Soviet Independent Trade Union," August 1981).
26 OSA, f.300, sf.85, c.44, b.25, t.4 ("Moscow-Warsaw," July 1979).
27 Russian Union of Solidarists, *O ruchu robotniczym w Rosji i Polsce* (Warsaw: UOW Brzask, 1985), 30–2, 70–1; *Materialy samizdata* (MS) (Samizdat Materials) 35/80, 13 October 1980, Document AS4092: A. Sakharov and nine other signatures, "'Message to the United Interfactory Strike Committee in Gdansk," Moscow, no date, probably 30 August 1980; MS 22/81, 8 June

1981, Document AS4321: Mykola Pohyba, a blue-collar worker, "Open letter to the Ukrainian Human Rights Group," vicinity of the Bucha train station, Kyiv oblast, 4 November 1980; see also O. Bazhan, "Zovnishn'o-politychni aktsii SRSR u 50- 80-ti rr. ta ikh vplyv na rozvytok opozytsiinoho rukhu v Ukraini," *Z arkhiviv VUChK-HPU-NKVD-KHB* 2/4 (2000).

28 E. Teague, *Solidarity and the Soviet Worker: The Impact of the Polish Events of 1980 on Soviet Internal Politics* (London: Croom Helm, 1988), 42–3.

29 Lewytzkyj, *Politics and Society*, 146–66.

30 MS 36/81, 25 September 1981, Document AS4429: Mikhail Zotov, member of SMOT, artist, "Extracts from a letter (November 1980) about reactions of Togliatti blue-collar workers to the Polish events," Moscow, no earlier than 27 January 1981; Russian Solidarity Union, *O ruchu robotniczym*, 51–2.

31 The authors of the survey conducted 618 informal conversations with inhabitants of the Moscow region – the respondents had no connection to the dissident movement and were not aware that they were taking part in an opinion poll. OSA, f.300, sf.85, c.46, b.5, t.1 (S. Pukhov, "Muscovites' attitudes towards the Solidarity trade union").

32 The 1962 unrest and massacre in Novocherkassk was one in a series of working class uprisings during the Thaw. Vladimir Kozlov argues that working-class protest in the late 1950s and early 1960s represented extreme frustration with the Soviet authorities and poor standards of living, yet also the belief that Soviet "communism" could be fixed that later dissipiated under Brezhnev. Kozlov, *Mass Uprisings*, 314.

33 OSA, f.300, sf.6, s.3, c.1 (Charles Allen, "Interview with Vladimir Borisov, Founding Member of Soviet Independent Trade Union," August 1981).

34 OSA, f.300, sf.6, s.3, c.2 ("Unevaluated Comments by Recent Emigrants," April 1982).

35 Ibid., May 1982.

36 Ibid., May 1982.

37 Ibid., December 1982.

38 OSA, f.300, sf.85, c.44, b.14, t.5 ("Information from SMOT to the International Labour Organisation, to all independent trade unions, and to the international community," no date, but probably 1982).

39 OSA, f.300, sf.85, c.46, b.6, t.1 ("Letter from Pavlov, Kudravtsev, and Ivanovskii," no date, but probably late 1982 or early 1983); OSA, f.300, sf.85, c.44, b.14, t.7 ("SMOT Information," February 1987).

40 OSA, f.300, sf.6, s.3, c.2 ("Attitudes of Soviet Citizens to the Strike Movement in Poland, September 1980–February 1981," May 1981).

41 OSA, f.300, sf.6, s.3, c.1 (Charles Allen, "Interview with Vladimir Borisov, Founding Member of Soviet Independent Trade Union," August 1981).

42 RGANI, f.5, op.89, d.82, ll. 37–50.
43 TsDAHOU, f.1, op.25, s.2228, ark. 7–14; RGANI, Moscow, f.5, op.77, d.105, ll. 2–7, 49–53.
44 Linda Cook and Elizabeth Teague already came to this conclusion, although not specifically with regards to the western borderlands. Linda Cook, *The Soviet Social Contract and Why It Failed: Welfare Policy and Workers' Politics from Brezhnev to Yeltsin* (Cambridge, MA: Harvard University Press, 1993); Teague, *Solidarity and the Soviet Worker*, 322.
45 TsDAHOU, f.1, op.25, s.2048, ark. 122–8.
46 TsDAHOU, f.1, op.25, s.2295, ark. 51–3.
47 OSA, f.300, sf.85, c.46, b.1, t.11 ("A Letter from V. Tomachinskii," December 1980).
48 TsDAHOU, f.1, op.25, s.2216, ark. 5–8; TsDAHOU, f.1, op.25, s.2048, ark. 84–8.
49 TsDAHOU, f.1, op.25, s.2048, ark. 114–17.
50 TsDAHOU, f.1, op.25, s.2295, ark. 51–3.
51 OSA, f.300, sf.6. s.3, c.2 ("Unevaluated Comments by Recent Emigrants," January 1983).
52 Igor Sinitsin, "The Great Strength of Unity," *Sovetskaia Rossiia*, 24 April 1981, from *CDSP* 33:17, 27 May 1981; author unknown, "A Socialist Poland Is Possible Only in Soviet Alliance, Grishin Says," *Pravda*, 18 July 1981, from *CDSP* 33:30, 26 August 1981; author unknown, "Where is the Gdańsk Congress Headed?," *Pravda*, 10 September 1981 and *Izvestiia*, 11 September 1981, from *CDSP* 33:36, 7 October 1981; Vladimir Bolshakov, "Socialism is Peace," *Pravda*, 13 September 1981, from *CDSP* 33:37, 14 October 1981; author unknown, "Polish Leaders Urged to Curb Anti-Sovietism," *Pravda*, 19 September 1981 and *Izvestiia*, 20 September 1981, from *CDSP* 33:38, 28 October 1981; author unknown, "On the Situation in Poland," *Pravda*, 11 December 1981, from *CDSP* 33:50, 13 January 1982. The imposition of martial law on 13 December 1981 put a rapid end to such alarming articles. Author unknown, "Soviet Leaders Pleased by Jaruzelski's Speech," *Pravda* and *Izvestiia*, 15 December 1981, from *CDSP* 33:50, 13 January 1982; author unknown, "Cooperation is Developing," *Pravda*, 26 January 1983, from *CDSP* 35:4, 23 February 1983.
53 RGANI, f.5, op.77, d.105, l. 8; TsDAHOU, f.1, op.25, s.2048, ark. 84–8.
54 TsDAHOU, f.1, op.25, s.2295, ark. 1–4.
55 Yurchak, *Everything Was Forever*, 164.
56 Ibid., 283.
57 RGANI, f.5, op.84, d.76, ll. 35–9.
58 TsDAHOU, f.1, op.25, s.2048, ark. 84–8.

59 OSA, f.300, sf.6, s.3, c.2 ("Soviet Citizens Attitudes Toward Poland Since Martial Law: Agitprop, Western Radio and the Evolution of Opinion," September 1982).
60 OSA, f.300, sf.6, s.3, c.2 ("Unevaluated Comments by Recent Emigrants," July 1982).
61 TsDAHOU, f.1, op.25, s.2295, ark. 1–4. Similar statements echoed in other parts of Ukraine. TsDAHOU, f.1, op.25, s.2048, ark. 84–8.
62 RGANI, f.89, 46, d.67, ll. 5–7; DALO, f.P3, op.44, s.77, ark. 2–4; DALO, f.P3, op.46, s.84, ark. 1–2.
63 AAN, z.1354, s.LVI, t.751 ("Cultural cooperation with socialist countries in 1981").
64 RGANI, f.89, 46, d.67, ll. 5–7; DALO, f.P3, op.44, s.77, ark. 2–4; DALO, f.P3, op.46, s.84, ark. 1–2.
65 Because officials in charge of tourism were reluctant to send Soviet citizens to simply rest in Poland, associated as it was with a prolonged stay in the country, they focused on promoting what they called "educational tourism" instead. RGANI, f.89, 46, d.67, ll. 2–3.
66 AAN, z.1037, s.13, t.13 ("Tourism perspectives for 1981," 18 July 1981).
67 AAN, z.1354, s.LVI, t.1848 ("Initial assessment of the Polish book days in the USSR that took place between 21 and 30 April 1981").
68 AAN, z.1354, s.LVI, t.967 ("Assessment of cultural cooperation with socialist countries").
69 Top CPSU officials reprimanded their subordinates when they failed to design talks for the Polish building brigades in the USSR or to make sure that their Soviet colleagues fulfilled their part of the work plans or to guarantee reliable supplies, which gave "the foreigners" a reason to voice "demagogic statements." TsDAHOU, f.1, op.25, s.2287, ark. 33–7.
70 TsDAHOU, f.1, op.25, s.2287, ark. 33–7; RGANI, f.5, op.89, d.67, ll. 12–14. CPSU officials claimed that their citizens could exert a very positive influence over the Poles: influenced by "bourgeois propaganda" and demoralised by a system where they were paid by the hour without taking into account the effectiveness of their labour, Polish workers could not keep up with the Soviet citizens' pace of work. This led CPSU leaders to suggest that Soviet workers' collectives should continue to visit Poland to rectify the situation. TsDAHOU, f.1, op.25, s.2600, ark. 51.
71 Gorsuch, "Time Travellers," 217, 222–4; DALO, f.P3, op.44, s. 85, ark. 7–8; TsDAHOU, f.1, op.25, s. 2608, ark. 18–22; TsDAHOU, f.1, op.25, s.2769, ark. 40–2; SWPW, t. 41/225 (Jerzy Piechowicz, "Report on trip number 7-2247 Warsaw-Moscow-Kyiv-Warsaw that took place from 24 to 31 March 1977,"

4 April 1977). P. Sowiński, *Wakacje w Polsce Ludowej. Polityka władz i ruch turystyczny (1945–1989)* (Warsaw: Trio, 2005), 166.

72 TsDAHOU, f.1, op.25, s.1884, ll. 17–23.

73 AAN, z.1354, s.XL, t.217 ("Information on some problems, observations, and activity of the customs services," January, February, and May 1978; "Information on customs crimes and currency crimes among Polish citizens travelling abroad in 1977," 28 July 1978).

74 RGANI, f.5, op.60, d.36, s. 45–8.

75 AAN, z.1354, s.LVI, t.930 (Letter from J. Nowicki, 17.4.73).

76 TsDAHOU, f.1, op.25, s.2287, ark. 8–10.

77 DALO, f.P3, op.46, s.85, ark. 4–9; RGANI, f.89, 46, d.67, ll. 5–7.

78 DALO, f.P3, op.46, s.85, ark. 84–6.

79 Ibid., 4–9; TsDAHOU, f.1, op.25, s.2295, ark. 1–4.

80 DALO, f.3, op.44, s.85, ark. 21–6.

81 TsDAHOU, f.1, op.25, s.2287, ark. 4–5.

82 DALO, f.3, op.44, s.85, ark. 21–6.

83 RGANI, f.5, op.84, d.76, ll. 35–9.

84 TsDAHOU, f.1, op.25, s.2048, ark. 96–100.

85 Ibid., 122–8.

86 DALO, f.P3, op.46, s.85, ark. 84–6.

87 DALO, f.P3, op.47, s.62, ark. 15–18.

88 TsDAHOU, f.1, op.25, s.2048, ark. 96–100.

89 In earlier decades, the term "bandits" was often used as a shorthand for Gulag returnees who included many former OUN-UPA members from west Ukraine. See Miriam Dobson, "Show the Bandits No Mercy!", 21–40.

90 DALO, f.P3, op.46, s.85, ark. 84–6.

91 TsDAHOU, f.1, op.25, s.2048, ark. 122–8.

92 In talking to other people queuing in front of a shop, for example, a local man from Lviv claimed, "the Poles are idiots who … do not know what they want. They will only harm themselves through not going to work." A telephone operator from Lutsk who, as the report underlined, had been born in Poland and still had relatives there, sounded more bitter: "The Poles have got used to a good life and good food, but they can't be bothered to work, which explains why they have such chaos in their country." TsDAHOU, f.1, op.25, s.2048, ark. 114–17; RGANI, f.5, op.77, d. 105, ll. 49–53.

93 TsDAHOU, f.1, op.25, s.2048, ark. 117–21.

94 Ibid., 96–100.

95 RGANI, f.5, op.77, d.105, l. 8.

96 TsDAHOU, f.1, op.25, s.2216, ark. 15–18.

97 RGANI, f.5, op.77, d.105, ll. 2–7.
98 TsDAHOU, f.1, op.25, s.2048, ark. 114–17.
99 Ibid.
100 Ibid., 96–100.
101 TsDAHOU, f.1, op.25, s.2541, ark. 23–5.
102 TsDAHOU, f.1, op.25, s.2048, ark. 121.
103 Ibid., 108.
104 DALO, f.P3, op.44, s.85, ark. 43–6.
105 Shelest, *Spravzhnii sud*, 331–3.
106 DAKO, f.5, op.7, s.1396, ark. 176–7, 179–80; TsDAHOU, f.1, op.25, s.355, ark. 47–50.
107 Ibid., 47–50.
108 Ibid., 58–60.
109 RGANI, f.89, 46, d.59, ll. 6–7.
110 In September 1981, for example, *Pravda* stated that the events in Poland demonstrated the necessity of utilising public opinion as a barometer to provide advance warning of "contradictions and conflict situations in socialist society." Similarly, Konstantin Chernenko's article in *Voprosy istorii KPSS* (*Issues of the History of the CPSU*) from February 1982 emphasised that "the Polish events showed the 'vital significance' of heeding popular opinion." Teague, *Solidarity and the Soviet Worker*, 69, 74.
111 DAKO, f.P5, op.86, s.243, ark. 106–7; TsDAHOU, f.1, op.25, s.2048, ark. 96–100; TsDAHOU, f.1, op.25, s.2216, ark. 15–18; TsDAHOU, f.1, op.25, s.2295, ark. 1–4.
112 TsDAHOU, f.1, op.25, s.2048, ark. 122–8.
113 RGANI, f.5, op.77, d.105, ll. 2–7, 49–53; DAKO, Kyiv, f.P5, op.86, s.243, ark. 106–7.
114 RGANI, f.5, op.77, d.105, ll. 49–53; TsDAHOU, Kyiv, f.1, op.25, s.2216, ark. 5–8; RGANI, f.5, op.84, d.76, ll. 20–3, 30–3, 35–9.
115 RGANI, f.5, op.77, d.105, ll. 49–53.
116 Ibid., 2–7.
117 Cook, *The Soviet Social Contract*, 65, 67, 79. They asserted that local bureaucrats should make a special effort to improve the material well-being of the Soviet industrial workers, increasing the supply of consumer goods and selling them directly at big factories. In October 1980, they also resolved to strengthen control over the building of hospitals and schools, housing, restaurants and canteens, as well as cultural institutions. RGANI, f.5, op.77, d.105, ll. 2–7.
118 TsDAHOU, f.1, op.25, s.2295, ark. 12–14.
119 Ibid., 10–11.
120 Teague, *Solidarity and the Soviet Worker*, 321–2.
121 AAN, z.1354, s.XI, t.472, ark. 4–10.

122 AAN, z.1354, s.LVI, t.1110, 25–44.
123 TsDAHOU, f.1, op.25, s.2600, ark. 51.
124 OSA, f.300, sf.6, s.3, c.3 ("Unevaluated Comments by Recent Emigrants," April 1983).
125 When Polish scouts travelled to the USSR in September 1984, for example, they met with Soviet war veterans and performed Polish folk songs. AAN z.1354, s.XLIII, t.39 (Władysław Kruk, "Information Provided by the Polish Consul General in Kyiv," 17 September 1984).
126 AAN, z.1354, s.XI, t.472, ark. 39.
127 AAN, z.1354, s.LVI, t.1860 ("Information on Wacław Janas's talks in Moscow between 9 and 12 January 1984").
128 AAN, z.1354, s.LVI, t.1860 ("A list of events organized as part of the Polish Culture Days in the USSR between 19 and 29 April 1984").
129 AAN, z.1354, s.LVI, t.1116 (Polish embassy in Moscow, "Report on cultural cooperation in 1985").
130 In the USSR, "Poland is slowly returning to the well-deserved top position it has previously occupied," one cocky embassy report claimed. AAN, z.1354, s.LVI, t.1116 (Henryk Jabłoński, "Cultural cooperation between the USSR and socialist countries," 27 November 1985).
131 AAN, z.1354, s.LVI, t.814 (Polish Embassy in Moscow, "Report on cultural cooperation," 13 December 1985); AAN, z.1354, s.LVI, tt.1116 (Polish embassy in Moscow, "Report on cultural cooperation in 1985").
132 AAN, z.1354, s.XI, t.993, ark. 350.
133 AAN, z.1354, s.LVI, t.1246 ("Report on the tour of the band 'String Connection' around the USSR between 20 January 1984 and 19 February 1984").
134 AAN, z.1354, s.LVI, t.967 ("Assessment of cultural cooperation with socialist countries").
135 AAN, z.1354, s.LVI, t.1118 ("Note from a meeting about the state and prospects of Polish-Soviet cultural cooperation," 21 November 1982).
136 AAN, z.1354, s.LVI, t.1116 (Polish embassy in Moscow, "Report on cultural cooperation in 1985").
137 TsDAHOU, f.1, op.32, d.2146, ark. 13–14.
138 AAN, z.1354, s.LVI, t.1119 ("Note from a meeting at the Writers' Union of Ukraine that took place on 15 February 1983").
139 AAN, z.1354. s.LVI, t.1116 (Władysław Kruk, "Letter to the Polish Foreign Ministry," 20 February 1986).
140 RGANI, f.5, op.89, d.67, ll. 12–14.
141 TsDAHOU, f.1, op.25, s.2600, ark. 60–1.
142 Ibid., 18–22; TsDAHOU, f.1, op.25, s.2769, ark. 40–2.

143 RGANI, f.5, op.89, d.67, ll. 12–14.
144 TsDAHOU, f.1, op.25, s.2769, ark. 40–2.
145 AAN, z.1354, s.LVI, t.1137 ("Information about the visit of a Soviet writers' delegation in Poand between 11 and 19 February 1983").
146 TsDAHOU, f.1, op.32, s.2146, ark. 15.
147 AAN, z.1354, s.LVI, t.1116 (Polish embassy in Moscow, "Report on cultural cooperation in 1985").
148 RGANI, f.5, op.89, d.154, ll. 75–8.
149 AAN, z.1354, s.LVI, t.1116 (Henryk Jabłoński, "Soviet cultural cooperation with socialist countries," 27 November 1985).
150 AAN, z.1354, s.LVI, t.1247 ("Report on citizen Zdzisław Pożarycki's trip to the USSR between 9 August and 6 September 1985").
151 AAN z.1354, s.XLIII, t.39 ("Note about a meeting at the Ukrainian Komsomol Central Committee in Kyiv").
152 AAN, z.1354, s.LVI, t.814 (W. Klaczyński, "Report on activities in the press and information sphere," 15 December 1985).
153 DALO, f.3, op.46, s.86, ark. 22–4.
154 Ibid.
155 TsDAHOU, f.1, op.25, s.2600, ark. 5–8.
156 Kalinovsky, *A Long Goodbye*, 1–2.
157 G. Kolankiewicz, "The Polish Question: Andropov's Answer?" in Leonard Schapiro and Joseph Godson, ed., *The Soviet Worker: From Lenin to Andropov* (London: Macmillan, 1984), 259, 272–5, 277.
158 G. Peteri, "The Occident Within – or the Drive for Exceptionalism and Modernity," *Kritika: Explorations in Russian and Eurasian History* 9:4 (Fall 2008): 934–5, 937.

Epilogue

1 The street has been renamed since 1991, but few local residents or street signs acknowledge this.
2 What I call "third Ukraine" here resembled Mykola Riabchuk's "second Ukraine" opposed to private ownership and radical economic reforms, the revival of Ukrainian language and culture, democratisation, and Ukraine's eventual membership in the European Union and NATO. M. Riabchuk, *Dvi Ukrainy: real'ni mezhi, virtual'ni viiny* (Kyiv: Krytyka, 2003), 303.
3 Riabchuk, *Dvi Ukrainy*, 302.
4 Roman Solchanyk, "The Radical Right in Ukraine," in S.P. Ramet, ed., *The Radical Right in Central and Eastern Europe Since 1989*, (University Park, Pennsylvania: Pennsylvania State University Press, 1999), 287–8.

5 B. Nahaylo, *The Ukrainian Resurgence*, (London: Hurst and Company, 1999), 318.

6 T. Kuzio and A. Wilson, *Ukraine: Perestroika to Independence* (Basingstoke: Macmillan, 2000), 117.

7 A. Wilson, *Ukrainian Nationalism in the 1990s: A Minority Faith*, (Cambridge: Cambridge University Press, 1997), 195.

8 S. Shulman, "Cultures in Competition: Ukrainian Foreign Policy and the 'Cultural Threat' from Abroad," *Europe-Asia Studies* 50:2 (March 1998): 293.

9 A. Wilson, "Ukraine's 2002 Elections: Less Fraud, More Virtuality," *East European Constitutional Review* 11:3 (2002): 94.

10 "*Pozacherhovi vybory narodnikh deputativ Ukrainy, 26 zhovtnia 2014 roku. Protokol tsentral'noi vyborchoi komisii pro rezul'taty vyboriv narodnykh deputativ Ukrainy u zahal'noderzhavnomu bahatomandatnomu okruzi*," accessed 24 February 2015, http://www.cvk.gov.ua/info/protokol_bmvo_ndu_26102014.pdf.

11 Rossoliński-Liebe, *Stepan Bandera*, 405, 457, 471, 483–6, 502–14, 761.

12 Ukrainian Nationalist Political Party "Svoboda," "Program for the Protection of Ukrainians," accessed 27 October 2015, http://en.svoboda.org.ua/about/program/.

13 M. Drohobysky, "The Lion Society: Profile of a Ukrainian Patriotic 'Informal' Group," Radio Liberty Research Report, RL 325/88, 18 July 1988. Held at School of Slavonic and East European Studies, London, Collection IND11 (Materials relating to the Ukrainian dissident movement).

14 Z. Gitelman, "Ethnopolitics and the Future of the Former Soviet Union," in Z. Gitelman, ed., *The Politics of Nationality and the Erosion of the USSR: Selected Papers from the Fourth World Congress for Soviet and East European Studies, Harrogate, 1990* (Basingstoke: Macmillan, 1992), 18.

15 Kuzio and Wilson, *Ukraine*, 54.

16 Ibid., 111.

17 Ibid., 81.

18 P. Potichnyj, "Elections in the Ukraine, 1990," in Gitelman, ed., *Politics of Nationality*, 178.

19 Kuzio and Wilson, *Ukraine*, 112.

20 O. Hnatiuk, *Pożegnanie z imperium: ukraińskie dyskusje o tożsamości* (Lublin: Wydawnictwo Uniwersytetu Marii Curie-Skłodowskiej, 2003).

21 Kuzio and Wilson, *Ukraine*, 217. Andrew Wilson suggests that Kuchma engineered the split in Rukh in 1999. A. Wilson, "Ukraine and Post-Soviet Europe: Authoritarian Consolidation or Renewed Reform?" in S. White et al., eds., *Developments in Central and East European Politics 3* (Basingstoke: Palgrave Macmillan, 2003), 99.

22 M. Riabchuk, "Civil Society and Nation Building in Ukraine," in T. Kuzio, ed., *Contemporary Ukraine: The Dynamics of Post-Soviet Transformation* (Armonk, New York: M.E. Sharpe, 1998), 86. Reformist forces were also divided. This was evident during the Gongadze affair, when Rukh (Kostenko) and Reforms-Congress failed to present a united front against Kuchma and "were internally divided about the actions to be taken as a result of the scandal." S. Whitmore, *State Building in Ukraine: The Ukrainian Parliament, 1990-2003* (London: Routledge, 2004), 109.

23 "Yushchenko portrayed the election as a choice between change (represented by himself) and a continuation of the status quo (Yanukovych)." To be sure, however, he also relied on the support of oligarchs concerned that Yanukovych's victory would overly strengthen the Donetsk clan vis-à-vis competing oligarchic groups. T. Kuzio, "From Kuchma to Yushchenko: Ukraine's 2004 Presidential Elections and the Orange Revolution," *Problems of Post-Communism* 52:2 (2005), 29–44.

24 The United Nations Refugee Agency. "*Zvit pro spil'nu otsinku potreb vnutrishn'o peremishchenykh osib (VPO), m. Kyiv ta Kyivs'ka oblast'* Ukraina," accessed 26 October 2015, http://unhcr.org.ua/attachments/article/1527/2015_PA_Kyiv_Ukr.pdf.

25 "*Gruppa po organizatsii pomoshchi bezhentsam iz Kryma i Donbassa,*" accessed 26 October 2015, http://vk.com/ua.crimea.

26 *Initsiativnaia gruppa kharkovchan-volonterov*, "Help Army," "About Us," accessed 26 October 2015, http://help-army.org.ua/o-nas/.

27 Wilson, "Ukraine and Post-Soviet Europe," 104.

28 Wilson, *Ukrainian Nationalism*, 126.

29 Mark Kramer, "The Collapse of East European Communism and the Repercussions Within the Soviet Union: Part Three," *Journal of Cold War Studies* 7:1 (2005): 67.

30 Communist apparatchiks in the republican capitals identified their political and economic interests with those of their republics, which helps account for what Mark Beissinger has described as a "tide of nationalism" that spread from the unstable Baltic republics to other parts of the USSR that witnessed relatively little popular support for national opposition to Soviet rule. M. Beissinger, *Nationalist Mobilisation and the Collapse of the Soviet State* (Cambridge: Cambridge University Press, 2002), 191–8.

31 On the role of republican-level elites in Soviet collapse, see Kuzio and Wilson, *Ukraine*, 3, 63, 127; Breuilly, *Nationalism and the State*, 347; Motyl, *Dilemmas of Independence: Ukraine after Totalitarianism* (New York: Council on Foreign Relations Press, 1993), 36–7.

32 Wilson, *Ukrainian Nationalism*, 128.

33 Y. Andrukhovych, "*Kraina mrii*," *Krytyka* 9–10 (2004): 2–3. See also Motyl, *Dilemmas*, 51–2.

34 J. Simon, "Ukraine Against Herself: To be Euro-Atlantic, Eurasian, or Neutral?" *Strategic Forum* 238 (2009).

35 Wilson, "Ukraine and Post-Soviet Europe," 94. For example, in the 1998 elections when communists became the largest single party in parliament, negative economic experiences since 1994 and anti-market values were associated with support for the left parties, the opposite with support for the centrist National Democratic Party (NDP) and Rukh. Sarah Birch and Andrew Wilson, "The 1998 Ukrainian Elections: Voting Stability, Political Gridlock," *Europe-Asia Studies*, 51:6 (September 1999): 1060.

36 Wilson, *Ukrainian Nationalism*, 132–43.

37 A. Motyl, "State, Nation and Elites in Independent Ukraine," in *Contemporary Ukraine*, ed. Kuzio, 6.

38 S. Plokhy, "Church, State and Nation in Ukraine," *Religion in Eastern Europe*, 9:5 (1999): 21.

39 Wanner, *Burden of Dreams*, 47.

40 S. Shulman, "National Identity and Public Support for Political and Economic Reform in Ukraine," *Slavic Review* 64:1 (2005): 85.

41 T. Kuzio, "Soviet Conspiracy Theories and Political Culture in Ukraine: Understanding Viktor Yanukovych and the Party of Regions," *Communist and Post-Communist Studies* 44:3 (2011): 221–32.

42 The Donbas region accounted for only 12 per cent of Ukraine's gross domestic product and consumed 21 per cent of government subsidies in 2010. Accessed 24 February 2014, http://thekievtimes.ua/economics/301541-donbass-ne-stolko-kormit-skolko-est-fotoreportazh-2.html.

43 Ian Traynor, Shaun Walker, "Russian Resurgence: How the Kremlin is Making its Presence Felt Across Europe," *The Guardian*, 16 February 2015, accessed 27 October 2015, http://www.theguardian.com/world/2015/feb/16/russian-resurgence-how-the-kremlin-is-making-its-presence-felt-across-europe; Tony Wesolowsky, "Czech President Breaks Ranks with Moscow Visit" Radio Free Europe – Radio Liberty, 11 May 2015, accessed 27 October 2015, http://www.rferl.org/content/czech-president-zeman-breaks-ranks-moscow-visit/27010077.html.

44 Olga Szpunar, Bartłomiej Kuraś, "Słowianie z Polski piszą do przyjaciół Moskali: Rola prezydenta Putina jest pozytywna." *Gazeta Wyborcza*, 17 May 2015 (accessed 27 October 2015).

Bibliography

Primary Sources

Archival Sources

Archiwum Akt Nowych (AAN), Warsaw

z.1037 "Orbis" Central Tourist Board in Warsaw

z.1354 Central Committee of the Polish United Workers' Party

Sygnatura XI	Chancellery of the Secretariat
Sygnatura XIA	Chancellery of First Secretaries of the Central Committee
Sygnatura XIB	Chancellery of Central Committee Secretaries and Members of the Political Bureau
Sygnatura XL	Department for Social Organisations, Sports and Tourism
Sygnatura XLII	Social-Professional Department
Sygnatura LVI	Department for Culture

z.1608 Council of Friendship Societies

z.1861 Youth Tourism Bureau of the Union of Polish Socialist Youth

Derzhavnyi arkhiv Kyivs'koi oblasti (DAKO), Kyiv

f.P5 Kyiv oblast committee of the Communist Party of Ukraine

Opisi: 6, 7, 47, 60, 76, 86, 90, 100

Derzhavnyi arkhiv Lvivs'koi oblasti (DALO), Lviv

f.P3 Lviv oblast committee of the Communist Party of Ukraine

Opisi: 5, 6, 10, 13, 44, 46, 47, 53

Derzhavnyi arkhiv Odes'koi oblasti (DAOO), Odesa

f.P11 Odesa oblast committee of the Communist Party of Ukraine

Opisi: 15, 18, 19, 20, 126, 129, 132, 150, 151, 153

Gosudarstvennyi arkhiv Rossiiskoi Federatsii (GARF), Moscow

f. 6903 USSR state committee for television and radio (Gosteleradio), 1933–1991

Opisi: 2, 32, 33, 37

f.9425 Supreme office for the protection of state secrets in publications by the USSR Supreme Soviet (Glavlit), 1922–1991

Opisi: 1, 2

f.9576 The union of Soviet societies for friendship and cultural relations with foreign countries (SSOD), 1958–1992

Opis 4

f.9612 Organisations for the management of foreign travel in the USSR, 1929-1991

Opis 3

Open Society Archives (OSA), Budapest

f.300–6 Radio Free Europe/Radio Liberty Research Institute, Media and Opinion Research Department, 1962–1994

f.300–85 Radio Free Europe/Radio Liberty Research Institute, Samizdat Archives, 1956–1994

Rossiiskii gosudarstvennyi arkhiv noveishei istorii (RGANI), Moscow

f.5 Apparatus of the Central Committee of the Communist Party of the Soviet Union

op.28 Department for relations with foreign communist parties
op.31 Department for union republics
op.33 Department of propaganda and agitation
op.55 Ideological commission
Opisi 58, 59, 60, 61, 62, 63, 66, 68, 73, 75, 77, 84, 88, 89, 90: Apparatus documents organised by year, 1966–1984

f.89 Collection of de-classified documents

Stowarzyszenie wspolpracy Polska-Wschod (SWPW), Warsaw

Files of the Polish-Soviet friendship society:

41/121; 41/144; 41/145; 41/176; 41/180; 41/181; 41/191; 41/202; 41/206; 41/219; 41/225

Tsentral'nyi derzhavnyi arkhiv hromads'kykh ob"ednan' Ukrainy (TsDAHOU), Kyiv

f.1 Central Committee of the Communist Party of Ukraine
op.24 General department, secret part, 1950–1967
op.25 General department, secret part, 1967–1988
op.31 General department, non-secret part, 1955–1970
op.32 General department, non-secret part, 1970–1991

Samizdat Materials

Khronika tekushchikh sobytii, issues 1–27 (Amsterdam: Fond im. Gertsena, 1979)
Khronika tekushchikh sobytii, issues 28–63 (New York: Khronika, 1974–83)
Materialy samizdata (Munich: Radio Liberty, 1972–91)
Sobranie dokumentov samizdata, vols. 1–16 (Munich: Radio Liberty, 1973)
Russian Solidarity Union, *O ruchu robotnicznym w Rosji i Polsce* (Warsaw: UOW Brzask, 1985)
Ukrains'kyi visnyk, issues 1–8 (Paris: Smoloskyp, 1970–4)

Soviet Press and Compilations of the Soviet Press

The Current Digest of the Soviet Press, vols. 8–27 (Columbus, OH: American Association for the Advancement of Slavic Studies, 1956–85)
Digest of the Soviet Ukrainian Press, vols. 5–13 (New York: Prolog Research and Publishing Association, 1961–9)
Literaturna hazeta
Literaturna Ukraina
Pravda Ukrainy
Zhovten'

Official Soviet Bloc Publications

Biriukov, I., *Chekhoslovakiia: liudi i gody* (Moscow: Izdatel'stvo politicheskoi literatury, 1986)
Bodrin, V.V. and Avdeichev, L.A., *Vengriia. Chekhoslovakiia* (Moscow: Geografgiz 1957)
Burlaka, P.N., *Mezh Tissoi i Dunaem* (Moscow: Geografgiz, 1959)
Gerasimov, V. and Gerasimova, G., *Servus, drug! Iz vengerskikh bloknotov* (Moscow: Izdatel'stvo politicheskoi literatury, 1980)
Inturist, *Posetite Vengriiu* (Moscow: Inturist, no date)
Kondufor, Iu. Iu., Kuras, I.F. et al., eds., *History Teaches a Lesson: Captured War Documents Expose the Atrocities of the German-facist Invaders and Their*

Henchmen in Ukraine's Temporarily Occupied Territory During the Great Patriotic War (1941-45) (Kyiv: Politvydav Ukrainy, 1986)
– *Istoriia Ukrains'koi RSR: Korotkyi narys* (Kyiv: Naukova dumka, 1981)
Korotich, V., *Most: Razmyshleniia o puteshestviiakh s piatnadtsat'iu otstupleniiami* (Moscow: Sovetskii pisatel', 1981)
Luka, L., ed., *Putevoditel' po muzeiam el'blongskoi zemli* (Gdańsk: Krajowa Agencja Wydawnicza, 1978)
– ed., *Putevoditel' po muzeiam gdan'skoi zemli* (Gdańsk: Krajowa Agencja Wydawnicza, 1977)
Makarenko, Ia., *Korni i vetvi* (Moscow: Sovetskaia Rossiia, 1977)
Mukhin, A.I., Glushakov, P.I. and Grave, L.I., *Germaniia. Pol'sha. Finlandiia* (Moscow: Geografgiz, 1958)
Nechkina, M.V. and Leibengrub, P.S., *Istoriia SSSR: Uchebnik dlia 7-go klassa* (Moscow: Prosveshcheniie, 1982)
Ravich, N., *Po dorogam Evropy* (Moscow: Sovetskaia Rossiia, 1964)
Slavin, L., *Portrety i zapiski* (Moscow: Sovetskii pisatel', 1965)
Ter-Grigorian, A., *Vengerskii dnevnik* (Moscow: Izvestiia, 1975)
Timashev, A.K., *Ot Karpat do Baltiki: Zametki geografa o Pol'skoi Narodnoi Respublike* (Moscow: Geografgiz, 1959)

Diaries and Memoirs

Honchar, O., *Shchodennyky* (3 vols., edited by Valentyna Honchar, Kyiv: Veselka, 2002–4)
Kozlov, A.S., *Dzhaz, rok i mednye truby* (Moscow: EKSMO, 2005)
Michalewska, W., *Sercem i Czynem* (Warsaw: Książka i Wiedza, 1981)
Pliushch, L., *History's Carnival: A Dissident's Autobiography* (London: Collins, 1979)
Shelest, P., *Spravzhnii sud istorii shche poperedu. Spohady, shchodennyky, dokumenty, materialy* (edited by Iurii Shapoval, Kyiv: ADEF Ukraina, 2003)

Source collections

Bazhan, O. (Ed.). ""Praz"ka Vesna" u dokumentakh Galuzevoho derzhavnoho arkivu Sluzhby Bezpeky Ukrainy', *Z arkhiviv VUChK-GPU-NKVD-KGB* 1/2 (2008)
Fursenko, A.A., *Prezidium TsK KPSS 1954–1964: chernovye protokol'nye zapisi zasedanii, stenogrammy, postanovleniia: v 3 tomakh* (Moscow: ROSSPEN, 2003–2008)
Karner, S., Tomilina, N., Tschubarjan, A. et al. (eds.), *Prager Fruhling: Das internationale Krisenjahr 1968* (Cologne: Bohlau, 2008)

Raleigh, D.J. (Ed.). *Russia's Sputnik Generation: Soviet Baby Boomers Talk about Their Lives* (Bloomington: Indiana University Press, 2006)

Tron'ko, P.T., Bazhan, O.G., and Danyliuk, Iu.Z. (eds.), *Ternystym shliakhom do khramu: Oles' Honchar v suspil'no-politychnomu zhytti Ukrainy, 60–80i rr. XX st.* (Kyiv: Ridnyi krai, 1999)

Secondary Sources

Aksiutin, Iu. *Khrushchevskaia 'Ottepel' i obshchestvennye nastroeniia v SSSR v 1953–1964 gg.* Moscow: Rosspen, 2004.

Alekseeva, G.D. *Istoricheskaia nauka v Rossii. Ideologiia. Politika (60-80-e gody XX veka).* Moscow: Institut rossiiskoi istorii RAN, 2003.

Amar, T. "Sovietisation as a Civilising Mission in the West." In Balazs Apor et al. eds., *The Sovietisation of Eastern Europe: New Perspectives on the Postwar Period*. Washington, DC: New Academia Publishing, 2008.

– *The Paradox of Ukrainian Lviv: A Borderland City between Stalinists, Nazis, and Nationalists*. Ithaca: Cornell University Press, 2015.

Anderson, B. *Imagined Communities: Reflections on the Origins and Spread of Nationalism.* London: Verso, 2006.

Andrukhovych, I. "Kraina mrii." *Krytyka* 9–10 (2004): 2–3.

Applebaum, R. "A Test of Friendship: Soviet-Czechoslovak Tourism and the Prague Spring." In Anne Gorsuch and Diane Koenker, eds., *The Socialist Sixties: Crossing Borders in the Second World.* Bloomington: Indiana University Press, 2013.

Atamanenko, A. "Ukrains"ka zarubizhna istoriohrafiia druhoi polovyny XX stolittia u svitovomu istoriohrafichnomu protsesi: perspektyvy doslidzhennia," *Warszawskie zeszyty ukrainoznawcze*, 25–6 (2008): 104–22.

Azadovskii, K. and Egorov, B. "From Anti-Westernism to Anti-Semitism: Stalin and the Impact of the 'Anti-Cosmopolitan' Campaigns on Soviet Culture." *Journal of Cold War Studies* 4:1 (2002): 66–80.

Babiracki, P. "Imperial Heresies: Polish Students in the Soviet Union, 1948–57." *Ab Imperio: Studies of New Imperial History and Nationalism in the Post-Soviet Space* 4 (2007): 199–236.

– "Interfacing the Soviet Bloc: Recent Literature and New Paradigms." *Ab Imperio: Studies of New Imperial History and Nationalism in the post-Soviet Space* 4 (2011): 376–407.

– *Soviet Soft Power in Poland: Culture and the Making of Stalin's New Empire, 1943–1957*. Chapel Hill: The University of North Carolina Press, 2015.

Bailey, S.C.M., "A Biography in Motion: Chokan Valikhanov and His Travels in Central Eurasia." *Ab Imperio: Studies of New Imperial History and Nationalism in the Post-Soviet Space* 1 (2009): 165–90.

Baker, K.M. "Defining the Public Sphere in Eighteenth-Century France: Variations on a Theme by Habermas." In Craig Calhoun, ed., *Habermas and the Public Sphere: Conference Papers*. Cambridge, MA: MIT Press, 1992.
Baran, V. *Ukraina: Novitnia istoriia* (Lviv: Instytut ukrainoznavstva im. Kryp'iakevycha, 2003)
Baranovs'ka, I.M. "Ukrains'ke zhurnalistykoznavstvo 1950–1980x rr." *Visnyk Kyivs'koho natsional'noho universytetu imeni Tarasa Shevchenka* 13 (2005): 50–3.
Barnes, S. "In a Manner Befitting Soviet Citizens: An Uprising in the Post-Stalin Gulag." *Slavic Review* 64:4 (2005): 823–50.
Bartov, O. "Wartime Lies and Other Testimonies: Jewish-Christian Relationships in Buczacz, 1939–44." *East European Politics and Societies* 25:3 (2011): 486–511.
Basarab, J. *Pereiaslav 1654: A Historiographical Study*. Edmonton: University of Alberta Canadian Institute of Ukrainian Studies, 1982.
Bazhan, O. "Represyvni zakhody radians'koi vlady shchodo hromadian evreis'koi natsional'nosti v URSR (1960ti–1980ti rr.)." *Z arkhiviv VUChK-GPU-NKVD-KGB* 1/2 (2004): 112–20.
– "Suspil'ni nastroi v Ukraini u khodi chekhoslovats'koi kryzy 1968 roku za donesenniamy radians'kykh spetssluzhb." *Z arkhiviv VUChK-GPU-NKVD-KGB* 1/2 (2008): 37–53.
– "Zovnishn'o-politychni aktsii SRSR u 50–80-ti rr. ta ix vplyv na rozvytok opozytsiinoho rukhu v Ukraini." *Z arkhiviv VUChK-GPU-NKVD-KGB* 2/4 (2000): 515–25.
Beissinger, M. *Nationalist Mobilisation and the Collapse of the Soviet State*. Cambridge: Cambridge University Press, 2002.
Bemporad, E. *Becoming Soviet Jews: The Bolshevik Experiment in Minsk*. Bloomington: Indiana University Press, 2013.
Bialer, S. "The Solidarity and the Soviet Union." In Steve Reiquam, ed., *Solidarity and Poland: Impacts East and West*. Washington, DC: Wilson Center Press, 1988.
Bilinsky, Y. "The Incorporation of Western Ukraine and Its Impact on Politics and Society in Soviet Ukraine." In Roman Szporluk, ed., *The Influence of Eastern Europe and the Soviet West on the USSR*. New York: Praeger, 1976.
– *The Second Soviet Republic: The Ukraine after World War II*. New Brunswick: Rutgers University Press, 1964.
Birch, S. and Wilson, A. "Voting Stability, Political Gridlock: The 1998 Ukrainian Elections" *Europe-Asia Studies* 51:6 (1999): 1039–68.
Blauvelt, T. "Status Shift and Ethnic Mobilisation in the March 1956 Events in Georgia." *Europe-Asia Studies* 61:4 (2009): 651–68.
Blium, A. *A Self-Administered Poison: The System and Functions of Soviet Censorship*. Oxford: Oxford University Press, 2003.

Bloom, W. *Personal Identity, National Identity, and International Relations.* Cambridge: Cambridge University Press, 1990.

Bociurkiw, B. *The Ukrainian Greek Catholic Church and the Soviet State (1939–1950).* Edmonton: Canadian Institute of Ukrainian Studies Press, 1996.

Bolton, J., *Worlds of Dissent: Charter 77, the Plastic People of the Universe, and Czech Culture under Communism.* Cambridge, MA: Harvard University Press, 2012.

Bonin, P. "Failures Compared: The State Nationalisms of Non-National States in Socialist Europe." In E. Jahn, ed., *Nationalism in Late and Post-Communist Europe.* Vol. 1: *The Failed Nationalism of the Multinational and Partial National States.* Baden-Baden: Nomos, 2008.

Boobbyer, P. "Truth-Telling, Conscience and Dissent in Late Soviet Russia: Evidence From Oral Histories." *European History Quarterly* 30:4 (2000): 553–85.

Brandenberger, D.L. *National Bolshevism: Stalinist Mass Culture and the Formation of Modern Russian Identity, 1931–1956.* Cambridge, MA: Harvard University Press, 2002.

– "Simplistic, Pseudosocialist Racism: Debates over the Direction of Soviet Ideology within Stalin's Creative Intelligentsia, 1936–39." *Kritika: Explorations in Russian and Eurasian History* 13:2 (2012): 365–93.

Brandenberger, D.L. and Dubrovsky, A.M. "The People Need a Tsar: The Emergence of National Bolshevism as Stalinist Ideology, 1931–41." *Europe-Asia Studies* 50:5 (1998): 873–92.

Bren, P. *The Greengrocer and His TV: The Culture of Communism after the 1968 Prague Spring.* Ithaca: Cornell University Press, 2010.

Breuilly, J. Introduction to *Nations and Nationalism* by E. Gellner, xiii–xlii. Ithaca: Cornell University Press, 2006.

– *Nationalism and the State.* Manchester: Manchester University Press, 1993.

Brooks, J. *Thank You, Comrade Stalin! Soviet Public Culture from Revolution to Cold War.* Princeton: Princeton University Press, 1999.

–"Socialist Realism in Pravda: Read All About It!" *Slavic Review* 53:4 (1994): 973–91.

Brown, K. *A Biography of no Place: From Ethnic Borderland to Soviet Heartland.* Cambridge, MA: Harvard University Press, 2004.

– "Gridded Lives: Why Kazakhstan and Montana are Nearly the Same Place." *The American Historical Review* 106:1 (2001): 17–48.

– *Plutopia: Nuclear Families, Atomic Cities, and the Great Soviet and American Plutonium Disasters.* Oxford: Oxford University Press, 2013.

– "Securing the Nuclear Nation." *Nationalities Papers* 43:1 (2015): 8–26.

Brubaker, R. *Nationalism Reframed: Nationhood and the National Question in the New Europe.* Cambridge, Cambridge University Press, 1996.

Brudny, Y. *Reinventing Russia: Russian Nationalism and the Soviet State, 1953–1991.* Cambridge, MA: Harvard University Press, 1998.

Budurowycz, B. "Poland and the Ukrainian Problem, 1921–1939." *Canadian Slavonic Papers* 25:4 (1983): 473–500.

Bushnell, J. "The 'New Soviet Man' Turns Pessimist." In S.F. Cohen, A. Rabinowitch and R. Sharlet, eds., *The Soviet Union since Stalin*, 179–99. Bloomington: Indiana University Press, 1980.

Calhoun, C. "Introduction: Habermas and the Public Sphere." In Craig Calhoun, ed., *Habermas and the Public Sphere: Conference Papers*. Cambridge, MA: MIT Press, 1992.

Chernyshova, N. *Soviet Consumer Culture in the Brezhnev Era*. London: Routledge, 2013.

Chushak, Kh. "Shliakhy vrehuliuvannia problemy pol's'ko-ukrains'koho kordonu v publikatsiiakh pol's'kykh opozytsioneriv (1976–1989)." In M. Lytvyn, ed., *Ukraina-Pol'shcha: istorychna spadshchyna i suspil'na svidomist,'* 3–4 (2010–11): 195–211.

Clark, K. *The Soviet Novel: History as Ritual.* Bloomington: Indiana University Press, 2000.

Cohen, S. "The Friends and Foes of Change. Reformism and Conservatism in the Soviet Union." *Slavic Review* 38:2 (1979): 187–202.

– "The Stalin Question since Stalin." In Stephen Cohen, ed., *Rethinking the Soviet Experience: Politics and History since 1917*. New York: Oxford University Press, 1985.

Cook, L. *The Soviet Social Contract and Why It Failed: Welfare Policy and Workers' Politics from Brezhnev to Yeltsin*. Cambridge, MA: Harvard University Press, 1993.

Corner, P. Introduction to *Popular Opinion in Totalitarian Regimes: Fascism, Nazism, Communism*, edited by Paul Corner, 1–20. Oxford: Oxford University Press, 2009.

Costanzo, S. "Amateur Theatres and Amateur Publics in the Russian Republic, 1958–71." *The Slavonic and East European Review* 86:2 (2008): 372–94.

Danyliuk, Iu. Z. "Vidrodzhuiuchy storinky mynuloho." In O.G. Bazhan et al., eds., *Zberezhemo tuiu slavu: hromads'kyi rukh za uvichnennia istorii ukrains'koho kozatstva w druhii polovyni 50x–80x rr. XX st*, 1–18. Kyiv: Ridnyi krai, 1997.

David-Fox, M. *Showcasing the Great Experiment: Cultural Diplomacy and Western Visitors to the Soviet Union, 1921–1941.* New York: Oxford University Press, 2011.

Davies, S. *Popular Opinion in Stalin's Russia: Terror, Propaganda, and Dissent, 1934–1941.* Cambridge: Cambridge University Press, 1997.

– "'Us Against Them': Social Identity in Soviet Russia, 1934–41." In Sheila Fitzpatrick, ed., *Stalinism: New Directions*. London: Routledge, 2000.

Dmytruk, V. "Nelehal'na informatsiina merezha v Chekhoslovachchyni ta ii vplyv na formuvannia opozytsiinykh nastroiv v Ukraini (kinets 60x – pochatok 70-x rr.)." In *Z arkhiviv VUChK-GPU-NKVD-KGB* 2/4 (2000): 525–32.

– "'Praz'ka vesna' i Ukraina." In *Z arkhiviv VUChK-GPU-NKVD-KGB* 1/2 (2008): 7–37.

– *Ukraina ne movchala: Reaktsiia ukrains'koho suspil'stva na podii 1968 roku v Chekhoslovachchyni.* Kyiv: Instytut Istorii Ukrainy NAN Ukrainy, 2004.

Dobson, M., *Khrushchev's Cold Summer: Gulag Returnees, Crime, and the Fate of Reform after Stalin.* Ithaca: Cornell University Press, 2009.

– "'Show the Bandit-Enemies No Mercy!' Amnesty, Criminality and Public Response in 1953." In Polly Jones, ed., *The Dilemmas of De-Stalinisation: Negotiating Cultural and Social Change in the Khrushchev Era.* London: Routledge, 2005.

Drachman, E.R. *Challenging the Kremlin: The Soviet Jewish Movement for Freedom, 1967–1990.* New York: Paragon House, 1991.

Drohobysky, M. "The Lion Society: Profile of a Ukrainian Patriotic 'Informal' Group." Radio Liberty research report, RL 325/88, 18 July 1988. Held at School of Slavonic and East European Studies, London, Collection IND11 (Materials relating to the Ukrainian dissident movement).

Dudzinskaia, E.A. *Mezhdunarodnye nauchnye sviazi sovetskikh istorikov.* Moscow: Nauka 1978.

Dvornichenko, V.V. *Turizm v SSSR i deiatel'nost' sovetskikh profsoiuzov po ego razvitiiu (1917–1984 gg).* Moscow: Vysshaia shkola profsoiuznogo dvizheniia VTsSPS im. N.M. Shvernika, 1985.

Dunham, V. *In Stalin's Time: Middleclass Values in Soviet Fiction.* Durham: Duke University Press 1990.

Ebon, M. *The Soviet Propaganda Machine.* New York: McGraw-Hill, 1986.

Edele, M. *Soviet Veterans of the Second World War: A Popular Movement in an Authoritarian Society, 1941–1991.* Oxford: Oxford University Press, 2008.

– "Strange Young Men in Stalin's Moscow: The Birth and Life of the Stiliagi, 1945–1953." *Jahrbucher fur Geschichte Osteuropas* 50:1 (2002): 37–61.

Edgar, A. "Bolshevism, Patriarchy, and the Nation: The Soviet 'Emancipation' of Muslim Women in Pan-Islamic Perspective." *Slavic Review* 65:2 (2006): 252–72.

– "Marriage, Modernity, and the 'Friendship of Nations': Interethnic Intimacy in Postwar Central Asia in Comparative Perspective." *Central Asian Survey* 26:4 (2007): 581–99.

Ekiert, G. "Rebellious Poles: Political Crises and Popular Protest under State Socialism, 1945–89." *East European Politics and Societies* 11:2 (1997): 299–338.

– *The State against Society: Political Crises and Their Aftermath in East Central Europe*. Princeton: Princeton University Press, 1996.

Epstein, D. "Soviet Patriotism: 1985–1991." In E. Jahn, ed., *Nationalism in Late and Post-Communist Europe*. Vol. 1: *The Failed Nationalism of the Multinational and Partial National States*, 201–23. Baden-Baden: Nomos, 2008.

Farmer, K. *Ukrainian Nationalism in the Post-Stalin Era: Myth, Symbols, and Ideology in Soviet Nationalities Policy*. The Hague: Hijhoff, 1980.

Fateev, A. *Obraz vraga v sovetskoi propagande: 1945–1954*. Moscow: RAN, 1999.

Feher, F. "Eastern Europe's Long Revolution against Yalta." *East European Politics and Societies* 2:1 (1987): 1–34.

Field, D. "Irreconcilable Differences: Divorce and Conceptions of Private Life in the Khrushchev Era." *Russian Review* 57:4 (1998): 599–613.

Filtzer, D. "From Mobilised to Free Labour: De-Stalinisation and the Changing Legal Status of Workers." In Polly Jones, ed., *The Dilemmas of De-Stalinisation: Negotiating Cultural and Social Change in the Khrushchev Era*. London: Routledge, 2005.

– *Soviet Workers and De-Stalinisation: The Consolidation of the Modern System of Soviet Production Relations, 1953–1964*. Cambridge: Cambridge University Press, 1992.

Fitzpatrick, S. "Ascribing Class: The Construction of Social Identity in Soviet Russia." *Journal of Modern History* 65:4 (1993): 745–70.

– *Everyday Stalinism: Ordinary Life in Extraordinary Times, Soviet Russia in the 1930s*. New York: Oxford University Press, 1999.

– "How the Mice Buried the Cat: Scenes from the Great Purges of 1937 in the Russian Provinces." *The Russian Review* 52:3 (1993): 299–320.

– "Popular Opinion in Russia under Pre-war Stalinism." In Paul Corner, ed., *Popular Opinion in Totalitarian Regimes: Fascism, Nazism, Communism*. Oxford: Oxford University Press, 2009.

– "Popular Sedition in the Post-Stalin Soviet Union." In V.A. Kozlov, S. Fitzpatrick, and S.V. Mironenko, eds., *Sedition: Everyday Resistance in the Soviet Union under Khrushchev and Brezhnev*. New Haven: Yale University Press, 2011.

– "Postwar Soviet Society: 'The Return to Normalcy,' 1945–1953." In Susan J. Linz, ed., *The Impact of World War II on the Soviet Union*. Totowa, New Jersey: Rowman and Allanheld, 1985.

– "Stalin and the Making of a New Elite, 1928–1939." *Slavic Review* 38:3 (1979): 377–402.

– *Tear Off the Masks! Identity and Imposture in Twentieth Century Russia*. Princeton: Princeton University Press, 2005.

Ford, C. *Creating the Nation in Provincial France: Religion and Political Identity in Brittany*. Princeton: Princeton University Press, 1993.

Frankel, E. *Novyi Mir: A Case Study in the Politics of Literature 1952–1958*. Cambridge: Cambridge University Press, 1981.

Frunchak, S. "Commemorating the Future in Postwar Chernivtsi." *East European Politics and Societies* 24:3 (2010): 435–63.

Furst, J. "The Arrival of Spring? Changes and Continuities in Soviet Youth Culture and Policy between Stalin and Khrushchev." In Polly Jones, ed., *The Dilemmas of De-Stalinisation: Negotiating Cultural and Social Change in the Khrushchev Era*. London: Routledge, 2006.

– "Prisoners of the Soviet Self? Political Youth Opposition in Late Stalinism." *Europe-Asia Studies* 54:3 (2002): 353–75.

Furst, J., P. Jones and S. Morrissey. "The Relaunch of the Soviet Project, 1945–1964." *The Slavonic and East European Review* 86:2 (2008): 201–7.

Garton-Ash, T. *The Polish Revolution: Solidarity*. New Haven: Yale University Press, 2002.

Gellner, E. *Nations and Nationalism*. Oxford: Blackwell, 2006.

Gitelman, Z. *Bespokoinyi vek: Evrei Rossii i Sovetskogo Soiuza s 1881 g. do nashikh dnei*. Moscow: Novoe literaturnoe obozrenie, 2008.

– "The Diffusion of Political Innovation: From East Europe to the Soviet Union." In Roman Szporluk, ed., *The Influence of Eastern Europe and the Soviet West on the USSR*. New York: Praeger, 1976.

– "Ethnopolitics and the Future of the Former Soviet Union." In Zvi Gitelman, ed., *The Politics of Nationality and the Erosion of the USSR: Selected Papers from the Fourth World Congress for Soviet and East European Studies, Harrogate, 1990*. Basingstoke: Macmillan, 1992.

Goff, K. "Why Not Love Our Language and Our Culture: National Rights and Citizenship in Khrushchev's Soviet Union." *Nationalities Papers* 43:1 (2015): 27–44.

Goode, L. *Jürgen Habermas: Democracy and the Public Sphere*. London: Pluto Press, 2005.

Gorenburg, D. "Soviet Nationalities Policy and Assimilation." In Dominique Arel and Blair A. Ruble, eds., *Rebounding Identities: The Politics of Identity in Russia and Ukraine*. Washington, DC: Woodrow Wilson Center Press, 2006.

Gorsuch, A.E. *All This Is Your World: Soviet Tourism at Home and Abroad after Stalin*. Oxford: Oxford University Press, 2011.

– "'There's No Place Like Home': Soviet Tourism in Late Stalinism." *Slavic Review* 62:4 (2003): 760–85.

– "Time Travellers: Soviet Tourists to Eastern Europe." In A.E. Gorsuch and D.P. Koenker, eds., *Turizm: The Russian and East European Tourist under Capitalism and Socialism*. Ithaca: Cornell University Press, 2006.

Gorsuch, A.E. and D.P. Koenker. "Introduction: The Socialist 1960s in Global Perspective." In Anne Gorsuch and Diane Koenker, eds., *The Socialist Sixties: Crossing Borders in the Second World*. Bloomington: Indiana University Press, 2013.

Granville, J. "'Ask for Bread, not Peace': Reactions of Romanian Workers and Peasants to the Hungarian Revolution of 1956." *East European Politics and Societies* 24:4 (2010): 543–71.

– "Poland and Hungary, 1956: A Comparative Essay Based on New Archival Findings." *The Australian Journal of Politics and History* 48:3 (2002): 369–95.

Gross, J. *Revolution from Abroad: The Soviet Conquest of Poland's Western Ukraine and Western Belorussia*. Princeton: Princeton University Press, 2002.

Grunberg, K. and B. Sprengel. *Trudne sąsiedztwo: Stosunki polsko-ukraińskie w X–XX wieku*. Warsaw: Książka i Wiedza, 2005.

Habermas, J. "Further Reflections on the Public Sphere." In Craig Calhoun, ed., *Habermas and the Public Sphere: Conference Papers*. Cambridge, MA: MIT Press, 1992.

– *The Structural Transformation of the Public Sphere: An Inquiry into a Category of Bourgeois Society*. Cambridge, MA: MIT Press, 1989.

Haga, L.P. "Coming to Terms with Europe: Konstantin Simonov and Oles' Honchar's Literary Conquest of East Central Europe at the End of World War II." In Patryk Babiracki and Austin Jersild, ed., *Socialist Internationalism in the Cold War: Exploring the Second World*. New York: Palgrave Macmillan, 2016.

Halfin, I. *From Darkness to Light: Class, Consciousness, and Salvation in Revolutionary Russia*. Pittsburgh: University of Pittsburg Press, 2000.

Haynes, R. "Work Camps, Commerce and the Education of the 'New Man' in the Romanian Legionary Movement." *The Historical Journal* 51:4 (2008): 943–67.

Hayward, M. "Introduction." In Leopold Labedz and Max Hayward, eds., *On Trial: The Case of Siniavskii-Tertz and Daniel-Arzhak*. London: Collins and Harvill Press, 1967.

Hazan, B. *Soviet Impregnational Propaganda*. Ann Arbor: Ardis, 1982.

Hellbeck, J. "Fashioning the Stalinist Soul." In S. Fitzpatrick, ed., *Stalinism: New Directions*. London: Routledge, 2000.

– *Revolution on My Mind: Writing a Diary under Stalin*. Cambridge, MA: Harvard University Press, 2006.

– "Speaking Out: Languages of Affirmation and Dissent in Stalinist Russia." In Michael David-Fox, Peter Holquist and Marshall Poe, eds., *The Resistance Debate in Russian and Soviet History*. Bloomington: Slavica Publishers, 2003.

Hessler, J. "Cultured Trade: The Stalinist Turn to Consumerism." In S. Fitzpatrick, ed., *Stalinism: New Directions*. London: Routledge, 2000.

Hillis, F. *Children of Rus': Right-Bank Ukraine and the Invention of a Russian Nation*. Ithaca: Cornell University Press, 2013.

Himka, J.P. "The Greek Catholic Church and Nation-Building in Galicia, 1772–1918." *Harvard Ukrainian Studies* 8:3–4 (1984): 426–52.

Hirsch, F. *Empire of Nations: Ethnographic Knowledge and the Making of the Soviet Union*. Ithaca: Cornell University Press, 2005.

– "The Soviet Union as a Work-in-Progress: Ethnographers and the Category of Nationality in the 1926, 1937, and 1939 Censuses." *Slavic Review* 56:2 (1997): 251–78.

– "Towards an Empire of Nations: Border-Making and the Formation of Soviet National Identities." *Russian Review* 59:2 (2000): 201–26.

Hixson, W. *Parting the Curtain: Propaganda, Culture, and the Cold War, 1945–1961*. New York: St. Martin's, 1997.

Hoffmann, D. "Was There a Great Retreat from Soviet Socialism?" *Kritika: Explorations in Russian and Eurasian History* 5:4 (2004): 651–74.

Hooper, C. "Terror of Intimacy: Family Politics in the 1930s Soviet Union." In C. Kiaer and E. Naiman, eds., *Everyday Life in Early Soviet Russia: Taking the Revolution Inside*. Bloomington: Indiana University Press, 2006.

– "What Can and Cannot Be Said: Between the Stalinist Past and New Soviet Future." *The Slavonic and East European Review* 86:2 (2008): 306–27.

Hnatiuk, O. *Pożegnanie z imperium: ukraińskie dyskusje o tożsamości*. Lublin: Wydawnictwo Uniwersytetu Marii Curie-Skłodowskiej, 2003.

Hodnett, G. and P. Potichnyj. *The Ukraine and the Czechoslovak Crisis*. Canberra: Australian National University, 1970.

Hosking, G. *Beyond Socialist Realism: Soviet Fiction since Ivan Denisovich*. London: Granada Publishing, 1980.

– *A History of the Soviet Union*. London: Fontana, 1990.

– *Rulers and Victims: The Russians in the Soviet Union*. Cambridge, MA: Belknap, 2006.

Hrycak, J. *Prorok we własnym kraju: Iwan Franko i jego Ukraina (1856–1886)*. Warsaw: Wydawnictwo Krytyki Politycznej, 2011.

Iakubets', O.A. "V. Shcherbyts'kyi ta ideolohiia: do pytannia shchodo prychyn 'Malanchukivshchyny.'" *Ukrain'skyi istorychnyi zhurnal* 5 (2014): 107–25.

Ivanova, K.S., Iu. V. Pomortseva. and E.A. Orlianskii. "Istoricheskoe znachenie pravozashchitnogo dvizheniia v SSSR." *Sibirskii torgovo-ekonomicheskii zhurnal* 3 (2011): 25–30.

Jersild, A. "The Soviet State as Imperial Scavenger: 'Catch Up and Surpass' in the Transnational Socialist Bloc, 1950-60." *American Historical Review*, 116:1 (2011): 109–32.

Johnston, T. "Subversive Tales? War rumours in the Soviet Union, 1945–47." In J. Furst, ed., *Late Stalinist Russia: Society between reconstruction and reinvention*. London: Routledge, 2006.

Jones, P. "From the Secret Speech to the Burial of Stalin: Real and Ideal Responses to De-Stalinisation." In Polly Jones, ed., *The Dilemmas of De-Stalinisation: Negotiating Cultural and Social Change in the Khrushchev Era*. London: Routledge, 2005.

– "Introduction: The Dilemmas of de-Stalinisation." In Polly Jones, ed., *The Dilemmas of De-Stalinisation: Negotiating Cultural and Social Change in the Khrushchev Era*. London: Routledge, 2005.

– *Myth, Memory, and Trauma: Rethinking the Stalinist Past in the Soviet Union, 1953–70*. New Haven: Yale University Press, 2013.

Kaiser, R. *The Geography of Nationalism in Russia and the USSR*. Princeton: Princeton University Press, 1994.

Kalinovsky, A. *A Long Goodbye: The Soviet Withdrawal from Afghanistan*. Cambridge, MA: Harvard University Press, 2011.

Kas'ianov, H., *Nezhodni: Ukrains'ka intelihentsiia v rusi oporu 1960x–80x rokiv*. Kyiv: Lybid, 1995.

Keck-Szajbel, M. "Show Around the Bloc: Trader Tourism and Its Discontents on the East German-Polish Border." In Paulina Bren and Mary Neuberger, eds., *Communism Unwrapped*. New York: Oxford University Press, 2012.

Kemp, W. *Nationalism and Communism in Eastern Europe and the Soviet Union: A Basic Contradiction?* Basingstoke: Macmillan, 1999.

Kenez, P. *The Birth of the Propaganda State: Soviet Methods of Mass Mobilisation, 1917–1929*. Cambridge: Cambridge University Press, 1985.

Kirasirova, M. "Sons of Muslims in Moscow: Soviet Central Asian Mediators to the Foreign East, 1955–1962." *Ab Imperio: Studies of New Imperial History and Nationalism in the Post-Soviet Space* 4 (2011): 106–32.

Koenker, D.P. "The Proletarian Tourist in the 1930s: Between Mass Excursion and Mass Escape." In A.E. Gorsuch and D.P. Koenker, eds., *Turizm: the Russian and East European Tourist under Capitalism and Socialism*. Ithaca: Cornell University Press, 2006.

– "Travel to Work, Travel to Play: on Russian Tourism, Travel, and Leisure." *Slavic Review* 62:4 (2003): 657–65.

Kohut, Z. *Rosiis'kyi tsentralizm i ukrains'ka avtonomiia: Likvidatsiia Het'manshchyny, 1760–1830*. Kyiv: Osnovy, 1996.

Kolankiewicz, G. "The Polish Question: Andropov's Answer?" In Leonard Schapiro and Joseph Godson, eds., *The Soviet Worker: From Lenin to Andropov*. London: Macmillan, 1984.

Komkov, G.D., B.V. Levshin and L.K. Semenov. *Akademiia Nauk SSSR: Kratkii istoricheskii ocherk, Tom Vtoroi, 1917–1976*. Moscow: Nauka, 1977.

Kotkin, S. *Armageddon Averted: The Soviet Collapse, 1970–2000*. Oxford: Oxford University Press, 2008.

– *Magnetic Mountain: Stalinism as a Civilisation*. Berkeley: University of California Press, 1995.
– "Mongol Commonwealth? Exchange and Governance across the Post-Mongol Space." *Kritika: Explorations in Russian and Eurasian History* 8:3 (2007): 487–531.
– "Modern Times: The Soviet Union and the Interwar Conjuncture." *Kritika: Explorations in Russian and Eurasian History* 2:1 (2001): 111–64.
– Review of *Popular Opinion in Stalin's Russia: Terror, Propaganda, and Dissent, 1934–41*, by Sarah Davies, *Europe-Asia Studies* 50:4 (1998): 739–42.
Kotsonis, Y. *States of Obligation: Taxes and Citizenship in the Russian Empire and Early Soviet Republic*. Toronto: University of Toronto Press, 2014.
Kozlov, D. "Naming the Social Evil: The Readers of *Novyi Mir* and Vladimir Dudintsev's *Not by Bread Alone*, 1956–59 and Beyond." In Polly Jones, ed., *The Dilemmas of De-Stalinisation: Negotiating Cultural and Social Change in the Khrushchev Era*. London: Routledge, 2005.
– *The Readers of Novyi Mir: Coming to Terms with the Stalinist Past*. Cambridge, MA: Harvard University Press 2013.
Kozlov, V.A. *Mass Uprisings in the USSR: Protest and Rebellion in the post-Stalin Years*. Armonk, NY: M.E. Sharp, 2002.
– "The Meaning of Sedition." In V.A. Kozlov, S. Fitzpatrick, and S.V. Mironenko, eds., *Sedition: Everyday Resistance in the Soviet Union under Khrushchev and Brezhnev*. New Haven: Yale University Press, 2011.
Koznarsky, T. "Ukrainian Literary Scholarship in Ukraine since Independence." *Canadian Slavonic Papers* 54:1–2 (2012): 433–60.
Kozovoi, A. "Eye to Eye with the 'Main Enemy': Soviet Youth Travel to the United States." *Ab Imperio: Studies of New Imperial History and Nationalism in the Post-Soviet Space* 2 (2011): 221–37.
Kramer, M., "The Collapse of East European Communism and the Repercussions within the Soviet Union: Part One." *Journal of Cold War Studies* 5:4 (2003): 178–256.
– "The Collapse of East European Communism and the Repercussions within the Soviet Union: Part Two." *Journal of Cold War Studies* 6:4 (2004): 3–64.
– "The Collapse of East European Communism and the Repercussions within the Soviet Union: Part Three." *Journal of Cold War Studies* 7:1 (2005): 3–96.
– "The Czechoslovak Crisis and the Brezhnev Doctrine." In Carol Fink, Philipp Gassert, and Detlef Junker, eds., *1968: The World Transformed*. Cambridge: Cambridge University Press, 1998.
– "The Early post-Stalin Succession Struggle and Upheavals in East-Central Europe: Internal-External Linkages in Soviet Policy-Making: Part Three." *Journal of Cold War Studies* 1:3 (1999): 3–55.

– "Soviet Policy during the Polish and Hungarian Crises of 1956: Reassessments and New Findings." *Journal of Contemporary History* 33:2 (1998): 163–214.

– "Spill-Over from the Prague Spring – a KGB Report." *Cold War International History Project Bulletin* 4 (1994): 67–8.

Krylova, A. "Identity, Agency, and the 'First Soviet Generation.'" In S. Lovell, ed., *Generations in Twentieth-Century Europe*. Basingstoke: Palgrave Macmillan, 2007.

– "Soviet Modernity: Stephen Kotkin and the Bolshevik Predicament." *Contemporary European History* 23:2 (2014): 167–92.

Kubik, J. "Who Done It? Workers, Intellectuals or Someone Else? Controversy over Solidarity's Origins and Social Composition." *Theory and Society* 23:3 (1994): 441–66.

Kudaibergenova, D. "'Imagining Community' in Soviet Kazakhstan. An Historical Analysis of Narrative on Nationalism in Kazakh-Soviet Literature." *Nationalities Papers* 41:5 (2013): 839–54.

Kula, M. "Poland: The Silence of Those Deprived of Voice." In Paul Corner, ed., *Popular Opinion in Totalitarian Regimes: Fascism, Nazism, Communism*. Oxford: Oxford University Press, 2009.

Kupczak, J. "Pojednanie polsko-ukraińskie na tle politycznej wizji Jerzego Giedroycia." In T. Zaretskaia, ed., *Rola Kultury paryskiej w kształtowaniu ukraińsko-polskiego zrozumienia wzajemnego*. Kyiv: Vydavnytstvo ukrains'koho fitosotsiolohichnoho tsentru, 2002.

Kuromiya, H. *Freedom and Terror in the Donbas: A Ukrainian-Russian Borderland, 1870s–1990s*. Cambridge: Cambridge University Press, 1998.

Kuzio, T. "From Kuchma to Yushchenko: Ukraine's 2004 Presidential Elections and the Orange Revolution." *Problems of Post-Communism* 52:2 (2005): 29–44.

– "The Polish Opposition and the Ukrainian Question." *Journal of Ukrainian Studies* 12:2 (1987): 26–58.

Kuzio, T. and A. Wilson. *Ukraine: Perestroika to Independence*. Basingstoke: Macmillan, 1999.

Lapierre, B. "Making Hooliganism on a Mass Scale: The Campaign Against Petty Hooliganism in the Soviet Union, 1956–1964." *Cahiers du monde russe* 47:1–2 (2006): 349–75.

– "Private Matters or Public Crimes: The Rise of Domestic Hooliganism in the Soviet Union, 1939–1966." In Lewis H. Siegelbaum, ed., *Borders of Socialism: Private Spheres of Soviet Russia*. Basingstoke: Palgrave Macmillan, 2006.

Lehmann, M. "Local Reinvention of the Soviet Project: Nation and Socialism in the Republic of Armenia." *Jahrbucher fur Geschichte Osteuropas* 59:4 (2011): 481–508.

Lewin, M. *The Soviet Century*. London: Verso, 2005.
Lewytzkyj, B. "Political and Cultural Cooperation between the People's Republic of Poland and the Ukrainian Soviet Socialist Republic." In P.J. Potichnyj, ed., *Poland and Ukraine: Past and Present*. Edmonton: Canadian Institute of Ukrainian Studies, 1980.
– *Politics and Society in Soviet Ukraine, 1953–1980*. Edmonton: Canadian Institute of Ukrainian Studies, 1984.
Liebich, A. and O. Myshlovska. "Bandera: Memorialization and Commemoration." *Nationalities Papers* 42:5 (2014): 750–70.
Lindenberger, T. "Tacit Minimal Consensus: The Always Precarious East German Dictatorship." In Paul Corner, ed., *Popular Opinion in Totalitarian Regimes: Fascism, Nazism, Communism*. Oxford: Oxford University Press, 2009.
Lipowski, M. "Rewindykacja społeczeństwa." In T. Zaretskaia, ed., *Rola Kultury paryskiej w kształtowaniu ukrainsko-polskiego zrozumienia wzajemnego*. Kyiv: Vydavnytstvo ukrains'koho fitosotsiolohichnoho tsentru, 2002.
Litvin, A.L. *Writing History in Twentieth-Century Russia: A View from Within*. Basingstoke: Palgrave, 2001.
Livschiz, A. "De-Stalinising Soviet Childhood: The Quest for Moral Rebirth, 1953–58." In Polly Jones, ed., *The Dilemmas of De-Stalinisation: Negotiating Cultural and Social Change in the Khrushchev Era*. London: Routledge, 2005.
Loewenstein, K. "Re-Emergence of Public Opinion in the Soviet Union: Khrushchev and Responses to the Secret Speech." *Europe-Asia Studies* 58:8 (2006): 1329–45.
Loiko, L.V. *Ispytanie na prochnost'. Obshchestvo pol'sko-sovetskoi druzhby: stanovlenie, razvitie*. Minsk: Belarus, 1989.
Lovell, S. "In Search of an Ending: *Seventeen Moments* and the Seventies." In Anne Gorsuch and Diane Koenker, eds., *The Socialist Sixties: Crossing Borders in the Second World*. Bloomington: Indiana University Press, 2013.
– *The Shadow of War: Russia and the USSR, 1941 to the Present*. Oxford: Wiley-Blackwell, 2010.
– "Soviet Russia's Older Generations." In S. Lovell, ed., *Generations in Twentieth-Century Europe*. Basingstoke: Palgrave Macmillan, 2007.
Lytvyn, V. et al., eds., *Ukraina: politychna istoriia, XX-pochatok XXI stolittia*. Kyiv: Parlaments'ke vydavnictvo, 2007.
Machcewicz, P. *Polski rok 1956*. Warsaw: Mówią wieki, 1993.
Magnusdottir, R. "'Be Careful in America, Premier Khrushchev!' Soviet Perceptions of Peaceful Coexistence with the United States in 1959." *Cahiers du Monde Russe* 47:1–2 (2006): 109–30.
Magosci, P. *The Roots of Ukrainian Nationalism: Galicia as Ukraine's Piedmont*. Toronto: University of Toronto Press, 2002.

Markus, V. "Religion and Nationality: The Uniates of Ukraine." In Bohdan R. Bociurkiw and John W. Strong, eds., *Religion and Atheism in the USSR and Eastern Europe*. London: Macmillan 1975.

Markwick, R.D. *Rewriting History in Soviet Russia: The Politics of Revisionist Historiography, 1956–1974*. Basingstoke: Palgrave, 2001.

Marples, D.R. *Heroes and Villains: Creating National History in Contemporary Ukraine*. Budapest: Central European University Press, 2007.

Martin, T. *The Affirmative Action Empire: Nations and Nationalism in the Soviet Union, 1923–1939*. Ithaca: Cornell University Press, 2001.

Mason, D. "Solidarity as a New Social Movement." *Political Science Quarterly* 104:1 (1989): 41–58.

Matthews, M. *Education in the Soviet Union: Policies and Institutions since Stalin*. London: Routledge, 2012.

McDermott, K. "Archives, Power and the 'Cultural Turn': Reflections on Stalin and Stalinism." *Totalitarian Movements and Political Religions* 5:1 (2004): 5–24.

– "A 'Polyphony of Voices'? Czech Popular Opinion and the Slánský Affair." *Slavic Review* 67:4 (2008): 840–65.

– "Popular Resistance in Communist Czechoslovakia: The Plzeň Uprising, June 1953." *Contemporary European History* 19:4 (2010): 287–307.

– "Stalinism 'From Below'? Social Preconditions of and Popular Responses to the Great Terror." *Totalitarian Movements and Political Religions* 8:3 (2007): 609–22.

McKenna, K. *All the Views Fit to Print: Changing Images of the U.S. in* Pravda *Political Cartoons, 1917–1991*. New York: Peter Lang, 1991.

McLellan, J. "'Even under Socialism, We Don't Want to Do without Love': East German Erotica." In David Crowley and Susan Reid, eds., *Pleasures in Socialism: Leisure and Luxury in the Eastern Bloc*. Evanston, IL: Northwestern University Press, 2010.

– "State Socialist Bodies: East German Nudism from Ban to Boom." *Journal of Modern History* 79:1 (2007): 48–79.

McMichael, P. '"After All, You're a Rock and Roll Star (at Least, That's What They Say)': Roksi and the Creation of the Soviet Rock Musician." *Slavonic and East European Review* 83:4 (2005): 664–84.

Mendelson, S.E. *Changing Course: Ideas, Politics, and the Soviet Withdrawal from Afghanistan*. Princeton: Princeton University Press, 1998.

Mick, C. "Incompatible Experiences: Poles, Ukrainians and Jews in Lviv under Soviet and German Occupation, 1939–44." *Journal of Contemporary History* 46:2 (2011): 336–63.

Milewicz, P. "National Identification in Pre-Industrial Communities: Peasant Participation in the November Uprising in the Kingdom of Poland, 1830–1831." *Jahrbücher für Geschichte Osteuropas* 58:3 (2010): 321–52.

Millar, J., "The Little Deal: Brezhnev's Contribution to Acquisitive Socialism." *Slavic Review* 44:4 (1985): 694–706.

Mitrokhin, N. *Russkaia partiia: Dvizhenie russkikh natsionalistov v SSSR 1953–1985*. Moscow: Novoe literaturnoe obozrenie, 2003.

Motyl, A. *Dilemmas of Independence: Ukraine after Totalitarianism*. New York: Council on Foreign Relations Press, 1993.

– "State, Nation and Elites in Independent Ukraine." In T. Kuzio, ed., *Contemporary Ukraine: Dynamics of Post-Soviet Transformation*. Armonk, NY: M.E. Sharpe, 1998.

Motyka, G. "Polsko-ukraińskie stosunki w XX wieku w ocenie ukraińskiej historiografii emigracyjnej." *Warszawskie zeszyty ukrainoznawcze* 25–6 (2008): 123–35.

Nahaylo, B. *The Ukrainian Resurgence*. London: Hurst and Company, 1999.

Neuberger, J. *Hooliganism: Crime, Culture and Power in St. Petersburg, 1900–1914*. Berkeley: University of California Press, 1993.

Neumann, I. "Russia as Central Europe's Constituting Other." *East European Politics and Societies* 7:2 (1993): 349–69.

O'Keefe, B. *New Soviet Gypsies: Nationality, Performance, and Selfhood in the Early Soviet Union*. Toronto: University of Toronto Press, 2013.

Ost, D. *Solidarity and the Politics of Anti-Politics: Opposition and Reform in Poland since 1968*. Philadelphia: Temple University Press, 1990.

Parthé, K., *Russian Village Prose: The Radiant Past*. Princeton: Princeton University Press, 1992.

Pastor, P. "Official Nationalism." In Gerasimos Augustinos, ed., *The National Idea in Eastern Europe: The Politics of Ethnic and Civic Community*. Lexington, MA: D.C. Heath, 1996.

Patterson, P.H. *Bought and Sold: Living and Losing the Good Life in Socialist Yugoslavia*. Ithaca: Cornell University Press, 2011.

Pauly, M., *Breaking the Tounge: Language, Education, and Power in Soviet Ukraine, 1923–1934*. Toronto: University of Toronto Press, 2014.

– "Soviet Polonophobia and the Formulation of Nationalities Policy in the Ukrainian SSR 1927–1934." In David Ransel and Bożena Shallcross, eds., *Polish Encounters, Russian Identity*. Bloomington: Indiana University Press, 2005.

Peteri, G. "The Occident Within – or the Drive for Exceptionalism and Modernity." *Kritika: Explorations in Russian and Eurasian History* 9:4 (2008): 929–38.

Petrescu, D. "Building the Nation, Instrumentalising Nationalism: Revisiting Romanian National Communism, 1956–89." *Nationalities Papers* 37:4 (2009): 523–44.

Plamper, J., "Beyond Binaries: Popular Opinion in Stalinism." In Paul Corner, ed., *Popular Opinion in Totalitarian Regimes: Fascism, Nazism, Communism*. Oxford: Oxford University Press, 2009.

Plokhy, S. "Church, State and Nation in Ukraine." *Religion in Eastern Europe* 9:5 (1999): 1–28.

– "In the Shadow of Yalta: International Politics and the Soviet Liquidation of the Ukrainian Greek Catholic Church." In Serhii Plokhy and Frank E. Sysyn, eds., *Religion and Nation in Modern Ukraine*. Edmonton: Canadian Institute of Ukrainian Studies Press, 2003.

– *Ukraine and Russia: Representations of the Past*. Toronto: University of Toronto Press, 2008.

Pohl, M. *The Virgin Lands between Memory and Forgetting: People and Transformation in the Soviet Union, 1954–60*. Doctoral diss, Indiana University, 1999.

Polak-Springer, P. "Landscapes of Revanchism: Building and the Contestation of Space in an Industrial Polish-German Borderland, 1922–1945." *Central European History* 45:3 (2012): 485–522.

Pollock, E. "'Real Men Go to the Bania': Postwar Soviet Masculinities and the Bathhouse." *Kritika: Explorations in Russian and Eurasian History* 11:1 (2010): 47–76.

Potichnyj, P. "Elections in the Ukraine, 1990." In Z. Gitelman, ed., *The Politics of Nationality and the Erosion of the USSR: Selected Papers from the Fourth World Congress for Soviet and East European Studies, Harrogate, 1990*. Basingstoke: Macmillan, 1992.

Prizel, I. *National Identity and Foreign Policy: Nationalism and Leadership in Poland, Russia, and Ukraine*. Cambridge: Cambridge University Press, 1998.

Ralis, M. "Workers' Social Perceptions." In Leonard Schapiro and Joseph Godson, eds., *The Soviet Worker: From Lenin to Andropov*. London: Macmillan, 1984.

Ramet, S.P. "The Interplay of Religious Policy and Nationalities Policy in the Soviet Union and Eastern Europe." In Sabrina Petra Ramet, ed., *Religion and Nationalism in Soviet and East European Politics*. Durham: Duke University Press, 1989.

Reddaway, P. "Policy towards Dissent since Khrushchev." In T. Rigby et al., eds., *Authority, Power and Policy in the USSR*. London: Macmillan, 1980.

Reid, S.E. "The Khrushchev Kitchen: Domesticating the Scientific-Technological Revolution." *Journal of Contemporary History* 40:2 (2005): 289–316.

– "Who Will Beat Whom? Soviet Popular Reception of the American National Exhibition in Moscow, 1959." *Kritika: Explorations in Russian and Eurasian History* 9:4 (2008): 855–904.

Remington, T. *The Truth of Authority: Ideology and Communication in the Soviet Union*. Pittsburgh: University of Pittsburg Press, 1988.

Riabchuk, M. "Civil Society and Nation Building in Ukraine." In T. Kuzio, ed., *Contemporary Ukraine: Dynamics of Post-Soviet Transformation*. Armonk, NY: M.E. Sharpe, 1998.

– *Dvi Ukrainy: real'ni mezhi, virtual'ni viiny*. Kyiv: Krytyka, 2003.

Rigby, T.H. "Soviet Communist Party Membership under Brezhnev." *Soviet Studies* 28:3 (1976): 317–37.

Risch, W.J. "A Soviet West: Nationhood, Regionalism, and Empire in the Annexed Western Borderlands." *Nationalities Papers* 43:1 (2015): 63–81.

– "Soviet 'Flower Children': Hippies and the Youth Counter-Culture in 1970s Lviv." *Journal of Contemporary History* 40:3 (2005): 565–84.

– *The Ukrainian West: Culture and the Fate of Empire in Soviet Lviv*. Cambridge, MA: Harvard University Press, 2011.

Ro'i, Y. "The Soviet Jewish Reaction to the Six Day War." In Y. Ro'i and B. Morozov, eds., *The Soviet Union and the June 1967 Six Day War*. Washington, DC: Woodrow Wilson Center Press, 2008.

Rossman, J. "The Teikovo Cotton Workers' Strike of April 1932: Class, Gender and Identity Politics in Stalin's Russia." *Russian Review* 56:1 (1997): 44–69.

Rossoliński-Liebe, G. *Stepan Bandera, The Life and Afterlife of a Ukrainian Nationalist: Fascism, Genocide, and Cult*. Stuttgart: Ibidem-Verlag, 2014.

Roszkowski, W. *Najnowsza historia Polski 1945–1980*. Warsaw: Świat Książi, 2003.

Roth-Ey, K.J. "Finding a Home for Television in the USSR, 1950–1970." *Slavic Review* 66:2 (2007): 278–306.

– *Moscow Prime Time: How the Soviet Union Built the Media Empire That Lost the Cultural Cold War*. Ithaca: Cornell University Press, 2011.

Rotkirch, A. "Traveling Maidens and Men with Parallel Lives: Journeys as Private Space during Late Socialism." In J. Smith, ed., *Beyond the Limits: The Concept of Space in Russian History and Culture*. Helsinki: SHS, 1999.

Rozenbaum, W. "The March Events: Targetting the Jews." *Polin: Studies in Polish Jewry* 21 (2009): 62–92.

Rusnachenko, A. "Sprotyv robitnytstva ta robitnychi protesty v Ukraini (kin. 50kh- poch. 80kh rr)." *Rozbudova derzhavy* 4 (1996): 51–7.

Sabrow, M. "Consent in the Communist GDR." In Paul Corner, ed., *Popular Opinion in Totalitarian Regimes: Fascism, Nazism, Communism*. Oxford: Oxford University Press, 2009.

Sahadeo, J. "Soviet 'Blacks' and Place Making in Leningrad and Moscow." *Slavic Review* 71:2 (2012): 331–58.

Sahlins, P. *Boundaries: The Making of France and Spain in the Pyrenees*. Berkeley: University of California Press, 1991.

Schattenberg, S. "'Democracy' or 'Despotism'? How the Secret Speech Was Translated into Everyday Life." In Polly Jones, ed., *The Dilemmas of De-Stalinisation: Negotiating Cultural and Social Change in the Khrushchev Era*. London: Routledge, 2005.

Schmid, U. "Between 'Narodnist' and 'Indyvidualnist': Ivan Franko's Theory of Literary Creativity." *Harvard Ukrainian Studies* 23:3–4 (1999): 45–62.

Schöpflin, G. "Poland in Eastern Europe." In Abraham Brumberg, ed., *Poland, Genesis of a Revolution*. New York: Random House, 1983.

Scott, J.C. *The Moral Economy of the Peasant: Rebellion and Subsistence in Southeast Asia*. New Haven: Yale University Press, 1976.

Serbyn, R. "Managing Memory in Post-Soviet Ukraine: 'Victory Day' or 'Remembrance Day.'" In S. Velychenko, ed., *Ukraine, the EU and Russia: History, Culture and International Relations*. Basingstoke: Palgrave Macmillan, 2007.

Shlikhta, N. *Tserkva tykh, khto vyzhyv. Radians'ka Ukraina, seredyna 1940x – pochatok 1970x rr.* Kharkiv: Akta, 2011.

Shulman, S. "Cultures in Competition: Ukrainian Foreign Policy and the 'Cultural Threat' from Abroad." *Europe-Asia Studies* 50:2 (1998): 287–303.

– "National Identity and Public Support for Political and Economic Reform in Ukraine." *Slavic Review* 64:1 (2005): 59–87.

Siegelbaum, L. "Cars, Cars, and More Cars: The Faustian Bargain of the Brezhnev Era." In L. Siegelbaum, ed., *Borders of Socialism: Private Spheres of Soviet Russia*. Basingstoke: Palgrave Macmillan, 2006.

Simon, J. "Ukraine against Herself: To be Euro-Atlantic, Eurasian, or Neutral?" *Strategic Forum* 238 (2009): 1–11.

Slezkine, Y. "The USSR as Communal Apartment, or How a Socialist State Promoted Ethnic Particularism." *Slavic Review* 53:2 (1994): 414–52.

Smith, A. *The Ethnic Origins of Nations*. Oxford: Basil Blackwell, 1986.

Snyder, T. "The Causes of the Holocaust." *Contemporary European History* 21:2 (2012): 149–68.

– "The Causes of Ukrainian-Polish Ethnic Cleansing 1943." *Past and Present* 179 (2003): 197–234.

– *The Reconstruction of Nations: Poland, Ukraine, Lithuania, Belarus, 1569–1999*. New Haven: Yale University Press, 2003.

– *The Red Prince: The Secret Lives of a Habsburg Archduke*. London: Bodley Head, 2008.

– *Sketches from a Secret War: A Polish Artist's Mission to Liberate Soviet Ukraine*. New Haven: Yale University Press, 2007.

– "'To Resolve the Ukrainian Problem Once and For All': The Ethnic Cleansing of Ukrainians in Poland, 1943–47." *Journal of Cold War Studies* 1:2 (1999): 86–120.

Solchanyk, R. "Polska a sowiecki zachód." *Suchasnist: zeszyt w języku polskim* 1–2 (1985): 79–100.

– "The Radical Right in Ukraine." In S.P. Ramet, ed., *The Radical Right in Central and Eastern Europe Since 1989*. University Park, PA: Pennsylvania State University Press, 1999.

Solomon, P. *Soviet Criminologists and Criminal Policy: Specialists in Policy Making*. London: Macmillan, 1978.

Sowiński, P. *Wakacje w Polsce Ludowej. Polityka władz i ruch turystyczny (1945–1989)*. Warsaw: Trio, 2005.

Spechler, D. *Permitted Dissent in the USSR: Novyi Mir and the Soviet Regime*. New York: Praeger, 1982.

Statiev, A. *The Soviet Counterinsurgency in the Western Borderlands*. Cambridge: Cambridge University Press, 2010.

Stitziel, J. "Shopping, Sewing, Networking, Complaining: Consumer Culture and the Relationship between State and Society in the GDR." In Katherine Pence and Paul Betts, eds., *Socialist Modern: East German Everyday Culture and Politics*. Ann Arbor: University of Michigan Press, 2008.

Subtelny, O. *Ukraine: A History*. Toronto: University of Toronto Press, 2000.

Suny, R. *The Revenge of the Past: Nationalism, Revolution, and the Collapse of the Soviet Union*. Stanford: Stanford University Press, 1993.

Suri, J. "The Promise and Failure of 'Developed Socialism': the Soviet 'Thaw' and the Crucible of the Prague Spring, 1964–1972." *Contemporary European History* 15:2 (2006): 133–58.

Sygkelos, Y. "The National Discourse of the Bulgarian Communist Party on National Anniversaries and Commemorations (1944–48)." *Nationalities Papers* 37:4 (2009): 425–42.

Sysyn, F. "The Changing Image of the Hetman: On the 350th Anniversary of the Khmel'nyts'kyi Uprising." *Jahrbucher fur Geschichte Osteuropas* 46:4 (1998): 531–45.

Szporluk, R. *Communism and Nationalism: Karl Marx versus Friedrich List*. New York: Oxford University Press, 1998.

– "Introduction." In Roman Szporluk, ed., *The Influence of Eastern Europe and the Soviet West on the USSR*. New York: Praeger, 1976.

– "The Making of Modern Ukraine: The Western Dimension." *Harvard Ukrainian Studies* 25:1–2 (2001): 57–90.

– "The Role of the Press in Polish-Ukrainian Relations." In P.J. Potichnyj, ed., *Poland and Ukraine: Past and Present*. Edmonton: Canadian Institute of Ukrainian Studies, 1980.

– "The Soviet West – or Far Eastern Europe?" *East European Politics and Societies* 5:3 (1991): 466–82.

– "The Strange Politics of Lviv: An Essay in Search of an Explanation." In Zvi Gitelman, ed., *The Politics of Nationality and the Erosion of the USSR: Selected Papers from the Fourth World Congress for Soviet and East European Studies, Harrogate, 1990*. Basingstoke: Macmillan, 1992.

– "Ukraina: od imperialnej peryferii do suwerennego państwa." In Roman Szporluk, ed., *Imperium, komunizm i narody: Wybór esejów*. Kraków: Arcana, 2003.

Teague, E., *Solidarity and the Soviet Worker: The Impact of the Polish Events of 1980 on Soviet Internal Politics*. London: Croom Helm, 1988.

Thomassen, L. *Habermas: A Guide for the Perplexed*. London: Continuum, 2010.

Thompson, E.P. "The Moral Economy of the English Crowd in the Eighteenth Century." *Past and Present* 50 (1971): 76–136.

Thum, G. "Ethnic Cleansing in Eastern Europe after 1945." *Contemporary European History* 19:1 (2010): 75–81.

Tillett, L. *The Great Friendship: Soviet Historians on the Non-Russian Nationalities*. Chapel Hill: University of North Carolina Press, 1969.

Tromly, B. "Soviet Patriotism and its Discontents among Higher Education Students in Khrushchev-era Russia and Ukraine." *Nationalities Papers* 37:3 (2009): 299–326.

– "An Unlikely National Revival: Soviet Higher Learning and the Ukrainian Sixtiers, 1953–65." *Russian Review* 68:4 (2009): 607–22.

Tsipursky, G. "Citizenship, Deviance, and Identity: Soviet Youth Newspapers as Agents of Social Control in the Thaw-era Leisure Campaign." *Cahiers du Monde Russe* 49:4 (2008): 629–49.

– "'As a Citizen, I Cannot Ignore these Facts': Soviet Whistleblowing and State Response, 1955–61." *Jahrbucher fur Geschichte Osteuropas*, 58:1 (2010): 52–69.

Tumarkin, N. *The Living and the Dead: The Rise and Fall of the Cult of World War Two in Russia*. New York: Basic Books, 1994.

Varga-Harris, C. "Forging Citizenship on the Home Front: Reviving the Socialist Contract and Constructing Soviet Identity during the Thaw." In Polly Jones, ed., *The Dilemmas of De-Stalinisation: Negotiating Cultural and Social Change in the Khrushchev Era*. London: Routledge, 2005.

Vari, A. "Re-territorializing the 'Guilty City': Nationalist and Right-Wing Attempts to Nationalize Budapest during the Interwar Period." *Journal of Contemporary History* 47:4 (2012): 709–33.

Velychenko, S. "Post-Colonialism and Ukrainian History." *Ab Imperio: Studies of New Imperial History and Nationalism in the post-Soviet Space* 1 (2004): 391–404.

– *Shaping Identity in Eastern Europe and Russia: Soviet-Russian and Polish Accounts of Ukrainian History, 1914–1991*. New York: St. Martin's Press, 1993.

Venken, M. "Nationalization Campaigns and Teachers' Practices in Belgian-German and Polish-German Border Regions (1945–56)." *Nationalities Papers* 42:2 (2014): 223–41.

Viola, L. "Popular Resistance in the Stalinist 1930s: Soliloquy of a Devil's Advocate." In Michael David-Fox, Peter Holquist, and Marshall Poe, eds., *The Resistance Debate in Russian and Soviet History*. Bloomington: Slavica Publishers, 2003.

Volkov, V. "The Concept of Kul'turnost': Notes on the Stalinist Civilizing Process." In S. Fitzpatrick, ed., *Stalinism: New Directions*. London: Routledge, 2000.

Wanner, C. *Burden of Dreams: History and Identity in Post-Soviet Ukraine*. University Park: Pennsylvania State University Press, 1998.

Wedgwood Benn, D. *Persuasion and Soviet Politics*. Oxford: Basil Blackwell, 1989.

Weiner, A. "Déjà Vu All Over Again: Prague Spring, Romanian Summer, and Soviet Autumn on Russia's Western Frontier." *Contemporary European History* 15:2 (2006): 159–94.

– "The Empires Pay a Visit: Gulag Returnees, East European Rebellions, and Soviet Frontier Politics." *The Journal of Modern History* 78:2 (2006): 333–76.

– *Making Sense of War: The Second World War and the Fate of the Bolshevik Revolution*. Princeton: Princeton University Press, 2001.

– "Robust Revolution to Retiring Revolution: The Life Cycle of the Soviet Revolution, 1945–1968." *The Slavonic and East European Review* 86:2 (2008): 208–31.

Wessely, A. "Travelling People, Travelling Objects." *Cultural Studies* 16:1 (2002): 3–15.

Westad, O.A. *The Global Cold War: Third World Interventions and the Making of Our Times*. Cambridge: Cambridge University Press, 2005.

White, A. *De-Stalinization and the House of Culture: Declining State Control over Leisure in the USSR, Poland, and Hungary, 1953–1989*. London: Routledge, 1990.

Whitmore, S. *State building in Ukraine: the Ukrainian Parliament, 1990–2003*. London: Routledge, 2004.

Wilson, A. "Ukraine and Post-Soviet Europe: Authoritarian Consolidation or Renewed Reform?" In Stephen White, Judy Batt and Paul G. Lewis, eds., *Developments in Central and East European Politics 3*. Basingstoke: Palgrave Macmillan, 2003.

– "Ukraine's 2002 Elections: Less Fraud, More Virtuality." *East European Constitutional Review* 11:3 (2002): 91–8.

– *Ukraine's Orange Revolution*. New Haven: Yale University Press, 2005.

– *Ukrainian Nationalism in the 1990s: A Minority Faith*. Cambridge: Cambridge University Press, 1997.

– *The Ukrainians: Unexpected Nation*. New Haven: Yale University Press, 2002.

Wojnowski, Z. "Communism and Nationalism: Poles' Perceptions of the West and Legitimacy of the Jaruzelski Regime, 1980–83." *Slovo* 19:1 (2007): 23–40.

– "De-Stalinization and Soviet Patriotism: Ukrainian Reactions to East European Unrest in 1956." *Kritika: Explorations in Russian and Eurasian History* 13:4 (2012): 799–829.

– "The Soviet People: National and Supranational Identities in the USSR after Stalin." *Nationalities Papers* 43:1 (2015): 1–7.

– "Staging Patriotism: Popular Responses to Solidarność in Soviet Ukraine, 1980–1981." *Slavic Review* 71:4 (2012): 824–48.
– "An Unlikely Bulwark of Sovietness: Cross-Border Travel and Soviet Patriotism in Western Ukraine." *Nationalities Papers* 43:1 (2015): 82–101.
Wolff, L." Inventing Galicia: Messianic Josephinism and the Recasting of Partitioned Poland." *Slavic Review* 63:4 (2004): 818–40.
– '"Kennst du das Land?' The Uncertainty of Galicia in the Age of Metternich and Fredro." *Slavic Review* 67:2 (2008): 277–300.
Yaremchuk, V. "Ukrains"ka radians'ka istoriohrafiia 50x–80x rokiv pro ukrains'ke natsiietvorennia: ofitsiina ta al'ternatyvni kontseptsii." *Naukovi zapysky. Seriia "Istorychni nauky"* 17 (2011): 266–75.
Yekelchyk, S. "Diktat and Dialogue in Stalinist Culture: Staging Patriotic Historical Opera in Soviet Ukraine, 1936–1954." *Slavic Review* 59:3 (2000): 597–624.
– "The Early 1960s as a Cultural Space: A Microhistory of Ukraine's Generation of Cultural Rebels." *Nationalities Papers* 43:1 (2015): 45–62.
– "The Location of Nation: Postcolonial Perspectives on Ukrainian Historical Debates." *Australian Slavonic and East European Studies* 11:1–2 (1997): 161–84.
– *Stalin's Citizens: Everyday Politics in the Wake of Total War*. Oxford: Oxford University Press, 2014.
– *Stalin's Empire of Memory: Russian-Ukrainian Relations in the Soviet Historical Imagination*. Toronto: University of Toronto Press, 2004.
– *Ukraine: Birth of a Modern Nation*. New York: Oxford University Press, 2007.
Yurchak, A. *Everything Was Forever, Until It Was No More: The Last Soviet Generation*. Princeton: Princeton University Press, 2006.
Zahra, T. "The 'Minority Problem' and National Classification in the French and Czechoslovak Borderlands." *Contemporary European History* 17:2 (2008): 137–66.
Zaitsev, I. "Pol's'ka opozytsiia 1970-80-kh rokiv pro zasady ukrains'ko-pol's'koho porozuminnia." In Iurii Slyvka, ed., *Deportatsii ukraintsiv ta poliakiv: kinets 1939- pochatok 50-kh rokiv*. Lviv: Instytut ukrainoznavstva im. Kryp'iakevycha, 1998.
Zhuk, S. *Rock and Roll in the Rocket City: The West, Identity and Ideology in Soviet Dniepropetrovsk, 1960–1985*. Washington, DC: Woodrow Wilson Center Press, 2010.
Zimmer, O. *A Contested Nation: History, Memory and Nationalism in Switzerland, 1761–1891*. Cambridge: Cambridge University Press, 2003.
Zisserman-Brodsky, D. *Constructing Ethnopolitics in the Soviet Union: Samizdat, Deprivation, and the Rise of Ethnic Nationalism*. New York: Palgrave Macmillan, 2003.
Zubok, V. *Zhivago's Children: The Last Russian Intelligentsia*. Cambridge, MA: Belknap, 2009.

Index

www.ingramcontent.com/pod-product-compliance
Lightning Source LLC
LaVergne TN
LVHW041112090826
844660LV00061B/746/J

* 9 7 8 1 4 4 2 6 3 1 0 7 6 *